TEXT- AIDED ARCHAEOLOGY

Barbara J. Little

CRC Press
Boca Raton   Ann Arbor   London

Library of Congress Cataloging-in-Publication Data

Text-aided archaeology / editor, Barbara J. Little.
       p.   cm.
     Includes bibliographical references and index.
     ISBN 0-8493-8853-8
     1. Archaeology and history — United States. 2. United States — History, Local — Sources.
3. United States — Antiquities.
I. Little, Barbara J.
E159.5.T48   1992
973—dc20   91-32228
                                                                                                                      CIP

Developed by Telford Press.

   Direct all inquiries to CRC Press, Inc., 2000 Corporate Blvd., N.W., Boca Raton, Florida, 33431.

© 1992 by CRC Press, Inc.

International Standard Book Number 0-8493-8853-8

Library of Congress Card Number 91-32228
Printed in the United States   1 2 3 4 5 6 7 8 9 0

Preface

My original and unrealistic plan for what would have become a quite unwieldy volume was to collect chapters that represented archaeological research from all over the world from the beginning of literacy to the present while maintaining a coherence based on archaeologists' use of text. I wanted to include not only the use of texts in archaeological interpretation itself, but also the influence of archaeologically produced texts (site reports, syntheses, etc.) on our continuing work. After realizing that all archaeology is text aided to some degree and that there is no nonliterate archaeology (even if its subject cultures are nonliterate), I decided that a different approach would be more worthwhile. I have organized this volume to address the structure of the ways that archaeologists actually use text to pose questions and to suggest interpretations. The case studies that illustrate the approaches to integrating our data sources were solicited from the viewpoint of a historical archaeologist working in the U.S. who wanted to challenge a narrowly conceived vision of "historical archaeology." I wanted to broadly define text-aided archaeology because my concern was the methods used to concoct such interdisciplinary study. The techniques of data gathering may be quite similar in these chapters, but the methodologies used to make sense of the data vary. The acceptance of different approaches as having equal validity aims to avoid arguing for one correct or orthodox method. The focus on methodology and sources is meant to contribute to understanding the articulations between method and theory; it is not an attempt to disassociate them. Interpretation, not "facts," is history, and it is our method and our theory that allow us to create interpretations.

I am grateful to Pat Kelly of Telford Press, who originally solicited this volume. I especially thank all the authors for their cooperation and patience, and for their splendid chapters. They may or may not categorize their work in the same way that I have; I request their indulgence. I am indebted to Paul Shackel for providing valuable comments and suggestions as this project took shape. In gratitude to and in memory of Beulah Oetjen (1904–1982), for a legacy of free thinking, I dedicate this book.

Barbara J. Little
University of Maryland

The Editor

Barbara J. Little, Ph.D., is currently a Faculty Research Associate in the Department of Anthropology at the University of Maryland, College Park.

Dr. Little obtained her training in anthropology from the State University of New York at Buffalo where she received her M.A. and Ph.D. in 1984 and 1987, respectively. Her B.A. is from the Pennsylvania State University. She was Visiting Assistant Professor at George Mason University from 1987 to 1989.

She is a member of the Society for American Archaeology, the Society for Historical Archaeology, the Council for Northeastern Historical Archaeology, and the Northeastern Anthropological Association, and is a Fellow of the American Anthropological Association. She has presented her research at meetings of those organizations and at the Smithsonian Institution, the American Studies Association, the International Organization for the Study of Group Tensions, and the Society for Applied Anthropology, as well as at other conferences. Her work is published in a dozen journal articles and book chapters. She has also acted as guest editor for special journal issues.

Dr. Little's research interests in archaeology include theory and method, feminist theory and practice, urban contexts, group interaction, and public interpretation. Her research in urban archaeology in Annapolis, Maryland has focused on printers and their craft, about which she is writing a monograph. Some of her research on printing was done while a predoctoral fellow at the Smithsonian Institution. She is currently coediting a book on historical archaeology in the Chesapeake Bay region.

Contributors

Charles E. Cleland
The MSU Museum
Michigan State University
East Lansing, Michigan

Julia G. Costello
Foothill Resource Associates
Mokelumne Hill, California

Janine Gasco
Institute for Mesoamerican Studies
State University of New York at Albany
Albany, New York

D. L. Hamilton
Nautical Archaeology Program
Department of Anthropology
Texas A&M University
College Station, Texas

Victor P. Hood
The Hermitage
Home of Andrew Jackson
Hermitage, Tennessee

Dorothy A. Humpf
Department of Anthropology
Pennsylvania State University
University Park, Pennsylvania

Sharon Macpherson
The Hermitage
Home of Andrew Jackson
Hermitage, Tennessee

Larry McKee
The Hermitage
Home of Andrew Jackson
Hermitage, Tennessee

Paul R. Mullins
Department of Anthropology
University of Massachusetts
Amherst, Massachusetts

Parker B. Potter, Jr.
New Hampshire Division of Historical Resources
Concord, New Hampshire

Margaret Purser
Anthropology Department
Sonoma State University
Rohnert Park, California

Robert J. Rowland, Jr.
Loyola University
New Orleans, Louisiana

Ellen-Rose Savulis
Department of Anthropology
University of Massachusetts
Amherst, Massachusetts

Paul A. Shackel
Division of Archaeology
Harpers Ferry National Historical Park
Harpers Ferry, West Virginia

Theresa A. Singleton
Department of Anthropology
National Museum of Natural History
Smithsonian Institution
Washington, DC

Robert Lindley Vann
School of Architecture
University of Maryland
College Park, Maryland

Bailey K. Young
Assumption College
Worcester, Massachusetts

In memory of my grandmother, Beulah Oetjen

Contents

1: Text-Aided Archaeology

Barbara J. Little
University of Maryland, College Park, Maryland

Archaeology is not a discipline that stands alone. Its scope is as broad as the diverse fields that claim it: anthropology, art history, classics, epigraphy, and history. Its sources are as varied and encompassing as the products of human actions. Depending on our questions and chronologies, many different sources may aid archaeological interpretation, whether they have become buried under earth or water, have survived above ground, have been protected in libraries and archives, have traveled across generations orally, or have been created through modern observation. Documents, oral testimony, and ethnographic description all play a role in text-aided archaeology, which in some broad sense includes all archaeology. Although some archaeological resources have directly associated documentation, even prehistoric archaeology relies on texts of ethnographic descriptions and texts of archaeological analyses and interpretive models to provide a context for interpretation.

This volume is intended as an exploration of relationships among some of our sources. The emphasis is on contexts in which archaeological resources have directly associated texts, but the use of texts for understanding prehistoric contexts is touched upon as well. The broad category of historical documentation and its use in archaeology is the subject of inquiry. Contributed chapters are therefore linked through a common concern with methodology: How can archaeology take the best advantage of its documentary sources of data to address the questions that interest us?

There are a fairly large number of books on methodology written to help the archaeologist analyze and interpret excavated materials. There are books on ceramics, lithics, bones, soils, glass, and metals. There are guides to computers, mathematics, spatial patterns, chemistry, demography, ecology, stratigraphy, nutrition, explanation, and philosophy. There are not many works that focus on the use of historical documentation for the archaeologist, although there are several collections of historical archaeology, organized under various themes,[1] and there is a good deal of excellent substantive work being done. There are, of course, guides to methodology for the historian,[2] and there are a few written for sociologists and social anthropologists who use historical data (e.g., Pitt 1972; MacFarlane 1977). There is also Dymond's (1974) useful "plea for reconciliation" between history and archaeology. Hodder (1986, 1987) has recently reemphasized historical thinking within archaeology, but there is no special emphasis on particular ways to use various texts. Many historical archaeologists have admonished their colleagues to pay closer attention to using documents. Among the most recent are Mary Beaudry, who writes "historical archaeologists must develop an approach towards documentary analysis that is uniquely their own" (1988:1), and Robert Schuyler, who writes "there is equal mystery, romance and potential richness to the document" (1988:42). Kathleen Deagan (1988) urges the development of a methodology specifically designed to take advantage of both documentary and artifactual data. There is a need for a book that is meant to help archaeologists weave together information and interpretation from documentary and other material culture sources.

Such a volume is necessary not only to "fill a gap," although it will help to do that, but also to provide ideas, information, and suggestions on the use of sources that have much to contribute to our interpretations. At least two trends in current scholarship also point to the need for such a volume. One is the rapid growth of historical archaeology as a subdiscipline. The precise definition and boundaries of this specialty have been much debated (e.g., Schuyler 1978a; Orser 1988:315). While historical archaeology logically encompasses human activity in any time or place for which documentation aids interpretation, other definitions focus the discipline on European expansion (especially in the New World) during and after the "Age of Discovery" (Schuyler 1970). As such it is somewhat ethnocentric, tending to treat all people only in terms of their relationships with Europeans. Gaining force is the viewpoint that refines this definition and sees capitalism as the specific focus for historical archaeology (Leone 1977; Leone and Potter 1988b:19–20; Orser 1988; Paynter 1988). Orser suggests that this focus on capitalism solves the long-standing problem of an atheoretical and eclectic stance in the subdiscipline. I have no intention of arguing against the need for theory in historical archaeology. Nor do I want to suggest that method and theory might be uncoupled and each encouraged to stand alone. There are important concepts to research within capitalism: colonialism, imperialism, frontier adaptation, and industrialization, to name a few; but "historical archaeology" thus conceived runs the risk of forgetting that there are many complex societies all over the globe with similarly interesting questions and with similarly interesting data. Text-aided archaeology is broader than this conception of historical archaeology. Whether one believes in cross-cultural comparisons and broadly applicable theoretical constructs or in particular, unique histories, it is important to compare and contrast methodologies in order to refine our questions and our analyses.

To help avoid isolation or unintentional provincialism, historical archaeologists need to take stock of the second trend of scholarship that necessitates this volume. That trend is the constantly growing recognition that history and anthropology need each other. Their mutual benefit has been clear for several decades,[3] and yet disciplinary boundaries can make interdisciplinary research difficult and unrecognized (i.e., unrewarding professionally). In spite of the difficulties and regardless of the particular focus on European capitalism, Roman imperialism, or some other problem, text-aided archaeology, as a historical and social enterprise, needs to place itself firmly and explicitly within this second trend of historical anthropology (or anthropological history). It has much to contribute.

The authors in this volume have much to contribute as well. Because methodology is a rather hollow topic without its theoretical and substantive sisters, there is an inevitable and welcome concern in each of the chapters with questions, ideas, perspectives, data, and interpretations. Within these pages theoretical orientations and historical contexts vary widely, tied together by the common appreciation of archaeology's rich and diverse sources. Archaeologists interpret material culture, and that material culture includes representations and remnants of culture, both objects and texts. The specific documents used and the approach taken to using both documentary and archaeological data vary according to the questions each author asks and perceptions of the relationships between types of data.

In an attempt to clarify relationships between archaeological data sources, Schuyler (1978b) proposed a categorization of sources according to the etic and emic viewpoints available in each. Ethnographic, written historical, oral historical, and archaeological sources were contrasted. The combination of directly available emic views from written sources (which also contained indirectly available etic views) with directly available etic views from archaeological sources (which contained indirectly available emic views) was to imitate ethnography, perceived as the most complete sort of observation possible, since both the emic and the etic were simultaneously available. While such a conceptualization of sources is heuristically useful, it does not account for different types of data within the written, oral, excavated, and observed records. It, therefore, cannot account for the intent of the source or the variety of viewpoints that may be available. It is beyond the scope of this volume to thoroughly expand Schuyler's typology. However, some of the variety within documentary data is considered, and different approaches to combining archaeological and documentary data are offered.

Texts may be categorized in different ways. Familiar typologies classify texts according to source as primary or secondary, acknowledged bias as objective reporting or subjective evaluation, and form as written, printed, or oral. In this volume Hamilton (Chapter 4) classifies documents according to their scope in providing information about regions or sites, persons or areas, artifacts, or some combination of these. Pitt (1972) lists categories by their source. Such a categorization is useful to Pitt because his purpose is to guide anthropologists and sociologists to historical documents in various locations. The same categorization is useful here, partly for the same general reason of pointing out the range of sources available. This categorization is also useful because it emphasizes the question of source and the influence of source on a document's intention, tone, and coverage. The expectation, for example, that private papers will embody different opinions and priorities than government documents should affect the way such documents are used to aid archaeological interpretation.

Pitt's 10 main categories of historical sources are listed in Table 1, along with the specific documentary sources used by the authors in this volume. Authors are often listed more than once. Statistical sources are listed under the sponsor who created them, rather than as a separate category, as in Pitt's listing. Pitt's "data bank" source is also omitted.

Public and official archives include government documents, such as minutes, journals, official papers, political records, policy documents, and court records, and statistics, such as census, taxes, and production figures. Also included are officially sponsored explorers' and travelers' accounts and government-sponsored research. Missions and church sources include letters, journals, parish and other records, and other related papers. Business and company sources include all pertinent records, including but not limited to account books, personnel records, union records, and insurance files. Scholarly institutions, as a source, hold acquired collections and unpublished notes. Pitt notes secondary sources as leads to primary documents, but for the purposes of text-aided archaeology, secondary sources, i.e., interpretive works, need to be considered as part of this category because of their impact on our questions and interpretations. Letters, diaries, and private papers compose a category that may include such other items as photo albums and memorabilia. Literature is defined by Pitt as "works written by people who are generally not professional social scientists and who present a subjective or fictitious picture" (1972:26). This source includes travel literature by outsiders and locals, as well as fiction, novels, short stories, and plays. For some purposes "literature" may include a catchall for written sources not claimed by other categories. Transient documents are items such as newspapers, pamphlets, brochures, broadsheets, directories, catalogs, or any other mass media with a limited circulation or life span. Local sources and opinions are "folk history," direct reporting by local people as found, for example, in court records (1972:29). Oral history also needs to be considered. Although Pitt does not include oral history, "local sources and opinions" may be expanded to include it. Maps, pictorial, and sound archives compose another category. At the risk of confusing the distinction between documents and artifacts, objects and structures might be included in this category.

Although several authors use the same source category and often similar types of specific documents, they rarely put them to similar uses. Most use more than one type of source. The heavy use of public and official archives suggests something of the sponsorship, preservation, and availability of such documents and also suggests something of the point of view often available from documents.

Table 1 shows the range of resources available and useful for text-aided archaeology. Table 1 also makes it clear that organizing these chapters by historical sources would be impossible and would produce an overly fragmented discussion of methodology. Instead I have created sections according to the author's basic message about text-aided archaeology. The first chapter, "Relationships Between Documents and Archaeology," is further divided into "Contradictory Data," "Complementary Data," and "Hypothesis Formation." The second section is "Documentary Myths and Archaeology" and the third is "Text and Context." Chapters in all sections demonstrate that the specific uses to which documents may be put to aid interpretation range from the identification of objects and their functions to the explication of a culture's world view. Several of the chapters also make it clear that history done without archaeology produces incomplete stories at best.

Table 1
CATEGORIES OF HISTORICAL SOURCES USED IN THIS COLLECTION

Category	Author	Specific Sources
Public and official archives	Cleland	Treaties, census
	Gasco	Probate records
	Hamilton	Wills, inventory, plats, census
	Humpf	Explorers' accounts
	Potter	Probate records
	Rowland	Census
	Shackel	Probate records
	Singleton	Tax records, census, inventory
	Vann	Commissioned history
Mission and church sources	Costello	Agricultural production figures
	Rowland	Jesuit records
	Savulis	Deaconess' journals
Business and company sources	Hamilton	Guild records
	Mullins	Ledgers, business letters
	Potter	Daybooks, store inventories
	Singleton	Plantation records — daybooks, ledgers, reports, hospital records
Scholarly institutions	Little	Archaeological discourse
	McKee, Hood, & Macpherson	Architectural history
	Rowland	19th-C. histories
	Vann	Autobiography
	Young	Historical interpretation
Letters, diaries, private papers	McKee, Hood, & Macpherson	Letters, contracts
	Mullins	Journal, ledgers, letters
	Singleton	Letters
Literature	Costello	Travelers' accounts
	Savulis	Poetry
	Shackel	Etiquette books
	Singleton	Journals
Transient documents	Potter	Newspaper
Local sources and opinions	Purser	Oral history
Maps, pictorial, sound archives	Cleland	Maps
	Hamilton	Markings on artifacts
	McKee, Hood, & Macpherson	Floor plans, structures
	Savulis	Spirit drawings, maps
	Vann	Drawings
	Young	Religious monuments

Relationships between Documents and Archaeological Data

Documentary and archaeological data may be thought of as interdependent and complementary, or as independent and contradictory. Oddly enough, both of these views are viable; the adoption of one or the other depends on the questions one is asking and the point of view of the interpretation.

Two authors, Potter and Purser, illustrate using "contradictory data," although in somewhat different ways. In his interpretation of 19th-century Rockbridge County, Virginia, Parker Potter makes a strong case for middle-range theory, wherein documents and artifacts are seen as independent sources of data that can be played off against one another. He is concerned, as are all the authors here, with appropriate matching of documentary information to the archaeological question, but the matching is not intended to "fill in the gaps." It is intended to identify anomalies that will lead to further questions. Margaret Purser argues for oral history as an essential part of text-aided archaeology. Informants for her study of 19th-century Paradise Valley, Nevada provided her with contradictory histories, which agreed in detail but not in meaning. The seeming contradictions between stories forcefully demonstrate that interpretations rather than facts are the essence of this history.

There are four authors who explicitly rely on the complementary nature of documentary and archaeological resources to create their interpretations. D. L. Hamilton describes the 17th-century site of Port Royal, Jamaica, whose data are rich in both types of resources. He uses a craftsman and family as a microcosm of city history, creating his interpretation by blending documentary and archaeological information and using each source to fill in where the other fails. Theresa Singleton examines the ways in which archaeology contributes to our understanding of Southern antebellum slavery, a topic that is conventionally regarded as being exhaustively documented. Her archaeological data from Butler Plantation in Georgia adds information that is otherwise unobtainable. Julia Costello and Janine Gasco take a somewhat different approach and focus their energies specifically on documents. Through her work with individual mission records, Costello cautions against the danger of generalizing about a region or type of site. The implications for archaeological interpretation of these sites are clear. Costello summarizes material excavated at several California missions, providing further specific information that refines the knowledge in the documents. Gasco describes the use of information recorded in probate records that allows archaeologists to compare objects and households. Objects unavailable in the archaeological record are supplemented to provide a fuller picture of colonial Soconusco's material culture.

Under the heading "Hypothesis Formation" are the chapters by Charles Cleland, Lindley Vann, and Dorothy Humpf. Cleland insists that the documentary and archaeological data be kept distinct to avoid circular arguments as one is tested against the other. Documents pertaining to the 19th-century Ojibwa and Ottawa in the Great Lakes region of the U.S. allow the creation of hypotheses about band territories, which may then be tested in the prehistoric archaeological record. Vann compares a historical eyewitness description to the archaeologically derived modern-day realities of an ancient harbor. Checking the facts of a long mistrusted historian against the physical evidence in Caesarea vindicates the historian and also provides some insights into the nature of historical reporting, facts, and interpretation (cf. Purser, Chapter 3). Humpf uses eyewitness observations and documented cultural changes that accompanied 16th-century Spanish contact in the southeastern U.S. to suggest alternative hypotheses for unexpected results of her osteological analysis of native populations.

Documentary Myths and Archaeology

Each of the three chapters in this section uses archaeological evidence to overturn a myth or myths created and perpetuated through documentary interpretation. These chapters contain more than simple corrections of historical "fact." They raise and address the issue of authority, not only of documentary versus archaeological resources, but also of the political and social authorities that help to create and uphold historical myths.

Bailey Young demonstrates that archaeology is able to suggest a much more complex and dynamic (and accurate) past when historians' preconceptions are reexamined. Reinterpreting the meanings of funerary deposits, he offers a new perspective on the barbarian invasions of the Roman Empire. Young also provides a much needed archaeological view of standing religious monuments. Robert Rowland, in a thorough overview of text-aided archaeology in Sardinia, attributes the standard interpretation of Bronze Age Sardinia to a ethnocentrically motivated myth and reinterprets both Bronze Age and Roman period Sardinia with the help of appropriate 19th-century documents. His work emphasizes the archaeological revision of text-based interpretations for the medieval period as well as the Roman and Bronze Ages. Larry McKee, Victor Hood, and Sharon Macpherson find archaeological evidence to challenge the standard interpretation of U.S. President Andrew Jackson's house, The Hermitage. Archaeology raises questions not only about architectural details, but also about the purposes of history and the selective writing of the past both to simplify and to gloss over social tensions.

Text and Context

These chapters use documents to create interpretive contexts for both archaeological and other historical work. Both Paul Mullins and Ellen-Rose Savulis are concerned with individual response to some of the disorienting, far-reaching changes of industrializing society. Mullins uses a potter's own writing to understand how an individual organized and responded to industrialization, both of his craft and of his whole way of life. Savulis examines alternative media to assess gender-specific response to the Shaker-built environment. The gender inequality born of industrialization is seen to affect both Shaker ideology and the landscape. Paul Shackel uses text to create context in a somewhat different way, concentrating on material culture within the historical record. Objects in an 18th-century Anglo-American colony are provided with social and ideological meaning through contemporary documents, allowing the proposed archaeological interpretations to take advantage of the rich historical contexts available. The final chapter is focused on no particular documentary or archaeological data beyond the realm of archaeological discourse. I have instead asked whether it would serve archaeological intent for text to go beyond providing context and become a model for our analyses; that is, can material culture be conceived of as text, should we subsume material culture data into methodology developed for interpreting texts?

Archaeologists well know that there is a "cult of authority" surrounding the written record (McKee, Hood, and Macpherson, Chapter 13). Some historians would rather believe "an off-the-cuff remark in the text of Pliny the elder [than]...hundreds of pages of archaeological reports" (Rowland, Chapter 12). Purser (Chapter 3) admonishes us that we privilege the written over the oral as we once privileged the documentary over the material. Text-aided archaeology has perhaps finally reached a stage wherein that once unquestioned privilege has been truly supplanted by a more equitable and fruitful arrangement.

The reader will immediately notice a Western bias and a predominance of the relatively recent in this collection. Text-aided archaeologies that use nonalphabetic texts are not included here. Colin Renfrew writes, "while archaeology may in a sense be the past tense of anthropology, it is not the past tense of anthropology alone" (1982:4). Be that as it may, this volume is strongly biased toward the contributions of archaeologists trained as anthropologists. In choosing topics for this volume, the challenge was to avoid an overly eclectic miscellany while still representing a useful range of areas, times, and perspectives to demonstrate text-aided archaeology. The reader will judge whether or not the challenge has been successfully met.

Notes

[1] Such collections include Beaudry (1988) on the New World, Dickens (1982) on North American urban contexts, Ferguson (1977) on material goods, Leone and Potter (1988a) on the interpretation of meaning, Schuyler (1980) on ethnicity, Schuyler (1978a) on contributions of historical archaeology, Singleton (1985) on slavery, South (1977) on pattern recognition, and Spencer-Wood (1987) on consumer choice.

[2] For example see the journals *Historical Methods* and *Historical Research*. Also see, among many, Beringer (1985), Chandler (1984), Stoffle (1979), and Topolski (1976).

[3] See Pitt (1972:11–13) for examples of anthropological studies that have relied on history. More recent examples include Dening (1988), Sahlins (e.g., 1981, 1985), and Wolf (1982). See also comments by Deetz (1988) and Young (1988) on relationships between history, anthropology, and archaeology.

References

Beaudry, M. C., Ed. (1988) *Documentary Archaeology in the New World*. Cambridge University Press, Cambridge.

Beringer, R. E. (1985) *Historical Analysis: Contemporary Approaches to Clio's Craft*. University Microfilms International, Ann Arbor, MI.

Chandler, W. J. (1984) *Science of History: A Cybernetic Approach*. Gordon and Breach Science Publishers, New York.

Deagan, K. (1988) Neither history nor prehistory: the questions that count in historical archaeology. *Historical Archaeology* 22(1):7–12.

Deetz, J. (1988) History and archaeological theory: Walter Taylor Revisited. *American Antiquity* 53:1:13–22.

Dening, G. (1988) *History's Anthropology, the Death of William Gooch*. University Press of America, Lanham, MD. Special publication of the Association for Social Anthropology in Oceania #2.

Dickens, R. S., Ed. (1982) *Archaeology of Urban America, the Search for Pattern and Process*. Academic Press, New York.

Dymond, D. P. (1974) *Archaeology and History; a Plea for Reconciliation*. Thames and Hudson, London.

Ferguson, L., Ed. (1977) *Historical Archaeology and the Importance of Material Things*. Special publication #2 of the Society for Historical Archaeology.

Hodder, I., Ed. (1987) *Archaeology as Long-Term History*. Cambridge University Press, Cambridge.

Hodder, I. (1986) *Reading the Past*. Cambridge University Press, Cambridge.

Leone, M. P. (1977) Foreward. In *Research Strategies in Historical Archaeology*. Stanley South, Ed. Academic Press, New York, pp. xvii–xxi.

Leone, M. P. and P. B. Potter, Jr., Eds. (1988a) *The Recovery of Meaning, Historical Archaeology in the Eastern United States*. Smithsonian Institution Press, Washington, D.C.

Leone, M. P. and P. B. Potter, Jr., (1988b) Issues in Historical Archaeology. In *The Recovery of Meaning*. M. P. Leone and P. B. Potter, Jr., Ed. Smithsonian Press, Washington, D.C., pp. 1–22.

Macfarlane, A. with S. Harrison and C. Jardine (1977) *Reconstructing Historical Communities*. Cambridge University Press, Cambridge.

Orser, C. E. (1988) Toward a Theory of Power for Historical Archaeoelogy: Plantations and Space. In *The Recovery of Meaning*. M. P. Leone and P. B. Potter, Jr., Eds. Smithsonian Press, Washington, D.C., pp. 313–343.

Paynter, R. (1988) Steps to an Archaeology of Capitalism: Material Change and Class Analysis. In *The Recovery of Meaning*. M. P. Leone and P. B. Potter, Jr., Ed. Smithsonian Institution Press, Washington, D.C., pp. 407–433.

Pitt, D. C. (1972) *Using Historical Sources in Anthropology and Sociology*. Holt, Rinehart and Winston, New York.

Renfrew, C. (1982) Towards an Archaeology of Mind. Disney Inaugural Lecture. Cambridge University Press, Cambridge.

Sahlins, M. (1985) *Islands of History*. University of Chicago Press, Chicago.

— (1981) *Historical Metaphors and Mythical Realities: Structures in the Early History of the Sanwich Islands*. University of Michigan Press, Ann Arbor, MI. Special Publication of the Association for Social Anthropology in Oceania, #1.

Schuyler, R. L., Ed. (1980) *Archaeological Perspectives on Ethnicity in America, Afro-American and Asian American Culture History*. Baywood Publishing Company, Farmingdale, NY.

— (1988) Archaeological Remains, Documents, and Anthropology: A Call for a New Culture History. *Historical Archaeology* 22:1:36–42.

— (1978a) *Historical Archaeology: A Guide to Substantive and Theoretical Contributions*. Baywood Publishing Company, Farmingdale, NY.

— (1978b) The Spoken Word, the Written Word, Observed Behavior and Preserved Behavior: The Contexts Available to Historical Archaeologists. Reprinted in *Historical Archaeology: A Guide to Substantive and Theoretical Contributions*. R. L. Schuyler, Ed. Baywood Publishing Company, Farmingdale, NY, pp. 269–277.

— (1970) Historical and Historic Sites Archaeology as Anthropology: Basic Definitions and Relationships. *Historical Archaeology* 4:83–89.

Singleton, T. A., Ed. (1985) *The Archaeology of Slavery and Plantation Life*. Academic Press, Orlando.

South, S., Ed. (1977) *Research Strategies in Historical Archaeology*. Academic Press, New York.

Spencer-Wood, S., Ed. (1987) *Consumer Choice in Historical Archaeology*. Plenum Press, New York.

Stoffle, C. J. (1979) *Materials and Methods for History Research*. Libraryworks, New York.

Topolski, J. (1976) *Methodology of History*. D. Reidel Publishers, Boston.

Wolf, E. (1982) *Europe and the People without History*. University of California Press, Berkeley.

Young, T. C. (1988) Since Herodotus, Has History Been a Valid Concept? *American Antiquity* 53:1:7–12.

Section I. Relationships between Documents and Archaeology

Part A: Contradictory Data

2: Middle-Range Theory, Ceramics, and Capitalism in 19th-Century Rockbridge County, Virginia

Parker B. Potter, Jr.
New Hampshire Division of Historical Resources
Concord, New Hampshire

As my title suggests, this article documents an application of middle-range theory to historical archaeology. However, the particular example of text-aided archaeology I report on here is a research project I conducted 4 or 5 years before I had ever considered using middle-range theory. Within that seeming contradiction lies the first point I want to make.

This article represents a retrofitting of middle-range theory onto a body of previously collected data. I am undertaking this exercise in part to demonstrate that the acceptance of a new theoretical paradigm does not automatically obligate us to throw away everything that has come before. Furthermore, once any statement of theory has been developed to the point where it can be announced as the Next Big Thing, there is usually at least a small body of existing research that conforms to the pattern of the new paradigm, lacking only the most up-to-date labels and terminology. In this particular instance, it is certainly the case that when Mark Leone started writing about middle-range theory (Leone 1988; Leone and Crosby 1987; Leone and Potter 1988), some historical archaeologists had already been thinking along the same lines that Leone was just beginning to articulate. Schmidt and Mrozowski's work on smuggling (Schmidt and Mrozowski 1983, 1988), which predates Leone's discussions of middle-range theory, is a good example of this phenomenon. By discussing my own middle-range theory "retrofit," I hope to encourage others to think about recasting old data in new terms, which will, at the very least, offer some relief to the ever-diminishing archaeological record. If some readers respond to this article by saying, "hey, I've been doing archaeology that

way all along," so much the better. More importantly, I want to argue for the value of middle-range theory by showing how this conceptual tool, had I known to use it, would have greatly simplified the analyses I report on here.

Having laid out the basic intellectual conceit that drives this paper, and my reasons for writing it, I need to explain what I mean by middle-range theory. The term *middle-range theory* has been woven into the archaeological literature over the last decade or so, primarily through the work of Lewis Binford (1977, 1981, 1987), though others have made important contributions to the development of this concept within archaeology (Raab and Goodyear 1984; Grayson 1986). In this article I follow Leone, who has formulated what he calls a historical archaeological analog of Binford's middle-range theory (Leone 1988; Leone and Crosby 1987; Leone and Potter 1988). While Binford has done ethnoarchaeology in order to create a line of evidence parallel to but independent from the archaeological record, Leone's key move is to array the archaeological record against the documentary record in order to tease new meaning from each. In each case, the vehicle for identifying the research questions that lead to new knowledge is the set of incongruities between the two lines of evidence. Rather than dismissing these data as faulty or extraneous, Binford and Leone call such data *ambiguity* and make these data a primary focus of research attention. At one level, historical archaeologists have *always* used the archaeological record and the documentary record to comment on one another, but usually one has been given primacy and has been used simply as a check on the other. Leone's innovation, which sets his version of middle-range theory apart from other attempts at text-aided historical archaeology, is the idea of the *independence* of the archaeological and documentary records.

Historical archaeologists typically make one of their two lines of evidence dependent on the other. Either the various components of the documentary record are homogenized into a kind of encyclopedia for artifact identification or the archaeological record is used simply to fill in gaps in the historical record. The idea that lies behind these two strategies is that the archaeological record and the documentary record are both imperfect representations of the same underlying reality, which makes the less intact of the two records dependent on the one that is more intact. While middle-range theory is an attempt to understand the past that in no way entails a radical epistemological skepticism, it *does* recognize that there is another set of realities at work here, namely, the processes by which these two lines of evidence have been created. Far more than we should, historical archaeologists act as if the documentary record was written just for us, with our analytical and interpretive uses in mind. This is, of course, absurd, but we fall into this fallacy by failing to pay adequate attention to the various reasons *why* the documents we rely on were created in the first place. A principal value of middle-range theory for archaeologists is that it contains a conceptual category for the activities that have structured the ethnographic record, the documentary record, and the archaeological record. These activities are called *organizational behavior,* and by recognizing organizational behaviors, we can begin to understand the documentary record in its own terms, rather than in terms of how well it seems to serve our archaeological needs.

Having introduced organizational behavior, which is the principal piece of middle-range theory I use in this paper, I would like to begin the real work of this paper, which is the use of middle-range theory to explore a body of data. Specifically, the documentary records that mention 19th-century ceramics reflect a wide variety of organizational behaviors. For a newspaper advertisement placed by a general store owner, the goal was to bring customers into the store. For a general store daybook, the purpose in writing about ceramic items was to describe a business transaction, and in particular, the assignment of a monetary value to a commodity. For a probate inventory, the task was to characterize an estate in a way that facilitated the settling of debts and the distribution of inheritance. Each of these organizational behaviors produced documentary records that mention ceramic items, but they cite different ceramic attributes and do so in varying degrees of detail.

Most newspaper advertisements in 19th-century Rockbridge County — except those that were printed just after the Civil War — describe in great detail the fabrics and groceries for sale while lumping all ceramics together in a phrase such as, "our usual assortment of hardware, Queensware, and dry goods" (Potter 1982:36–38). But the daybooks kept by these same merchants listed ceramic items rather more specifically, by size, shape, decoration, ware type, and, of course, price. One response to this phenomenon is to reject newspaper ads as useless and to concentrate on daybooks. However, by understanding the different organizational behaviors that created these different documents, it is possible to move beyond judging them in terms of the richness of their detail and, instead, think about them in terms of the original purposes for which they were intended. For example, if we replace the assumption that more detail makes for a better document with the assumption that Rockbridge general store advertisements must have been effective because their pattern did not change for decades, then we can learn about Rockbridge from the ads. Specifically, the ads suggest quite strongly that ceramics did not play a significant role in 19th-century material culture, and certainly could not be counted on to attract general store customers.

The technique for using the idea of organizational behavior as a research tool is relatively straightforward. Instead of searching out every documentary reference to a particular category of material culture — as I did with ceramics in Rockbridge — a more efficient strategy is to seek the documents created by people in the past who had needs and interests that mirror those of the present-day analyst. For archaeologists interested in using ceramics as a guide to socioeconomics, probate inventories are not a very useful document. Their usefulness is diminished not so much by their lack of detail, but rather by the fact that, in most cases, ceramic items had lost a good bit of their economic value by the time they were probated. Unlike cattle, crops, or slaves, ceramic items had relatively little resale value and were frequently passed on to survivors, along with clothing, linens, and other consumable personal property. On the other hand, general store daybooks list ceramic items at precisely the point where their economic value is the greatest and at the point where it is most important to characterize their attributes in terms of dollars and cents. There is another way to think about the difference between probate inventories and general store daybooks. Consider the life spans of people and ceramic items as two variables. With probates, the ceramic items are usually a mixture of old and new, while the persons whose inventories are probated are *all* at the ends of their lives. Among other things, this means that probated ceramic items have lost *varying* amounts of their economic value. However, in the general store daybooks, the ceramics are all at the same point in their careers, and *uniformly* at their peak of value, while their purchasers are both young and old. To learn about ceramics and their economic values, it seems sensible to use elements of the documentary record in which the age of ceramics is well controlled. Importantly, in each of these cases, it is organizational behavior and not the level of detail that makes general store daybooks better than probate inventories for socioeconomic studies of ceramics.

These various insights, presented here in two neat paragraphs, are the major conclusions of a 90-page masters thesis (Potter 1982), researched and written over a 12-month period. Had I gone into the field armed with the idea of organizational behavior, I would have begun with these two paragraphs and then spent 12 months and 90 pages actually trying to prove something or another about 19th-century Rockbridge County, instead of devoting all my attention to a methodological issue. I am writing this paper in the hope that this retrofitting of the idea of organizational behavior onto my Rockbridge County data will help other people avoid reinventing this wheel yet again.

The balance of this paper consists of three main parts. I begin with the historical problem that sent me into the field in Rockbridge County. I follow this with a discussion of an archaeological problem that flows from the historical problem. I conclude with solutions to the archaeological problem, based on the concept of organizational behavior.

A Historical Problem

The data presented in this paper were collected in 1981 as a part of the Washington and Lee University High Hollows Research Project. In 1974, under the direction of John McDaniel, Washington and Lee began an ongoing program of historical archaeology in Rockbridge County, Virginia (McDaniel 1984; McDaniel and Potter 1984). The first stage in this research program was an investigation of the campus of Liberty Hall Academy. Located just west of Lexington, Liberty Hall Academy was a late 18th-century precursor of today's Washington and Lee University (McDaniel 1977; McDaniel, Watson, and Moore 1979). A principal goal of the Liberty Hall project has been to use archaeological data to test a series of myths about the Scotch-Irish Presbyterians who settled the Valley of Virginia and who founded the school that became Washington and Lee (McDaniel and Potter 1980).

Early in the Liberty Hall project, McDaniel and his colleagues realized that the excavation of a site as specialized as an academic complex would provide only one part of the data necessary to understand Scotch-Irish history and culture in Rockbridge County (McDaniel and Patter 1984:67). In recognition of this, plans were made to move beyond the Liberty Hall campus and out into the county. Augmenting this strong interest in the Scotch Irish, a second interest lead to the founding of the High Hollows project. Specifically, the mountain hollows of Rockbridge County are full of cellar holes and chimneys

marking the centers of working farms that have since been reclaimed by forest regrowth. Even casual observation demonstrates that the county's steep mountain hollows were occupied much more intensively in the past than they are today and that this occupation was largely agricultural. In the popular versions of history that circulate throughout the county, these tumbledown cabins are attributed to three different groups: (1) early (mid-18th-century) settlers, (2) Civil War deserters, and (3) poor 19th-century farmers and squatters. There is a good bit of evidence that argues against 18th-century settlers and Civil War deserters as the builders and inhabitants of these vanished farms (Potter 1982:26–27; Babits 1984), which leaves the third attribution, poor 19th-century farmers and squatters.

The High Hollows Research Project was designed, in part, as an attempt to test this popular historical notion. The project focuses on a 9000-acre area of Rockbridge County located approximately 10 miles west of Lexington. This area contains the four major landform types found in the county: floodplains, hollows, steep slopes, and ridge tops. The High Hollows Project is a standard regional study that has entailed documentary research, extensive survey, and intensive excavation (McDaniel and Potter 1984:68–69; McDaniel and Adams 1984). Stated broadly, the project has sought "to determine *when* hollows were occupied, *by how many persons* they were occupied and most importantly, specifically *what* the occupants of the hollows were doing there, particularly with regard to subsistence and participation in the local economy" (Potter 1982:23). Leone (1984:97) characterizes this project as an attempt to study "the ebb and flow of capitalism into and out of the area." Stated in other terms, the project has been interested in examining just how people were able to live in areas that are now considered too isolated or unproductive to support intensive occupation.

In order to answer these questions about hollow dwellers, the project has been set up as a comparative analysis in which the principal comparisons are between hollow sites and sites in the floodplain. This comparative analysis was originally stated as a pair of propositions:

Important cultural contrasts can be identified between the inhabitants of our research area and those of Liberty Hall and other sites within towns,

and:

Significant variations in economic adaptation existed between the inhabitants of sites in the hollows and those in the floodplains (McDaniel and Potter 1984:69).

This second proposition was subsequently reformulated as a testable hypothesis:

The larger and/or more farmable the landholdings of a household, the larger, more expensive, or more highly elaborated will be the inventory of material culture items maintained by that household (Potter 1982:28).

This is a fairly straightforward hypothesis, and it certainly mirrors the local popular histories, which would suggest its archaeological confirmation; that is, local popular history would predict the recovery of "expensive" assemblages from floodplain sites and the recovery of "poor" assemblages from sites up in the hollows. As for actually testing the hypothesis, measurement of the first variable is a relatively easy matter; tracts of farmland can be measured in terms of acreage, elevation, degree of slope, soil quality, nearness to water, and access to lines of transportation — judged either in 20th-century terms or according to 19th-century norms and preferences, as stated in a wide range of historical literature on farming. What is less easy to measure is the size, expense, and degree of elaboration of the material culture maintained by a household. Measurement of this second variable is, in fact, the archaeological problem that is the subject of the next section.

An Archaeological Problem

The High Hollows hypothesis presented in the previous section postulates a relationship between the quality of farmland and the value of portable material culture. If we assume that we can define with confidence the characteristics of "good" farmland, then the discovery of "expensive" assemblages on hollow sites will suggest something counterintuitive, namely, that poor farmers spent their limited resources on expensive tableware and their household furnishings. There is, however, a second way to "read" such a "disconfirmation," namely, "expensive" assemblages on hollow sites may indicate that land in the hollows was not "bad" farmland in the 19th century. In either case, this hypothesis is intended to explore the translations of farmland into crops, crops into cash, and cash into household furnishings. To test this hypothesis, it is essential to have a reliable way of measuring the value of the artifactual record, a task usually undertaken with the assistance of the documentary record. But before it is possible to use the documentary record to attach values to the archaeological record, it is necessary to attach names to artifacts. This problem of naming is the archaeological problem referred to by the heading of this section, and in particular, I will focus on the problem of naming ceramic artifacts in a way that makes them useful data for socioeconomic analyses (see also Beaudry 1980 and Beaudry et al. 1983 for a sophisticated linguistic approach to the problem of archaeological naming).

There is a well-established precedent in historical archaeology for concentrating on a single artifact category. My decision to deal with ceramics is reasonable, given the fact that this paper stands in a long line of socioeconomic analyses based largely, or even exclusively, on the ceramic record. Even so, and at the risk of arguing against the value of my own paper, it is important to place ceramics in the context of all the other things people could buy, sell, and own in 19th-century Rockbridge County. As I have already noted, general store advertisements mentioned ceramics in a perfunctory fashion, suggesting that they were ordinary, everyday items. Fabrics and groceries were the exciting items, listed in great detail, presumably to attract customers. Moving from advertising to inventory, I examined four annual inventories from H. L. Wilson's general store, taken from 1846 through 1849 (Wilson, 1846, 1847, 1848, 1849). The value of Wilson's ceramics, as a percentage of the total value of his inventory, ran from a high of 2.6% in 1846 to a low of 1.1% in 1849. Clearly, ceramics were not a major part of what Wilson had for sale. Finally, if we turn to the end of the line for ceramic items, in terms of the documentary record, we see a similar pattern. Of the 10 inventories probated in Rockbridge County in 1850 (Rockbridge County Will Books), 7 have ceramic assemblages that account for less than 0.5% of the total cash value of the estate. In the other 3 estates, ceramics accounted for between 2.0 and 5.7% of the estate value, but interestingly, these were by far the 3 least valuable estates in the sample. Furthermore, the seven most valuable estates were left by men, while all three of the least valuable estates were left by women. The conclusion here is that the present archaeological visibility of ceramics as an artifact type is considerably in excess of the past behavioral visibility of ceramic items; that is, it seems that ceramics are far more important to historical archaeologists today than they were to the people who used them in the past.

This conclusion leads directly to an important question: Is it appropriate for historical archaeologists to place so much analytical weight on the ceramic record, given its seemingly small place in the lives of the people we study? Or, to paraphrase the famous question once put to Freud, "is a plate ever just a plate?" Happily, I have found an answer to this question in my Rockbridge probate data, and in particular, in the 1841 inventory of John F. Caruthers. The standard pattern in Rockbridge probates was for property of economic utility, principally cattle and slaves, to be listed first, while domestic items such as linens and housewares — including ceramics — were listed near the end of the inventory. Furthermore, cattle and slaves were individually listed with a good bit of descriptive detail, while housewares were often lumped together in lots and left relatively undescribed. Caruthers' inventory does not follow this pattern. Instead, it begins with a detailed listing of a large number of ceramic items. Caruthers' inventory treated ceramics in the same way that cattle and slaves were treated in the inventories of most other men. At first I took this anomaly to be a meaningless idiosyncrasy, but on further examination I was able to find an explanation. A marginal notation indicated that John Caruthers was a merchant, that is, a man for whom ceramics were economic and not simply domestic. By treating this anomaly as data, as what Binford would call ambiguity, I was able to postulate an explanation, and more importantly, a justification for the analytical weight historical archaeologists place on ceramics. There is no doubt that for people in 19th-century Rockbridge County, ceramics were sometimes domestic items and sometimes economic items. Therefore, while we should be careful about the degree to which we allow ceramics to stand for an entire economic system, we are indeed acting reasonably when we attempt to gain socioeconomic insights from the analysis of ceramics.

Having justified and qualified the use of ceramic artifacts as indices of socioeconomics, we are back where we were two paragraphs ago, facing the archaeological problem of determining how best to name ceramic artifacts in order to extract socioeconomic meaning from them. As a theoretical issue, the naming problem has been recognized by archaeologists, at least prehistorians, for decades. The problem is that for any archaeological find, even the smallest shard of creamware, there are dozens of variables that can be measured, dozens of attributes that can be used to construct a name (Hill and Evans 1972; Fontana 1973; Dunnell 1971; Clarke 1968; Kaplin 1964; Binford 1965; Potter 1989:230–267). Obviously we cannot call every artifact by a name made up of all the things we can learn about it. Thus we must abbreviate. But how? Is it creamware or is it a plate? Or is it a creamware plate? Does it matter that it is a dinner plate and not a dessert plate? What about the shape of the rim? Or the color of the decoration? These are only some of the variables we typically pay attention to, and, on top of these, there are many more we have trained ourselves to ignore or have never bothered to think about (Deetz 1983:29–30; Potter 1982:91–92). The obvious solution to this large number of variables, identified as such many years ago, is that we should measure variables, attend to attributes, and name artifacts in accordance with the questions we want to urge them to answer. Given my adherence to this position, I disagree strongly with Noel Hume's statement that: "The potters' written observations describing the names, distribution, and popularity of their wares are likely to be a good deal more accurate than are, say, the advertisements of American china shops whose proprietors bought them from middlemen and had no contact with the factories" (Noel Hume 1973:217–218). For a variety of reasons, positions like Noel Hume's still predominate, and the idea of naming artifacts in relation to particular analytical problems has not trickled down to, and through, historical archaeology nearly as thoroughly as it should have. For one thing, historical archaeologists are faced with a vast artifactual record and an equally vast documentary record. But a big pile of artifacts is truly a big pile of nothing when the artifacts in the pile have no names or have irrelevant names. Given

the priority of naming in the process of turning nothing into something, and the size of the task, it is no wonder that historical archaeologists are often quite happy to use whatever naming scheme is available, and it is also no wonder that, in many cases, the identification of artifacts is taken to be the end of the line, rather than the beginning of an analytical process. Beaudry (1980:12–13) makes a similar point. Furthermore, there is the unhappy fact that learning how to identify historic artifacts in one or two ways is virtually a rite of passage in historical archaeology. One is not considered a true historical archaeologist without the ability to identify ceramics the way Noel Hume does (Noel Hume 1970:98–145) and to manipulate their dates of manufacture the way South does (South 1977:201–274). These skills are certainly important to know, or at least know about, but it is a mistake to see them as existing independent of a particular analytical problem. Sometimes it is valuable to be able to identify ceramics in the same way that their makers would have, which is largely what Noel Hume does (Noel Hume 1973:217) but, as Rubertone (1976, 1979:64) has argued for prehistoric ceramic studies, there are many situations in which it would be far more helpful to replicate some other knowledge of those same ceramics.

Here is where middle-range theory comes in. Any piece of creamware we dig up today has gone through a long series of transformations. That archaeological artifact was once a lump of clay, then it was prepared, poured into a mold, decorated, baked, crated, shipped, sold at wholesale, inventoried, displayed, sold at retail, used, broken, and then discarded. At many of these points, people had the opportunity and the need to write about the objects that are now our artifacts. People who handled ceramic items wrote pattern books, advertisements, price-fixing lists, bills of lading, store inventories, invoices, daybooks, ledgers, wills, and probate inventories, to name some, but not all, of the documents that mention ceramics. When people created these documentary records, they were not doing so for archaeologists 200 years later, they were writing about plates in order to do something with them, make them, advertise them, buy them, sell them, and so on. These are all organizational behaviors and they determined the degree of detail in various documents, as well as the attributes selected in place of those that were ignored. For a teamster, the notation "one crate of plates" probably contained sufficient detail to ensure the carting of several sets of plates. However, to sell plates to merchants, people at the potteries needed to discuss in some detail things like rim shapes, plate sizes, and even the specific designs on transfer-printed plates. Given this, the question for archaeologists is not which documents are the "best," but rather, which documents are the best *for what*. Josiah Wedgwood had a great deal to say about the ceramics he designed, made, and sold in the late 18th century, but despite what Noel Hume might say, that does not make Wedgwood's records any better than any other document that mentions those same ceramic pieces. The key is to match historic documents and the names they contain with archaeological needs on the basis of the similarities between a particular archaeological analysis and the organizational behavior that structured a particular documentary record. To answer a broadly framed question about overland shipping, it might be sufficient to use names derived from teamsters' records and to lump *all* ceramics together, to weigh them, and then to compare ceramics to other artifact classes on the basis of weight. Alternatively, to answer a very specific chronological question or a question about the worldwide distribution of particular Staffordshire transfer print motifs, it is appropriate to use pattern books and other pottery records to construct an elaborate scheme for naming ceramic artifacts based on the designs they bear. The point is, there are no "right" names or "wrong" names for artifacts in the absence of a particular analytical problem. If widely implemented, the use of organizational behavior to link contemporary analytical needs with specific appropriate historical documents could help historical archaeology to be a little less formulaic, a little less routinized, and a little more creative.

Having discussed the problem of naming, I would now like to turn to the analytical problem of making historic ceramics useful for socioeconomic analysis. The historical issue I am trying to understand is the relationship between landholdings and the expenditure of income on household goods. In other words, I am trying to understand the translation of farmland into the kinds of objects we recover from the archaeological record. On the archaeological side, a number of approaches have been developed for assessing the social or economic value of archaeologically recovered ceramics, including those put forward by Wise (n.d.); Outlaw, Bogley, and Outlaw (1977); Otto (1975, 1977, 1980, 1984); and Miller (1980, 1984). Each of these analysts has attempted to isolate a single socially or economically relevant variable that may be used to determine a socioeconomic "signature" or "profile" for assemblages of archaeologically recovered ceramics. Wise's "Status Index I" and "Status Index II" were based on ware type (refined ware vs. coarseware, and porcelain vs. refined earthenware), as were the analyses of Pettus and Utopia conducted by Outlaw, Bogley, and Outlaw. Both Otto and Miller, on the other hand, have isolated decoration as the most socioeconomically sensitive variable, at least for 19th-century ceramics. While each of these strategies has its strengths and weaknesses (Potter 1982:42–56), they all share the same pattern, the identification of the single variable that is the "prime mover" in determining the cost of a ceramic item and the value of a ceramic assemblage.

Of these four approaches, there is little question that Miller's has been the most influential, and I would like to use Miller's work as a jumping-off point. Miller's great contribution is a careful and sophisticated reading of the ceramic price-fixing lists made and used by the Staffordshire pottery factories. From these lists he has determined that decoration was the variable that moved most consistently with ceramic cost, with undecorated pieces at the bottom of the scale, transfer-printed pieces at the top, and edge-decorated pieces somewhere in between. Furthermore, using the value of undecorated vessels as a baseline, Miller has formulated a series of scalings for different years, representing the varying relationships between the costs of undecorated pieces and the various kinds of decorated pieces. For example, if on one price-fixing list, plain plates sold for $1.50 per set, shell-edged plates for $2.25 per set, and transfer-printed plates for $4.50, the "CC index" for shell-edged plates would be 2.25/1.5 or 1.5, while the CC index for transfer-printed plates would be 4.5/1.5 or 3. To use these scales archaeologically, all one needs to do is select the scale for the year closest to the date of occupation, and then for each decorative category multiply the number of specimens by the CC index for that decorative type, add the products, and divide by the total number of specimens. The result is a single CC index that characterizes the overall price of the assemblage on a scale that runs from one (the absolute minimum for an assemblage of all undecorated pieces) to the CC index value for the most expensive decorative type on the particular scale that was used (indicating an assemblage in which all pieces exhibited the most expensive type of decoration). The value of Miller's work is that it provides a precise and reliable way of assessing the costs of ceramic assemblages.

Miller's work stands out from most other attempts at assessing the costs of ceramic artifacts because Miller is very careful to identify the specific documents from which he draws the data he uses to attach names to artifacts. Price-fixing agreements are an appropriate set of documents to use for this purpose, because they were written at a point in the life spans of ceramic items when these items did indeed possess economic value. The only problem with Miller's work, from the standpoint of an archaeological analyst attempting to answer a question about *local* economics, is that there is no guarantee that the cost ratios Miller identified in price-fixing agreements between potteries held up, intact, through the processes of wholesaling and retailing. This is not a criticism of Miller, only a caution to those who would use his work. I am arguing that it would be a good idea, if possible, to verify Miller's indices through *local* documentation of *retail* trade before assuming that they are appropriate in a particular context. Again, organizational behavior is the key here. Price-fixing agreements represent what the potteries wanted to happen in the marketplace, while general store daybooks represent what actually took place at the point where consumers got their hands on what the potteries produced.

Archaeological Solutions

To this point I have framed a historical problem, measuring the participation of Rockbridge County hollow dwellers in the local market economy, and I have discussed several of the issues that complicate the use of the archaeological record to solve this historical problem. In this third and final section, I will discuss three parts of an archaeological solution to the historical problem I have framed. These parts do not constitute a fully formed archaeological solution, but instead represent three insights into the documentary record I have gained as a result of thinking about the documentary record along the lines suggested by middle-range theory.

CREATING CERAMIC SCALINGS FOR ROCKBRIDGE

The first of these insights is specific and flows from my trying to follow George Miller's lead, using 19th-century Rockbridge County data to establish an attribute scaling for assigning relative purchase costs to archaeological ceramics. In examining 10 general store daybooks spanning the period from 1796 through 1869, I read and analyzed several hundred strings of data in the following format:

1/2 doz dinner plates 3/-

In this case, Wilson & Irvine sold John Croddy a half dozen dinner plates for three shillings (about 50¢) in March of 1843 (Wilson & Irvine, 1842). At the most basic level, this entry documents the translation of a certain amount of merchandise into a certain amount of money. This entry is about average in terms of the degree of detail it provides, and there is no question that Miller's price-fixing agreements provided considerably more detail than even the most elaborate Rockbridge general store daybooks. From the perspective of what Miller and Noel Hume know about ceramics on the basis of English pottery records, this entry is unsatisfactory because it tells us only that Croddy's new plates are dinner plates (as opposed to breakfast plates or dessert plates), while failing to inform us as to ware type or decoration. What makes these daybooks seem even more suspect is the fact that some entries give no description of the basic form, they say only "plates," with no value for size/shape, ware type, or decoration, while other entries list values for two or even all three of these variables.

The ideal or fully elaborated data string for a general store transaction follows the following format:

quantity + decoration + ware type + size/shape + basic form = price

An example would be:

12 blue china breakfast plates, $1.50

In this example *blue* is the decoration, *china* is the ware type, and *breakfast* is the size/shape. Taken together, *blue china breakfast* constitutes a description of *plate*, which is the basic form. While this is the ideal format, all that was *necessary* to document a transaction was a quantity, a basic form, and a price, as in

6 plates, $1.00

But while

quantity + basic form = price

could describe any ceramic transaction, decoration and ware type are variables for which *every* ceramic item has a value, and most ceramic items had a size/shape. Wilson & Irvine did not indicate a decoration or a ware type for the plates they sold John Croddy, but those plates *had* to have been made out of some kind of ware, and they *had* to have been decorated or undecorated (white); they could not have been "ware neutral" or "decoration neutral." Without a ware type or a decoration, they would not have been plates. Therefore, even when general store merchants did not list values for these four variables, there were values available to have been listed.

As I have already noted, Wilson & Irvine's description of their sale to John Croddy was about average in its level of detail. Croddy's transaction was one of 551 extracted from 10 different daybooks (Caruthers, 1796; Dold, 1854, 1858, 1860, 1869; Dold & Son, 1867; White & Wilson, 1861; Wilson, 1860; Wilson & Company, 1844; Wilson & Irvine, 1842). Of these entries, 22.3% mention decoration, while only 11.4% mention ware type. A majority of these daybook entries, 52.3%, contain no descriptive term at all. Data from 193 general store inventory entries are similar to the daybook records. In the inventories, 43.5% of the entries contain a term for description, and 11.1% contain a term for ware type. Of these 193 entries from general store inventories, 16.1% contain no descriptive term at all. The majority of the entries from both sources contain no descriptions or have one descriptive term, for size/shape *or* decoration *or* ware type. Some entries have terms for two descriptive categories, while very few have terms for all three.

Given the range of information that *could* have been recorded in any given transaction, but was not, we are faced with the problem of dealing with data strings in which so much information seems to be missing. If we move beyond the outward appearance of this database, and make the assumption that whatever else it is, Wilson & Irvine's daybook was useful to Wilson & Irvine, then we can make some headway. Here is the key question: What was the organizational behavior that produced this document? Wilson & Irvine needed to indicate how and why they accomplished each of their transactions, each of their translations of merchandise into cash. Furthermore, they needed to do so quickly and efficiently. They did not have time to write down everything they knew about the things they sold, and it is more than likely that they confined their written commentary to those things that affected value. Thus, it is reasonable to assume that the "gaps" in general store daybooks are not random, but rather, represent merchants' conscious decisions not to write down ceramic attributes they could easily identify, but that were irrelevant because they did not affect value. Finally, organizational behavior is the key to turning this assumption into a testable hypothesis, and it is also the key to deriving an analytical payoff from it.

The organizational behavior that produced general store daybooks was the assignment of cash values to quantities of merchandise, and these assignments of value are basically a set of equations. To test the assumption that the entries on the merchandise side of the equation represent a sensible "shorthand" created by merchants, we can set up a hypothesis that links a measurable variation on the merchandise side with a measurable variation on the value side. Such a hypothesis would be: the greater the cost of a ceramic item, the more elaborately it will be described. This hypothesis follows my initial observation that for any particular basic form, the items with the fewest descriptive terms were the cheapest, while those with the most descriptive terms were the most expensive.

A test of this hypothesis may be made using data on the sales of plates, abstracted from Wilson & Irvine's 1842 daybook. In the 1 year covered by this book (April 1842 to April 1843), Wilson & Irvine recorded the sales of 26 sets of plates with a total value of $16.42. The lowest priced plates were $37\frac{1}{2}$¢ per set; the highest priced plates were $87\frac{1}{2}$¢ per set. The mean price paid for a set of plates was about 63¢. Of the 26 sets of plates, 14 had no descriptive term listed in the daybook entry, while the remaining 12 had only a single descriptive term. Of the 14 sets of plates with no descriptive term listed, 13 sold for the lowest possible price, $37\frac{1}{2}$¢, while the other sold for $62\frac{1}{2}$¢. For the 12 sets of plates with a single descriptive term, five different descriptive terms were used. They are *soup, breakfast, dinner, injn'd,* (presumably engine-turned annular wares), and *Liverpool*. The first three terms are values for "size/shape;" the last two are values for "decoration." Seven sets of plates have no terms for "size/shape" listed, five have terms for "decoration." No sets of plates had terms for "ware type" applied to them.

When the prices paid for sets of plates in this daybook are scaled and the terms for those plates are compared to the scaling, a pattern emerges. As noted above, 13 of the 14 sets of plates with no descriptive term sold for prices less than or equal to the mean price for a set of plates. On the other hand, each of the five sets of plates with a term

listed for "decoration" sold for a price greater than or equal to the mean price. Of the seven sets of plates with a term for "size/shape," six sold for less than the mean price and one for more than the mean. Stated differently, the range of prices paid for sets of plates was from $37\frac{1}{2}$¢ to $87\frac{1}{2}$¢. The mean price for plates with no descriptive terms was 39.3¢; plates referred to with a term for "size/shape" had a mean price of 52.5¢; and plates referred to with a term for "decoration" had a mean price of 75.0¢.

In a rough way, these data confirm the hypothesis; plates with descriptive terms were demonstrably more expensive than plates without descriptive terms. This, in turn, suggests a broader conclusion. Descriptive terms were used primarily to indicate why a particular set of plates sold for more than the minimum price, and they were not used when the value for any particular descriptive variable was the least expensive of the available options. This is the general store merchants' shorthand. According to this shorthand, John Croddy's "1/2 dozen dinner plates 3/-" were probably "1/2 doz white earthenware dinner plates 3/-." The "codebook" to this shorthand is important, because it allows us to see meaning in a collection of data that we might otherwise reject as random and incomplete. Merchants did not leave out descriptive terms because they were stupid or lazy, they left out terms that did not contribute to cost, which was the basis of meaning in a book composed of sales records.

One archaeological payoff from cracking this code is a cost profile for 19th-century ceramics in Rockbridge County. The value of this profile is that it will allow for a determination of the relative expensiveness of ceramic assemblages from 19th-century sites in the county. As I have noted, most analysts have isolated single variables that affect ceramic socioeconomics. Wise and Outlaw, Bogley, and Outlaw focused on ware type, while Otto and Miller have focused on decoration. On the basis of my daybook data, I have opted for a multivariable approach (see also Friedrich 1970; S. Plog 1973; Redman 1978; Rubertone 1979; and Whallon 1972 for similar approaches with different data). In the 1842 Wilson & Irvine daybook, cited above, two different variables affected price. Plates that differed from the standard in size/shape cost were, on the average, 13¢ per set more expensive than the plates with no descriptive terms. Plates with a term for decoration were about 35¢ per set more expensive than the standard plates and about 22¢ per set more expensive than the plates with a term for size/shape. At least in the eyes of Wilson & Irvine, a variation in size/shape made plates a little more expensive, while a difference in decoration made a set of plates much more expensive. References to the third category of description, ware type, are relatively rare, occurring in only about 11% of my 551 daybook entries. However, when ware type is mentioned, it usually makes a set of plates even more expensive than a set of plates given a term for decoration. In the 1854 S. M. Dold daybook, the average price for sets of plates with no description was 46.3¢. Plates with a term for size/shape sold for 75¢ per set. Plates with a term for decoration sold for an average of 50¢ per set (owing to the fact that in all three cases the term for decoration was *white*, the value for this variable that was usually suppressed). Finally, plates with a term for ware type sold for an average cost of 83.3¢ per set.

Taken in sum, these data suggest that a variation in size/shape added a little to the cost of a set of otherwise standard plates, a variation in decoration added somewhat more to the cost, and a variation in ware type added a good bit more. There was also an additive quality to the application of descriptive terms. Entries with two or three descriptive terms are rare, but when they do occur sets of plates with more than one term tend to be more expensive than even the costliest of the single-variable sets. In the 1844 H. L. Wilson & Company book, the average prices were no description, 39.1¢; size/shape description, 50.0¢; decoration description, 67.7¢, and size/shape *and* decoration description, 78.1¢.

This multivariable cost profile for Rockbridge ceramics leaves one problem unresolved and leads to one additional archaeological payoff. The problem is establishing the standard values for size/shape, decoration, and ware type, or in other words, the values understood by the shopkeepers and left unrecorded. I have no insights to offer with regard to the standard value for size/shape. This is the most complex descriptive category, because it is the only one that varied along with basic form. The terms *dinner* and *dessert* applied to plates, but not to bowls or to pitchers. The best I can do with decoration and ware type is to work backward from the terms that are used, in an attempt to guess the term that was usually suppressed. With regard to decoration, *edged* and *Liverpool* appear frequently, while *white* is used only rarely, despite the frequent discovery of white or undecorated ceramic shards. It seems a safe surmise that *white* or *undecorated* is the decoration in entries without a decorative term. As for ware type, the terms *china* and *stoneware* sometimes appear, while the term *earthenware* never does. Again, it seems safe to conclude that *earthenware* is the value for ware type when ware type is left unspecified.

The additional archaeological payoff from this profile is that it allows historical archaeologists working in Rockbridge to make informed decisions about which ceramic attributes matter in particular cases. For example, the daybooks give no indication that the particular pattern on a Liverpool plate had any effect on price. A careful matching of archaeological specimens to Spode/Copeland transfer-print pattern books may offer chronological insights, but it would be a meaningless exercise if the task at hand is local economic analysis. Given the relatively small impact of variations in size/shape on the cost of plates, it is not all that important for an archaeologist with basic economic questions to be able to distinguish between dessert plates and breakfast plates. However, when the goal is to answer economic questions, in Rockbridge County, it is relatively important to be able to identify *edged* or *Liverpool* plates, and it is very important to be able to distinguish between *china* and all the other ware types. *Liverpool* ceramic decoration is a signature of moderate expenditure on ceramic items, while *china* is a signature of the greatest possible expenditure on ceramics in 19th-century Rockbridge.

In summary, this section is directed toward two objectives, one methodological, the other substantive. On the methodological side, I have created a way of recovering greater meaning from general store daybooks than these documents appear to contain on the surface. On the substantive side, I have proposed a set of general characteristics for an economic scaling of Rockbridge County ceramic artifacts from the 19th century. There is nothing in these scalings that is especially radical or surprising. I did not discover some sort of strange "inverse economic stratigraphy" in which transfer-printed plates cost less than plain ones. My scalings are pretty much what one would expect, based on a reading of Noel Hume and Miller, but this lack of surprises does not argue against the value of these findings to an archaeologist asking local economic questions in Rockbridge County. This sort of local verification of broader national or international patterns is an essential first step in adapting work such as Noel Hume's or Miller's for local use. Furthermore, variations between the documents maintained at these two different levels of analysis — and there will be some — should be treated as "ambiguity," in the middle-range theory sense, and made the object of future inquiry and investigation.

COUNTING CERAMICS IN ROCKBRIDGE

My second archaeological solution flows from one of the most important qualities of ceramic as an artifact type. While ceramic as a material is nearly indestructible in the archaeological record, ceramic fragments enter the archaeological record in the first place because ceramic *objects* are relatively fragile (Fontana 1973:3). This wonderful paradox points up a key issue in ceramic analysis, the fact that ceramic artifacts may be counted by the fragment or by the vessel. In addition, there is yet a *third* way to count ceramics. This issue is an important one, because without the ability to quantify our assemblages, it is impossible to apply any of the kinds of scalings discussed in the previous section.

Consider again John Croddy's ceramic purchase of:

1/2 dozen dinner plates 3/-

To answer the kinds of economic questions I posed earlier in this paper, it would be useful to have a way of

Table 1
Wilson & Irvine's 1842 Ceramic Sales

Basic Form	Purchasable Units	Vessels	Cash Value
Bowl	40 (30.3)	40 (7.2)	$ 3.40 (7.1)
Plate	28 (21.1)	181 (32.6)	16.42 (34.5)
Cup & saucer	19 (14.4)	228 (41.0)	4.75 (10.0)
Dish	12 (9.1)	12 (2.2)	6.87 (14.4)
Pitcher	11 (8.3)	11 (2.0)	4.02 (8.6)
Mug	10 (7.6)	10 (1.8)	1.81 (2.5)
Chamber pot	3 (2.3)	3 (0.5)	.75 (1.6)
Jug	3 (2.3)	3 (0.5)	.60 (1.3)
Salt stand	2 (1.5)	2 (0.4)	.12 (0.3)
Wash bowl	2 (1.5)	2 (0.4)	.44 (0.9)
Set of china	2 (1.5)	64 (11.5)	9.00 (18.9)
	132 100%	556 100%	$47.59 100%

characterizing the cost of archaeologically recovered ceramic assemblages, and transactions like Croddy's offer considerable assistance. Once a ceramic assemblage is described as a series of minimum vessel counts, all that is necessary is a little algebra and the knowledge that 1 shilling equals 12 pence:

$$1/2 \text{ dozen plates} = 6 \text{ plates} = 3 \text{ shillings} = 36 \text{ pence}$$
$$6 \text{ plates} = 36 \text{ pence}$$
$$1 \text{ plate} = 6 \text{ pence}$$

The only problem is that this final equation is not one that can be found in Rockbridge County general store daybooks. In my examination of several hundred transactions involving plates, I found fewer than five instances where plates were sold in any quantity other than some multiple of the standard set of six (see Potter 1982:30–31 for a discussion of the number of plates in a set). While it is easy enough to calculate the cost of a plate, useful in attaching dollar values to ceramic assemblages described in terms of minimum vessel counts, such an exercise would not mirror any kind of 19th-century behavior. Merchants like Wilson & Irvine sold individual plates about as often as they sold the shards of broken plates. My point is that neither shard counts nor minimum vessel counts necessarily allow us to understand assemblages of 19th-century ceramics in terms of their acquisition.

Again, the key here is organizational behavior. General store daybooks tell us precisely the units in which ceramic items were bought and sold, and this part of the documentary record should be our guide to determining the analytical units we use. The term I would like to coin here is *purchasable unit*. For many items the purchasable unit was the individual vessel; one could buy a single pitcher, dish, or teapot. For these basic forms, a minimum vessel count would also be a minimum count of purchasable units. However, for plates, the purchasable

unit seems to have been the set. This means two things. First, when somebody broke a plate, they also broke a *set* of plates. More importantly, the discovery of a plate fragment indicates not only the purchase of a plate, but also the purchase of five more. The discovery of a teacup fragment indicates the purchase of *12* vessels, 6 cups and 6 saucers. Ceramic artifacts can be counted by the fragment, by the vessel, or by the purchasable unit, and if the goal is to answer questions about local economics, the purchasable unit seems to be the most appropriate unit of analysis.

This distinction between vessels and purchasable units could be dismissed as just another example of the formation processes of archaeological jargon, if not for the fact that the daybooks themselves indicate that this distinction is deeply meaningful. Consider, for example, the following summation of Wilson & Irvine's 1842 daybook. In Table 1, Wilson & Irvine's ceramic sales are listed, by basic form. The three columns of the table represent three ways of characterizing the store's ceramic sales. The first column lists sales by purchasable units, the second, sales by the number of vessels, and the third, sales by dollar value. In each column, raw numbers are listed first, followed by percentages in parentheses.

These data suggest three very different ways of understanding Wilson & Irvine's ceramic sales. For example, the basic form Wilson & Irvine call *dish* accounted for 9.1% of the 132 purchasable units of ceramics Wilson & Irvine sold in 1842, 2.2% of the 556 ceramic vessels that went out the door of their shop, and 14.4% of the $47.59 spent on ceramics that went into their till. At the very least, these data demonstrate the danger in equating vessel counts with counts of purchasable units, and therefore, the danger of stopping at minimum vessel counts when using ceramic artifacts to perform economic analyses, particularly analyses such as Miller's procedure for calculating assemblagewide CC index values. The archaeological solution here is straightforward. If we are to answer local economic questions, we need to count our finds the same way that merchants counted ceramic items, 1 at a time, 6 at a time, or 12 at a time, depending on which basic form we are dealing with. This approach to the artifactual record solves the discrepancy between the first two columns in Table 1.

Q

In an earlier section, I discussed the creation of attribute-based cost profiles against which to measure assemblages of archaeologically recovered ceramics. In that discussion I followed Miller, and for the most part elaborated on his decoration-based ceramic scalings. My elaboration consisted of adding two other descriptive variables to the analysis: size/shape and ware type. Whether one uses one, two, or all three descriptive variables, Miller's scalings and my own work so far have been based on a comparison of apples to apples, edge-decorated plates to transfer-printed plates. In this section I discuss a way of comparing apples and oranges, or plates to pitchers, in an attempt to gain economic insights.

This third archaeological solution comes from my attempts at manipulating data of the sort presented in Table 1. Specifically, I was interested in finding a way of understanding, and making use of, the sometimes wild discrepancies between the column for purchasable units and the column for cash value. Obviously, there is no one-to-one relationship here, not when 30.3% of the purchasable units (bowls) brought in 7.1% of the money and 1.5% of the purchasable units (sets of china) brought in 18.9% of the money. This means that a large number of ceramic artifacts does not automatically indicate a large expenditure for ceramic items. One shard of a plate from a $4.50 set of china is worth far more, economically, than 50 shards of a single 10¢ bowl.

The technique I have developed for dealing with this phenomenon is called q. Q is a quotient that relates the relative amount of money spent on any particular basic form to the relative number of purchasable units represented by that same basic form, in the same set of documentary records. Q values for any particular basic form are calculated from data like those presented in Table 1, using the following formula:

$$q = \frac{\text{percentage of total cash value}}{\text{percentage of purchasable units}}$$

A q value of 1 indicates that the amount of money spent on a particular basic form is exactly commensurate with its representation among all other purchasable units, in a particular source document. A q value between 0 and 1 indicates a relatively inexpensive basic form, while a q value greater than 1 indicates just the opposite. Working again from the Wilson & Irvine book of 1842, the q value for bowls is 7.1 divided by 30.1, or 0.23; while for

pitchers q = 8.6/8.3 = 1.04; and for sets of china, q = 18.9/1.5 = 12.6. As purchasable units go, bowls were pretty cheap and sets of china were pretty expensive.

In most cases, the q values one would calculate are not particularly surprising, but taken individually, none of Miller's ceramic scalings is very surprising either. The value comes after building up a comprehensive set of these data, with wide coverage in both time and space. For a start, my original study contains 16 lists of q values, from 10 daybooks and 6 general store inventories, kept from 1796 to 1869 (Potter, 1982: 102–107). As Miller demonstrates, the price relationships between transfer-printed plates and CC plates changed over time, and so too do the q values in my data. Furthermore, and I think Miller would agree, it is important to follow up his work at the point of manufacture with specific local studies. Such studies will test the hypothesis that the relationships Miller identified remained intact as ceramics moved from manufacture to wholesale to retail, and they will also provide appropriate local baselines for answering local economic questions.

There are problems with the q statistic. For one, it does not successfully isolate basic form from size/shape, decoration, and ware type; that is, for any general store daybook, the q for bowls is based on prices paid for all bowls, regardless of ware type, decoration, or size/shape. If we assume that variations in size/shape, decoration, and ware type are distributed evenly across all basic forms, then this is not a problem, but if in one daybook all the bowls were undecorated earthenware and all the plates were decorated porcelain, then the disparity in q values for these two basic forms would be inappropriately large. I have no solution here, only my trust in the Great God Random, and the suggestion that q be used as a general rather than a specific way of characterizing assemblages. Another problem is based on the apples and oranges metaphor I introduced earlier. Specifically, transfer-printed plates and edge-decorated plates are interchangeable in a way that chamber pots and vegetable dishes are not. Stated another way, the knowledge that a set of Liverpool plates was purchased instead of a set of shell-edged plates or a set of white plates is different from the knowledge that a chamber pot was purchased instead of a vegetable dish. A list of basic forms, with their corresponding q values, is not necessarily a meaningful contrast set.

Problematic or not, the q statistic does provide interesting new information relating to a material culture problem of long standing. Briefly, the problem is understanding the meaning of two distinct complexes of ceramic items. One complex is composed of shared bowls for food and communal mugs for beverages. The other complex is composed of sets of plates for food and sets of cups and saucers for beverages. Deetz (1973, 1977) and Brown (1973) began their consideration of this problem with a solution, Deetz's celebrated postulate of a shift, over time, from a Stuart yeoman to a Georgian mind-set. Deetz discovered in the archaeological record and Brown discovered in the documentary record of Plymouth, Massachusetts that this shift in mind-sets was accompanied by, or marked by, a shift in the material record from the use of ceramic tableware items (mugs and bowls) to the use of individual items of ceramic tableware (plates and cups and saucers).

Otto also began with the solution to a material culture problem, the known statuses of the three kinds of sites on Cannon's Point Plantation. He discovered that these known statuses were marked in the material record by differences in ceramic assemblages. Planter assemblages were characterized by high percentages of transfer-printed flatware pieces. Slave assemblages had high percentages of banded ware bowls. Otto suggests that a possible reason for this variability was the difference between the planters' roast meat diet and the slaves' liquid-based diet. Interestingly, Otto's low status assemblages seem quite similar to Deetz's "Stuart yeoman — communal — asymmetrical" assemblages, while his high status assemblages resemble Deetz's "Georgian — individual — symmetrical" assemblages. While Deetz is content to call the shift from one complex to another a matter of mind-sets, and while Otto can only call the differences between his assemblages a matter of status, my data and the q index allow me to add another layer to the analysis of this problem.

If we assume that a 19th-century Rockbridge shopper would have chosen between bowls and plates to fill the same general function, and between mugs and cups and saucers to fill similar functions, then my data and the q index can offer new insight into the meanings of these two complexes of ceramic items.

In 9 of the 10 daybooks I examined and in 5 of the 6 general store inventories, both plates and bowls are listed. In 12 of these 14 instances of co-occurrence, plates have a higher q value than bowls. Cups and saucers and mugs are both listed in 6 of 10 daybooks and in 4 of 6 inventories. In 9 of these 10 cases, cups and saucers have a higher q value than mugs. This is ample evidence that in Rockbridge, communal items of tableware, purchased one at a time, were less expensive than individual items sold in sets that served the same basic functions. Given this relation between the prices of these four basic forms, it would seem that the occurrence of plates or teacups and saucers in the archaeological record should be considered a reliable signature of relative expensiveness; the occurrence of mugs or eating bowls should be considered a signature of relative inexpensiveness.

This conclusion is not intended to replace Deetz's or Otto's, only to add another dimension to their analyses. Bowls instead of plates, and mugs instead of cups and saucers, may well be indicative of culturally based foodways and mind-sets, but there is also, clearly, an economic dimension to the choices structured by these two binary oppositions.

Conclusions

I would like to conclude by returning to the themes I laid out in my title, capitalism, ceramics, and middle-range theory. Simply stated, this paper documents a single, local attempt to use the principles of middle-range theory to make archaeological ceramics into a tool for studying the impact of capitalism on a local, agricultural economy. The observant reader will have noticed that the symmetry of my section headings is flawed by my failure to balance "a historical problem" with "historical solutions" in the way that I was able to pair off "an archaeological problem" with a set of "archaeological solutions." That failure is also to be found in my initial study, and as I noted in my introduction, one reason for writing this paper is to help other people take the step I did not take in 1982.

That is, this paper is largely methodological. Within the realm of methodology I have attempted to do two things. First, I have tried to rehabilitate a class of documents that has sometimes been judged narrowly and wrongly dismissed as inferior to other kinds of documents. My syntactical or grammatical approach to daybook data strings, my discussion of ceramic counting, and my invention of q are all attempts, based on organizational behavior, to understand general store daybooks on their own terms, those terms being the operational logic that structured their creation. Secondly, I have used middle-range theory, and principally the idea of organizational behavior, to reiterate an important archaeological idea that bears constant repeating: the ways in which we use particular attributes to name and classify the artifactual record are necessarily dependent on the questions we intend to answer by analyzing the artifacts we recover. This point was being made long before middle-range theory ever entered the archaeological literature, but it is worthwhile to cast this old problem in new terms, because the idea of organizational behavior solves this problem so well in historical archaeology. For historical archaeologists, the "best" historical documents are those created by the people whose interests in material culture most clearly match the interests of the analyst. The enactment of these interests in material culture is organizational behavior. My research problem in Rockbridge County was to learn about one part of the emergence and impact of capitalism in a 19th-century rural economy. My central obstacle was the fact that a heap of broken household discards recovered from a cellar hole in a mountain hollow says absolutely nothing about capitalism *or anything else* until the objects in the heap are named, interpreted, translated, and spoken for. In this particular case, I have used a small part of middle-range theory to begin the process of translating 19th-century ceramics into economic understandings.

The broader point is that for most analytical purposes there is no ready-made, one-size-fits-all analytical scheme. In historical archaeology this means that the discovery of a "good" historical document is the beginning of things, not the end of the line. The archaeological line of evidence needs to be worked over, as does the documentary, to bring about a successful translation of one into the other. In this paper I introduced q. To study the penetration of capitalism into Annapolis, Maryland, Paul Shackel created a statistic based on the variability in plate diameters (Shackel 1987:264–285; Little and Shackel 1989:501–504; Leone, Potter, and Shackel 1987:288–289). Moreover, there are hundreds of locally relevant questions that could be answered, or at least addressed, by analyzing the archaeological record, but at the same time, most of the techniques for conducting these analyses are still to be formulated. These particular techniques will be the practical outcome of applying middle-range theory to historical archaeology, and any one of them will represent a successful fusion of a theory, a body of data, and a meaningful research question.

For historical archaeology to produce meaningful results, its practitioners must dare to be creative. In the case I report on here, middle-range theory has been proven to be a useful tool for shaping and structuring a set of novel archaeological solutions to a particular complex of archaeological and historical problems. More broadly, there is every reason to believe that further applications of middle-range theory will help to bridge the gap between the totalizing theories (and formats for pattern recognition) that seem to dominate contemporary historical archaeology and the particular sites and regions that are not especially well served — or well understood — by those overarching schemes.

Acknowledgments

In reverse chronological order of their assistance with this paper, I would like to thank Nancy Jo Chabot for improving everything I do; my colleagues in the New Hampshire Division of Historical Resources for providing a supportive and stimulating environment in which to work; Barbara J. Little for allowing me to invite myself into this volume and for her helpful comments and suggestions; Mark Leone for introducing me to middle-range theory as a tool for historical archaeology; Richard Gould, Patricia Rubertone, and Peter Schmidt for serving on the academic committee that helped me shape my original study into an acceptable M.A. paper; and John McDaniel for giving me the opportunity to conduct the research on which this paper is based. To all these people I owe thanks as well as plausible deniability for any shortcomings in the paper, which are my responsibility alone.

References

Beaudry, M. C. (1980) "Or What Else You Please to Call It": Folk Semantic Domains in Early Virginia Probate Inventories. Ph.D. thesis, Department of Anthropology, Brown University. University Microfilms, Ann Arbor, MI.

Beaudry, M. C., J. Long, H. M. Miller, F. D. Neiman, and G. W. Stone (1983) A Vessel Typology for Early Chesapeake Ceramics: The Potomac Typological System. *Historical Archaeology* 17(1):18–43.

Babits, L. E. (1984) Historical Archaeology and the Analysis of a Region. In *Historical Archaeology West of the Blue Ridge: A Regional Example from Rockbridge County* (The James G. Leyburn Papers in Anthropology, Vol. 1). J. M. McDaniel and K. C. Russ, Eds. Liberty Hall Press, Lexington, VA, pp. 78–90.

Binford, L. R. (1965) Archaeological Systematics and the Study of Culture Process. *American Antiquity* 31(2):203–210.

— (1977) Introduction. In *For Theory Building in Archaeology*, L. R. Binford, Ed. Academic Press, New York, pp. 1–10.

— (1981) *Bones: Ancient Men and Modern Myths*. Academic Press, New York.

— (1987) Researching Ambiguity: Frames of Reference and Site Structure. In *Method and Theory for Activity Area Research*, S. Kent, Ed. Columbia University Press, New York, pp. 449–512.

Brown, M. R. III (1973) Ceramics from Plymouth, 1621–1800: The Documentary Record. In *Ceramics in America* (Winterthur conference report, 1972), I. M. G. Quimby, Ed. University Press of Virginia, Charlottesville, pp. 41–74.

Caruthers, J. (1796) General store daybook. Privately owned. Photocopies and photographs on file, Laboratory of Archaeology, Washington and Lee University, Lexington, VA.

Clarke, D. L. (1968) *Analytical Archaeology*. Methuen, London.

Deetz, J. F. (1973) Ceramics from Plymouth, 1635–1835: The Archaeological Evidence. In *Ceramics in America* (Winterthur conference report, 1972), I. M. G. Quimby, Ed. University Press of Virginia, Charlottesville, pp. 15–40.

— (1977) *In Small Things Forgotten*. Anchor Doubleday, Garden City, NY.

— (1983) Scientific Humanism and Humanistic Science: A Plea for Paradigmatic Pluralism in Historical Archaeology. *Geoscience and Man* 23:27–34.

Dold, S. M. (1854) General store daybook. Part of the Dold papers, owned by the Rockbridge County Historical Society, curated in Special Collections, The University Library, Washington and Lee University, Lexington, VA.

— (1858) General store daybook. Part of the Dold papers, owned by the Rockbridge County Historical Society, curated in Special Collections, The University Library, Washington and Lee University, Lexington, VA.

— (1860) General store daybook. Part of the Dold papers, owned by the Rockbridge County Historical Society, curated in Special Collections, The University Library, Washington and Lee University, Lexington, VA.

— (1869) General store daybook. Part of the Dold papers, owned by the Rockbridge County Historical Society, curated in Special Collections, The University Library, Washington and Lee University, Lexington, VA.

Dold, S. M. & Son (1867) General store daybook. Part of the Dold papers, owned by the Rockbridge County Historical Society, curated in Special Collections, The University Library, Washington and Lee University, Lexington, VA.

Dunnell, R. C. (1971) Sabloff and Smith's The Importance of Both Analytic and Taxonomic Classification in the Type-Variety System *(American Antiquity 34:278–286)*. *American Antiquity* 36(1):115–118.

Fontana, B. L. (1973) The Cultural Dimensions of Pottery: Ceramics as Social Documents. In *Ceramics in America* (Winterthur conference report, 1972), I. M. G. Quimby, Ed. University Press of Virginia, Charlottesville, pp. 1–13.

Friedrich, M. H. (1970) Design Structure and Social Interaction: Archaeological Implications of an Ethnographic Analysis. *American Antiquity* 35:332–343.

Grayson, D. K. (1986) Eoliths, Archaeological Ambiguity, and the Generation of "Middle-Range" Research. In *American Archaeology Past and Future: A Celebration of the Society for American Archaeology. 1935–1985*, D. J. Meltzer, D. D. Fowler, and J. A. Sabloff, Eds. Smithsonian Institution Press, Washington, D.C., pp. 77–133.

Hill, J. N. and R. K. Evans (1972) A Model for Classification and Typology. In *Models in Archaeology*, D. L. Clarke, Ed. Methuen, London.

Kaplin, A. (1964) *The Conduct of Inquiry: Methodology for Behavioral Science*. Chandler, San Francisco.

Leone, M. P. (1984) Varied Epistemologies in Historical Archaeology. In *Historical Archaeology West of the Blue Ridge: A Regional Example from Rockbridge County* (The James G. Leyburn Papers in Anthropology, Vol. 1), J. M. McDaniel and K. C. Russ, Eds. Liberty Hall Press, Lexington, VA, pp. 91–98.

— (1988) The Relationship Between Archaeological Data and the Documentary Record: 18th-Century Gardens in Annapolis, Maryland. *Historical Archaeology* 22(1):29–35.

Leone, M. P. and C. A. Crosby (1987) Epilogue: Middle-Range Theory in Historical Archaeology. In *Consumer Choice in Historical Archaeology*, S. Spencer-Wood, Ed. Plenum Press, New York, pp. 397–410.

Leone, M. P. and P. B. Potter, Jr. (1988) Introduction: Issues in Historical Archaeology. In *The Recovery of Meaning: Historical Archaeology in the Eastern United States,* M. P. Leone and P. B. Potter, Jr., Eds. Smithsonian Institution Press, Washington, D.C., pp. 1–22.

Leone, M. P., P. B. Potter, Jr., and P. A. Shackel (1987) Toward a Critical Archaeology. *Current Anthropology* 28(3):283–302.

Little, B. J. and P. A. Shackel (1989) Scales of Historical Anthropology: An Archaeology of Colonial Anglo-America. *Antiquity* 63(240):495–509.

McDaniel, J. M. (1977) Liberty Hall Academy: The Application of Archaeology in the Investigation of an Eighteenth Century Virginia Academy Site — An Interim Report. *Quarterly Bulletin of the Archaeological Society of Virginia* 31:141–167.

— (1984) Historic Site Research at the Undergraduate Teaching Institution. In *Historical Archaeology West of the Blue Ridge: A Regional Example from Rockbridge County* (The James G. Leyburn Papers in Anthropology, Vol. 1), J. M. McDaniel and K. C. Russ, Eds. Liberty Hall Press, Lexington, VA, pp. 1–11.

McDaniel, J. M. and J. T. Adams (1984) The Research Area Approach to Historic Sites in Western Virginia. In *Historical Archaeology West of the Blue Ridge: A Regional Example from Rockbridge County* (The James G. Leyburn Papers in Anthropology, Vol. 1), J. M. McDaniel and K. C. Russ, Eds. Liberty Hall Press, Lexington, VA, pp. 12–22.

McDaniel, J. M. and P. B. Potter Jr. (1980) Historical Archaeology and the History of a Specific Section of Western Virginia. *Quarterly Bulletin of the Archaeological Society of Virginia* 35(1):28–34.

— (1984) A Review of Historic Site Work Conducted by Washington and Lee University over the Last Decade. In *Upland Archaeology in the East. A Symposium*, Vol. II (Cultural Resources Report No. 4), M. B. Barber, Ed. U. S. Department of Agriculture, Forest Service, Southern Region, Atlanta, pp. 67–74.

McDaniel, J. M., C. Watson, and D. T. Moore (1979) *Liberty Hall Academy: The Early History of the Institutions Which Evolved into Washington and Lee University*. Liberty Hall Press, Lexington, VA.

Miller, G. M. (1980) Classification and Economic Scaling of 19th Century Ceramics. *Historical Archaeology* 14:1–41.

— (1984) George M. Coates, Pottery Merchant of Philadelphia, 1817–1831. *Winterthur Portfolio* 19(1):37–49.

Noel Hume, I. (1970) *A Guide to Artifacts of Colonial America*. Alfred A. Knopf, New York.

— (1973) Creamware to Pearlware: A Williamsburg Perspective. In *Ceramics in America* (Winterthur Conference Report, 1972), I. M. G. Quimby, Ed. University Press of Virginia, Charlottesville, pp. 217–254.

Otto, J. S. (1975) Status Difference and the Archaeological Record — A Comparison of Planter, Overseer, and Slave Sites from Cannon's Point Plantation (1794–1861), St. Simon's Island, Georgia. Ph.D. dissertation, Department of Anthropology, University of Florida, Gainesville. University Microfilms, Ann Arbor, MI.

— (1977) Artifacts and Status Difference — A Comparison of Ceramics from Planter, Overseer, and Slave Sites on an Antebellum Plantation. In *Research Strategies in Historical Archaeology*, S. South, Ed. Academic Press, New York, pp. 91–118.

— (1980) Race and Class on an Antebellum Plantation. In *Archaeological Perspectives on Ethnicity in America: Afro-American and Asian American Culture History*, R. L. Schuyler, Ed. Baywood Publishing Company, Farmingdale, NY.

— (1984) *Cannon's Point Plantation 1794–1860: Living Conditions and Status Patterns in the Old South*. Academic Press, New York.

Outlaw, M. A., B. A. Bogley, and A. C. Outlaw (1977) Rich Man, Poor Man: Status Definition in two Seventeenth Century Ceramic Assemblages from Kingsmill. Manuscript on file, Virginia Historic Landmarks Commission, Research Center for Archaeology, Richmond.

Plog, S. (1973) Variability of Ceramic Design Frequencies as Measures of Prehistoric Social Organization. Manuscript, Department of Anthropology, University of Michigan, Ann Arbor.

Potter, P. B., Jr. (1982) The Translation of Archaeological Evidence into Economic Understandings: A Study of Context, Naming, and Nineteenth Century Ceramics in

Rockbridge County, Virginia. M. A. research paper, Department of Anthropology, Brown University, Providence, RI.

— (1989) Archaeology in Public in Annapolis: An Experiment in the Application of Critical Theory to Historical Archaeology. Ph.D. thesis, Department of Anthropology, Brown University. University Microfilms, Ann Arbor, MI.

Raab, L. M. and A. C. Goodyear (1984) Middle-Range Theory in Archaeology: A Critical Review of Origins and Applications. *American Antiquity* 49(2):225–268.

Redman, C. L. (1978) Multivariate Artifact Analysis: A Basis for Multidimensional Interpretations. In *Social Archaeology: Beyond Subsistence and Dating*, C. L. Redman et al., Eds. Academic Press, New York, pp. 159–192.

Rockbridge County Will Books (1778–) Bound manuscript "will books," held in the Rockbridge County Court House, Lexington, VA.

Rubertone, P. E. (1976) Interaction in Archaeology: Inferences from Ceramic Attribute Analysis. Paper presented at the annual meeting of the Society for American Archaeology, St. Louis, Missouri.

— (1979) Social Organization in an Islamic Town: A Behavioral Explanation of Ceramic Variability. Ph.D. dissertation, Department of Anthropology, State University of New York at Binghamton.

Schmidt, P. R. and S. A. Mrozowski (1983) History, Smugglers, Change, and Shipwrecks. In *Shipwreck Anthropology*. R. A. Gould, Ed. University of New Mexico Press, Albuquerque, pp. 143–171.

— (1988) Documentary Insights into the Archaeology of Smuggling. In *Documentary Archaeology in the New World*, M. C. Beaudry, Ed. Cambridge University Press, Cambridge, pp. 32–42.

Shackel, P. A. (1987) A Historical Archaeology of Personal Discipline. Ph. D. dissertation, Department of Anthropology, State University of New York at Buffalo. University Microfilms, Ann Arbor, MI.

South, S. (1977) *Method and Theory in Historical Archaeology.* Academic Press, New York.

Whallon, R. (1972) A New Approach to Pottery Typology. *American Antiquity* 37:13–33.

White & Wilson, H. L. (1861) General store daybook. Part of the Wilson papers, owned by the Rockbridge County Historical Society, curated in Special Collections, The University Library, Washington and Lee University, Lexington, VA.

Wilson, H. L. (1846) General store inventory. Part of the Wilson papers, owned by the Rockbridge County Historical Society, curated in Special Collections, The University Library, Washington and Lee University, Lexington, VA.

— (1847) General store inventory. Part of the Wilson papers, owned by the Rockbridge County Historical Society, curated in Special Collections, The University Library, Washington and Lee University, Lexington, VA.

— (1848) General store inventory. Part of the Wilson papers, owned by the Rockbridge County Historical Society, curated in Special Collections, The University Library, Washington and Lee University, Lexington, VA.

— (1849) General store inventory. Part of the Wilson papers, owned by the Rockbridge County Historical Society, curated in Special Collections, The University Library, Washington and Lee University, Lexington, VA.

— (1860) General store inventory. Part of the Wilson papers, owned by the Rockbridge County Historical Society, curated in Special Collections, The University Library, Washington and Lee University, Lexington, VA.

Wilson, H. L. & Co. (1844) General store daybook. Part of the Wilson papers, owned by the Rockbridge County Historical Society, curated in Special Collections, The University Library, Washington and Lee University, Lexington, VA.

Wilson, H. L. & Irvine (1842) General store daybook. Part of the Wilson papers, owned by the Rockbridge County Historical Society, curated in Special Collections, The University Library, Washington and Lee University, Lexington, VA.

Wise, C. L. (n.d.) Date and Status in Eighteenth Century Delaware: An Archaeologists' View. Unpublished manuscript.

3: Oral History and Historical Archaeology

Margaret Purser
Anthropology Department, Sonoma State University, Rohnert Park, California

The only way to preserve the fantasy of the inarticulate masses is never to listen to members of the masses when they are articulate.

Glassie 1982:86

[Oral history] forces people to make their lives anthropologically strange.

Grele 1985:206

See what a change time does? There's no building, there's no people, there's nothing.
F. C. Buckingham, Sr., Paradise Valley, Nevada, December 1981

This paper is not about how to do oral history as a historical archaeologist. Methodological treatises on oral history written by a range of scholars have covered that ground far better, and with greater expertise, (Allen and Montell 1981; Dunaway and Baum 1984; Henige 1982; Thompson 1978). Rather, this is a plea for historical archaeologists to do more oral history, and to do a great deal more *with* it than is current practice. It defines a broader range of information oral history could make available to us as archaeologists. It casts oral history as a crucial bridge between historical archaeology and contemporary developments in social theory, ethnography, and approaches to the interpretation of the past. Finally, it pays some debts to the people who taught me to listen to stories about the past, by acknowledging both the value and the authority of their labor.

Oral History and Historical Archaeology

The formal incorporation of local oral tradition, family histories, and ethnohistorical material in historic site analysis began in the early 1970s. At that time, the work of people like William Adams at Silcott, Washington (1976), Marley Brown at Mott Farm in Rhode Island (1973), and Robert Schuyler at Sandy Ground, New York (1974, 1977) set the pattern for integrating oral accounts with archaeological and documentary data.

While the methodology accommodated a wide range of research questions and theoretical orientations, two central issues unified such efforts. Oral history was used in the first instance as a component of site history, to identify and describe specific archaeological components, and to enliven them with a more detailed account of their creators and occupants. This began with the more focused "who lived in that house, and where did they put their garbage?" data. But the approach had broader interpretive implications. As interviewers, historical archaeologists elicited an oral history marked by the discipline's emphasis on the interpretation of objects, structures, and small-scale economic patterns, a kind of "oral history of material culture" (Brown 1973:347).

The second issue addressed with oral history took historical archaeologists beyond the bounds of their own subdiscipline. Historical archaeologists used oral historical sources to join discussions in the emerging fields of ethnohistory, ethnoarchaeology, and folklife studies. They borrowed, collaborated on, and debated the relative merit of these new sources of information on how best to identify past social processes from their material remains, and to specify the connections linking a given historical community to the material world it had created and used.

This dual role of oral history, as a source of specific archaeological data, and as a bridge between historical archaeology and other fields, has continued through the 1980s. Applications of oral history in historical archaeology have grown broader and more sophisticated in recent years, as the discipline itself has expanded. In the U.S., an increasing interest in contact period sites generally, and particularly in non-Anglo cultural expansion in the New World, has renewed the incorporation of ethnohistorical sources in the work of historical archaeologists, (cf. Crosby 1988; Deagan 1983). Such work builds on an existing corpus of ethnohistorical literature, as well as a growing theoretical interest in incorporating ethnohistorical documents in ethnographic research (Simmons 1986, 1988; Marcus and Fischer 1986:101–108). It also draws upon a long-standing practice of incorporating oral tradition, folklore, and ethnohistory in the archaeological interpretation of New World prehistoric and protohistoric sites, (e.g., Marquardt 1987; cf. Winters 1987).

Another important development has been the extension of American historical archaeology beyond North America. Beginning in the late 1970s, historical archaeologists working in the U.S. were drawn to the comparative contexts of other sites of European colonization, particularly in Africa. Oral tradition had long been recognized as integral to the historical record of many African nations (Daaku 1973; Vansina 1985). Historical archaeologists working in a range of African contexts have been quick to incorporate both individual oral sources and the sophisticated textual and historical analyses of these sources that existed (cf. Donley 1983; Posnanski and Decorse 1986; Schmidt 1978).

Finally, oral history recently has begun to play a role in mitigation processes and historical preservation work conducted by historical archaeologists as part of a number of individual public programs, as well as general cultural resource management (Costello 1981; Costello and Cunningham 1988). Oral history has been a regular component of public history programs, such as those operated by historians working for national parks, since the late 1960s (Bearss 1990). The expanding scope of cultural resource management practices for historical resources, and the continued popularity of public interpretive programs for historical sites and districts, have encouraged increasingly collaborative research between historians and historical archaeologists. Oral history is one of the methodologies being incorporated into such research.

While historical archaeologists were redefining their discipline in ways that incorporated oral tradition, the field of oral history itself was undergoing a similar shift towards greater methodological complexity and intellectual sophistication. One source summarizes current trends in oral historical research as moving towards a greater emphasis on the "process, public use, and interdisciplinary applications" of oral texts (Dunaway and Baum 1984:xiii). Of these, the growing interdisciplinary nature of the field is probably the most significant. Oral history as research technique has long been borrowed by many disciplines (including archaeology); at annual meetings of the Oral History Association, psychologists, anthropologists, and folklorists rub shoulders with historians of women, labor, communities, medicine, families, and a United Nations of ethnic groups (Dunaway and Baum:xix). Current anthologies bring together au-

thors who consider themselves to be first novelists, biographers, and filmmakers, as well as members of more traditional academic disciplines (cf. Dunaway and Baum 1984; Grele 1985).

The interdisciplinary debates among this diverse mix of practitioners has guided the direction other current trends in oral history have taken. This is particularly true for the cited interest in the "process" and "public use" of oral history. Following the recent popularity of hermeneutics and critical theory in many of the social sciences and literary criticism, much of recent research has focused on the functions of oral narratives in social discourse. New work by folklorists and ethnographers, (e.g., Glassie 1982; Price 1983; Vansina 1985) has heightened the awareness of oral history as purposeful texts that are constantly being created, revised, contested, and validated in complex living communities.

Work from similar perspectives has tried to make more explicit and self-critical the oral historians' role in creating and manipulating such narratives (e.g., Friedlander 1984:131–141). Greater attention to the processes of eliciting, collecting, and interpreting oral history has forced scholars working with narratives to confront their own role in shaping content. Constrained by their own biases and research agendas, oral historians can "ask questions which we know our respondents are going to want to answer, and they begin to give us answers which they know we are going to want to hear" (Grele 1985 [1975]:203).

Like others in the social sciences, oral historians have begun to explore "the role of history in the culture in general and among different populations in particular" (Grele 1985 [1975]:205). Oral history speaks to the structure of the past itself, and the cognitive impact of perceptions of the past on individuals and cultures. Ethnographers like Renato Rosaldo and Tzvetan Todorov have defined oral narrative as organizing key features of current social and cultural reality, and have used the content, structure, and performance of oral traditions to document the existence of (and conflict between) multiple systems for describing and explaining the past (Marcus and Fischer 1986:98–107; Rosaldo 1980; Todorov 1984 [1982]).

Applications of Marxist-materialist theory have examined the differential power to control the uses of history in more focused community contexts, as well as broader social and political ones. The information provided by oral tradition has been used to argue against the appropriation of "history" by western cultures, and the relegation of nonwestern cultures to a cultural and political status "without" either legitimate pasts or the means by which to make their pasts comment on the present (Wolf 1982).

On a smaller scale, oral historical research intended to recover voices of disenfranchised or misrepresented groups, like much of the similarly motivated historical archaeology of the 1970s, has on occasion been powerful and evocative. Specialized oral histories of individual groups, such as women (Gluck 1984:221–237) and African-Americans (Montell 1970; Rosengarten 1974), have fluoresced from case studies to subdisciplines. Oral narratives also have been collected to recover otherwise unrecorded (or unevenly recorded) events, such as the American labor movement (Friedlander 1975), or to provide depth and detail for understanding social institutions, such as the family and community (Hareven and Langenbach 1978; Thompson 1978).

As in historical archaeology, this approach has provoked considerable debate, particularly when the issue of the underlying assumptions that structure these histories are examined. On the one hand, the most articulate of such oral histories have provided rich alternative pictures of groups or events that also escape the anonymous terms of the "statistical aggregate" common in many social histories (Thompson 1978:3). On the other, the same approach "has also given us a pile of racist or sentimental trash," in which an overly naive attribution of "truth" to oral narratives fails to discern "how the larger culture impinges upon the imaginations" of local individuals and communities (Grele 1985 [1975]:201).

The problems of integrating individual accounts at any larger social scale remains an ongoing interpretive dilemma for the field. Oral history's inevitable focus on the individual can make it difficult to synthesize specific oral texts with broader social and cultural events. The particularistic focus reinforces our own cultural tendencies to privilege independent human action over "institutions or social forces," creating a version of the past that is "simply one more version of Protestant individualism" (Grele 1985 [1975]:206).

One approach to resolving the dilemma has been to begin at the smallest interpretive scale, by examining the importance of oral history to the individuals who tell the stories. Psychological research on memory has added considerable dimension to the interpretation of recounted stories, as a means by which individuals order the events of their own lives, and position themselves with respect to local communities (Lowenthal 1985:193–210). It has also indicated that the role of memory in an individual's life changes as much over the course of a lifetime as do the contents of that memory (Lo Gerfo 1984:314–323; Neuenschwander 1984:324–332).

Memory is also notoriously variable and is subject to frequent revision. Furthermore, memories can differ radically in the telling, and can be tailored to the audience, to the context of recent events, and to the purposes of the moment. This situational, functional approach to memory has provided a means of integrating individual accounts with at least the broader social context of audience: the people to whom stories are told (and who tell stories of their own), the community in which stories (and story-tellers) are known. In telling and listening to stories, people "say what they know to discover what they think" (Glassie 1982:34). Oral historians have long been concerned with methods for evaluating the historical accuracy of individual memories; most standard manuals include a chapter on verification (e.g., Allen and Montell 1981:67–100), and the Oral History Association's published guidelines include a section on "evaluation criteria" (Dunaway and Baum 1984:415–423). But in the broader context of remembering and recounting, historical "facts" are articulated through more immediate personal and political "truths," and analytical measures of validity must encompass both.

There are two general implications that this wide-ranging interpretive discourse has for historical archaeologists who work with oral history. First and foremost, there are accepted ways of doing oral history. There are acknowledged criteria to apply, ethical and legal considerations, skills, and specialized knowledge that can sort good from bad techniques, useful from wasteful interpretation, and constructive from meaningless evaluation. Furthermore, there is an established dialogue on relevant definitions, interpretation, and evaluation. Historical archaeologists need to join in this exchange, if only to avoid reinventing wheels in the course of our own exploration of the method. The formal incorporation of oral history as a field technique in historical archaeology requires the formulation of clearly stated methods, priorities, and ethical guidelines specifically geared to the organizational frameworks that affect our discipline, including archaeological fieldwork, material culture studies, public interpretation, and cultural resource management policy, to name a few.

Secondly, historical archaeology has a good deal to contribute to current practice in oral history. The potential contributions derive from our focus on things, from the more prosaic acts of digging holes in the ground and identifying objects to the more interpretive realm of understanding material culture as a reflexive part of cultural expression and social discourse. The objects, structures, and places that are the stuff of memory are also the stuff of archaeology. Historical archaeology provides a critique on the texts of oral history that is distinct from, but related to, both the written past of the documentary record and the narrative past of present memory. It tells the stories in another way.

Historical archaeologists should have no difficulty talking to other students of oral history: we share a great deal of vocabulary, read many of the same books, and have begun to haunt many of the same kitchen tables, backyards, crossroads, and street corners. Many of the current trends and debates in oral history have obvious parallels in our field. Historical archaeologists also struggle to come to terms with the epistemological standing of our disparate data sources (cf. Schuyler 1988; Leone and

Crosby 1987; Beaudry, Cook, and Mrozowski, 1991). "Text" and "voice" are among our own current analytical devices of choice. We also debate the best means to self-critical approaches, seek to recover unrepresented people from the past, and struggle to integrate highly particularistic data with broadly generalist interpretive schemes.

Yet despite such similar intellectual inheritance, epistemological challenges, and complementary goals, oral history remains a largely marginal and incidental factor in the practice of historical archaeology. This marginality persists in spite of growing interest in the field technique and a sense that "if we could, we would" use it in the interpretation of any given site. Much of how we see the applicability of oral history can be phrased in terms of a series of disjunctions. The primary gaps are logistical. They stem from the belief that we simply cannot get there from here, either because our site sits too far back in time from any living potential narrator, or because current local communities have no lineal connections to the people who created the archaeological components we want to interpret.

The second set of disjunctions are less obvious, and in some cases less conscious, but may be far more difficult to overcome. There are the ever-present incongruities between forms of data. We are familiar with the problems of integrating written documents with archaeological remains. Oral texts represent yet another form of information, with yet another set of difficulties, constraints, and grammars to learn. Like historians of a generation ago, we have yet to develop explicit frameworks for either recognizing or critiquing the complex legitimacy and validity of oral texts (Thompson 1978:19–64). In the absence of such frameworks, archaeologists continue to privilege written texts over oral ones, much as we once privileged the same texts over material culture.

There is also a further question of legitimacy and authority. Historical archaeologists are academically trained professionals whose disciplinary locus at the bridge points between multiple academic fields has bequeathed a certain intellectual uneasiness as well as flexibility (Glassie 1977). We zealously defend our authority, be it in terms of science, epistemology, or theoretical expertise.

Yet oral history is an inherently collaborative process, between interviewer and interviewee, between storyteller and audience (Friedlander 1984:133–136). Historical archaeologists who want to employ oral history in their work must enter into that collaboration, and the consequences of that move can be great. Paul Thompson has written that when historians begin to do oral history, "the process of writing history changes along with the content. The use of oral evidence breaks through the barriers between the chroniclers and their audience; between the educational institution and the outside world" (Thompson 1978:7–8).

If the authority of voices outside the professional discipline is accepted uncritically, the result can be "a reenactment of community myth" that leaves in place not only the myth itself, but the barrier between professional and "amateur," producing a paean to the quaint and the "common," articulated by the academic (Thompson 1978:16–18). But if historical archaeologists do involve themselves in genuine collaboration with the people who can tell them more about their sites and artifacts, they will inevitably raise questions about the authority with which their discipline speaks, and for whom.

There are ways to pull these disjunctions into focus. In part help comes from the intellectual histories of other disciplines, such as history, folklore, and ethnography, which have developed their own means of incorporating oral history into their work. In part, resolution must come from historical archaeologists *doing* oral history, for ours will be a somewhat different practice.

Paradise Valley

An extended case study provides an opportunity to examine how such an integration might proceed. The ideas presented here grew from my own experience with using oral history as part of a 6-year project in north central Nevada. Paradise Valley is a small ranching community in northern Humboldt County, 40 miles south of the Idaho border. Euro-American settlers who arrived in the 1860s prospered through commercial-scale grain agriculture and a local silver boom, and built a central town that survived the economic vicissitudes of the late 19th century relatively intact. The small town and surrounding ranch lands continue to support a resident population of around 300 to 400 people.

Paradise's history between 1860s and 1920s was to provide me with grist for a dissertation on the impact of later 19th-century American industrialization and the birth of a "consumer society" (Purser 1987). The research followed on the heels of a much larger project on valley ranching practices sponsored by the American Folklife Center of the Library of Congress (Marshall and Ahlborn 1980). Following in these footsteps encouraged the use of oral history from the very beginning of the archaeological research, but initial interviews were focused very narrowly. I wanted quick information to guide excavation and to help identify specific artifacts, structures, and sites.

So, tape recorder in hand, I arrived in town in the fall of 1981, with a ream of very specific questions about this house, that store, and where was the garbage dump, anyway? Among the first people who agreed to contribute to the project was Mr. Frederick Charles Buckingham, Sr., a life-long resident of Paradise Valley, and acknowledged expert on local history, at that time 88 years old. I would ask Mr. Buckingham what I considered to be a very directed, specific question, and he would begin what seemed to me to be a long, rambling, and somewhat unfocused answer. At some point along the way, with a certain amount of frustration, I would interrupt to repeat my original question. With considerably greater frustration, Mr. Buckingham would say something like, "Well, that's what I'm *trying* to tell you!," and would start all over, at the beginning (Interviews with F. C. Buckingham, Sr., Paradise Valley, 1981).

Luckily for the project, further graduate work in folklore with Alan Dundes of the University of California, Berkeley brought home the significance of relevant concepts like tale sequences, oral tradition, and life history. As work in Paradise Valley proceeded, Folklife Center specialists, such as Howard W. Marshall and Carl Fleischhauer, provided further guidance on methodology. All these experiences forced me to adopt a more inclusive method and broader focus.

I learned to see oral history as performance, as communication, as collaboration, and as authority. Oral history ceased to be a source of supplemental or second-choice information consulted in the absence of sufficiently specific written records. It became instead the primary source of a very *different* information, valid in its own terms.

The unique character of this information lay not so much in the specificity or accuracy of its recollected facts, as in their recounting. When he told his complex stories, Mr. Buckingham *was* answering my specific question. But his answer did not consist of a series of randomly remembered "facts" about the past, from which I was free to select the ones I considered appropriate. His history of a particular building, or event, or of the valley community as a whole, was instead a carefully constructed *interpretation* of such facts, and the "answer" to my questions, in his mind, lay in that interpretation, and not in the facts alone.

Furthermore, his interpretation took its shape in the context of an ongoing dialogue within the valley community at large over past events in Paradise Valley and their significance. A major learning experience of the dissertation involved learning to incorporate this broader, more contextual information into my study of the valley's material culture, as well as more specific data on house construction dates and garbage pits.

In the process, a fundamental shift occurred in my position with respect to the valley community and to my own research. I entered into the ongoing debate as student and participant. Individual valley residents ceased to be "informants" and became authorities, and sometimes colleagues. I checked their facts; they questioned my interpretations. We did not always agree. It was my project, and the ultimate decisions were mine. Some individuals still question the final version of the dissertation, and the debate continues. But in general, the more we acknowledged expertise on both sides of the discus-sion, the more genuinely collaborative that discussion became. I quit discovering, and began to learn.

Oral History and Material Culture

Over the course of 4 years of research in Paradise Valley, I encountered two coexisting and competing versions of the community history. Which history you told depended on how old you were, and to a lesser extent on whether you or your family were generally identified as a "town" family or a family from one of the surrounding ranches, or had come to the valley before or after 1900. Often, the histories told by a particular individual could shade from one version to another over time. This kind of transition appeared to be linked more to the development of my own research and depended on how long I had known the person and how many interviews we had done together.

In iconographic terms, the first history described an early community of socially and technologically sophisticated entrepreneurial settlers arriving from the eastern U.S. and Europe, on the forefront of their society and its great technologically driven progress, who set up a bustling, well-connected, "in-the-know" community on the western frontier. This history was told generally by people age 70 and older, people whose lifetime residence patterns focused more on town than on ranches, and people of any age or residence whose families had arrived in the valley prior to 1900. To a certain extent, more details of this version of history tended to emerge in anyone's narrative, the more interviews they gave.

The second history described a violent, environmentally marginal wilderness peopled by murderers, bandits, and hostile Native Americans against whom the determined individuals of the community struggled in hardship and isolation. Younger people most often told stories of this type, as did people who identified themselves more as ranchers than townspeople, or whose families had come to Paradise after 1900. In addition, stories about specific murders, Indian attacks, and accounts of isolation and hardship were among the first stories that everyone told me when I first began work in the valley, and a nearly identical set of such stories was repeated often in the first interviews with many individuals as the project continued.

The two groups did not necessarily restrict their interpretations to their own experience. The histories told by the second generation often extended backward in time to cover the earliest periods of the town settlement. Furthermore, they consciously selected from individual tales told by the older generation for their data, and reinterpreted these stories to conform to and to support their own description of the period.

Coming to terms with this situation transformed my

own approach to the work in Paradise Valley, not only with specific oral historical data, but with the central research question of the project. I decided to use these discrepancies in the two histories to do more than illuminate the archaeological record or to put specific people in particular houses. The two histories did more than identify material culture, they sought to explain it. The discrepancies in the competing explanations spoke directly to the changing relationship between the community and its material culture, and beyond that to the changing nature of the community itself.

What follows is an account of the way analysis of the Paradise Valley material proceeded. The articulation of oral historical data with both the written record and the valley's surviving material culture has gone through several phases and continues to change. The kinds of logistical, interpretive, and authoritative disjunctions described earlier recurred at several levels of analysis and are not fully resolved yet. Perhaps because of these apparent flaws, it makes a provocative case study for the use of oral history in historical archaeology.

My initial analysis of Paradise Valley material culture focused on two broad categories, the built environment and the consumer goods purchased and used by valley residents. Transitions in the built environment included a greater physical and formal segregation of public and private space. The functions of all kinds of structures and spaces generally became more specialized and exclusive, and the control exercised by commercial property owners, in particular, over the public uses of town structures and open spaces grew more explicit and comprehensive.

Town stores, hotels, and shops had encouraged informal public use of their porches, yards, and upper floors in the early years and had incorporated a wide range of activities into any given building. By the turn of the century, the same owners had begun to fence off their lots from the street, to limit the different ways their extra rooms or floors were used, and to restrict access to public areas to paying customers.

Private space experienced the same increasing specialization and control. Property ownership became concentrated in the hands of two or three dominant town families, who rented or leased homes and businesses to an increasing percentage of town residents. Earlier building patterns that had mixed commercial and residential structures, including urban-style combined shop-residences, gave way to streets of exclusively residential buildings radiating from an exclusively commercial crossroads hub.

This transition extended well beyond the scale of individual buildings to include spatial organization of the community as a whole. For example, valley settlers had built an original road system that ran from ranch dooryard to dooryard across the valley, which had been maintained and extended on an *ad hoc* basis with private labor through the late 19th century. Beginning in the 1890s, county officials systematically replaced this earlier road network with a far more restricted one based on county-owned rights of way that followed the section line grid. This new public road system isolated the previously connected ranch houses from one another and severely limited the connections between the Paradise community and other settlements in the region (Purser 1989).

The same transitional period of the 1890s through the early 20th century saw an ever-increasing consumption of processed and mass-produced goods, both in town and out on the ranches, documented in the archaeological record and in contemporary account books available for Paradise stores. This increasing consumption on the part of individual households took place in the context of the declining commercial power of Paradise Valley as a whole. In particular, as the local town lost its power to compete with the larger town of Winnemucca in prices and services, many Paradise tradespeople left for the more economically stable county seat and railroad depot. The departed businesses included most of the people who had provided local distribution, processing, and maintenance services: shoemakers, saddlers, butchers, blacksmiths, millers, carpenters, traveling peddlers, tinkers, and the sellers of seasonal goods, such as fruits and vegetables. As the smaller shopowners left, the remaining larger storekeepers tried to replace the lost services, to keep their own customers from taking their business to Winnemucca.

But the storekeepers replaced processing services with already-processed goods, and maintenance services with mass-produced goods, agricultural equipment, household articles, and even vehicles made with replaceable, catalogue-order parts. Processing and maintenance activities shifted out of a diversified local commercial context, and into either the individual household or the distant manufacturing center, with the local storekeeper acting as middleman (cf. St. George 1983).

Neither of these two phenomena are unusual for the time and place; on the contrary, changing spatial organization and consumption patterns are the hallmarks of 19th-century site interpretation. But the trends in these two categories of material culture are interpreted very differently in the two historical traditions of Paradise Valley. Generally stated, the historical explanations of older or more town-oriented residents describe the process as a decline and fall of the local community, while younger or more ranch-oriented residents do not describe any change at all. Instead, they project the smaller, more isolated, economically reduced community of the period following 1900 backward in time as having been the conditions of valley life all along.

The original interpretation of this discrepancy and its implication for the material culture of Paradise Valley sharpened the terms of difference between the two sets of stories and the two sectors of the population they represented. In general, younger or more recently arrived valley residents "read" from the current, post-1900 material conditions of Paradise back into the past, and sought *from* the past information that explained social and economic isolation as "that which has always been." They selected from among the stories of older or more established residents those people and events that helped to construct such an explanation. They interpreted these stories in terms framed by their current material surroundings and spoke of frontier-sponsored independence, personal autonomy, and individualism.

They did not seem to see that the material conditions under which those earlier people lived and those events occurred were in fact fundamentally different than the buildings, roadways, and consumption patterns that they had seen around themselves since 1910, or 1920, or 1950. Older residents *did* recognize a change. They assembled the same stories about the same people and events in very different ways, because for them the issue was to explain the causes and consequences of that change.

Yet this was not particularly a matter of greater or lesser accuracy in the stories themselves, or in how a history "should" be constructed from them. In fact, both versions carried great degrees of accuracy, particularly with respect to the actual descriptions of specific events, as those could be corroborated from available documentation. Even at a more general level, there were certainly rowdy, gun-slinging buckaroos, Indian skirmishes and raids, and episodes of frontier justice in the town's earliest days, (a fact downplayed and occasionally ignored in the accounts from the older generation). It is equally true that the post-1900 period actually saw a considerable increase in local concern with things nationally fashionable, stylish, and technologically progressive, at least among the more successful valley families, a fact universally ignored in second-generation accounts, in spite of the fact that the tellers are themselves members of those families.

Rather, the discrepancy in the two histories of Paradise Valley was significant to an archaeological interpretation because it clearly and explicitly defined the changes in the relationships between the Paradise community and its material world between 1860 and 1920. It was not that the second generation had gotten its "facts" concerning specific people or events "wrong." It was that the physical and material context of those past people's lives was fundamentally different than the one that exists in the valley today. This earlier, different material life underlay the relationships between people and was articulated through those relationships between shopkeeper and customer, neighbor and neighbor, or resident and traveler. When compared, the points of conflict between the two histories pinpointed the ways in which not only the material culture had changed, but the way this articulation of human interaction and the material world had changed.

This interpretation proved adequate for the original

purposes at hand: it allowed me to integrate data from a wide range of material culture categories, from archaeological and documentary records, and across 60 years of Paradise settlement. But as a treatment of oral history, it suffered from oversimplification. Because it emphasized the differences between the two sets of stories, it implied that Paradise residents are somehow unaware of the discrepancies between different accounts of local history, when in fact people invest considerable time and effort in identifying and debating points of interpretive difference. Because it portrayed the process of local history-making as relatively naive and unself-conscious, my interpretation left out the highly sophisticated awareness Paradise Valley residents have of the links between the events of their community history and the mythic structure of the American "West." Both these flaws narrowed the scope of local oral history in crucial ways, particularly in describing how local accounts identify and explain change.

The first corrective to my analysis came from ethnography. In 1987 Nancy Howell presented a paper that identified certain parallels between the emerging Tasaday controversy and a series of archival revelations about historical !Kung involvement in long-distance trade, pottery-making, and metallurgy. She used these parallels to reassess anthropological approaches to "isolated" cultural groups, particularly hunter-gatherers (Howell 1987). One of the points she made struck a chord: if the !Kung had once traded over great distances, manufactured pots, and exploited rich copper mines, why did they now tell the visiting ethnographers that their current, "isolated," technologically limited situation was how things had always been? And how willing were the ethnographers to hear any other version, trapped in the temporal framework of an ethnographic present that had never really existed? At the time, I found myself wondering if I had not employed an analogous "ethnographic past" in interpreting Paradise oral histories, neatly breaking a continuum of memory into before and after, then and now.

Howell's cautionary tale sent me back to the Paradise Valley material with two concerns. I needed a less mechanical (and less patronizing) view of how contemporary Paradise residents perceived and interpreted the changes that had occurred there since the 1860s. I also needed to acknowledge the complex interweaving of Paradise oral histories with a wide spectrum of academic texts, novels, politician's speeches, Hollywood movies, television characters, and cigarette advertisements that inextricably linked Paradise to the outside world.

This reevaluation is as yet unfinished. In general, the original interpretation of the valley's changing material culture remains valid. But the clear dichotomy between who told which story has proved much less reliable. In listening again to the interviews, it is easy to realize my own role in shaping story content: when I asked questions about change, I got answers about change. As the project went on, I asked more and more such questions, because they increasingly framed my own research interests.

I also triggered similar interests among some of the people interviewed, because documentary or archaeological research began to provide new information that had not been available before and had to be incorporated into existing explanations of the valley's past. In this respect, my project on Paradise Valley material culture became a component of valley oral history, as had the American Folklife Center project that preceded me. These influences from outside added new information, ideas, and heightened awareness of local history in general. But there remained ample room for disagreement and variation. Defining and evaluating change had always been a central feature of local oral history, and it continued to be.

The role of the larger outside world in Paradise oral history has proved even more complex. For example, so many people told a nearly identical set of stories about Indian skirmishes, local murders, and environmental hardship during their first interviews because they had all read the stories in Myron Angel's *History of Nevada*, first published in 1881. Angel, in turn, had included the stories as a way of heightening the sense of progress and prosperity he found in the valley, and throughout the state, in 1879 and 1880. Furthermore, his was a subscription history, and many of the more established Paradise citizens paid small sums to have their personal or family histories included in the text.

All of which leads to the conclusion that Angel's material was itself the stuff of oral history, collected from valley ranchers and farmers in the course of recording their "subscription" (Angel 1881). One hundred years later, the "oral history" of these events spans the generations, from people who heard the stories from their parents, many of whom had lived the actual events (and whose names appear in Angel's subscription list), to people who read Angel's accounts on their arrival in the valley in the 1960s.

Many of these newer residents cite these stories as evidence that Paradise belonged to the West of myth and legend, further amplifying the connections between their local history and some broader frame of reference. But then, it is not inconceivable that Angel also chose these particular stories for their "wild West" connotations, playing to the popular market of the 1880s that first brought such images into vogue (Smith 1978[1950]).

Did Angel's original subscribers tell him these stories for the same reasons he wrote them in his published history, to provide dramatic markers for subsequent progress and change? Are these the same reasons why those same stories are still the *first* stories told to the outsider, who comes asking about the valley's past? How can the telling of the same stories, to describe essentially the same sets of changes, encompass two such different understandings of the valley's material culture, and *its* history? My exploration of what these people told me about their community's past continues to shape subsequent research in places far removed from Paradise Valley. In like manner, Paradise residents continue to comment on my interpretations, debate my word choices, and provide alternative views.

Discussion

The lessons of Paradise Valley provide two avenues for approaching oral history in historical archaeology. The first is the most directly methodological: how can oral narratives of the past speak to the analysis of past material culture? At its most particularistic, people who remember can identify how specific objects were once produced, distributed, and consumed in local contexts long gone. Such memories also have the potential to explain relationships *between* objects and their broader social and material contexts, paralleling and critiquing archaeological interpretation as it moves from definition to analysis. Furthermore, when archaeologists ask others to explain material culture, they open up their discipline to a wide range of highly contested alternative interpretations of past objects, spaces, and technologies, and their relevance to the present. As in Paradise, because many *different* histories are told, the archaeologist is forced to come to terms with disagreement, ambiguity, and discontinuity, as well as conformity and validation (Leone and Crosby 1987).

The second theme involves how and why we do historical archaeology. We have become increasingly sophisticated at describing historical archaeology as the anthropology of *what*: of changing world views, of European expansion, of gender, of mercantile and industrial capitalism, of ethnicity, and so on. It has come less easily, to identify historical archaeology as the anthropology of *whom*, done *by* whom, on what authority.

Part of the confusion may stem from the discipline's parentage. American prehistoric archaeology has always been an archaeology of a distinct "other," in contrast to European schools, which approached the archaeological record as an account of their own cultural past. But with historical archaeology, we are studying the immediate past of our own society. Historical models for this are numerous, but anthropological ones are less well developed.

Current ethnographic interest in "writing culture," and the emerging post-modern critiques of archaeology, suggest that a dialogue between the archaeologist and storyteller could open up an avenue for confronting whose anthropology the historical archaeologist is doing. James Clifford has described an emerging ethnography which has lost its clearly defined, objectified "other," an ethnography that "now...encounters others in relation to itself, while seeing itself as other" (Clifford 1986:23). At the same time, there is a renewed interest in using anthropology to provide a "cultural critique" of our own society, a critique in which historical perspectives can play crucial roles (Marcus and Fischer 1986:111–131).

In much the same way, and for similar reasons, archaeology has lost its single, distant "past." Post-structural critiques borrowed from Bourdieu, Giddens, and Foucault, and specific theoretical premises from Marxist materialism, cognitivism, psychology, and feminist theory, have created multiple, alternative pasts. At the same time, hermeneutics and critical theory have broken down the objective barriers between past and present, as well as subject and object (Hodder 1986:156–169).

The links between anthropological approaches to the past, to other cultures, and to its own cultural milieu are complex. Johannes Fabian has examined anthropological conceptions of time as they relate to the discipline's understanding of other cultures (Fabian 1983). In part, he argues that ethnographers distance themselves from their subject culture by fixing it in an evolutionarily ordered "other" time. The process denies the contemporaneity, or "coevalness" of other cultures with the anthropologist's own. Cultures thus fixed at some point outside western time can be brought up to the "present" through colonization, development, or some other form of cultural co-option. Fabian argues that this distancing device is not a methodological accident, but an integral part of the intellectual history of anthropology. It has shaped, and continues to shape, perceptions of other cultures, through generally social evolutionary theories and concepts, such as the ethnographic present or cultural relativity. It is an inheritance that must be overcome before the discipline can serve any critical function (Fabian 1983:156–165).

In this context, American historical archaeologists work in a potentially very powerful arena. The intellectual tools inherited from American archaeology encourage a treatment of the past as "other," as inhabitants of a truly "foreign country" (Lowenthal 1985). To some extent, we have accomplished just this: we have reified a specific sense of distance from the past by ordering an evolutionary series of cultural "others" in our own history. These can be understood in terms of shifting mind-set or world view, medieval to Georgian to Victorian (e.g., Deetz 1977; Hardesty and Hattori 1983), or as the cultural consequences of the episodic transitions in socioeconomic systems, such as mercantile, industrial, and post-industrial capitalism, (cf. Handsman 1981; Leone and Shackel 1990; Leone and Potter 1988).

And yet we work primarily in a context that we also have defined as our own broader culture, although much of *how* we define that identity remains problematic and unexpressed. That premise has justified work in historical archaeology that takes an overtly critical stance on the social and economic processes that created contemporary society (e.g., Leone and Potter 1988). It underlay studies that identified the origins of contemporary cognitive patterns or world view in the transformation of earlier societies (e.g., Deetz 1977). Because of this underlying premise, the one comparative context that historical archaeology-as-anthropology emphatically cannot escape is that of the present.

Finally, we also work back and forth across a powerfully and literally objectified temporal boundary between familiar and unfamiliar things, the recognizable and the strange. Material culture has served as the means of translation between culture and time. The power of material culture as an inherent component of social discourse is well documented in the anthropological literature and is an integral feature in the work of recent social theorists (e.g., Bourdieu 1984; Giddens 1979; cf. Beaudry, Cook, and Mrozowski 1991). But the intellectual history of our discipline has meant that we have approached this materially defined temporal boundary by moving from the most distant point — European exploration and colonization — towards ourselves. Authority develops as specialized knowledge about the previously unknown objects, unidentified technologies, and unfamiliar landscapes. Ignoring the more conventional lessons of stratigraphy, we move from least known towards the most familiar.

Oral history forces us to begin from the other end, with ourselves, and to look back. Furthermore, we do not look alone, but must acknowledge the perspective of other memories and other expertise. These other narratives can not only disagree with our own, but amongst themselves. In the process of such debate, the temporal boundary created and reinforced by our approaches to material culture becomes far less absolute, more contested, and is ultimately redefined.

Questioning the boundary from this side calls forth useful questions about both the nature and the subject of our research. To what extent is our operating division between past and present real, or just an artifact of individual combinations of bias and birth date, expertise, and ignorance? How far back from the present is the past? Where, when, and how often does the past really become an "other" culture, truly different from our own, in spite of its ancestral role? How real is the perceived cultural consensus against which this "other" is defined? How different is different enough? What is the nature of the change that separates then from now?

It has been said that oral history is not the past, but what the present remembers about the past (Grele 1985 [1975]:206). When historical archaeologists take the odd, known-yet-unknown artifacts they excavate into the negotiated dialogue of oral history, both parties can compare what has been remembered with what was forgotten. The history that results undoubtedly still serves present purposes, but those purposes are vastly different than those served by histories constructed either by archaeologists or storytellers alone.

The anthropology that results can address fundamental questions about the nature of culture and history, and the relationship between them. In particular, it brings the historical archaeologist face to face with the issue of *whose* anthropology we are doing. From its inception, "American" historical archaeology has been composed of "Americans" telling stories about an "American" past. Efforts to achieve any *real* representativeness have varied greatly over time and among practitioners, but the ethos has remained. Even as the field expanded from its elite biography and culture history origins to incorporate different ethnic, social, and gender groups, some sense of an "anthropology of us," set in the past, continued.

It is in this respect that oral history can contribute most to historical archaeology. It is not just that it allows the inclusion of a wider range of voices, and so helps to justify, or challenge, the collective "us" from which we claim to speak. It is that the historical accounts of others outside our field force a reappraisal of our own authority, and the grounds on which we make such claims, either as academic professionals, government policy administrators, or public educators. In the process, these stories about things from the past will bring us into the thick of an ongoing debate over the present status of anthropology itself as an intellectual discipline and the roles it is to play in the future.

References

Adams, W. (1976) Silcott, Washington: Ethnoarchaeology of a Rural American Community. Ph.D. dissertation, Washington State University, Department of Anthropology, Pulman, Washington.

Allen, B. and W. L. Montell (1981) *From Memory to History: Using Oral Sources in Local Historical Research.* The American Association for State and Local History, Nashville, Tennessee.

Angel, M. (1881) *The History of Nevada.* Thompson and West, San Francisco.

Bearss, E. C. (1990) Oral History: A Challenging and Provocative Experience. National Park Service, *Cultural Resource Management Bulletin* 13(2):1.

Beaudry, M. C., L. J. Cook, and S. A. Mrozowski (1991) Artifacts and Active Voices: Material Culture as Social Discourse. In *The Archaeology of Social Inequality.* R. Paynter and R. H. McGuire, Eds. Basil Blackwell, Oxford, pp. 150–191.

Bourdieu, P. (1984) *Distinction: A Social Critique of the Judgement of Taste.* Richard Nice, trans. Harvard University Press, Cambridge, MA.

Brown, M. R. (1973) The Use of Oral and Documentary Sources in Historical Archaeology: Ethnohistory at the Mott Farm. *Ethnohistory* 20:347.

Buckingham, F. C. (1981) Interview, December 6–7, 1981, Paradise Valley, Nevada, tape on file, American Folklife Center, Library of Congress, Washington, DC.

Clifford, J. (1986) Introduction: Partial Truths. In *Writing Culture: The Poetics and Politics of Ethnography.* J. Clifford and G. E. Marcus, Eds. University of California Press, Berkeley, pp. 1–26.

Costello, J. G. (1981) *Los Olivos Market: Initial Impact Assessment.* Submitted to Planning Department, County of Santa Barbara, CA.

Costello, J. G. and J. Cunningham (1988) *Inventory and Evaluation of Historic Resources.* A Cultural Resource Survey of the Proposed Royal/Mountain King Mine and National Register Evaluations of Historic Properties, Calaveras County, California, Vol. 2. Foothill Resource Associates, submitted to Meridian Minerals, Inc., Denver, CO.

Crosby, C. A. (1988) From Myth to History, or Why King Philip's Ghost Walks Abroad. In *The Recovery of Meaning, Historical Archaeology in the Eastern United States.* M. P. Leone and P. B. Potter, Eds. Smithsonian Institution Press, Washington, DC, pp. 183–209.

Daaku, K. Y. (1973) History in the Oral Traditions of the Akan. In *Folklore and Traditional History.* R. M. Dorson, Ed. Mouton Press, The Hague, pp. 42–54.

Deagan, K. (1983) *Spanish St. Augustine: The Archaeology of a Colonial Creole Community.* Academic Press, New York.

Deetz, J. (1977) *In Small Things Forgotten: The Archaeology of Early American Life.* Anchor Press/Doubleday, Garden City, New York.

Donley, L. (1983) House Power: Swahili Space and Symbolic Markers. In *Symbolic and Structural Archaeology,* I. Hodder, Ed. Cambridge University Press, Cambridge.

Dunaway, D. K. and W. K. Baum Eds. (1984) *Oral History: An Interdisciplinary Anthology.* American Association for State and Local History, Nashville, TN.

Fabian, J. (1983) *Time and the Other: How Anthropology Makes Its Object.* Columbia University Press, New York.

Friedlander, P. (1975) *The Emergence of a UAW Local, 1936–1939: A Study in Class and Culture.* University of Pittsburgh Press, Pittsburgh.

— (1984) Theory, Method, and Oral History. In *Oral History: An Interdisciplinary Anthology,* D. K. Dunaway and W. K. Baum, Eds. American Association for State and Local History, Nashville, TN, pp. 131–141.

Giddens, A. (1979) *Central Problems in Social Theory.* University of California Press, Berkeley.

Glassie, H. (1977) Archaeology and Folklore: Common Anxieties, Common Hopes. In *Historical Archaeology and the Importance of Material Things,* L. Ferguson, Ed. Society for Historical Archaeology Special Publications Series, #2.

— (1982) *Passing the Time in Ballymenone: Culture and History of an Ulster Community.* University of Pennsylvania Press, Philadelphia, PA.

Gluck, Sherna (1984 [1977]) What's So Special About Women? Women's Oral History. In *Oral History, An Interdisciplinary Anthology,* D. K. Dunaway and W. K. Baum, Eds. American Association for State and Local History, Nashville, TN, pp. 221–237.

Grele, R. J. (1985[1975]) *Envelopes of Sound: The Art of Oral History.* Precedent Publishing, Chicago.

Handsman, R. (1981) Early Capitalism and the Center Village of Canaan, Connecticut: A Study of Transformations and Separations. *Artifacts* 9:1.

Hardesty, D. L. and E. M. Hattori (1983) An Archaeological Model of Victorianism on the Nevada Mining Frontier. Paper presented at the 16th annual meeting, Society for Historical Archaeology, Denver, Colorado.

Hareven, T. K. and R. Langenbach (1978) *Amoskeag: Life and Work in an American Factory City.* Pantheon Press, New York.

Henige, D. (1982) *Oral Historiography.* Longman Group, London, England.

Hodder, I. (1986) *Reading the Past: Current Approaches to Interpretation in Archaeology.* Cambridge University Press, Cambridge, England.

Howell, N. (1987) The Tasaday and the !Kung: Reassessing Isolated Hunter-Gatherers. Paper presented at the annual meeting, Society for American Archaeology.

Leone, M. P. and C. A. Crosby (1987) Epilogue: Middle Range Theory in Historical Archaeology. In *Consumer Choice in Historical Archaeology,* S. Spencer-Wood, Ed. Plenum Press, New York, pp. 397–410.

Leone, M. P. and P. B. Potter, Eds. (1988) *The Recovery of Meaning, Historical Archaeology in the Eastern United States.* Smithsonian Institution Press, Washington, DC.

Leone, M. P. and P. A. Shackel (1990) The Georgian Order in Annapolis. In *New Perspectives on Maryland Historical Archaeology,* R. J. Dent and B. J. Little, Eds. *Maryland Archaeology* 26:69–84.

Lowenthal, D. (1985) *The Past is a Foreign Country.* Cambridge University Press, Cambridge.

Lo Gerfo, M. (1984) Three ways of reminiscence in theory and practice. In *Oral History: An Interdisciplinary Anthology.* D. K. Dunaway and W. K. Baum, Eds. American Association for State and Local History, Nashville, TN, pp 314–323.

Marcus, G. E. and M. M. J. Fischer (1986) *Anthropology as Cultural Critique: An Experimental Moment in the Human Sciences.* University of Chicago Press, Chicago.

Marquardt, W. H. (1987) The Calusa Social Formation in Protohistoric South Florida. In *Power Relations and State Formation,* T. C. Patterson and C. W. Gailey, Eds. Archaeology Section, American Anthropological Association, Washington, D.C., pp. 98–116.

Marshall, H. W. and R. E. Ahlborn (1980) *Buckaroos in Paradise: Cowboy Life in Northern Nevada.* Library of Congress, Washington, DC.

Montell, L. (1970) *The Saga of Coe Ridge: A Study in Oral History.* University of Tennessee Press, Knoxville.

Neunschwander, J. (1984 [1978]) Oral Historians and Long-Term Memory. In *Oral History: An Interdisciplinary Anthology,* D. K. Dunaway and W. K. Baum, Eds. American Association for State and Local History, Nashville, TN, pp. 324–332.

Posnansky, M. and C. R. Decorse (1986) Historical Archaeology in Sub-Saharan Africa — A Review. *Historical Archaeology* 20:1.

Price, R. (1983) *First-Time: The Historical Vision of an Afro-American People.* Johns Hopkins University Press, Baltimore.

Purser, M. (1989) All Roads Lead to Winnemucca: Local Road Systems and Community Material Culture in Nineteenth Century Nevada. In *Perspectives in Vernacular Architecture, III.* T. Carter and B. L. Herman, Eds. University of Missouri Press, Columbia, MO, pp. 120–134.

— (1987) Community and Material Culture in Nineteenth Century Paradise Valley, Nevada. Ph.D. dissertation, University of California Berkeley, Department of Anthropology, Berkeley.

Rosaldo, R. (1980) *Ilongot Headhunting, 1883–1974: A Study in Society and History.* Stanford University Press, Stanford, CA.

Rosengarten, T. (1974) *All God's Dangers: The Life of Nate Shaw.* Knopf, New York.

St. George, R. B. (1983) Maintenance Relations and the Erotics of Property. Paper presented at annual meeting, American Historical Association.

Schmidt, P. R. (1978) *Historical Archaeology: A Structural Approach in an African Culture.* Greenwood Press, Westport, CT.

Schuyler, R. L. (1988) Archaeological Remains, Documents, and Anthropology: A Call for a New Culture History. *Historical Archaeology* 22:36.

— (1974) Sandy Ground: Archaeological Sampling in a Black Community in Metropolitan New York. *Papers of the Conference on Historic Site Archaeology* 7:12.

— (1977) The Spoken Word, the Written Word, Observed Behavior and Preserved Behavior: The Contexts Available to the Archaeologist. *Papers of the Conference on Historic Site Archaeology* 10:99.

Simmons, W. S. (1988) Culture Theory in Contemporary Ethnohistory. *Ethnohistory* 35:1.

— (1986) *Spirit of the New England Tribes, Indian History and Folklore, 1620–1984.* University Press of New England, Hanover, NH.

Smith, H. N. (1978 [1950]) *Virgin Land: The American West as Symbol and Myth.* Harvard University Press, Cambridge, MA.

Thompson, P. (1978) *The Voice of the Past: Oral History.* Oxford University Press, Oxford, England.

Todorov, T. (1984 [1982]) *The Conquest of America.* Harper and Row, New York.

Vansina, J. (1985) *Oral Tradition as History.* University of Wisconsin Press, Madison.

Winters, C. L. (1987) *The Role of Oral Tradition in Archaeological Research.* Masters thesis in folklore, Department of Anthropology, University of California Berkeley.

Wolf, E. (1982) *Europe and the People Without History.* University of California Press, Berkeley.

Part B: Complementary Data

4: Simon Benning, Pewterer of Port Royal

D. L. Hamilton

Department of Anthropology, Texas A & M University, College Station, Texas

Historic documents and the excavation of historic sites represent the two primary sets of data that archaeologists use and mesh in order to interpret the cultural history of a site. Each of these data sets has its own particular problems, pitfalls, and potential contributions. The use of only the archaeological data from an excavated site, aside from being a farce, would be analogous to studying human anatomy by looking only at the skeleton. In historical archaeology, the written records and documents flesh out the skeletal archaeological data into a viable cultural reconstruction.

Most 17th- and 18th-century English sites have a comparable compliment of public records, such as maps, censuses, land plats, wills, inventories, port records, and various other documents. It is immaterial if the site happens to be in England, New England, Maryland, Virginia, or Jamaica. In fact, information concerning one area is often found in other areas.

Generally speaking, relevant historic records and documents fall into four broad areas:

1. Records that shed light on the region or site as a whole
2. Records that shed light on a given person or area
3. Records that shed light on selected artifacts
4. Some combination of the above

The secret, or more accurately the problem, is to find records that pertain to a particular research area and question. Each search has its own detective trail as the archaeologist looks for clues that relate a deed transaction, a will, or an inventory to specific questions. Often the initial part of the search is aimed at finding the documents that will identify the people associated with the artifacts, for example, the property owners of a specific site or the makers and/or owners of particular objects. During the quest, one must try to determine just how many different ways the simplest of surnames can be spelled. One must also determine how many of the similar spellings represent the same person. In time, the researcher feels that he or she is more familiar with the people, places, and period of research than with his or her own town and neighbors. Presented below is just one of the many historic investigations that have resulted from the archaeological excavations at Port Royal, Jamaica.

Background History of Port Royal

During the late 17th century the two largest English towns in the Americas were Boston, Massachusetts and Port Royal, Jamaica. Most archaeologists who work with historic sites in the U.S. are familiar with the archaeological work carried out in New England, but relatively few are familiar with Port Royal and its role in the history of the 17th century English colonies.

In December 1654, Cromwell, Lord Protector of England, as part of his "Western Design," sent a invasion force under the commands of Admiral Penn and General Venable to capture Hispaniola (Taylor 1965:XI). The Spanish were forewarned of the invasion and soundly defeated the invading forces attempting to capture the city of Santo Domingo. Failing miserably in their attempt to capture Hispaniola, and fearing to return empty handed, they sailed to Jamaica, and in May of 1655 captured the poorly defended island with relatively little resistance. Jamaica became a consolation prize to appease Cromwell.

Port Royal was born within weeks of the conquest, when construction on a fort was begun. Situated at the tip of the sand spit separating Kingston Harbor from the Caribbean, Port Royal could control all access to the harbor through the narrow entrance. A small community, consisting of mariners, merchants, craftsmen, and prostitutes, built up around it. In its early days, the settlement was known as The Point or Point Cagway (Pawson and Buisserct 1975:7). After the restoration of Charles II and the monarchy in England in 1660, the

Point was renamed Port Royal and the fort, which had been called Passage Fort or Fort Cromwell, was renamed Fort Charles (Taylor 1965:131; Pawson and Buisseret 1975:9).

Although Port Royal was designed to serve as a defensive fortification, guarding the entrance to the harbor, it assumed much greater importance. Because of Port Royal's location within a well-protected harbor, its flat topography, and deep water close to shore, large ships could be easily serviced, loaded, and unloaded. Ships' captains, merchants, and craftsmen established themselves in Port Royal to take advantage of the trading and outfitting opportunities. As Jamaica's economy grew and changed between 1655 and 1692, Port Royal grew faster than any town founded by the English in the New World, and it became the most economically important English port in the Americas. Its story up to 1692 is that of Jamaica itself.

Coinciding with this early development, in the period between 1660 and 1671, was the age of officially sanctioned privateering for which the city was so notorious. In 1689, approximately 1200 of the 4000 whites in the town were privateers (Zahedieh 1986b:220). The buccaneer era greatly enriched the port, but it was a short-lived and colorful period that England was supposed to end by the conditions of the 1670 Treaty of Madrid. Privateering and/or piracy, however, continued in one form or another into the 18th century. Throughout the 17th century, the Spanish money flowing into the coffers of Port Royal, through trade and plunder, made the port what it was.

After 1670, the importance of Port Royal and Jamaica to England was increasingly due to trade in slaves, sugar, and raw materials. Port Royal became the mercantile center of the Caribbean. Vast amounts of goods flowed in and out of the port through an expansive trade network, which included extensive trading and/or looting of coastal Spanish towns throughout Spanish America. It was a wealthy city of merchants, artisans, ships' captains, slaves, and, of course, notorious pirates. From this latter citizenry, it derived its reputation of being the "wickedest city in the world."

Only Boston, Massachusetts rivaled it in size and importance. In 1690, Boston had a population of approximately 6000 (Henretta 1965:73). The population estimates for Port Royal in 1692 range from a low of 6500 to a high of 10,000 (Buisseret 1966:26; Claypole 1972:242; Pawson and Buisseret 1975:99; Taylor 1688:260). Pawson and Buisseret, using the census of 1680, arrive at a population of about 7000 inhabitants — 4500 whites, and 2500 black and Indian slaves. I personally think a population estimate of 6500 to 7000 is probably the most realistic. If even the lowest of these population estimates is reliable, then at the time of Port Royal's destruction, it was the largest English town in the New World. The town had as many as 2000 buildings densely packed into 51 acres at the tip of the Palisadoes,

as the spit is called. Many of the buildings were constructed of brick, and some were four stories tall. It may be debated whether Boston or Port Royal was larger, but there is no doubt that in the late 17th century, Port Royal was more important economically. This statement is easily verified by the number of ships that visited the two ports. In 1688, 213 ships visited Port Royal, while 226 ships made port in all of New England (Zahedieh 1986a:570). Port Royal's affluence is indicated by the large number of ships calling there, the privateers, the large number of merchants, the greater value of the inventories, and the observation that, unlike the other English colonies, Jamaica used coins for currency instead of commodity exchange, as was common for most English colonies in the Americas (Zahedieh 1986a:585; Claypole 1972:144–145, 216–217). Port Royal was the most successful entrepot in the English New World. The town had a social milieu quite different than anything in either New England, with its religiously ordered towns, or in the tobacco-driven economy of Maryland and Virginia. This difference is clearly indicated in Taylor's (1688) preearthquake description of the town in 1688 and again in the two postearthquake travelogues written by Edward Ward (1699, 1700) after visits to both Port Royal and Boston. Port Royal was more tolerant and its *laissez faire* attitude toward life allowed for a diversity of religious expression and life styles. Thus we find early mention of merchants who were Quakers, "Papists," Puritans, Presbyterians, Jews, and of course, Anglicans, practicing their religion openly alongside the free-willing sailors and pirates who frequented the port.

Throughout most of Port Royal's early history (1660 to 1692), it was the *de facto* capital of the island. Until 1692, it was Jamaica's only legal port of entry, and its merchants controlled the economic affairs of the island. By this time, the merchants had been investing the profits derived from trading and looting to finance and develop emerging plantations (Claypole 1972:174–195; Zahedieh 1986b:221). Thus we see the beginning of the transition from the domination of the economy by the Port Royal merchants to the domination and control of the economy by the equally strong plantation owners of the 18th century. Still, by New World standards, Port Royal, in 1692, was the most affluent town at or near its peak of prosperity (Pawson and Buisseret 1975:111).

Everything was to come to a sudden and frightful end. Shortly before noon on June 7, 1693, 33 acres (66%) of the "storehouse and treasury of the West Indies" sank into Kingston Harbor in a disastrous earthquake. Interestingly, a pocket watch made circa 1686 by Paul Blondel, a Frenchman living in the Netherlands, was recovered in underwater excavations near Fort James by Edwin Link (Link 1960:173). The hands of the watch were frozen at 11:43 a.m., recording the time of the earthquake — a first for archaeology. Of course there are numerous eye witness accounts that survive in the archives that verify the time of the disaster. An estimated 2000 persons were killed immediately by the earthquake and the seismic sea waves that followed. An additional 3000 citizens died of injuries and disease in the following days (Pawson and Buisseret 1975:121). Salvage and outright looting began almost immediately and continued off and on for years.

After the 1692 earthquake, Port Royal underwent a dramatic revival, which was to end when it was ravaged by a fire in 1703. In the following years, it was hit by hurricanes in 1712, 1722, 1726, 1744, 1751, 1782, 1786, 1787, 1805, 1818, 1830, 1867, 1884, 1886, 1903, and 1951; and had damaging earthquakes in 1770, 1812, 1824, 1858, 1867, and 1956 (Cox 1984:Appendix B). Following a severe storm, a hurricane, and two earthquakes in 1722, the town went into a decline from which it never emerged. Most recently, the town suffered some damages form Hurricane Gilbert in 1988. With each disaster, fewer people chose to live in the town.

Today, as one walks along the narrow streets of the poor fishing village of Port Royal, it is hard to imagine that in the late 17th century it was the largest and most economically important English settlement in the Americas. Port Royal remains today as an isolated town at the end of the spit. It has a population of roughly 1800 inhabitants, who view themselves as unique "Port Royalists," rather than simply Jamaican. The town survives as a quiet fishing village. However, beneath its surface, both on land and water, lies an unparalleled archaeological record with a massive array of *in situ* materials. Archaeologically, it is acknowledged as being one of the most important 17th-century English sites in the world, but only a small portion of the town has been investigated.

Port Royal is different from most archaeological sites. It belongs to that group of sites that includes Pompeii and Herculaneum in Italy and Ozette in the state of Washington in the U.S.. I have coined the term *catastrophic site* to describe those sites created by some disaster that preserves both the cultural features and material and the all-important archaeological context (Hamilton and Woodward 1984:38). In these undisturbed sites, the archaeologist is not dealing with a situation where — over a span of time — houses, shops, warehouses, churches, and other buildings were constructed, expanded, neglected, abandoned, eventually collapsed, were razed, and then possibly were built over. Port Royal is strikingly different: after only 37 years of existence this bustling city literally sank into the harbor in only a matter of minutes during a severe earthquake. Shipwrecks, which are also catastrophic sites, dating from the 17th century are relatively common, but Port Royal is the only such site of its kind in the Americas.

There has been considerable work conducted on the part of the town that remains submerged below the water of present day Kingston Harbor (Link 1960; Marx 1973; Hamilton 1984, 1985, 1986, 1988). For various reasons, these data have not been used by archaeologists working on contemporaneous 17th-century English colonial sites in North America. Much can be learned from this site, for the underwater excavations of the submerged 17th-century remains of Port Royal have resulted in remarkable parallels and even more interesting contrasts with the contemporaneous English colonists in North America.

Archaeological Excavations at Port Royal

In 1981, the Institute of Nautical Archaeology (INA), in cooperation with Texas A&M University (TAMU) and the Jamaica National Heritage Trust (JNHT), began the underwater archaeological investigation of the submerged portion of the 17th-century town of Port Royal, Jamaica. Present evidence indicates that the areas of the town that lay along the edge of the harbor before the earthquake slid and jumbled as they sank, destroying most of the archaeological context. The area investigated by INA/TAMU, which is situated away from the harbor, sank vertically, with minimal horizontal disturbance, during the earthquake through a process called liquefaction.

Accordingly, unlike other 17th-century sites, at Port Royal we deal with artifacts and even furniture within the rooms and buildings where they were used. On some occasions the occupants of the rooms are found where they were trapped by fallen brick walls. In contrast to most archaeological sites, we are not working exclusively with trash and discarded items — although this component is present. Also, because the part of Port Royal being excavated is underwater, a considerable amount of perishable, organic artifacts that are missing from most terrestrial sites are preserved. With intact artifacts and a full range of cultural data present, distributional studies and patterns are more meaningful. The underwater archaeological excavations and the vast treasury of complimentary historical documents allow us to reconstruct a detailed picture of everyday life up to the time of the destruction in 1692. Through the historic documents and the archaeological record, we are able to conduct a detailed synchronic study of Port Royal at the time of the town's destruction in 1692, when it was near or at its peak of prosperity and still reigned as the mercantile capital of the English New World.

I have concentrated the excavations for the past 10 years on the submerged 17th-century remains on Lime Street near its intersection with Queen and High Streets in the commercial center of the town (Figure 1). This decade of underwater excavations has resulted in a more detailed body of data on the buildings in the town and their *in situ* artifacts than any previous excavations in the town — on land or underwater. To date five buildings have been investigated (Figure 2).

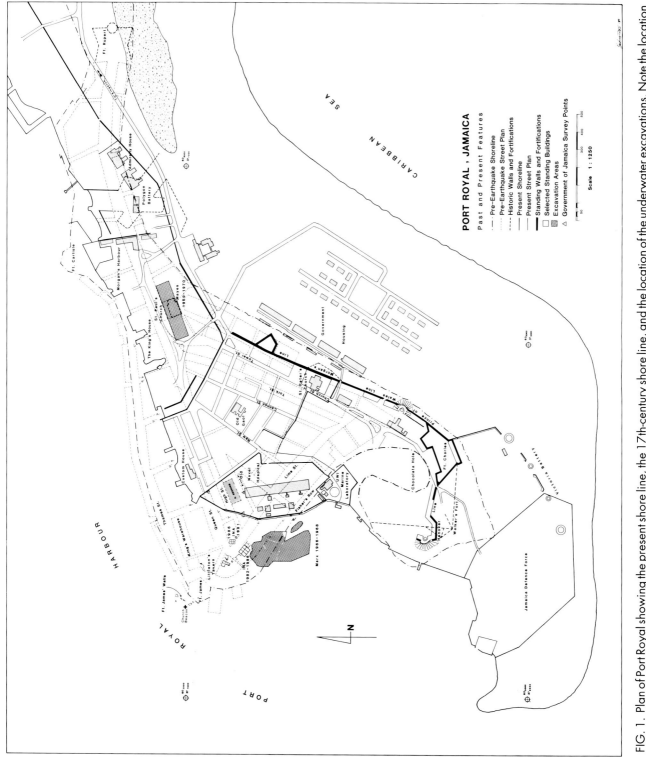

FIG. 1. Plan of Port Royal showing the present shore line, the 17th-century shore line, and the location of the underwater excavations. Note the location of Simon Benning's property on High Street, just north of the Old Naval Hospital Building.

42

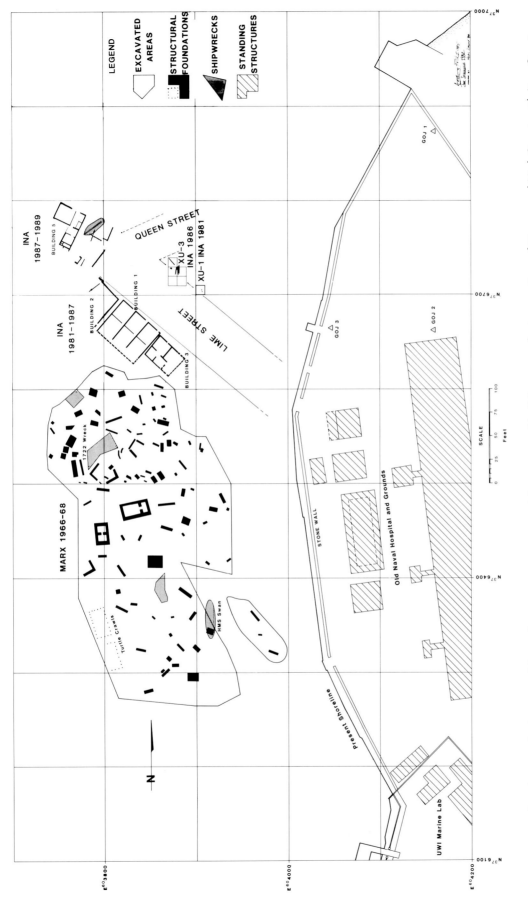

FIG. 2. Plan showing the location of the underwater excavations and the excavated buildings near the intersections of Queen and High Streets with Lime Street.

43

The construction features of the five investigated buildings exemplify the variety of architectural styles found in the center of the town. Some were well-built, multistoried, brick structures, while others were simple, earth-bound, frame buildings, hastily built with no intention for them to last for any length of time. In several instances, a small, core building was constructed, and then rooms were tacked on as the need arose, until the structure formed a complex. Both Building 1 and Building 5 clearly show this building sequence. The information from the excavated buildings have contributed significantly to our understanding of 17th-century town planning, architecture, diet, cooking activities, and other aspects of daily life at Port Royal.

To date, four adjacent buildings have been investigated, on the south side of Lime Street. Each has its own architectural detail and associated artifacts. Each has a compliment of records that pertain in some way to either the owners, occupants, or the makers of the associated artifacts. Building 1 is a well-built brick building consisting of two construction phases and having six ground floor rooms divided into three separate two-room combinations, including a probable pipe shop, a tavern, and a combination wood turner/cobbler's shop. Building 2 is a poorly preserved building to the west of Building 1. Nothing much can be said about it, other than that it was a frame building with a plaster floor. Building 3 is to the east of Building 1. It had raised sills on a mortar foundation, with interrupted floor sills at the corners and at major intersections. The front rooms had plastered floors and one room had a sand floor. The final building that has been excavated is Building 5. There actually is no Building 4. What was once thought to be Building 4 was found be part of Building 5, which is a large rambling complex of at least eight rooms (Figure 3).

The initial construction phase of Building 5 consisted of Rooms 1 and 2 and the sidewalk at the front of the building. Room 1, the large room to the west, has a plaster floor, while the smaller Room 2 has a herringbone brick floor and a stairwell. Tacked to the south of Room 2 are Rooms 3 and 4, which were added in a later construction phase, whose purpose may have been to join an exterior kitchen, represented by Room 4, to the building. Both back rooms have common bond, brick floors, and Room 4 contains a large hearth and oven. To the east of Rooms 2 and 3 are Rooms 5 to 8 with a second hearth behind Room 7. The presences of half-brick-wide interior walls dividing Rooms 5 to 8 indicate a much less substantial, one-story building addition. Horizontal displacements, seen most readily at the east end, in Room 7, have skewed the floor and walls several feet. The Building 5 complex is approximately 65 ft wide across the front of the building and is over 40 ft deep. It represents at least two, and possibly three, different houses or combination houses/shops.

The Building 5 excavations have produced more *in situ* artifacts than any building thus far excavated. To the front of the building, in what would have been a part of Lime Street, a large section of a fallen wall was discovered, which may have fallen out from Building 5, or from a building to the north that would have been located on the block between Thames and Queen Street.

In the area of the fallen exterior wall, we found the wood frame of a four-partition window with leaded glass panes within a wrought iron frame. In and around the window were two sets of Chinese porcelain Fo Dogs and a minimum of 28 Chinese porcelain cups and bowls. Pewter plates, candlesticks, a brass mortar, a delft vase, a Dutch Faience plate, a gold ring, a pearl with a gold attachment, silver forks and spoons, and many encrusted metal objects that are awaiting identification, conservation, and analysis were found in the same area.

At the start of the excavations in 1990, the building consisted of four core rooms, one being a kitchen with a hearth, and at least four rooms constructed to the east. Building 5 is a well-preserved brick building with plastered walls, brick floors, wooden door sills, and even the lower portion of one of the doors and the accompanying milled door jambs. Just outside the two, adjacent front doorways with *in situ* door sills, a young child was uncovered under the bricks of the fallen front wall. The remains of two more children were found in Rooms 3 and 4 of the same building. Numerous artifacts were found in association with the structure, including organic objects, such as hafted tools, wood buckets, shoe fragments, 3 candlesticks, 2 oil lamps, 37 pewter plates or bowls, 4 silver spoons, 2 calabash gourd dippers, another window frame with lead caming and shattered glass, and even textile fragments. Even more interesting is the remains of a ship, which appears to date from the time of the earthquake, which ripped through the front walls and tore through the floors of the four rooms on the east side of the building complex.

The investigation of Building 5 concluded in 1990 with the excavation of the area, which was found to be a paved yard, south of Room 1 in the main building. I concentrated on determining the alignment of the building in relation to Lime and Queen Streets and on determining the identity of the occupants of the structure in 1692. It was only with the excavation of Building 5, after 9 years of excavations, that we were finally able to pinpoint the exact location of the plat being excavated. It is now known that the structure is located on an extension of Lime Street that is not recorded on any of the maps of Port Royal. These archaeological findings are dictating changes in the plan of Port Royal that are not fully incorporated in Figure 1. Knowing about the existence of this extension of Lime Street will make the job of reconstructing the plats from the land patents and deed records simpler.

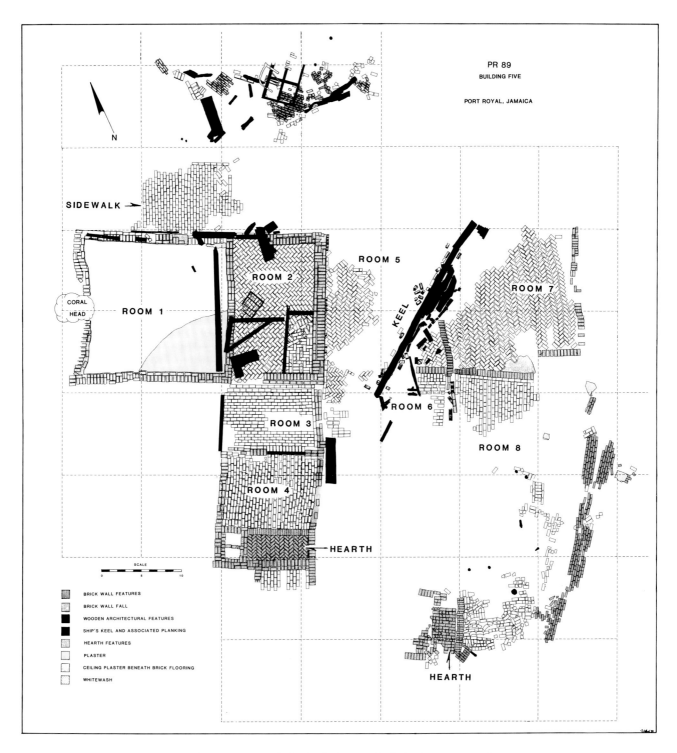

FIG. 3. Plan of Building 5, with the keel of a wrecked ship lying across the east rooms.

Historic Documents and Focused Historic Research

A brief outline of the excavation of Building 5 was presented above to give the reader a better appreciation for the uniqueness of the submerged site. The recon-structions that are possible from just the archaeological data are also unparalleled by any other 17th-century site, but it is still the historic documents that bring these data alive and attach names to them.

Relevant historic documents were sought from the first year of excavation in 1981, but this research increased significantly in the summers of 1988 to 1990,

45

when the Jamaica Archives and the Island Records Office in Spanish Town were thoroughly searched and relevant material was microfilmed for use by the project. Presently the microfilms of the land patents, wills, and inventories of the period 1660 to 1720 are being studied to determine the owners of specific building lots and to get a better appreciation for the estates left in wills and the contents of households and businesses in both Port Royal and the rest of Jamaica. The documentary research has allowed us to compare and contrast the Jamaica historic data with the archaeological record and with contemporaneous documents from other English colonies and England herself. Specifically, my students and I have been comparing and contrasting the 17th-century records of Port Royal; Bristol, England; and Boston, Massachusetts. These comparisons have allowed us to investigate common patterns, and differences have helped identify common cultural elements characteristic of 17th-century English sites, regardless of location.

The amount of documentation available on Port Royal is enormous. Comprehensive histories, survivor's accounts, and general background were thoroughly consulted prior to excavation, but much of the data had little direct relevance until there was a focus to the research. It is difficult to focus this research unless one can identify the exact land plat that is being excavated and associate it with a given person at the time of the earthquake. If any of this is known, then the document searches can be directed. It is much easier to trace back to any previous occupants if the land is occupied or exists as real estate at the present time. Then it is just a matter of working backwards. This is not possible for occupied land that ceased to exist because it sank beneath the water. The paper trail stops in the 17th century, with no continuity to the present. The problem of establishing ownership of given plats of land is compounded when one is dealing with an urban environment, such as Port Royal, that had no consistent means of referring either to property or maps depicting the location of properties in the deeds and patents. It can be very frustrating.

Quite often it is recovered artifacts, especially those that contain any identifying marks, that focus the historic research and identification process. This approach is detailed here.

During the excavations of Building 5 in 1989, 25 pewter plates were found near the stairwell in Room 2. Twenty-three of these plates were 9-in. diameter, narrow-rimmed plates, and they had the touch mark of Simon Benning, the maker, and either of the ownership marks NCI or IC. The same ownership marks were found on the silver spoons, silver forks, and a brass nutmeg grinder in the same room. It is obvious that the occupants of the building at the time of the earthquake in 1692 were a man with the initials NC and his wife with the initials IC, but the search for their identity is another story for another article. Here I am going to concentrate on the

historic documents that tell the story of Simon Benning, pewterer of Port Royal. In many ways the story of Simon Benning is a microcosm of the story of Port Royal itself.

Simon Benning, Pewterer of Port Royal

The name of Simon Benning was first encountered in the book, *Port Royal, Jamaica* by Pawson and Buisseret (1975:105, 183). The reference to Benning merely stated that there was a pewterer in Port Royal by that name in 1667. There was no reason to continue ferreting out the story of Simon Benning until the excavation of Room 5 in Building 1 yielded a pewter platter with an unusual and unidentified touch mark: a pineapple surrounded by an oval rope braid with the initial S to the left of the pineapple and the initial B to the right (Figure 4). We were reasonably confident that this was the touch mark of Simon Benning, for there were no parallels in the standard references on English pewterers (Cotterell 1963; Peal 1976, 1977). We knew that in the 17th century the pineapple was commonly identified with Jamaica and that it was incorporated into the seal of Jamaica in the 1660s. Then in 1989, 22 more Simon Benning pewter plates were recovered from Room 2 of Building 5. This provided the incentive to find out everything we could about Simon Benning, and we were fortunate enough to actually find what we were looking for.

The search for Simon Benning began in London. Since he was listed as being a pewterer, it was logical to start our search in the records of the Worshipful Company of Pewterers of London, for it was assumed that any pewterer working in Jamaica in 1665 would have received his training in England. A search of the index files records by Shirley Gotelipe-Miller (1990) found that the only Benning recorded was Tobias Benning. He was listed as being a freeman of the company. Tobias was the brother of Simon Benning. The records list Tobias as being the son of Francis Benninge of Totnham (sic) [Tottenham], Middlesex. Tobias was apprenticed to Peter Duffield in 1652 (Guildhall Library ms. 7090), was given leave to strike his touch in 1660, and was dead in 1664/5 (Guildhall Library ms. 7095). The only reference to Simon Benning was found on an index card that merely noted that he was not a freeman of the company, but that in his will he was described as a pewterer and he died abroad. This gave us the lead to a will in England.

Simon Benning's London will was found in the Perrogative Court of Canterbury. The Perrogative Court of Canterbury handled the probates of all individuals with estates in two or more parishes, for individuals who died overseas, at sea, or for any individual who had property in both England or Wales and in the colonies (Walne 1964:19). Benning's London will, which was written on February 19, 1656, states, "I Simon Benning of London, pewterer," was taking a voyage to Barbados. He left property to his brothers William, Francis, Tobias, and John, and to an individual by the name of John Duffield, who was probably some relation to the Peter Duffield to whom Tobias was apprenticed at the time. There is no mention of a wife, so we can assume that he was not married at this time. Simon Benning was apparently presumed to be dead by his family, for the will was executed June 25, 1664 (Public Record Office Chancery Lane:1664).

PR89

A

B

FIG. 4. The touch mark of Simon Benning. A: Line drawing of SB mark (scale 1:2). B: Photograph of SB mark on a pewter plate.

This will is significant for a number of reasons. Along with Tobias' apprenticeship records, it establishes Simon's immediate family members and places the family as being from Tottenham, Middlesex. Assuming that Simon was a pewterer, it shows that, despite the rigid rules and regulations of the Worshipful Company of Pewterers, some individuals managed to learn the trade without this being recorded in the company. Perhaps it can be assumed that he received his training through his brother Tobias or the Duffield pewterers, to whom Tobias was apprenticed and with whom Simon had some business relationship in a shipping venture, as recorded in his

London will. Because of the rules and regulations of the Worshipful Company of Pewterers, it is doubtful that Simon could have ever been a freeman pewterer in England (Hornsby, Weinsten, and Homer 1989:10–14), and perhaps that is one of the reasons he left for Barbados.

Simon Benning was clearly young and unmarried; he went to Jamaica via Barbados, which was a thriving colony in the 1650s (Dunn 1972:46–116) and was the source of many of the first settlers of Jamaica. When Simon Benning made his London will in February of 1656, it was less than a year after Admiral Penn and General Venables had captured Jamaica in May of 1655, with the help of several hundred citizens and indentured servants recruited from Barbados (Black 158:50). In the 1660s many more Barbadians moved to the larger island of Jamaica, situated strategically in the center of the Caribbean, where there were more opportunities to prosper (Dunn 1972:153–155).

There are probably public records concerning Simon Benning in Barbados, but they have not yet been sought. It is probable that Benning practiced the pewtering trade in Barbados during the 6 to 7 years he spent there. It is also possible that he married there.

The first record we have of Simon Benning being in Jamaica is found in the land patent records in the Jamaica Public Archives. The various plat books, along with the *Grantors, Deeds* records are the basic sources for determining who owned what land and how it changed hands through the years. Although these records are indispensable, they can be contradictory and confusing when used to reconstruct consecutive lots on a street for a given time period. We do know that in 1663 he was patented a small piece of land on Queen Street (Jamaica Public Archives, Port Royal Plat Book, Plat 216). Later a plat of land facing northward on High Street was patented in 1665, where he located his pewter shop. The two adjacent lots were acquired in 1667 and 1670 (Plats 248 and 349). The location of the Benning property is indicated in Figure 1 by the shaded area on the southeast side of High Street, just north of what is presently the old Naval Hospital, which was closed in 1906.

The next record we have of Simon Benning is in the 1680 census taken at Port Royal (Public Record Office at Kew, Colonial Office Series, I/45, fols 97–109). In this census his household is listed as having five white males, two white females, one white male born, and two black females. Other than Simon and his wife, we cannot reliably identify the other individuals. One must refer to Benning's Jamaican will for additional information to shed light on the occupants of his home.

Simon Benning's Jamaican will was written on March 8, 1683 and was entered into the Island Record Office on December 17, 1687, soon after the time of his death (Island Record Office: Wills, Vol. 3–5 folio 180). In this will, only 4 of the 10 individuals counted in the 1680 census are tentatively identified. They are Simon Benning, his wife Susanna (who was appointed the executrix of the three underage children), two sons, Symon and Thomas, and a daughter, Sarah. Simon is one of the five white males counted, and Symon the son (also spelled *Simon*, but I consistently use the *Symon* spelling to distinguish him from his father) has to be the white male born in Jamaica. If this son, or any child, had been born in Barbados, he would have been at least 23 and would not have been underage at the time of the writing of the will in 1683. Following this reasoning, I assume that Thomas and Sarah had not yet been born. Mary Benning, the daughter of Tobias Benning, was given £30, so she may have been living in Jamaica with the family, for she is not listed as being of London, only being the daughter of Tobias Benning of London, who we know died in 1664. If she were living with her uncle, she would be the second white female. The other white males in the household must have been either apprentices or workers helping Benning in his pewtering. The two black females were obviously slaves who assisted around the shop, in the house, or both.

Simon Benning's Jamaica will is also informative in other ways. We have specific information on the property

given to each of his children. Symon, the eldest son, although underage, inherited the house, shop, and tools on High Street. Thomas inherited two houses or taverns on High Street. Sarah received a parcel of land on High Street containing houses, yards, and tenements that were leased out. Aside from an annual support of £50, his wife received 120 acres of land in St. Elizabeth parish. The information in the will is useful in that it lists the property owned by Simon Benning at the time of his death and how he distributed it. All the property listed in the Port Royal Plats, except the property on Queen Street, is accounted for in his will. The property holdings that were distributed indicate that he was prosperous. Furthermore, and of equal significance, it shows that he, like many of the merchants and businessmen of Port Royal at this time, had begun to invest his money in land holdings that were to become the large sugar plantations in the 18th century.

Simon Benning's inventory provides us with very detailed information on the only definitely identified pewterer working in Jamaica in the late 17th century. Because of its significance, it is transcribed in its entirety, exactly as it was written:

Port Royall February 19th 1689

Simon Benning's Inventory

An Inventory of the Goods and Chattles of the Dedisseased Mr. Simon Benning as there was apprais by Mq Richard Greene and John Roswell and are as followeth (viz_)

	li// s// d
To 1//7^{li2}//mould weighed 150//at 1^s p^3 li	07//10//—
To 1/4^{li}//mould 115//at 1^s p li	05//15//—
To 1//4^{li}//Duep 117 at 1^s p li	05//17//—
To 1//midle plater mould at //1^{l}//112 p li	05//12//—
To 1//bason and 1 Plate mould at 1^{l}//117 p li	05//17//—
To 1//Plate mould at 1^{l}:35 p li	01//15//—
To 74 pound of Iron working tooles	01//04//—
To 14 pound of old mettel at	00//08//09
To 50 pound Scruf pewter	01//11//03
To 2 anvils & 12 hammers at	02//10//—
To 1 wheele and Spindle^4	03//00//—
To Blocks & old things in the workhouse	01//10//—
To 250 of cast Rufe plates at 8^d p li	07//16//—
To 60 pound of old brass at	01//17/6
To 3 //hundred of old pewter Lay at 6^d p li	05//13/6
To 190^{t5}//28^{li} at Seven pence half penny p li	60//05//03^6
To 113// of alloy at 4^d half penny p li	02//02//8
To 20//pound of old pewter at 7^{d 1/2} p li	//12//6
To 3_//pound of new pewter at 12^d p li	1?//12//—
To 1 case of glass bottls at	—//05//—
To 1//cestern^7 of pewter at	—//07//—
To 2 pair of old Scales & weight at	—//15//—
To 26^{ct}:45^{li}//pound of pewter at 1^s p li	132// 5//—
To 2 old beds & bedstead	02//10//—
To 1 bead & bedstead at	03//—//—

To 1 Table Looking glass 2 chairs & a box	01//—//—
To 1 bead & bedstead curtins & vallians	07//—//—
To 2 Chest of Drawers Tables 6 Chers and 1 Looking Glass	10//—//00
To 2 chests and Linnen 1 close Stoole and Hammerkar[8]	05//—//—
To 1 Jack 1 Kittle & sume old things in the Coockroom	02//15//—
To cash 3li 10s to 28 ounces of Plate	10//10//—
To 1 grinstone water cask & tools	01//—//—
To 3 Tables Desk the Furniture of the Low room	07//—//—
To 1 Large Looking glass at	01// 5//—
To 1 Bead & beadstead curtins & valliance	05//—//—
To 6 chaares and a Table	02//—//—
To old Copper & brass 121li: at 7p 1/2 p li	03//15//01
To course brass 21li at 4p 1/2 p li	00// 7//11
To book debts Standing out	28// 8//0
To bad debts Standing out	29//18//0

the marke of ————————
Richard R. Greene 376//11//10
John Rosswell ————————

Source: Jamaica Public Archives: *Inventories*, Vol 3, folio 64.

1   20 shilling (s) = 1 pound (li), 16 pence (d) = 1 shilling
2   li = libri (pound)
3   Per
4   Lath to spin pewter
5   Here, ct = 10-pound units. This works out to be 1900li (plus 28li) for a total of 1928li.
7   Probably cistern, which in this context means a chest or box.
8   Hammock

In order to fully appreciate Benning's inventory, it is necessary to examine it in terms of what was going on in the pewtering trade at this time in England. I sent a copy of Benning's inventory to Dr. Ronald F. Homer (1989), a well-known authority on English pewter, for his comments, which are excerpted here.

He notes that the inventory is in very familiar form and resembles those of many English provincial pewterers of the period. It is, however, interesting in that it details his molds individually. In English inventories these are usually lumped together under a heading of so many pounds of molds. Typically this might be in the range of 800 to 1200 lbs.

By comparison to comparable pewterers in England at this time, Benning was prosperous; his inventoried estate of £360 is at the top end of the worth of English provincial pewterers of the period. Generally these range from about £100 to £400. The presence of mirrors and bedstead curtains in his home indicates a comfortable life-style for the period.

Dr. Homer was particularly interested to see that the values put on the metal and molds were almost the same as those found in England. For example, in the inventory of Richard Plummer of Ludlow, 1692, molds are valued at 10d per pound and in the inventory of Sampson Bourne of Worcester, 1689 molds are valued at 9d. Plummer's inventory values old pewter at 7d per pound and Sampson Bourne's at 6d. Bourne also had some inferior alloys valued at 3d and 4d. Benning's molds would have cast plates and dishes of about 20 in., 16 in., 11 in., and 9 in. in diameter. The word *plate*, if not qualified, normally means 9 in. in diameter, weighing about 1 lb each. Accordingly, this would fit with the valuation put on the 250 "Rufe" (rough, i.e., unfinished) plates of about $7\frac{1}{2}$d each.

The entry of 26ct:45li of pewter at 1s per pound is significant for it must relate to his stock of new wares ready for sale, which would equate with the then current English price. At that price, it would be equivalent to 2957 nine inch plates, which is a very large amount of stock! This is in addition to the 250 rough, unfinished plates.

The large stock of pewter on hand indicates a surprisingly large business scale. It is much larger than that of English pewterers of comparable total worth. It also represents an enormous investment of time, considering that only one lathe upon which to turn it all is mentioned in the inventory (Homer, personal communication, 1989).

The tools of the pewterer, such as molds, anvils, iron

49

FIG. 5. The three forms of pewter recovered from the INA/TAMU excavation. Left to right, $9^3/_8$-in. diameter narrow-rimmed plate, 15-in. diameter narrow-rimmed platter, $16^1/_2$-in. diameter broad-rimmed charger.

working tools, wheele and spindle (lathe), old and new pewter metal, grind stone, and scales, are all common tools of the pewtering trade. The presence of the copper and brass indicates that Benning, like many pewterers, also worked in these metals.

Although not related to pewter, I want to point out a particularly Jamaican trait mentioned in Benning's inventory and many other Jamaican inventories, but never listed, as far as I am aware, in England or the North American colonies. This is "hammerkar," which is a hammock, which was often preferred over the overstuffed and hot bedsteads. Hammocks were commonly used in the West Indies and were adopted by the English, if not for themselves, for slaves and servants in the household.

Archaeological Analysis and a New Focus

It was at this stage of the research that we were back analyzing the 34 pewter plates bearing the Simon Benning touch mark. When we found that first pewter platter in 1983 in Building 1, we were confident in attributing the new mark to Simon Benning. As a result of the excavations, we were able to connect a previously unknown touch mark to a pewterer known to have lived in Port Royal.

Over the next 8 years, 27 more Simon Benning pewter pieces were found. Forms represented in the INA/TAMU excavations are twenty-six $9^3/_8$-in. narrow-rimmed plates, one 15-in. narrow-rimmed dish, and one $16^1/_2$-in. broad-rimmed charger (Figure 5). Note the distinctive hammering marks in a concentric pattern on the surface of the pieces. Five $9^5/_8$-in broad-rimmed plates were found in Marx's excavations. At a minimum, we have

found examples of the pewter produced from three of the six molds listed in Benning's inventory.

As mentioned earlier, 25 pewter plates (22 in one pile) were found around the stairwell in Room 2 of Building 5. After proper conservation and cleaning, all the surface details were very evident, and we began a detailed analysis and physical examination of them. What is interesting is that 20 of the 25 plates found in one room were made from the same mold, had the Simon Benning maker's mark on them, and had one of two sets of ownership marks on them. There were two obviously different sets. One set of 9 plates had the ownership mark "N^CI" on the back surface of the plate, along with the pineapple touch. All of the N^CI plates had numerous knife cut marks on the eating surface and, generally speaking, looked very used and worn. The other 11 plates were much newer looking and had considerably fewer cut marks on the eating surface. All of the newer looking set had the owner's mark IC in the center of the eating surface and the pineapple mark on the center of the back. Conventionally, the mark N^CI indicates that a man with the initials NC and his wife IC were the owners of the plates. Given this, then we can say that the IC marked plates are the initials of the wife appearing alone. It is possible that the husband in this union died and the wife had a new set of plates made for her use. It was the realization that there were two obvious sets of Simon Benning pewter plates made from the same mold — one older N^CI set with lots of use and one newer IC set with much less signs of use — that made me search further for historic records on the Benning family to prove a hypothesis: Symon Benning the son was also a pewterer.

Simon Benning died in 1687. The probability that 5 years later there would still be 11 plates around showing few signs of use seems low. This observation led to the realization that Simon Benning's son, Symon, who inherited the house and shop, must have taken over his father's pewterer's trade. Now the problem was to find a written record that confirmed this.

A search of the *Grantors, Deeds* records (Island Record Office), which contain deeds, mortgages, bonds, and indentures, yielded two records. One, "Benning to Darby," entered on August 25, 1695, records the sale of two slaves to William Darby (Island Record Office, *Grantors/Deeds* Vol. 25, O.S. folio 178). In this record it states that "I Simon Benning of Port Royall in the island of Jamaica aforesaid Puiser..." I thought that *puiser* probably meant pewterer, but it was not definite. A second record, "Benning to Bradford" entered July 15, 1696, was the proof that I was looking for within the text it states, "Symon Benning of Port Royall on the island of Jamaica pewterer of the one part..." (Island Record Office, *Grantors/Deeds* Vol. 25, O.S. folio 247). This was the documentary proof validating the speculation first formulated from the archaeological data that led me to seek out additional documents long past the year that Simon Benning, Sr. had died. Now we know that there were two Simon Benning, pewterers — father and son. The Simon Benning pineapple touch in Jamaica has a date range of 1663 to 1696.

"Benning to Bradford," other than conclusively proving that Symon Benning, Jr. was a pewterer, also gives us more information on the family. In this record, Benning is selling all the property he inherited from his father, as well as the inherited property of his now deceased brother, Thomas, to Edward Bradford. The document is a complete abstract with specific details on the acquisition of the each of the pieces of property being sold. It also tells us that Thomas Benning is deceased, possibly a victim of the earthquake in 1692. Only the property inherited by Sarah, daughter of Simon Benning, was excluded from the sale.

This is the last record we have of Symon Benning. Where did he go after selling all of his property in 1696? This question remains to be answered, but we do know what happened to his sister, Sarah. She shows up on May 23, 1698, when she arrives from South Carolina with her husband, Thomas Barker, to settle her father's estate (Claypole 1972:244). As of this writing, I have not had a chance to consult the record, "Barker to Bradford," but I feel sure that it records the selling of the property Sarah inherited from her father to Edward Bradford, the same man that her brother sold his property to in 1696. Thus ends the story of the Benning family in Port Royal.

The question of what happened to Symon Benning, Jr. is left unsolved, but we know that Sarah was now married and living in South Carolina, along with other former Port Royal residents (Claypole 1972:244). The Benning family was taking part in yet another movement shared by many other English subjects, ever on the move to lands offering more opportunity. First Simon Benning, Sr. followed the English masses that were emigrating to Barbados in the 1650s. Then in the 1660s he followed the Barbadians that migrated to Jamaica. Arriving in Port Royal by 1663, he prospered and became one of the many small land owners with property in the interior of Jamaica. At Simon Benning Sr.'s death in 1687, his eldest son was underage, but he probably took over his fathers pewter shop, if not at his death, then soon after. He may have even prospered, but the earthquake in 1692 probably spelled the beginning of the end. By 1695, he was selling property. Perhaps he joined in yet another trend that of resettling in the North American colonies after the great earthquake in 1692. Many citizens of Port Royal and Jamaica, including his sister, are known to have moved to South Carolina and other northern colonies. As noted by Dunn (1972:150–151):

> By the end of the century when the buccaneers had left, most of the small planters were gone also. Jamaica, the one English island which seemingly offered good prospects to ex-servants and small freeholders, had been taken over entirely by the large planters who consolidated the arable land into huge plantations manned by armies of slaves.

A search in the records of South Carolina may continue the history of the Benning family and their descendants, but that is another story.

The most intriguing question confronting me now is the identification of N.C. and I.C. The marks, "N^{C}I" or "IC," appear on pewter plates, silver forks, silver spoons, and even a nutmeg grinder, all of which were found in Room 2 of Building 5. In all probability, the N&I Cs lived in the building at the time of the earthquake, but their identity is not known. No suitable plat records have been found, so they possibly were renting the premises from the property owner. I am searching the wills, deeds, and inventories for a "NC" who had a wife "IC" who lived on the south side of Lime Street, where it intersected the northwest side of Queen Street. Time will tell if they are to be identified, but it all depends on the written record, not the archaeological record. So it goes in historical archaeology.

Conclusion

Directed historic research resulting from the attempt to answer specific archaeological questions was presented above. Such research shows how documents such as wills, inventories, deed transactions, and guild records all contribute to our understanding of the archaeological data from this excavation. I have shown how it takes a number of different documents to understand what has actually happened. One record is seldom conclusive, and quite often one record is meaningful only in the light of another document. Each document adds to the story, one piece at a time, just as each piece of archaeological data adds to the story.

We have seen how documents are not always where they should be and that craftsmen in the colonies practiced their trade without going through the prerequisite training required by the crafts guilds back in England. Thus no apprentice documents on Simon Benning appear in the Worshipful Company of Pewterers, other than a statement that Simon Benning claimed to be a pewterer in his will and that he died overseas. Still, the scant records on Simon Benning in the Worshipful Company led to his London will and the apprenticeship and free status records of his brother Tobias Benning in the Worshipful Company of Pewterers. Each of these provided significant details concerning the Benning family. Once in Jamaica, the *Patents* records and *Inventories* in the Jamaica Public Archives and the *Wills* and *Grantors, Deeds* in the Island Record Office complete the story of the family in Jamaica.

As a result of the archaeological excavation and research using the historic documents, we have been able to

1. Locate the Benning family's property on High Street (Figure 1).
2. Identify the touch mark of Simon Benning (Figure 4).
3. Identify at least three examples of pewter plates, dishes, and chargers made from the six pewter molds listed in Simon Benning, Sr.'s inventory (Figure 5).
4. Conclusively prove that Symon Benning, Jr. was a pewterer.
5. Offer a number of plates, probably made by both Simon Benning, Sr. and Symon Benning, Jr.

The archaeological data and the historic documents, separately and in combination, provide us with a story of the two Simon Bennings, father and son, pewterers of Port Royal.

This is just one of many stories that archaeological excavations and historic documents research contribute to our knowledge and understanding of the English colonization in the New World in the 17th century. Many more stories are merely waiting for the questions to be asked by archaeology and then to be researched and told.

References

Black, C. V. (1958) *History of Jamaica*. Collins Educational, London.

Buisseret, D. J. (1966) Port Royal 1655–1725. *The Jamaican Historical Review* 6, 21–28.

Claypole, W. A. (1972) The Merchants of Port Royal 1655 to 1700. Unpublished thesis, University of the West Indies, Kingston, Jamaica.

Cotterell, H. H. (1963) *Old Pewter, Its Makers and Marks in England, Scotland, and Ireland*. Charles E. Tuttle, Rutland, VT.

Cox, O. (1984) *Upgrading and Renewing a Historic City: Port Royal, Jamaica*. British Overseas Development Administration.

Dunn, R. S. (1972) *Sugar and Slaves: The Rise of the Planter Class in the English West Indies, 1624–1713*. W. W. Norton & Co., New York.

Gotelipe-Miller, S. (1990) Pewter and Pewterers from Port Royal Jamaica: Flatware before 1692. Masters Degree thesis at Texas A&M University.

Guildhall Library, London (ms) *Worshipful Company of Pewterers of London, Company's Court Books*, Guildhall ms 7090.

—(ms) *Worshipful Company of Pewterers of London, Company's Livery and Yeomanry Lists*, Guildhall ms 7095.

Hamilton, D. L. (1984) Preliminary Report on the Archaeological Investigations of the Submerged Remains of Port Royal, Jamaica, 1981–1982. *International Journal of Nautical Archaeology and Underwater Exploration* 13(1):11–25.

—(1985) The City Under the Sea. In *Science Year 1986*. World Book Encyclopedia, Chicago, pp 92–109.

— (1986) Port Royal Revisited. In *Underwater Archaeology: The Proceedings of the Fourteenth Conference on Underwater Archaeology*, Calvin R. Cummings, Ed. Fathom Eight, Special Publication #7, pp 73–81.

—(1988) Underwater excavations of 17th-century building at the intersection of Lime and Queen Streets. In *Underwater Archaeology: Proceedings from the Society for Historical Archaeology Conference*, Reno, Nevada, January 1988. Society for Historical Society Special Publication Series No. 7, pp. 9–12.

Hamilton, D. L. and R. Woodward (1984) A sunken 17th-century city: Port Royal, Jamaica, with Robyn Woodward. *Archaeology* 37(1):38–45.

Henretta, J. A. (1965) Economic development and social structure in colonial Boston. *William and Mary Quarterly*, 3rd. Ser. XXII, 1, pp. 75–92.

Homer, R. F. Personal communication. Gorse Croft, West Hill Road, West Hill, Ottery St. Mary, Devon EX11 1TU, England. Phone (0404) 812379.

Hornsby, P. R. G., R. Weinstein, and R. F. Homer (1989) *Pewter: A Celebration of the Craft 1200–1700*. The Museum of London, London.

Island Record Office: *Grantors, Deeds*, Old Series. Vol. 25. Spanish Town, Jamaica.

— Wills, Vol. 3–5. Spanish Town, Jamaica.

Jamaica Public Archives: *Port Royal Plat Book*, Vol. 28, 1661–1713, 1B/11/2, Spanish Town, Jamaica.

— Inventories, Vol. 3, 1686–1694, 1B/11/3, Spanish Town, Jamaica.

Link, M. C. (1960) Exploring the drowned city of Port Royal. *National Geographic* 117(1):151–183.

Marx, R. (1973) *Port Royal Rediscovered*. Doubleday & Co. New York.

Pawson, M. and D. J. Buisseret (1975) *Port Royal, Jamaica*. Clarendon Press, Oxford.

Peal, C. (1976) *More Pewter Marks*. Price Glover, New York.

— (1977) *Addendum to More Pewter Marks.* Price Glover, Inc. N.Y.

Public Records Office, Chancery Lane, London, England (1664) Simon Benning's Will, Perogative Court of Canterbury Probate Records: Prob 11/314, fo. 210–211.

Public Records Office at Kew, London, England (ms) *The Port Royal Census of 1680,* Colonial Office Records, P.R.O.C.O. 1/45/97–109.

Taylor, S. A. G. (1965) *The Western Design: An Account of Cromwell's Expedition to the Caribbean.* The Institute of Jamaica and the Jamaica Historical Society, Kingston, Jamaica.

Taylor, J. (1688) Second Part of the Historie of his Life and Travels in America. Manuscript on file at the Institute of Jamaica, Kingston, Jamaica.

Walne, P. (1964) *English Wills.* The Virginia State Library.

Ward, E. (1699) *A Trip to New England: With a Character of the Country and People, Both English and Indians.* Republished in 1938 in *Five Travel Scripts Commonly Attributed to Edward Ward.* The Facsimile Text Society, Columbia University Press.

Ward, E. (1700) *A Trip to Jamaica: With a True Character of the People and Island.* Republished in 1938 in Five Travel Scripts Commonly Attributed to Edward Ward. The Facsimile Text Society, Columbia University Press.

Zahedieh, N. (1986a) The merchants of Port Royal, Jamaica, and the Spanish contraband trade, 1655–1692. *William and Mary Quarterly,* 3rd Series, Vol. XLIII, pp. 570–593.

— (1986b) Trade, plunder, and economic development in early English Jamaica, 1655–89. Economic Hist*ory Reveiw,* 2nd Series XXXIX, 2, pp. 205–222.

5: Using Written Records in the Archaeological Study of Slavery, an Example from the Butler Island Plantation

Theresa A. Singleton
Department of Anthropology, National Museum of Natural History,
Smithsonian Institution, Washington, DC

A historian recently noted that scholarship of slavery "seems to be in a perpetual state of reinterpretation and renewal" (Dew 1987:120). Archaeology offers the potential to reinterpret slave life, particularly in the study of colonial and early federal period slavery, where little information exists on slave material life from above-ground, visual, written, oral, or other historic sources. The contribution of archaeology to antebellum slavery (dating from approximately 1820 to 1865) may be more questionable. Critics claim that the information derived from archaeology is already known from written and oral sources (Joyner 1989). Antebellum slavery is generally better documented than slavery of earlier time periods, and these historic sources often contain a wealth of information on slave material life that frequently cannot be recovered from the archaeological record, such as descriptions of clothing or furnishings.

How can archaeology uniquely contribute to the study of antebellum slavery? What kinds of written sources are most useful in solving archaeological problems related to the study of slavery? What kinds of questions can archaeologically successfully address in cases where there are few written sources for the plantation under investigation? This essay addresses these questions by examining the archaeological and historical sources of a well-documented antebellum plantation. The purpose here is not to point out the deficiencies in the archaeological and written records, but to suggest how the two bodies of data best complement each other, and how together they can be used to achieve a more complete picture of slave life.

The use of written records in the archaeological study of slavery is complicated by at least two factors. The first,

and perhaps the most obvious, is that few of these sources originated from the slaves themselves. Records concerning slave life were often created by persons whose understanding of slave life was flawed and one dimensional. For example, plantation owners and managers only wrote about subjects that interested them, such as the slaves' capacity to do work, their health, and behavior considered deviant. Plantation visitors recorded information on slaves that often went unnoticed by slaveholders, such as work routines, material life, and cultural expressions. However, because visitors' observations were often of a short duration, it is sometimes difficult to assess if their accounts describe everyday life or unusual circumstances. Moreover, it is also possible that they did not always understand what they observed. Even documents derived from former slaves are problematic, as both slave narratives and ex-slave testimony suffer from the passage of time. Most of these former slaves were enslaved as children, and their reminiscences of slavery were recorded years later, often as elderly adults, when their memory of specific events and experiences had faded. Thus, any of these sources must be closely scrutinized before they can be offered as evidence to support an interpretation.

The second problem in using written sources in archaeological studies of slavery concerns the search for information on slave material culture. This search can be particularly arduous, because descriptions of slave housing, household objects, or foodways were not systematically recorded in written sources traditionally used in archaeological analysis, such as probate inventories. As chattel property, slaves themselves are listed and often are described on probate inventories, but not the objects they made and used. References to slave material life are more likely to occur as incidental or occasionally descriptions in correspondence, diaries, traveler accounts, slave narratives, or ex-slave testimony.

In this essay, written records used in the archaeological study of a slave community at Butler Island Plantation, McIntosh County, Georgia, are analyzed and evaluated. Butler Island Plantation was one of several plantations of a large Georgian estate, which operated with slave labor from 1801 to 1864, and with wage labor from 1866 to 1878. The period of operation from approximately 1803 to 1850 is well documented through correspondence, diaries, plantation daybooks, ledgers, annual reports, and traveler accounts. This well-documented period corresponds with the major period of occupation represented by archaeological resources.

Descriptions of slave life can be obtained from numerous sources, but it is imperative that all sources are properly evaluated. The written sources for the Butler Island Plantation were created for various purposes and offer several perspectives, sometimes with conflicting information. Archaeological investigations of the slave settlements provided information on the Butler Island slaves that was found to be either totally absent in written records or was described infrequently. In some cases, archaeological data were capable of supporting or discrediting written documents. Archaeology is not without bias. Like written records, archaeological data must be carefully evaluated before it can be used as evidence to offer an interpretation. This paper emphasizes the evaluation of written sources that are essential to archaeological study of slavery.

Historical Background of Butler Island Plantation

Butler Island is one of several "brackish marsh Islands" located within the Altamaha Estuary in McIntosh County, Georgia (Figure 1). These islands form part of the tidal swamps that become covered with saltwater when tides are pushed by high wind and are inundated from freshwater when rivers overflow to cause floods known as *freshets*. The tidal swamps, considered ideal for the cultivation of lowland or "wet rice," were transformed into rice fields with the ingenious construction of canals, dikes, ditches, and floodgates that permitted the inflow of freshwater back up at high tide and the outflow at low tide. These irrigation systems, built entirely by hand with slave labor, flooded and drained the rice fields as desired.

Reclamation of brackish marshes in the Altamaha drainage into arable land began at the close at the 18th century. Planters from South Carolina, where rice cultivation had been introduced in 1680 and had become a well-established and lucrative enterprise by 1740, moved southward to Georgia in search of new lands for rice growing. Butler Island became a rice plantation under

the ownership of Major Pierce Butler, a South Carolinian, who acquired the island through a land grant in the 1780s (Bell 1987:117–120). In 1802, the first year the annual rice crop yield was recorded, the island produced approximately 76,800 lb of rice (Butler Papers 1803, hereafter referred to as BP).

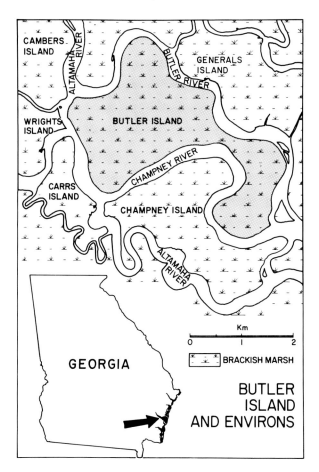

FIG. 1. Location of Butler Island in Georgia.

Born in Ireland, Major Pierce Butler came to America in 1766 as an officer in the British Army. He liked the colonies and decided to stay. In 1771, he married Polly Middleton, the daughter of a wealthy South Carolina planter. He and Polly had one son and four daughters. During the American Revolution, Major Butler sided with the revolutionaries and became an important political figure in South Carolina. In 1787, he served as a delegate to the Constitutional Convention in Philadelphia, and he was elected twice as senator from South Carolina to the United States Senate (Bell 1987:66–80; Scott 1978:6–7).

At the Constitutional Convention, Major Butler was one of the principal proponents arguing that state representation in the House of Representatives should be proportional to the total population, both slave and free. Butler and his supporters believed that the slave states needed this type of representation in order to prevent the possibility that a majority of representatives from the free states would attempt to abolish slavery. The major's view epitomized that of the small but powerful elite who desired to perpetuate and expand the institution of slavery (Scott 1978:7).

In 1790, Polly died and Major Butler moved his planting operation to Georgia. By 1800, he had acquired several thousand acres (Figure 2) within the Altahama Estuary, which included Butler Island and surrounding marshlands, Butler Point (also known as Hampton Plantation) located on St. Simons Island, Little St. Simons Island, and Woodville located on the mainland (Page 1799). Major Butler acquired vast numbers of slaves to work these large landholdings and became one of the largest and wealthiest slaveholders in Georgia.

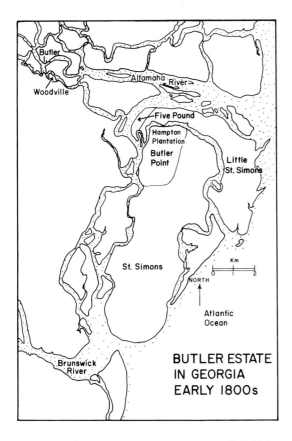

FIG. 2. Butler estate in Georgia in the early 1800s.

Major Butler's descendants continued his planting interests and held onto the Georgia properties until 1878. At its peak in 1859, the estate included over 900 slaves, of whom approximately 500 resided at Butler's Island (BP 1859). Slaveholding of this magnitude was clearly in a class by itself. Slaveholders who owned from 500 to 1000 slaves represented less than 2% of all the slaveholding in the entire South. In Georgia this unusually large slaveholding was confined to less than 1% of all planters in the state (Gray 1941:530–538).

Unlike other planters of the Altamaha basin who were full-time residents of Georgia, Major Butler and his descendants made Philadelphia their permanent home. As absentee landlords, the Butlers relied upon overseers to manage the day-to-day operations of their Georgian plantations. From approximately 1802 to 1847, the operation of the plantation is well documented through correspondence, plantation daybooks, ledgers, and annual reports. The plantation was managed for much of that time by Roswell King, Sr. and later his son Roswell King, Jr. The Kings kept detailed records of their management activities and corresponded regularly with the Butlers. The survival of many of these records makes the Butler Plantations among the best documented in Georgia. While most of the information contained in these records are primarily concerned with planting, harvesting, and marketing activities, valuable information on the slaves is also provided, including name, age, monetary value and skill level, general health, birth and death rates, disease and health care, amount of food rations, and a miscellany of other topics.

The Butler's Georgian Plantations are perhaps best known by both laymen and scholars as the plantations visited by Frances (Fanny) Anne Kemble, a famous British actress who in 1834 married Pierce Butler, Jr., Major Butler's grandson. During Fanny Kemble's first and only trip to these plantations, she recorded her observations in a journal published 24 years later in 1863, entitled *A Journal of a Residence on a Georgian Plantation in 1838–1839* (Scott 1961). Fanny's journal describes slave life at both Butler Island and Hampton Plantations, where Fanny, Pierce, and their two young daughters spent approximately 4 months, 2 months at each plantation. The journal contains details on many aspects of slave life, from grueling work routines to work songs; diet, health care, housing, and household objects; handicrafts made by slaves; their religious fervor; and their suffering, particularly the suffering endured by slave women.

From time to time, the accuracy and authenticity of the journal has been questioned. Apologists for slavery have tended to be very critical of the journal's accuracy (e.g., Phillips 1929:259–265); other historians have found a great deal of accuracy in Ms. Kemble's descriptions (e.g., Stampp 1956; Genovese 1974; Owens 1975), although most acknowledge that the journal is overromanticized and is the product of an "impassioned observer" (Bell 1987:286).

Fewer records are available on the operation of Butler's Island Plantation during and after the Civil War. The plantation continued to be worked by slaves as late as 1864, in spite of an effort by the Confederate government to confiscate the Butler's Island slaves in 1861. Because the Butler heirs were residents of Pennsylvania and not of Georgia, they were considered "alien enemies" to the Confederacy (CSA 1862). The Confederacy seized property from those whom they considered unsympathetic to its cause as a means to raise funds for support of the war effort. The overseer of Butler Island at the time, Alexander Blue, attempted to smuggle some of the slaves from the island (CSA 1862). Blue's actions, as well as those of the Confederacy, were possibly curtailed by the Union Army occupation of coastal Georgia beginning in the fall 1862.

In 1866 Frances Butler Leigh, the daughter of Fanny Kemble and Pierce Butler, Jr., restored rice planting at Butler's Island with wage laborers, many of whom were former slaves. She and her husband James Leigh pursued their interest in rice planting until 1876, in spite of changed labor relationships, a depressed rice market, freshets, and a fire. Frances Leigh recorded their efforts in the journal, *Ten Years on a Georgia Plantation*, published in 1883 (Leigh 1883). Her journal is one of the few first-hand accounts on the reorganization of labor in the South during the early years following the Civil War.

Between 1878 and 1910, parcels of the Butler lands were leased to rice planters, who in turn contracted with tenants to farm small plots for a portion of the crop. According to local informants, by the end of the 1880s tenants no longer lived at Butler Island. Instead, they lived in newly established settlements on the mainland and commuted daily by small boats to Butler and other islands in the Altamaha estuary (Singleton 1980:55). In the 1920s, fruit and vegetable farming supplanted rice cultivation on the island. Butler Island became a state wildlife preserve for waterfowl in 1954 and still functions in that capacity.

Archaeological Investigations at Butler Island

The purpose of archaeological fieldwork undertaken at Butler Island in 1978 and 1979 was twofold: first, to provide an inventory of the cultural resources at Butler Island and second, to conduct a study of slave life at Butler Island. As part of the Altamaha Waterfowl Management Area, Butler's Island is subject to periodic management practices, such as seasonal flooding, plowing, and dredging activities, which would modify or destroy archaeological sites. An inventory of sites provided waterfowl management personnel with the location of sites that need be avoided in future management activities.

The study of slavery at Butler Island utilized archaeological and archival sources to examine similarities and differences between slave life at a rice plantation with slave life at cotton plantations of the Altamaha estuary (Singleton 1980). Investigations at Butler Island provided the first opportunity to systematically compare and contrast the archaeological resources associated with slavery at a rice plantation with those previously studied at cotton plantations located on nearby St. Simons Island (see McFarlane 1975; Moore 1981, 1985; Otto 1975,

1984). It was hoped that the study of Butler Island would produce evidence of slave cultural expression that the studies at St. Simons failed to produce. The slave community at Butler Island was considered an excellent candidate for producing material evidence of ethnicity for several reasons. A sizable number of the slaves were African born, oral traditions suggest that slave community at Butler Island held on to their African ways, and the slave community lived in relative isolation most of the year from the watchful eye of either a resident planter or overseer. Unfortunately no discernible evidence of ethnicity was recovered, but excavations generated important new data on slave craft practices, foodways, and household objects.

A secondary goal of the research at Butler Island examined to what extent the descriptions in Fanny Kemble's journal were accurate. Fanny Kemble described many aspects of slave material life, such as slave houses, slave-made objects, food preparation, and serving practices, the remains of which could potentially be found in the archaeological record. The archaeological record provided detailed information on housing and foodways that greatly elaborated on Fanny Kemble's observations. In a few cases, the archaeological data did not support her observations. Such findings do not necessarily suggest that her observations were incorrect. Some of what she observed perhaps would not endure in the archaeological record.

Written historic resources associated with Butler Island were utilized from the very beginning in devising strategies for locating, identifying, and dating archaeological resources. In addition to the journals of Fanny Kemble and Frances Leigh, several documents proved very useful in indicating site locations of the pre-Civil War era: a sketch drawn by Roswell King, Sr. in 1813 that identified two of the plantation mills (King, Sr. 1813a), a map of Butler Island showing the locations of the four slave settlements (Anonymous 1877), and an 1815 inventory of the Butler Estate that lists the kinds of structures located at each of the four settlements at Butler's Island (BP 1815a). These 19th-century records, in combination with aerial photographs, previous archaeological assessments, surface reconnaissance, and subsurface testing, contributed to the creation of the site location map depicting sites associated with the antebellum occupation of Butler Island (Figure 3).

Archaeological evidence supporting these site locations ranged from mere artifact scatters to substantial intact structural remains. Virtually no archaeological evidence was found that could be identified as the overseer's house, slave settlement #2, or the sugar mill. In the 1920s, the owner of Butler Island built a two-story house that is still standing on the presumed site of the overseer's cottage (Singleton 1980:58). Slave settlement #2 was completely obliterated by the construction of

Interstate 95, but a few antebellum artifacts, including pipebowls, shell-edge pearlware, and locally made bricks of the period, were found in the vicinity where I-95 crosses Butler Island. The site of the presumed sugar mill contained no structural features, but the location of an impounding pond (used to store water for an undershot waterwheel turned by the rise and fall of the tide) was identical to the impounding pond found associated with the excavated tidal rice mill. Additionally, Roswell King, Sr. in 1816 referred to the location of the "sugar works" as halfway between slave settlements #3 and #4 (King, Sr. 1816). From surface reconnaissance this area was the only possible location for the sugar mill in that area of the island.

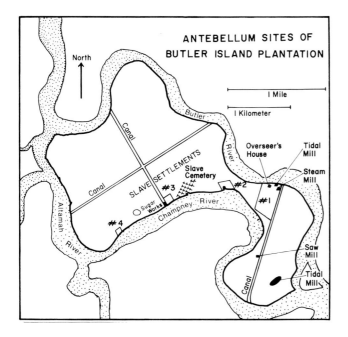

FIG. 3. Antebellum archaeological sites of the Butler Island Plantation.

More substantial archaeological resources were found in association with settlements #1, #3, and #4, and the southernmost tidal mill. At settlement #1, the former administrative nucleus for the plantation, remains of the steam rice mill, tidal mill, and landing were evident in above-ground remains. Subsurface testing designed to locate slave houses and the slave hospital yielded antebellum artifacts but no structural remains. These artifacts, however, were mixed with modern debris and, therefore, could not be reliably used to interpret life at Butler's Island during the antebellum period. The tidal mill located in the southeastern corner of the island was partially excavated, and information on its size, construction, and mode of operation was recovered. The slave cemetery mentioned by both Fanny Kemble (Scott 1961:141) and Frances Leigh (1883:72) was located, identified, and partially excavated in 1956 (Caldwell n.d.;

Sanders n.d.). A break in the dike surrounding the cemetery left it partially submerged in water. For this reason, the cemetery was not restudied in 1978–1979.

Slave settlements #3 and #4 contained the best preserved remains of slave houses. Test excavations were conducted at settlement #4, because chimney remains of five of the original eight slave houses were identified during the surface reconnaissance at #4, while only two of the original six slave dwellings were identified at #3. Additionally, settlement #4 was chosen over #3, because both the approximate beginning and ending dates of occupation were suggested from written sources. Diking and construction of settlement #4 was completed in 1803 (King, Sr. 1803), and at least 86 slaves were living there in 1811, as indicated by a provision list (BP 1811). By 1815, settlement #4 was in full operation, as indicated by the 1815 inventory, and it continued to function as a slave settlement until the end of the Civil War. After the war, the site appears to have been abandoned. Frances Leigh's journal suggests that settlement #4 was not restored as a wage labor settlement, as were the other three slave settlements (Leigh 1883:242–244). Analysis of the recovered artifacts, particularly a Mean Ceramic Date of 1835, strongly supports the suggestion that settlement #4 was temporally antebellum, thereby making it a slave site (Singleton 1980:156). Field research at settlement #4 consisted of a combination of subsurface shovel tests taken every 5 m at 10 m intervals, resulting in a total of 222 tests and partial excavations of three slave dwellings. The recovered artifacts, along with information obtained from written sources, were used to interpret slave life at Butler Island.

Interpreting Slave Life at Butler Island

Through the examination of both the archaeological record and written sources for Butler Island, the information on the slave community can be subdivided into four categories: first, slave demography obtained entirely from written records, but potentially estimated from archaeological sources; second, slave provisioning obtained primarily from archaeology, but interpreted with the aid of written records; third, slave disease and health care information obtained primarily from written records, but supported by the archaeological record; fourth, slave behavior used here as an "all other" category, which includes several topics that received varied treatment in written sources but lack archaeological evidence. The analysis of each category is examined separately in the following discussion.

SLAVE DEMOGRAPHY

Information on the size of the slave population at

Butler Island comes from tax assessments, census, and plantation records (Table 1). Because all the slaves of the entire estate were frequently lumped together, it was often difficult to discern the slave population for Butler Island alone. Two documents list by name each slave at Butler Island in 1821 and in 1844 (King, Jr. 1821, 1844). These lists, however, only indicate the slaves considered to be part of the working force and do not include children under 10, who usually averaged 100 in number, or elderly slaves involved in menial tasks, who usually added another 25 to 30 to the total population. Census records, on the other hand, provide better indications of the total number and age distribution of the slaves, but census figures are organized by county and do not designate the name of the plantation. Fortunately, the Butler estate was located in both Glynn and McIntosh counties, and the majority of slaves recorded on the McIntosh county census resided at Butler Island. Therefore, it is possible to identify the approximate number of slaves at Butler Island and to distinguish them from slaves at the plantations located on St. Simons and Little St. Simons islands in Glynn County.

Table 1
THE SLAVE POPULATION AT BUTLER ISLAND

Date	Male	Female	Total
1811	—	—	295
1820	209	207	416
1830	188	207	395
1840	196	179	375
1850	284	240	524
1860	261	244	505
Average			411

Sources: Butler Family Papers, 1811.
U.S. Bureau of Census 1820, McIntosh County, GA.
U.S. Bureau of Census 1830, McIntosh County, GA.
U.S. Bureau of Census 1840, McIntosh County, GA.
U.S. Bureau of Census Slave Schedules 1850, McIntosh County, GA.
U.S. Bureau of Census Slave Schedules 1860, McIntosh County, GA.

In 1799, Major Butler's entire slave force on his Georgian properties numbered 359 (Page 1799). Through purchases of slaves made between 1801 and 1804 (BP 1801–1803), his slaveholdings increased by 1811 to 638 slaves, of whom 295 lived at Butler Island. Natural increase and occasional purchases of new slaves added to the slave population; few slaves were sold. By 1859 the total number of slaves for the entire estate was 919, approximately 500 of whom lived at Butler Island. These demographic factors indicate not only the growth of the slave population at Butler Island, but also suggest that the slave community was virtually unchanged from 1811 to 1860. In other words, by 1860 the slave community consisted primarily of descendants and survivors of the 1811 slave population. This factor suggests an element of cultural continuity. The implications for the archaeology are that the excavated materials represent the activities of the stable slave community, rather than activities of a highly transient slave labor force that fluctuated in size as owners bought and sold slaves, as was common on many plantations. Demographic patterns similar to those of the Butler estate appear to have been characteristic of rice and other plantations along the southeastern seaboard (House 1939; Friedlander 1985).

Analysis of slave demographic patterns at a particular plantation requires written records. However, it may be possible to calculate the approximate size of the slave population without the aid of slave lists and census data. An approximate count could be estimated from the number of slave houses. For example, the 1815 inventory for Butler Island indicates that 38 slave houses were located on Butler Island (18 at Settlement #1, 6 each at #2 and #3, and 8 at #4). These houses, identified as double-pen or duplex structures from historic photographs, contemporary descriptions, and archaeological evidence, housed two slave households, making a total of 76 households. If 5.2 is used as an average number of slaves in a household unit, as suggested by Fogel and Engerman (1974:115), then the total slave population for Butler Island would be approximately 395.2 slaves. The figure 395, though lower than the documented average of 411 slaves, demonstrates that a useful approximation for the size of the slave force could be made if there were no records. The 5.2 figure may well be too low for many plantations, but appears to be consistent with contemporary descriptions of the number of slaves occupying a slave household on antebellum rice plantations (Scott 1961:67; Olmsted 1856:422).

Determining the size of a slave community can be derived from several kinds of records, including tax records, census, plantation ledgers, and probate records. It may be possible to estimate size from the number of slave dwellings. The demography of a slave population is important; not only for background information in an archaeological study, but also for determining the structure of the slave population whose activities are represented in the archaeological record.

SLAVE PROVISIONING

The use of the term *provisioning* refers here to all aspects of slave material life, including food, housing, clothing, and household objects and personal possessions, whether provided by the slaveholder or acquired by slaves through gift, purchase, theft, or other means. Archaeological sources provide detailed information on slave material life at Butler Island, while written sources supply the context for interpreting these archaeological findings.

Information on slave provisioning in written sources is more uneven than information on slave demography or health and disease. Food provisions receive the greatest attention, housing and clothing the next, and household objects and personal possessions are scarcely mentioned. Entries in plantation ledgers and annual expense lists identify purchased provisions and indicate the frequency of such purchases. Comments in overseer correspondence, daybooks, and Fanny Kemble's observations shed light as to how purchased supplies were augmented.

Food

Supplying the slaves with food was apparently the major provisioning concern of the owners and managers at Butler Island. Two provision lists indicate how food rations were distributed among the Butler Island slaves. Apparently the amount of rations varied according to the slave's occupation (BP 1811, 1815b). Ditchers received the greatest amount of food rations; next in line were the slave foremen, known as "drivers," and the skilled artisans; then came the field workers; and last in line were the invalids and elderly slaves, who received the least amount of food (BP 1815b). Only ditchers received rations of meat on a regular basis and, according to Fanny Kemble, those meat rations were modest (Scott 1961:169).

Archaeological studies of slave life have contributed important information on slave diet. The recovery of zooarchaeological data and food procurement artifacts indicate that slaves supplemented plantation rations with foods collected through hunting, trapping, and fishing. References to these activities in written accounts, however, do not indicate the high frequency of supplemental food collection suggested in the archaeological record. On the other hand, written accounts can help to clarify or explain practices associated with food collecting activities such as slaves' access to firearms for hunting. Archaeological evidence at Butler Island established that slaves had access to guns, but the following account by Roswell King, Jr. explains the limitations of that access:

> At Butler Island, a fellow asks me permission to get a gun for ducks. Plenty of which are at the landing and in the fields. I have sometime since taken all firearms from them as I think they have forfeited their charter from the swamps and their conduct. I am often glad my philanthropy in allowing them guns did not extend further than this (1829c).

Ten years later, when Fanny Kemble visited Butler Island, she observed that the slaves had no access to firearms and had to resort to using traps to capture ducks and other waterfowl (Scott: 1961:58). Both accounts suggest that slaves' access to guns at Butler Island was indeed limited, a situation that may explain why birds, ducks, and deer, and other animals generally taken with guns comprised an insignificant percentage of the total nondomestic food bone recovered. On the other hand, animals collected

with nets, hooks, or traps, such as fish, turtles, and small mammals, represented the highest percentages of nondomestic food bone recovered (Singleton 1980:178–185).

Archaeology supplied limited information on the kinds of fruit and vegetables slaves consumed at Butler Island. Numerous peach pits were recovered, but no other botanical samples were collected or analyzed (Singleton 1980:177). Numerous references to provision gardens in plantation records suggest that provision gardens regularly augmented food rations. Yet, Fanny Kemble observed that the areas around houses intended for gardens were "untended and uncultivated" (Scott 1961:67). Given the frequent references to slave gardens in the plantation records, it is highly possible that her observation reflected a short-lived occurrence rather than ongoing practice.

The greatest discrepancy between Fanny Kemble's journal and other forms of evidence is found in her description of central kitchens, where slave's meals were prepared at each settlement (Scott 1961:55,100). The recovery of substantial quantities of charred bone, cast iron kettles and cauldrons, and serving and storage vessels suggest that large quantities of food were prepared and served from the cabins of individual households, rather than from a central plantation kitchen. Similar evidence for the preparation of food in individual cabins has been recovered from other slave sites in the Altamaha estuary and elsewhere along the coast. Thus far, no archaeological evidence of a central plantation kitchen has been reported (Singleton 1988:349). This finding is significant, not because it discredits a written account, but because it suggests that slaves prepared their food to suit their own tastes, perhaps incorporating aspects of their traditional cuisine.

Housing

References to housing in plantation records are few and generally describe new construction rather than indicate repairs or other alterations. The most graphic verbal descriptions of slave houses come from plantation visitors, but their descriptions are contradictory. Fanny Kemble describes the slaves houses as "filthy and wretched hovels," consisting of "one room about twelve feet by fifteen feet, with a couple of closets smaller and closer than staterooms of a ship divided off from the main room and each other by rough wooden partitions in which the inhabitants sleep" (Scott 1961:67–68). Seven years later Charles Lyell briefly visited Butler Island and described the slave houses in his journal as "neat, and whitewashed, all floored with wood, each with an apartment called the hall, two sleeping rooms, and a loft for children" (Lyell 1849 vol. I:249). Both accounts describe the general appearance of slave dwellings structures when they were occupied. Excavations of the slave dwellings confirmed that the structures were duplexes, raised off the ground, and floored with cypress planks. No evidence of whitewashing was uncovered. But the recovery of household refuse, particularly organic materials, within and around slave houses does suggest that the houses were more often "filthy and wretched" than "neat" and clean.

Clothing

Most rice plantations distributed annually two sets of clothing to the slaves, one set for winter and the other for summer (Allston 1858; House 1954; Phillips 1969:114–130). This annual distribution of clothing was not systematically recorded for the Butler estate, so it is questionable whether slaves received this provision on a regular basis. In the early years of operation, all clothing was produced on the plantation. Slave weavers wove the fabric, seamstresses made the clothes, and shoemakers tanned raw hides that they made into shoes. By the 1820s, these plantation-made provisions were apparently replaced with purchased items. Fewer references to making these items appear after that date, and there is more evidence of purchased items on annual expense lists. Additionally, fragments of shoe soles recovered from the slave settlement appeared to have been machine stitched rather than nailed, suggesting that the shoes were purchased and not produced on the plantation (Singleton 1980:190).

Household Objects

References to purchased household objects and miscellaneous objects, such as tobacco and pipes, rarely appeared in written accounts. A reference to the "purchase of 50 crates of crockery" (King, Jr. 1829b) suggests that the slaves were provisioned with ceramics at least once. References to tobacco and "negro pipes" occur more often on annual expense lists, indicating that these items were occasionally provided to the slaves. Other kinds of objects recovered from cabins include beads, a parasol attachment, eye glass lens, drawer pull, comb fragments, and a bone-handled pocket knife. These items are not mentioned in any written record, since they were most likely obtained through the slaves' own efforts. Written sources, however, do suggest how slaves acquired these items. Most personal items were purchased with money earned by selling produce, poultry, and handicrafts, or by "hiring out," that is, working for wages. Some items were possibly acquired through trade and theft.

SLAVE DISEASE AND HEALTH CARE

No single topic concerning the slaves dominated correspondence between the overseers and owners of the Butler estate as much as the health and physical well-being of the slaves. This concern held especially true for the slaves at Butler Island, where malaria and other diseases festered in the swampy lowlands. Although unknown to antebellum medicine, modern medical research has shown that many populations exposed to malarial climates like those in tropical Africa display a genetic trait, the "sickle-cell" allele, which produces a partial but heritable immunity to malaria. Individuals who are heterozygous for the sickle-cell trait are apparently better able to survive and reproduce in a malarial region (Livingstone 1958, 1960). Slaveholders had no knowledge of the sickle-cell trait, but they observed that some slaves fared better in swampy lowlands than others. For the managers of the Butler estate, identifying slaves who could withstand the rice swamp was an ongoing concern, as is indicated in the following passage:

> It appears that you have few Negroes here [Hampton] that are suitable for the rice swamp. We have at least 20 at the rice island which I would like to move if we had suitable highland for them. When you purchase more of course some of them will not be so profitable in a rice swamp and it is necessary we should arrange for land more suitable (King, Sr. 1813b).

Yet, in spite of efforts to place slaves at Butler Island who were in good health and exhibited the capacity to survive in the swampland, disease and sickness were prevailing problems. An array of ailments plagued the slaves, including cholera, intestinal disorders, influenza, pneumonia, rheumatic diseases, and whooping cough, among others. Of these, cholera, pneumonia, and intestinal disorders were the most dreaded, as these diseases frequently followed annual occurrences of freshets. Flood waters from the freshet contaminated food and water supplies, which when consumed caused illness and occasionally death (Singleton 1980:79).

The Butler Island slaves were often relocated to higher ground to reduce debilitating disease. This was particularly true when a freshet threatened (King, Jr. 1835). As a general practice, invalids were removed to St. Simons, because the sea air and sandy soil were considered to be more favorable for recuperation than the marshlands of Butler Island (Scott 1961:146).

By far the greatest sufferers among the slave population at Butler Island were infants and children. The infant mortality rate was higher there than at any other plantation of the Butler estate: "the mortality among infants is very high particularly at this place [Butler Island] the state of the atmosphere is certainly injurious to infants" (King, Jr. 1829a). Deaths among infants at the Butler estate often comprised 50% or more of the annual deaths, as indicated in Table 2. Evidence of a high infant mortality rate was supported by the archaeological assessment made of the slave cemetery in 1954 (Caldwell n.d.; Sanders n.d.). At that time, a dragline used for dredging a canal cut through and exposed the southern edge of the cemetery, smashing several wooden coffins and exposing others in the profile north of the dragline. The archaeologists noted that most of coffins were those of infants (Singleton 1980:90).

Table 2
MORTALITY RATES OF INFANTS AND CHILDREN OF SLAVES ON THE BUTLER ESTATE, 1819–1834

Year	Number (All Deaths)	Infants #	Infants %	Children (1–4) #	Children (1–4) %	Children (5–14) #	Children (5–14) %	Total #	Total %
1819	19	9	47	3	16	3	16	15	79
1820	16	7	43	2	13	0	0	9	56
1821	27	3	11	5	19	3	11	11	41
1822	22	3	14	7	32	3	14	13	60
1823	14	12	86	0	0	0	0	12	86
1824	18	9	50	2	11	0	0	11	61
1825	28	9	32	5	18	1	3	15	53
1826	23	15	65	1	4	2	9	18	78
1827	39	24	62	5	13	2	5	31	80
1828	25	21	84	3	12	2	12	25	100
1829	16	8	50	3	19	2	12	13	82
1830	25	10	40	3	12	2	8	15	60
1831	20	15	75	2	10	1	5	18	90
1832	29	12	41	5	17	1	3	18	61
1833	34	21	62	5	14	0	0	26	76
1834	34	17	50	5	15	1	3	23	68
Total	389	200	51	56	15	25	6	281	72

Source: Births and Deaths, BP, 1819–1834

Sick slaves were kept at the plantation infirmary located at Settlement #1 on Butler Island. The plantation managers administered treatment for minor ailments, but a physician was brought in for more severe medical problems. Fanny Kemble described the infirmary building as a large two-story building "built of whitewashed wood and contains four large-sized rooms" (Scott 1961:69). Unfortunately, this structure was not identified from archaeological resources, therefore, the only evidence that can be used to describe the physical structure and the activities that took place there are derived from written records. Since the completion of the Butler Island study, hospital ledgers for the Butler Island slave infirmary dating from 1838 to 1843 have surfaced at an archives in Louisiana. These ledgers give a day-to-day account of the sick at Butler Island. The listings include dates, names, settlement number, the disease, and remarks (Butler Island Hospital Books 1838–1843). As few as 2 slaves and as many as 60 were checked in during the course of a day. An examination of these ledgers revealed several patterns: most of the patients were slave women and children; certain ailments occurred on a seasonal basis, for example, "bowel complaint" (possibly dysentery or cholera) was most prevalent in the summer and rheumatic pains were more prevalent in the cold months; few incidences of injuries (burns, cuts, broken bones) were treated. Careful analysis of these ledgers will make it possible to conduct a detailed examination of slave health at Butler Island.

Information indicating the prescribed treatment for a particular ailment is absent from the hospital ledgers. Indications of medications used are found on annual expense lists and include rhubarb, spirits of turpentine, red lavender, aloes, alum, magnesia, camphor, peppermint, castor oil, opium, and patent medicines. A favorite patent medication requested by Roswell King, Jr. was "Swain's Panacea." King had a very high opinion of this medication (Bell 1987:237), claiming that it cured a slave with ulcers in the summer and within a few months restored him to perfect health (King Jr. 1823).

Numerous fragments of discarded medicine vials recovered from slave dwellings indicate that slaves regularly consumed patent medicines. The consumption of brewed alcoholic beverages in considerable quantities is suggested by the recovery of dark green bottles. The liquor may have been used for its medicinal effects. In fact, rum was produced at Butler Island and periodically issued to the slaves as a preventative for rheumatic ailments (King, Sr. 1803). Because rum was also occasionally issued to the slaves for holidays, some of this consumption reflects recreational consumption of alcohol (Singleton 1980:158–159).

Data on disease and health care among the Butler Island slaves were derived primarily from written sources. Archaeological resources supported interpretations derived from written records. However, archaeology could have offered a valuable perspective to this topic had the human remains from the slave cemetery been analyzed or if the slave infirmary had been located and excavated. Because the health status of the slaves at Butler Island was recorded, that aspect of slave life can be interpreted.

Slave Behavior

The final category refers to activities that received limited treatment in written sources for Butler Island but have no archaeological correlates. These activities include resistance, cultural expressions, and family and community relations. It is unfortunate that none of these activities could be interpreted from archaeological resources, as these topics provide insights into slave life from the slaves' perspective, as well as some indications of how slaves responded to enslavement.

In the plantation records, primarily in the overseer correspondence, the aspects of slave behavior that received the most attention were those considered deviant, such as stealing, running away, and refusal to work. Of these incidences, stealing was recorded most frequently and was perhaps considered the primary disciplinary problem. Most thefts were of warehoused produce that was sold for cash to merchants in the nearby town of Darien. The stealing of plantation produce by slaves had become so widespread in the Altamaha estuary that planters attempted to prosecute local merchants for buying from slaves. Runaway attempts were second to stealing as a disciplinary problem. Most of these attempts were apparently intended to be short-term absences from the plantation. Occasionally, one or two slaves, usually male, would go to another plantation or sneak into town without permission. Few efforts toward permanent escape are indicated, and the one incidence described in the plantation records was an unsuccessful attempt (1804b). Refusal to work ranked third but probably occurred more often than is indicated in plantation records. Faking illness was the primary way slaves resisted hard labor in the fields.

Punishment for these offenses included flogging with a lash, forced labor on Sundays, and denial of fish, meat, molasses, clothes, and rice. Chronic offenders were exiled to "Five Pound," a remote settlement on Little Simons Island where slaves worked a narrow patch of swampland (Scott 1961:195)

Not only is information on cultural expressions, family life, and community life limited, but the most often recorded behavior was considered negative, such as family disputes and other conflicts among slaves. Similarly, descriptions of cultural expressions are always conveyed from an ethnocentric perspective, such as the seeking out of "negro doctors" for cures to health problems (King, Sr. 1814, 1815) or comments on slaves' religious life (King, Sr. 1804a). In contrast to the overseer brief references to slave behavior, Fanny Kemble's journal contains detailed information on slave songs, a funeral ceremony, and incidences of rape and other abuse to slave women. While her comments are more sympathetic than the overseers' accounts, they are equally ethnocentric. Both records are difficult to use to interpret slave behavior. Any detailed discussion of slave behavior at Butler Island must also consider other sources, such as oral testimony, in order to better understand these aspects of slave life from the slaves' perspective.

Summary and Conclusion

The interpretation of slave life at Butler Island offered here demonstrates that information obtained from archaeology and information obtained from written records complement each other. The archaeological data presented evidence that either offered new information or helped to clarify the written information. Only in a few cases did the information simply reinforce what was already described in the written record. The same held true for the written record: most of the information either was unobtainable from the archaeological record or facilitated the interpretation of the archaeological data. Few plantations are as well documented as Butler Island, particularly with records that describe slave life. Yet, in spite of written sources, there is very little information concerning aspects of slave life that are preserved in the archaeological record. Archaeology provides the most detailed information on slave provisioning, the primary area where written accounts were fewer, lacked information, or provided ambiguous information. On the other hand, written records were the sole source for information on the size, age distribution, and sexual division of the slave population. Relative population size could have been calculated from estimates of the number of houses or perhaps other archaeological resources, but this is the only demographic factor that could be potentially estimated without written information.

A great deal of information was recorded on slave health, particularly the number of sick and the kinds of ailments at Butler Island. Such detailed documentation is rare, particularly the hospital ledgers, which give a day-to-day account of the sick over a period of several years. If the slave cemetery and the infirmary had been available for archaeological study, these archaeological resources would no doubt have shed light on aspects of slave health not revealed from the written sources. Analysis of skeletal remains could have supplied information on slave health resulting from disease, nutritional intake, occupational stresses, and injuries affecting the skeleton. Deaths resulting from cholera and yellow fever epidemics are less detectable in human skeletons, but written records, such as the hospital ledgers, would fill that void. Excavations of the slave infirmary would have produced data on the nature of slave health care, such as the kinds of medical instruments used, the kinds of medications administered, and possibly evidence of the kinds of foods prepared for ill slaves. This information was only vaguely described in the written sources.

The aspects of slave life categorized as slave behavior are beginning to receive serious attention in the historiography of slavery. Such studies generally utilize information from written records of several, if not numerous, plantations. It may be that slave behavior is a topic that cannot be sufficiently addressed within the context of a single plantation, unless there is an abundance of information describing these activities. Recent archaeological investigations have recovered information on cultural expressions. Studies have produced information on folk medicine (Brown 1989), culinary practices (Ferguson 1991), and possibly folk beliefs (Adams 1989). It has also been argued that material evidence of African traditions can be viewed as a form of resistance (Ferguson 1991). Archaeological findings such as these do provide insights as to how slaves responded to enslavement.

Written sources are vital to any study of slavery, but some records are of more use to archaeological studies than others. At Butler Island, the sources that proved to be most useful for locating, identifying, and interpreting archaeological data included the plantation inventory, overseer letters, and Fanny Kemble's accounts. Unfortunately, these sources are unique and uncharacteristic of written records generally associated with a plantation. Other sources, such as the slave lists, daybooks, and ledgers, are more characteristic of plantation records. The search for written descriptions of slave material life, however, continues to an arduous task, because such information is not found in any one kind of record.

The archaeological record offers a unique contribution to the study of antebellum slavery by providing information on material life that for most plantations was not systematically recorded. While the Butler Island study only addressed questions concerning slave provisioning, archaeological data can be used to address any question for which material culture can serve as a primary source of data. Recent studies in plantation archaeology are beginning to address new and provocative topics, such as cultural change, power relations, and slave resistance. In time, other topics will be added to this list, making archaeology a significant contributor to the reinterpretation of slavery.

References

Adams, W. H.(1989) Black American Heritage and Archaeology: Theoretical Paradigms and Methodological Practices in the Search for Ethnic Heritage, paper presented at the conference, Digging the Afro-American Past: Archaeology and the Black Experience, May 18, University of Mississippi, Oxford, MS.

Allston, R. F. W. (1858) Notes on the Management of a Southern Rice Estate. *DeBows Review* 24:324–326.

Anonymous (1877) Map of Butler Island, McIntosh County, Surveyor General Department, Georgia State Archives, Atlanta, GA.

Bell, M. C. (1987) *Major Butler's Legacy: Five Generations of a Slaveholding Family*. University of Georgia Press, Athens, GA.

Brown, K. L. (1989) From Slavery to Wage Labor Tenancy: Structural Continuity in an Afro-American Community, paper presented at the conference, Digging the Afro-American Past: Archaeology and the Black Experience, May 18, University of Mississippi, Oxford, MS.

Butler Papers [BP] (1801–1803) Slave Transactions. Folders 16, 17, 18, 19, Box 10, BFPC, PHS.

— (1803) Crop and Livestock Report. Folder 6, Box 7, BFPC, PHS.

— (1811) Number of Negroes & Statement of Allowance per Week. Folder 20, Box 10, BFPC, PHS.

— (1815a) Inventory of the Butler Estate, Folder 8, Box 31, WFPC, PHS.

— (1815b) Provisions for Negroes. Folder 20, Box 10, BFPC PHS.

— (1819–1834) Births and Deaths. Folders 13, 14, 15, Box 10, BFPC, PHS.

— (1859) A List of Slaves Belonging to John Butler. Folder 5, Box 41, WFPC, PHS.

Butler Island Hospital Books (1838–1843) Record Group 100, Louisiana State Museum, New Orleans, LA.

Caldwell, S. (n.d.) Report on Butler Island Burial Site. Report on File, Historic Preservation Section, Georgia, Department of Natural Resources, Atlanta, GA.

CSA (1862) Confederate States of America versus Gabriella Butler and Alexander Blue, CSA, District Court, Southern District Georgia, Sequestration Docket #269, 208, Regional Archives Branch, Atlanta.

Dew, C. (1987) The Slavery Experience. In *Interpreting Southern History: Historiographical Essays in Honor of Sanford Higginbotham*, J. B. Boles and E. T. Nolen, Eds. Louisiana State University Press, Baton Rouge, LA, pp. 120–161.

Ferguson, L. G. (1991) Struggling with Pots in Colonial South Carolina. In *The Archaeology of Inequality*, R. Paynter and P. H. McGuire, Eds. Basil Blackwell, Cambridge, MA, pp. 28–39.

Fogel, R. W. and S. L. Engerman (1974) *Time on the Cross: The Economics of American Negro Slavery*. Little, Brown, and Company, Boston.

Friedlander, A. (1985) Establishing Historical Probabilities for Archaeological Interpretations: Slave Demography of Two Plantations in the South Carolina Lowcountry, 1740–1820, In *The Archaeology of Slavery and Plantation Life*, T. A. Singleton, Ed. Academic Press, Orlando, FL, pp. 215–238.

Genovese, E. D. (1974) *Roll Jordan Roll: The World the Slaves Made*. Pantheon Books, New York.

Gray, L. C. (1941) *History of Agriculture in the Southern United States to 1860*, 2 vols. Peter Smith, New York.

House, A. J. (1939) The Management of a Rice Plantation in Georgia 1834–1861, as Revealed in the Journal of Hugh Fraser Grant. *Agricultural History* 13:208–217.

— (1954) Labor Management Problems on a Georgian Rice Plantation, 1840–1860. *Agricultural History* 28:148–153.

Joyner, C. (1989) Digging Common Ground: African American History and Historical Archaeology. Paper presented at the Digging the Afro-American Past: Archaeology and the Black Experience, May 18, University of Mississippi, Oxford, MS.

King, R. Jr.(1821) Letter to Francis Butler, February 18, Folder 17, Box 3, BFPC, PHS.

— (1823) Letter to Francis Butler, December 8, Folder 4, Box 4, BFPC, PHS.

— (1829a) Letter to Thomas Butler, January 5, Folder 12, Box 4, BFPC, PHS.

— (1829b) Letter to Thomas Butler, March 18, Folder 3, Box 33, WFPC, PHS.

— (1829c) Letter to Thomas Butler, June 28, Folder 13, Box 4, BFPC, PHS.

— (1835) Letter to Thomas Butler, February 15, Folder 5, Box 33, WFPC, PHS.

— (1844) Daybook, Estate of John and Pierce Butler in Georgia, MDCC, Folder 205, GHS.

King, R. Sr. (1803) Letter to Major Butler, October 22, Folder 12, Box 2, BFPC, PHS.

— (1804a) Letter to Major Butler, March 30, Folder 12, Box 2, BFPC, PHS.

— (1804b) Letter to Major Butler, May 12, Folder 12, Box 2, BFPC, PHS.

— (1813a) Letter to Major Butler, January 3, Folder 23, Box 2, BFPC, PHS.

— (1813b) Letter to Major Butler, August 22, Folder 25, Box 2, BFPC, PHS.

— (1814) Letter to Major Butler, June 5, Folder 26, Box 2, BFPC, PHS.

— (1815) Letter to Major Butler, August 20, Folder 2, Box 3, BFPC, PHS.

— (1816) Letter to Major Butler, April 20, Folder 6, Box 3, BFPC, PHS.

Leigh, F. B. (1883) *Ten Years on a Georgian Plantation since the War.* Bentley and Sons, London.

Livingstone, F. B. (1958) Anthropological Implications of Sickle Cell Gene Distribution in West Africa, *American Anthropologist* 60:533–562.

— (1960) The Wave of Advance of an Advantageous: The Sickle Cell Gene in Liberia, *Human Biology* 32(2):197–202.

Lyell, C. (1849) *A Second Visit to the United States of America*, 2 vols., Harper & Brothers, New York.

McFarlane, S. (1975) The Ethnoarchaeology of a Slave Cabin Community: The Couper Plantation Site. Masters Thesis, University of Florida, Gainesville.

Moore, S. M. (1981) The Antebellum Barrier Island Plantation: A Search for an Archaeological Pattern, Ph.D. dissertation, University of Florida, Gainesville.

— (1985) Social and Economic Status on the Coastal Plantation. In *The Archaeology of Slavery and Plantation Life*, T. A. Singleton, Ed. Academic Press, Orlando, FL, pp. 141–160.

Olmsted, F. L. (1856) A Journey in the Seaboard Slave States with Remarks on Their Economy. Reprint, Negro Universities Press, Detroit.

Otto, J. S. (1975) Status Differences and the Archaeological Record — A Comparison of Planter, Overseer, and Slave Sites from Cannon's Point Plantation, 1794–1861, St. Simons Island, Georgia. Ph.D. Dissertation, University of Florida, Gainesville.

— (1984) *Cannon's Point Plantation 1794–1860: Living Conditions and Status Patterns in the Old South.* Academic Press, Orlando, FL.

Owens, L. H. (1975) *This Species of Property: Slave Life and Culture in the Old South.* Oxford University Press, New York.

Page, W. (1799) Copy of Taxable Property, McIntosh and Glynn Counties, Georgia, Folder 23, Box 10, BFPC, PHS.

Phillips, U. B. (1929) *Life and Labor in the Old South.* Little, Brown, and Company, Boston.

Phillips, U. B., Ed. (1969) *Plantation and Frontier.* Burt Franklin, New York.

Sanders, W. T. (n.d.) Report on Excavations on Butler Island, July 1956. Report on File Archaeology Laboratory, University of Georgia, Athens.

Scott, J. A. (1978) *Hard Trials on My Way: Slavery and the Struggle Against It, 1800–1860.* Mentor Books, New York.

Scott, J. A., Ed. (1961) *A Journal of A Residence On a Georgian Plantation, 1838–1839 by Francis Kemble 1863.* Alfred A. Knopf, New York.

Singleton, T. A. (1980) The Archaeology of Afro-American Slavery: A Regional Perception of Slave household and Community Patterns, Ph.D. Dissertation, University of Florida, Gainesville.

— (1988) An Archaeological Framework for Slavery and Emancipation. In *The Recovery of Meaning: Historical Archaeology in the Eastern United States.* M. P. Leone and P. B. Potter, Eds. Jr. Smithsonian Institution, Washington, DC, pp. 345–370.

Stampp, K. M. (1956) *The Peculiar Institution: Slavery in the Antebellum South.* Alfred A. Knopf, New York.

United States Bureau of Census (1820) Fourth Census of the United States 1820. Microfilm on file at the National Archives, Washington, DC.

— (1830) Fifth Census of the United States 1830. Microfilm on file at the National Archives, Washington, DC.

— (1840) Sixth Census of the United States 1840. Microfilm on file at the National Archives, Washington, DC.

— (1850) Seventh Census of the United States, Slave Schedules, Georgia. Microfilm on file at the National Archives, Washington, DC.

— (1860) Eighth Census of the United States, Slave Schedules, Georgia, Microfilm on file at the National Archives, Washington, D.C.

Abbreviations used in References

BFPC Butler Family Papers Collection, Record Number 1447
CSA Confederate States of America
GHS Georgia Historical Society, Savannah Georgia
MDCC Margaret Davis Cate Collection
PHS Pennsylvania Historical Society, Philadelphia, PA
WFPC Wister Family Papers Collection (Butler Section)

6: Not Peas in a Pod: Documenting Diversity among the California Missions

Julia G. Costello
Foothill Resource Associates
Mokelumne Hill, California

This paper explores some of the economic changes in the Franciscan Missions of Alta California between about 1790 and 1835 (see Costello 1990a for larger study). During this time period, the Spanish colony was transformed from a string of struggling agricultural settlements to a significant participant in international trading networks. How this integration took place and its effect on individual mission economies was reconstructed using both archaeological and documentary data sources. The analytic strategies and results of the documentary research are the topic of this paper.

Archaeological research in California has traditionally treated the entire mission system as a unified entity, with homogeneous conditions over time and between missions. Recently, however, researchers have argued that the mission system was not static over time but went through several developmental stages that affected social, technological, economic, and religious aspects of mission life (Hornbeck 1989). My research suggests that aspects of mission life in California not only changed over time, but differed between regions and between individual missions. Responses of each mission institution to external political and economic events were not uniform, but were affected by local ecological, geographical, and historical factors that resulted in a range of institutional adaptations. Evidence for an increase in this mission individuation after 1821 was found in archaeological remains, as well as in two separate types of documentary sources. This corroboration was vital to the recognition of these divergence mission economies, as no one of these sources could have identified the economic patterns as fully and persuasively as did the combination.

In this chapter I briefly describe some of the archaeological comparisons and then discuss at length the documentary evidence of mission economic productivity. I have limited my detailed discussion to the Monterey and Santa Barbara Presidio Districts because all of the relevant archaeological collections come from missions in these regions (Figure 1).

Archaeological Synopsis

The archaeological data for the larger study of mission economics was drawn from excavations conducted at five mission sites in California: La Purisima (Deetz 1978); San Buenaventura (Greenwood 1975, 1976); San Antonio (Hoover and Costello 1985); La Soledad (Farnsworth 1987); and Santa Ines (Costello 1989b). At all of these sites, stratigraphically discrete collections were identified that satisfied two important criteria: (1) they represented discrete time periods that fell between ca. 1790 and 1835; and (2) they were associated with a specific subpopulation at the mission (Indian Residents, Hispanic Specialists, or Clerics).

To examine differences between individual missions, the variables of time and subpopulations had to be held constant. Three of the archaeological collections represented both the same general time period (ca. 1810–1835) and the same population (Indian residents) (Table 1). The ceramics (vessels) from each collection were compared for variability in proportion of ceramic types, production dates, and prices.

Identification of some significant differences between missions resulted. The occurrence of ceramic types was not uniform between the Indian populations at the three missions. Nearly half of the pottery at San Buenaventura (47%) and San Antonio (50%) Missions consisted of mission-made wares, while quantities of this type were negligible at La Purisima (4%). Correspondingly, La Purisima Indian residences displayed greater percentages of imported English (55%) and Chinese (22%) wares, in proportions similar to those associated with clerics and Hispanic specialists (Costello 1990a: Table 54).

Differences between the dates ceramics were manufactured (mean ceramic dates) and when they were thrown away (artifact deposition dates) reflect purchasing patterns that were consistent for all the missions studied: prior to the 1810 Mexican War of Independence, large purchases of Hispanic wares were made; after this time, Hispanic wares were replaced by English ceramics (Costello 1990a:Table 61). All of the mean ceramic dates for the ca. 1810–1835 Spanish-colonial collections were in the 1790s, nearly a quarter century earlier than the mean dates of the artifact deposits; these Hispanic wares were archaic remnants of prior trading patterns. For the English wares at San Buenaventura and La Purisima, however, mean ceramic dates for collections were close to the dates for the archaeological deposits, reflecting regular purchases of these wares over the time period represented by the refuse. At Mission San Antonio, however, the mean date for the English ceramic collection is 1842, indicating that these items were nearly all purchased at the end of the 1810 to 1835 time period of the deposit (Costello 1990a: Table 61).

The study of historic documents that accompanied these archaeological inquiries provided unique and independent information on economic variability between the California missions. The economic setting of the California mission system will be briefly reviewed below and then data will be presented that was obtained from two types of documents: (1) mission agricultural production records; and (2) descriptions of California missions made by foreign travelers.

Economic Setting

The California missions were founded between 1769 and 1823, the final episode in Spain's frontier colonization. The Alta, California colony was to hold this territory against Russian and English expansion in the North Pacific using a combination of missions, presidios, and pueblos that had succeeded in other parts of New Spain. The 21 missions eventually founded were administered by Franciscan priests, who introduced agriculture and simple industries to the converted Indians and developed communities of 500 to 1200 inhabitants. Four presidios attended to the defense and governmental activities of their districts. The three pueblos established to supply agricultural produce to the presidios were generally unsuccessful until after the mission period had ended.

Geographically removed from international activities and restricted to trading with Spanish ships, Alta California developed in relative isolation. By the early years of the 19th century, mission industries and agricultural production were well established and major building

programs were largely completed. Prosperity and surplus production increased the trading potential of the colony. After 1810 and the beginning of the Mexican War of Independence, Spanish economic and political support were virtually severed, and California was increasingly dependent on its own resources to obtain necessary manufactured goods.

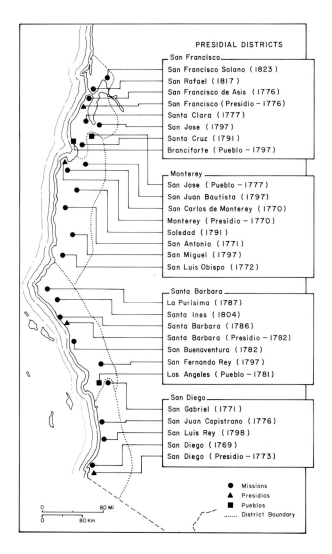

FIG. 1. The California missions, presidios, and pueblos, 1769–1823.

After 1821, the victorious Mexican government opened California to foreign trade, a change that profoundly affected the economy of the colony. Most missions signed exclusive 3-year contracts with the British firm of McCulloch, Hartnell, and Company in 1823. Although trading with foreigners and Spanish nationals had been carried on both illegally and legally for nearly two decades, California missions had long suffered a lack of transport for their increasing surplus production, and these contracts for the first time guaranteed that all hides

Table 1
PERCENT DISTRIBUTION OF CERAMICS BY ORIGIN

Mission (Coll. Date)	N	New Spain	China	England	Mission	Unknown	Total
Buenaventura (1805–1840)	131	34	9	6	47	4	100
San Antonio (1810–1835)	161	20	6	24	50	—	100
La Purisima (1813–1835)	123	18	22	55	4	1	100
Total	415	23	12	28	36	1	100

and a certain volume of tallow would be purchased each year at set prices. Imported goods were now readily available in exchange for California products. The colony's primary exports were mission cattle products, particularly hides and tallow, which were exchanged for manufactured items and cash and shipped to England, the Atlantic states, and the Pacific rim. The missions' virtual monopoly of land and livestock excluded private individuals from participating in this new export economy, fostering resentment among the growing secular population.

In response to public pressure, and in keeping with the tenants of the Mexican independence movement, in 1832 the missions were allowed to be secularized and land was leased to private parties. After 1834, mission lands were increasingly granted outright to individuals, ending the mission as an institution. Most of the Indian residents dispersed to towns and ranchos, livestock was sold or appropriated, and fields and orchards gradually succumbed to neglect. The mission period in California ended and the era of the ranchos began.

Agricultural Production at the Missions

PRODUCTION STATISTICS

In 1777, a format was established for mission annual reports that included livestock and agricultural statistics, as well as a census of the mission population (Archibald 1978:70–71). This standardized reporting was universally used between 1784 and 1832 (Engelhardt 1915:535) and provides invaluable data on mission production and population that is comparable both over time and between individual missions (Costello 1989a).

There are obvious differences in the accuracy of figures, as some clerics apparently enumerated livestock down to single animals, while others rounded herds off to the nearest hundred or thousand. Especially in the case of cattle and sheep, which grew to exceed 10,000 animals at individual missions, reports of numbers of range animals

must certainly be approximations. However, local military officials were vitally interested in the accuracy of mission reports on population and agricultural production, as these affected mission and presidio economic transactions (Archibald 1978:20–21). Annual figures were verified by the soldiers and significant errors in the annual reports would not have been tolerated.

Most of the original mission annual reports have survived and are archived in various repositories in California (Bowman 1958:138–139). The most accurate publication of these statistics was made by Fr. Zephyrin Engelhardt, O.F.M. for his series of books on 16 of the 21 California missions (only one of the San Francisco Presidio District missions is included) (Engelhardt 1920–1973). Although some small discrepancies have been noted in Engelhardt's figures, they are relatively minor (Bowman 1958:140; Jackson 1988:269–270), and these published statistics were used for the present analysis.

Annual crop production consists of the total number of *fanegas* (1 *fanega* = 1.57 bushels) harvested of the major crops of wheat and corn plus the minor crops of barley, beans, and peas. Annual livestock production consists of the total animal holdings, which are dominated by sheep and cattle with horses, goats, mules, and pigs in decreasing quantities. Production statistics were normalized by dividing both the total annual volume of crops harvested and the total annual numbers of livestock by the size of the population. The resulting figures represent annual per-capita crop and livestock resources; the numbers of *fanegas* of wheat, or numbers of animals, theoretically available to each person. Comparisons can then be made between missions of diverse population sizes to determine the relative abundance of food resources per person — the relative ability of the missions to feed their inhabitants or trade in surplus produce. Crop statistics can be further analyzed by comparing the reported annual amount harvested to that sown. While the annual crop production per-capita ratio measures how much food was actually produced per inhabitant, the harvest-to-sown ratio indicates how successful farming efforts were each year. Because of numerous factors influencing harvests, such as vicissitudes of climate, ver-

Table 2
AVERAGE ANNUAL MISSION PRODUCTION PER CAPITA BY PRESIDIO DISTRICT

Years Averaged	Santa Barbara		Monterey		Calif. Average[b]	
	Crops[a]	Livestock	Crops[a]	Livestock	Crops[a]	Livestock
1784–1790	3.1	3	2.4	4	2.6	5
1791–1800	3.3	7	2.5	7	3.1	9
1801–1805	3.7	10	3.2	10	3.5	12
1806–1810	2.9	14	2.8	17	3.0	16
1811–1816	4.8	18	2.7	22	3.6	19
1817–1821	4.9	20	4.1	25	4.5	22
1822–1827	3.0	17	2.8	23	2.7	19
1828–1832	2.4	19	2.2	24	2.2	22
Average	3.6	14	2.8	17	3.2	15

[a] In fanegas: 1 fanega = 1.57 bushels.
[b] Includes all missions from Santa Barbara, Monterey, and San Diego Districts.

min, and pestilence, crop production values have much greater fluctuations than do livestock statistics.

A detailed presentation of livestock and crop statistics, and their changes over time, are presented elsewhere (Costello 1990a), and only a summary of the analysis results have been given below. First discussed are general trends in California as a whole: the "homogenized" mission approach. Then individual economic behavior at missions in the Santa Barbara and Monterey Presidio Districts will be examined.

GENERAL PRODUCTION TRENDS OF THE CALIFORNIA MISSION SYSTEM

Throughout Alta California, crop production for missions founded prior to 1776 evidenced the worst per-capita crop production rates of the entire mission period, certainly a result of the lack of governmental support and problems inherent in starting farming enterprises in a new geographic area. Missions founded after 1776 began with much higher per-capita crop production rates, reflecting the refinement of growing techniques, regular governmental assistance, and available help from previously established missions. By 1790, per-capita crop production attained relatively stable values, which then rose markedly between 1811 and 1821 (Table 2). The period from 1822 to 1827 saw a dramatic drop in per-capita crop production throughout California; the largest number of single worst-years for individual missions occurred in this time period.

This major drop in crop production resulted from a major decline in harvest-to-sown ratios after 1821, breaking a pattern of relative stability that had prevailed since at least 1784 (Table 3). Even though the quantity of seed sown during this same period increased markedly, former production levels could not be maintained. Although

this pattern seems to prevail throughout the colony, it does not appear to be a result of decreased rainfall: climate reconstructions for southern California do not show any abnormal drought patterns for this time period (Meko et al. 1980; Rowntree 1985a, 1985b). Other ecological variables that may have contributed to the decline include increase in pestilence, disease, and weeds, and decrease in soil nutrients, which often accompany the introduction of agriculture to a region (Nye and Greenland 1960:75). An alternative explanation proposed in this study associates the drop in crop production with the introduction of new economic opportunities in exporting cattle hides and tallow, and with a corresponding shift in the allocation of mission labor away from tending the planted crops.

Table 3
AVERAGE ANNUAL MISSION HARVESTED-TO-SOWN RATIOS BY PRESIDIO DISTRICT

Years Averaged	Santa Barbara	Monterey	California Average[a]
1784–1790	32	23	28
1791–1800	27	13	22
1801–1805	25	19	21
1806–1810	21	14	18
1811–1816	29	15	21
1817–1821	21	20	26
1822–1827	14	11	14
1828–1832	14	9	11
Average	22	15	20

[a] Includes all missions from Santa Barbara, Monterey, and San Diego Districts.

Table 4
AVERAGE ANNUAL MISSION LIVESTOCK AND PERCENT OF CHANGE BY
PRESIDIO DISTRICT

Years Averaged	Santa Barbara		Monterey		Calif. Average[a]	
	n	%	n	%	n	%
1784–1790	862	—	2,968	—	3,062	—
1791–1800	4,586	+432	4,832	+69	7,242	+142
1801–1805	10,855	+137	7,746	+54	11,041	+49
1806–1810	15,376	+42	13,300	+71	15,492	+40
1811–1816	19,160	+25	15,455	+13	18,269	+17
1817–1821	19,847	+4	16,492	+10	20,151	+12
1822–1827	12,381	–38	13,955	–14	17,514	–13
1828–1832	10,361	–16	11,379	–19	17,083	–3
Average	12,198		10,784		13,814	

[a] Includes all missions from Santa Barbara, Monterey, and San Diego Districts.

Livestock holdings and per-capita livestock ratios show steady increases from the earliest years of the California missions until 1821 (Tables 2 and 4). Unlike per-capita crop production, which began high at later-founded missions, initial per-capita livestock figures begin low for each mission; livestock holdings apparently had to be built up at each institution from small herds. After 1821, when foreign trade was legalized, total average numbers of livestock dropped for the first time (–13%), reflecting a liquidation of cattle for the production of hides and tallow (Table 4). Declining populations at the missions mitigated the depletion of herds and per-capita ratios rose again by the 1828 to 1832 period.

In summary, two major changes in agricultural production correspond with the change to a Mexican government in 1821 and development of the trade in hides and tallow after 1822: (1) a dramatic decline in total numbers of livestock and (2) a decline in both crop and livestock production per capita. The phase from 1821 to 1832 is therefore generally characterized by a shift toward ranching and away from agriculture.

PROFILES OF INDIVIDUAL MISSIONS

Analysis of the individual missions in the Santa Barbara and Monterey Presidio Districts provide evidence of economic variation between institutions within the general patterns of the colony. Per-capita crop and livestock statistics are presented in Table 5, along with a ranking of individual missions as low, medium, or high in each category. Most missions are not equally successful in livestock and crop productivity and therefore do not exhibit similar ratings in both categories. San Juan Bautista, for example, had high livestock holdings per capita and low crop production, whereas the opposite conditions existed at San Carlos. Some missions, however, are low in

both categories, such as Santa Barbara and San Antonio. These data indicate that productivity of animal and plant resources varied between missions. As a result, efforts required to obtain food and produce export commodities must also have been unequal between institutions.

The response of individual missions to the economic opportunities offered by the hide-and-tallow trade can be compared by looking at changes in the size of their cattle herds (Table 6). Between 1810 and 1816, four ships from Spanish-American countries trading in cattle products were known to have called in California (Costello 1990a: Table 2). The only mission showing an actual decrease in herd size at this time is San Carlos, implying that exports were obtained from this mission, the closest one to the capital at Monterey. Other missions may have been involved in some trading, but this did not deplete their herds to any visible extent. Between 1817 and 1821, San Buenaventura was apparently the primary supplier of cattle products in California, with Santa Barbara second in volume, while herd size at San Carlos began to increase again. During this period the export center seems to have shifted from Monterey to the Santa Barbara Presidio District. San Antonio Mission also shows only a modest increase in livestock, although its remote distance from a port makes it an unlikely early trader.

Although it seems reasonable that missions with the largest cattle surpluses (largest per-capita livestock ratios) would be the early traders, this does not appear to be true. Of the two missions that showed evidence of substantial trading activities prior to 1821, Santa Barbara had the lowest per-capita livestock ratios in the colony, while San Buenaventura had only an average rating (Table 5). There also does not appear to be a correlation between size of herds and active trading. In the 1817 to 1821

Table 5
SANTA BARBARA AND MONTEREY PRESIDIO DISTRICT MISSIONS RANKED BY PER-CAPITA CROP AND LIVESTOCK PRODUCTION

Ranking	Presidio District	Mission	Average Rate
a. Annual Crop Production Per Capita			
High	Santa Barbara	Santa Ines	4.5
	Santa Barbara	San Buenaventura	4.3
	Monterey	San Carlos	3.7
Medium	Monterey	La Soledad	3.6
	Santa Barbara	La Purisima	3.3
	Santa Barbara	San Fernando Rey	3.3
	Monterey	San Luis Obispo	3.1
Low	Santa Barbara	Santa Barbara	2.7
	Monterey	San Juan Bautista	2.5
	Monterey	San Miguel	2.2
	Monterey	San Antonio	1.8
b. Annual Livestock Per Capita			
High	Monterey	San Luis Obispo	21
	Monterey	La Soledad	21
	Monterey	San Juan Bautista	19
	Santa Barbara	La Purisima	18
Medium	Santa Barbara	San Buenaventura	17
	Santa Barbara	Santa Ines	17
	Monterey	San Miguel	16
Low	Monterey	San Carlos	13
	Monterey	San Antonio	12
	Santa Barbara	San Fernando Rey	12
	Santa Barbara	Santa Barbara	8

period, Santa Barbara had the second lowest total number of cattle of the missions studied, while San Buenaventura had an average amount (Table 7). La Purisima, never an active trader, had the largest cattle herds of all missions from 1822 through 1832.

During the early boom of hide and tallow exporting between 1822 and 1827, all of the missions except San Antonio showed evidence of active trading. San Fernando Rey, the second largest trader, liquidated a good portion of its cattle herds during this time, coincidentally allowing its formerly good crop production to fall to one of the lowest of all the missions. This suggests that either agricultural labor was being allocated to export production or general crop failures were being compensated for by increased exports.

Toward the end of the mission period, 1828 to 1832, San Buenaventura, San Juan Bautista, and San Miguel still appear among the most active traders. San Luis Obispo is the new leader in trading, however, with the largest drop in cattle herds. Mission San Antonio has also left its apparent trading isolation of the previous years and is among the largest exporters. San Fernando Rey appar-

ently terminates its previously active export industry, and Santa Ines also allows its herds to increase.

SUMMARY OF SANTA BARBARA DISTRICT MISSIONS
San Buenaventura

Prior to 1821 this mission was the best overall provisioner in the district and one of the best in California. San Buenaventura was active in the hide and tallow trade between 1817 and 1821, and continued as the largest volume trader in cattle products in the district through the end of the mission period. Corresponding with escalating trade after 1821, crop production suffered considerably.

Santa Barbara

Santa Barbara was the most populous and also the poorest economic producer of all the missions in the district. This mission began modest trading in hides and tallow between 1817 and 1821, and continued this level of export following the lifting of trade restrictions in

Table 6
SANTA BARBARA AND MONTEREY PRESIDIO DISTRICT MISSIONS
RANKED BY AVERAGE ANNUAL CATTLE REDUCTIONS

Presidio District	Mission	Implied Change in Herd Size	Trading Activity
		a. 1811–1816	
Monterey	San Carlos	–197	Moderate
		b. 1817–1821	
Santa Barbara	San Buenaventura	–5,155	Very high
Santa Barbara	Santa Barbara	–1,275	High
Monterey	San Antonio	+587	Moderate
Monterey	San Carlos	+613	Moderate
Monterey	San Miguel	+1,184	Low
Monterey	San Luis Obispo	+1,306	Low
Monterey	La Soledad	+1,510	Low
Santa Barbara	Santa Ines	+2,300	Low
Santa Barbara	La Purisima	+2,450	Low
Santa Barbara	San Fernando Rey	+2,792	Low
Monterey	San Juan Bautista	+3,060	Low
		c. 1822–1827	
Santa Barbara	San Buenaventura	–10,737	Very high
Santa Barbara	San Fernando Rey	–6,210	Very high
Monterey	San Miguel	–3,237	Very high
Monterey	San Juan Bautista	–2,768	High
Santa Barbara	Santa Barbara	–1,131	High
Monterey	San Carlos	–994	High
Monterey	San Luis Obispo	–939	High
Monterey	La Soledad	–122	Moderate
Santa Barbara	Santa Ines	0	Moderate
Santa Barbara	La Purisima	+267	Moderate
Monterey	San Antonio	+1,825	Low
		d. 1828–1832	
Monterey	San Luis Obispo	–4,410	Very high
Monterey	San Juan Bautista	–1,650	High
Santa Barbara	San Buenaventura	–1,477	High
Monterey	San Antonio	–1,136	High
Monterey	San Miguel	–990	High
Monterey	San Carlos	–158	Moderate
Santa Barbara	Santa Barbara	–67	Moderate
Monterey	La Soledad	+7	Moderate
Santa Barbara	La Purisima	+8	Moderate
Santa Barbara	Santa Ines	+984	Low
Santa Barbara	San Fernando Rey	+1,250	Low

1822; the largest reductions in livestock were made in the sheep flocks.

La Purisima Mission

La Purisima was a respectable producer of both crops and livestock; crop production improving significantly after 1812, when the mission moved to its second site.

Evidence indicates only minimal participation in the hide and tallow trade, although major reductions were made in sheep holdings after 1821.

San Fernando Rey

Like Santa Barbara, San Fernando Rey's per-capita livestock statistics never substantially improved over time,

Table 7
Santa Barbara and Monterey Presidio District Missions, Ranked by Average Annual Size of Cattle Herds

Presidio District	Mission	Herd Size
	a. 1822–1827	
Santa Barbara	La Purisima	9,467
Monterey	San Juan Bautista	7,892
Monterey	San Luis Obispo	7,050
Monterey	San Antonio	6,536
Santa Barbara	Santa Ines	6,200
Santa Barbara	San Buenaventura	6,187
Santa Barbara	San Fernando Rey	5,350
Monterey	San Miguel	4,931
Monterey	La Soledad	4,305
Santa Barbara	Santa Barbara	2,317
Monterey	San Carlos	1,946
	b. 1828–1832	
Santa Barbara	La Purisima	9,475
Santa Barbara	Santa Ines	7,184
Santa Barbara	San Fernando Rey	6,600
Monterey	San Juan Bautista	6,242
Monterey	San Antonio	5,400
Santa Barbara	San Buenaventura	4,710
Monterey	La Soledad	4,312
Monterey	San Miguel	3,941
Monterey	San Luis Obispo	2,640
Santa Barbara	San Buenaventura	2,250
Monterey	San Carlos	1,788

a situation that may be due to poor soils or to early loss of mission lands to private ranchos. San Fernando Rey was an active participant in the hide-and-tallow trade after 1821, second only to San Buenaventura, although it later began to accumulate cattle surpluses. This mission had good crop production prior to 1821, after which it fell to the lowest rates in the district.

Santa Ines Mission

This mission had one of the best crop production records in California and had respectably sized livestock herds. Large reductions in sheep herds were made at the inception of legal trade in 1822, although cattle sales were restricted to maintaining herd size, suggesting minimal trading activities. Between 1828 and 1832, trade diminished further as cattle herds again increased.

SUMMARY OF MONTEREY DISTRICT MISSIONS
San Carlos

San Carlos has the highest per-capita crop production and one of the lowest per-capita livestock ratios in the

district. With populations in serious decline by the 1810 to 1817 period, this mission made large reductions in sheep herds and apparently exported cattle products. Export activity slows down in the 1817 to 1821 period and then continues modestly through the end of the mission tenure.

San Antonio

The most populous mission in the district, San Antonio has one of the poorest records for crop production and the poorest for per-capita livestock. There is some suggestion of early trading in the 1817 to 1821 period although major reductions in cattle herds do not occur until after 1827.

San Luis Obispo

San Luis Obispo is one of the best producers of both crops and livestock in the district. Reductions in sheep flocks began prior to 1821, although exporting of cattle products did not apparently begin until after this date. After 1827, reductions in cattle herds quadrupled, identifying this mission as by far the most active trader in the district.

La Soledad

The smallest mission in the district, La Soledad was one of the best provisioners of crops and livestock per capita. Trading began after 1821 but never reached proportions large enough to significantly reduce the average size of cattle herds.

San Juan Bautista

One of the largest missions in the district, its population reached a late peak in 1823. Although sheep flocks were being reduced prior to 1821, trading in cattle products apparently began after that date and continued at respectable, although decreasing, levels until the end of the mission period.

San Miguel

San Miguel was, with San Antonio, the poorest provisioner in the district. The mission was, however, the largest district trader between 1821 and 1827, and continued to be active until the end of the mission period, showing large decreases in sheep flocks as well as cattle herds.

Traveler's Comments

Historic documentary accounts were examined for references to mission economic activities and for observations on the relative economic success between institutions. Although evaluations made by different people at different times cannot reliably be equated, a series of evaluations made of several missions by one individual are assumed to represent valid comparisons. Observations on the general economic success and quality of life at individual missions help to define variation between institutions.

All known historic accounts made by foreign travelers to Alta, California between 1786 and ca. 1835 were examined (Costello 1990b). Over 30 chroniclers provided descriptions of missions, and 12 of these specifically visited the Santa Barbara and Monterey Districts. Although there are voluminous accounts by Spanish priests and officials that might also be useful, most Spanish written material is of an official nature and occasional remarks on relative mission conditions are difficult to extract from the lengthy correspondence. Travelers and visitors, however, regularly record descriptive information on the places they visit and often compare one mission institution to another. They are, therefore, a convenient source for this type of information.

Summaries of these chroniclers' economic observations were organized by topics commonly addressed in the narratives. These include the condition of buildings and housing, attributes of clothing, abundance and types of food, general cleanliness, Indians' health, and personal attributes of the padres, as well as more directly economic topics, such as land and climate, cultivation, production, livestock, industries, and trading (Costello 1990a).

Using visitors' observations to determine differences between missions is difficult, as the depth of accounts are uneven between chroniclers, and the same individual often does not make similar observations at each establishment. Nevertheless, an appreciation is gained for the diversity of living conditions and management at the different mission institutions in California at any one time. In an effort to determine relative economic conditions for individual missions, and change in these conditions over time, those accounts are summarized that include missions from the Santa Barbara and Monterey Districts, address more than one mission, and make some comparative statements between establishments.

1792: Vancouver (1954)

Vancouver ranks San Buenaventura highest among the missions for buildings, gardens, produce, and cultivated land. San Juan Capistrano and Santa Clara rank second, with excellent land and superior agricultural produce; San Juan Capistrano also has extensive livestock holdings and Santa Clara has fine buildings. San Antonio is also noted for having superior land, with San Luis Obispo and Soledad additionally located on good ground. Santa Barbara ranks above average, with its poor land being offset somewhat by good food and fine buildings. San Carlos is undistinguished in its accommodations and agriculture, while the lowest ranking mission is San Francisco, primarily due to poor agricultural production.

1792: Menzies (1924)

San Buenaventura, with enormous production, was ranked first of the missions, while Santa Clara and San Juan Capistrano were second. Santa Barbara appeared to be taking better care of resident Indians than other missions, although it had small livestock holdings. San Diego and San Carlos had average production, with the former having relatively small numbers of livestock. San Francisco had the lowest evaluation due to the poor climate for growing crops.

1804: Shaler (1808)

All of the missions were variously described as productive, except San Diego, which was deemed inferior.

1825: Morrell (1832)

The conditions and attributes of the Indians, and the nature of the priests, are praised at both Santa Clara and San Antonio; San Carlos is noted as having a small population.

1826–1827: Beechey (1831)

Mission San Jose ranks highest, particularly for health and general living conditions, with Santa Clara close behind. Santa Cruz and San Juan Bautista also rank among these most productive missions, while Santa Barbara is noted as making a good wine. San Francisco has fallen into disrepair and is being decimated by disease.

1827–1828: Duhaut-Cilly (1929)

The richest missions in the south are identified as San Gabriel and San Luis Rey, while in the north they are San Jose and Santa Clara. San Luis Obispo and Santa Barbara also ranked highly, the latter primarily due to the attentions of the padres. Santa Cruz is only mentioned as having more cattle than San Francisco, which is identified as the poorest in the country. San Carlos, Solano, and San Raphael also receive poor evaluations: San Carlos being nearly depopulated and Solano because it is new and yet undeveloped. San Buenaventura is also dismissed with a poor rating.

1828: Khlebnikov (1940)

The highest rated mission is San Luis Rey for agriculture, livestock, and the management of an "enlightened" padre. Cattle are most abundant at San Diego, San Gabriel, San Luis Obispo, and San Jose, while gardens are praiseworthy at Santa Cruz, Santa Barbara, and San Gabriel. San Juan Bautista is recognized as having an exceptional padre.

1829: Green (1915)

He only observes that San Carlos is in better condition than San Francisco.

1829–1831: Robinson (1944, 1969)

The largest, "best," and most productive missions on the coast are identified as San Luis Rey and San Gabriel, with San Jose and Santa Clara also ranking among the highest. Missions that were once great but were now in a state of decay are San Juan Capistrano, San Luis Obispo, and La Purisima, although there is still a great deal of livestock at the latter. San Francisco is also in a dilapidated state, although still trading in hides. San Fernando Rey is suffering from a tight-fisted priest who refuses to trade, while the wealth of San Luis Rey is accompanied by harsh enforcement of church discipline. Santa Barbara and San Antonio are noted as being particularly tidy and well run, while productive gardens and sizable livestock are observed at Santa Ines and San Buenaventura. La Soledad and San Miguel receive little mention, except that the latter, along with San Antonio, apparently has limited resources due to its inland location and the small size of its territories.

1832: Coulter (1951)

San Gabriel was identified as the best suited to support a large population, while San Carlos' crops were harmed by the mildew on the coast. The only population where young girls did not die in disproportionate numbers was at San Luis Rey.

1833–1834: Leonard (1934)

San Jose is the largest mission encountered with about 900 Indians; San Juan Bautista, with 600 to 700 Indians, has a church that is both larger and better decorated than that at San Jose.

1835–1836: Dana (1980)

San Buenaventura is the finest mission in the whole country, while Santa Barbara and San Diego are nearly deserted. San Jose and Santa Clara do a better business in hides than any other mission; San Francisco has no trade at all.

COMPARISON OF PRODUCTION STATISTICS AND HISTORIC ACCOUNTS

Correlation of levels of trading activity in the Santa Barbara and Monterey Districts, as indicated by declines in cattle herds (Table 6) and the historical assessments of mission economies is given in Table 8. There is agreement between high visitors' assessments of economic life and active hide-and-tallow trading at San Juan Bautista and San Buenaventura, and poor conditions and little trading at San Fernando Rey. The low evaluation that Duhaut-Cilly gives San Buenaventura in 1827 is surprising, as this mission is praised by most. In 1792, Menzies reports that the mission is in "a higher state of improvement than any they had yet seen in the Country" (Menzies 1924:328),

Robinson praises the agriculture in 1829 (Robinson 1969:49–50), and in 1835 Dana describes it as the finest mission in the whole country (Dana 1980:184). Duhaut-Cilly's comment,

> ...We passed in front of Mission San Buenaventura. This establishment is a poor one, and the anchorage there is bad; so we did not stop (Duhaut-Cilly 1929:1:164),

likely simply includes second-hand, erroneous information.

There are several instances, however, where high and moderate trading levels were accompanied by low evaluations of mission conditions: at San Carlos, San Luis Obispo, and La Purisima. The low evaluation for San Carlos Mission was given by Duhaut-Cilly in 1828:

> Mission San Carlos is built upon a little bay, open to the southwest and offering neither shelter nor anchorage. It is poor and almost depopulated of Indians (Duhaut-Cilly 1929:1:151).

The large cattle reductions between 1821 and 1828 are probably in response to this mission's dramatically shrinking population: 234 Indians in 1828 and only 185 in 1832. Livestock reductions here, therefore, do not represent a lively economy as much as the drastic decreases in labor, resulting in early deterioration of this establishment.

San Luis Obispo was also given a poor economic assessment by travelers at the same time it was by far the most active trader in the Santa Barbara and Monterey Districts (1828–1832) (Table 6). These massive reductions in cattle resulted in lowering the per-capita livestock ratio to pre-1810 levels, a serious depletion of resources. In ca. 1830 Robinson describes San Luis Obispo:

> This Mission, though formerly a wealthy establishment, is now of little importance. The buildings are in a decayed state, and every thing about them appears to have been much neglected....This mission possesses excellent horses, and a great many good mules; but, owing to want of attention, many of them are permitted to stray away, and mix with the wild cattle of the mountains (Robinson 1969:84–85).

The reason for the lack of upkeep of the mission in view of their apparently large income from trading is not known. It may be that mission assets were being liquidated and dispersed to the Indians. In 1834,

> ...The padre of S. Luis Obispo was ordered by his prelate to convert the mission wealth as rapidly as possible; and he bought $20,000 worth of cotton, woolen, and silk goods which he distributed among the neophytes [Indians]... (Bancroft 1966:349).

La Purisima was still conducting some moderate trad-

Table 8
COMPARISON OF TRADING ACTIVITIES (TABLE 6) AND ETHNOGRAPHIC RATINGS OF MISSION ECONOMIES

Mission	ca. 1821–1828		ca. 1828–1832	
	Trading	Economy	Trading	Economy
San Carlos	High	Low	Moderate	—
San Antonio	Low	—	High	—
San Luis Obispo	High	—	Very high	Low
San Buenaventura	Very high	Low	High	High[a]
Santa Barbara	High	—	Moderate	—
La Purisima	Moderate	—	Moderate	Low
La Soledad	Moderate	—	Moderate	—
San Juan Bautista	High	High	High	
San Miguel	Very high	—	High	—
San Fernando Rey	Very high	—	Low	Low
Santa Ines	Moderate	—	Low	—

[a] 1835: Dana (1980).

ing when Robinson visited in 1829 and described the mission:

> ...though possessing abundant wealth, in cattle and planting grounds, yet it has been much neglected, and the Indians generally are ill clothed, and seem in the most abject condition (Robinson 1969:49).

Here, as at San Luis Obispo, the proceeds from trading were not apparent in the mission facilities or the condition of the Indians. It is evident from the above information that active participation in foreign trade did not ensure better living conditions for the Indian residents.

Summary of Findings

TRADING ACTIVITIES AND AGRICULTURAL PRODUCTION

Production statistics and descriptions by visitors have highlighted the range of economic conditions that existed at the California missions. Some of the general differences in agricultural production between missions of the Monterey and Santa Barbara Presidio Districts can be attributed to ecological factors. Crops do better in the central district of Santa Barbara, which has longer growing seasons than the north, while livestock do better on the cooler and more verdant lands of the Monterey District. However, local ecological factors could override regional trends. The poor crop-production records of the Santa Barbara Mission are corroborated by visitors' comments about the poor croplands at this location. San Fernando Rey is also identified as having unproductive country. San Carlos' crops were mentioned by one visitor as being hurt by fogs, although its croplands were located away from the coast and it had one of the best per-capita crop ratios of all the missions studied. Fogs and winds at the first La Purisima site were improved by removal to a new location in 1812, resulting in a dramatic increase in crop production.

There does not appear to be any drought-related cause for the decline in crop production felt at virtually all missions after 1821. Some ecological explanations may be found in infestations of birds, gophers, and crickets noted by travelers (Khlebnikov 1940:320–322; Coulter 1951:22–25). Declines in yields may also have resulted from soil depletions and increases in pests, disease, and weeds (Nye and Greenland 1960:75), but these variables have yet to be investigated.

Some geographic variables were influential in the economies of individual missions. Access to coastal resources was important for the Santa Barbara Mission, which supplemented its poor agricultural yields with regular harvesting of sea resources by the Indians (Vancouver 1954:227; Menzies 1924:326). Isolation from the coast was also identified as an important factor in limiting the resources of San Antonio and San Miguel Missions. Proximity to presidios and pueblos also appears to have been influential in mission economic development. San Carlos' location near the capital of Monterey may account for it being the earliest and only large exporter of cattle products between 1811 and 1816. San Buenaventura and Santa Barbara were the only significant hide-and-tallow traders between 1817 and 1821, an activity that must have been uniquely encouraged by the promotion of favorable trading policies by the Santa Barbara Presidio. During this same time period, northern missions were developing export specialties in agricultural produce, supplying the Russians through the ports of San Francisco, Monterey, and Santa Cruz. San Fernando Rey was unique in California for suffering loss of extensive tracts of land to private ranchos prior to 1804, an activity that may have contributed to its poor livestock holdings.

For some missions, the onset of active foreign trading more than compensated for the end of economic support from Spain. It brought in a larger volume of goods than had previously been available, and transactions conducted in cash or through direct bartering were more efficient and immediate than the old system, where all purchases, sales, and accounts were handled in Mexico City. Mission participation in this new trade was not equal, however, and some suffering occurred where exports were minimal.

Richness of cattle assets did not appear to influence levels of trading activity, as the most active missions often had very low or moderate herd sizes and per-capita livestock ratios (Tables 6 and 7). It is also somewhat surprising that the district with the best crop production statistics, Santa Barbara, would exhibit the greatest reduction in cattle, while the northern district of Monterey, with the highest per-capita livestock holdings, maintained its crop production. The reason for this latter anomaly may be found in the extensive trading in agricultural products with the Russians, which between 1817 and 1825 took place primarily through the port of Monterey.

Although the general decline in crop production after 1821 may have some ecological causes, the demonstrated correlation between poorer harvests and increased trading activities is compelling. It is likely that the new reallocation of Indian labor from tending crops to preparing cattle products for export contributed to falling agricultural yields.

THE PADRES AND THEIR MISSIONS

During the final decade of the missions, historical accounts indicate an increasing disparity between living conditions at individual missions that do not appear related to the environment. There is an increase in the number of institutions in the Santa Barbara and Monterey Districts that, although once productive and prosperous, are in a state of decay by the late 1820s: San Carlos, San Luis Obispo, La Purisima, and San Fernando Rey. The decline of these missions apparently is not directly related to either their level of trading activity or their crop and livestock production.

Under the trading contracts after 1823, missions were first introduced to the world of international trading: they developed a product that could be sold abroad, methods of transport to ports, skills at negotiation, and a better idea of the value of both their own and imported goods. At least in general they did. It is at this point that the mercantile skills and motivations of individual padres appear to have began to produce significant differences between institutions. Although discrepancies in produc-

tion had existed prior to the introduction of the export economy, the ready availability of cash and consumer goods appeared to heighten economic differences. After the end of the British company's contracts by 1827, missions were free to trade on their own, and the discrepancies between them widened further. Some missions practiced regular depletions of cattle, implying controlled trading; others had episodic participation, which lowered herd size drastically in a short period of time; and a few, such as San Buenaventura, were always large-volume traders.

At least as significant as variables of ecology and geography, the economic success and living conditions at individual missions were dependent on the character and administrative abilities of the senior priest. Most missions retained their director-padres for many years, and his influence on the development of the mission, especially in these later, critical years of economic change, was profound. The new trading-based economy, unsupported by church funds, relied on individual mission economic strategies, which were, in turn, dependent on the skills of the clerics. Substantial differences between these men resulted in an increased range of mission economic performances.

The relationship between physical comforts at the missions and the well-being of the inhabitants was noted by travelers (Beechey 1831:20), as was the absolute power that the senior clerics held over their institutions (Leonard 1934:162; Peard 1974:218). Jose Bandini observed in 1828:

> All the missions of Alta California are under the care of Franciscan missionaries, of whom there are at present twenty-seven, most of them of advanced age. Each administers one mission and in it has absolute authority. The labor of the fields, the harvest of grain, the slaughter of cattle, the work of the shops, and all of those things that may concern the mission are directed by the Padre; and he alone attends to the sales, purchases, and business agreements, without interference from anyone. Thus if a mission is fortunate enough to have a hard-working and capable minister its neophytes will enjoy an abundance of the necessities of life; but poverty and misery in a mission give palpable evidence of the inactivity of him who directs it (Bandini 1951:6).

Ethnohistoric accounts provide numerous examples of mission conditions throughout California that are directly attributed to the influence of individual Franciscans. San Fernando Rey, where conditions could have been improved by trading, suffered under the miserly hand of Fr. Francisco Ibarra (1820 to 1835), who, surrounded by tradable commodities, kept his establishment in a state of poverty (Robinson 1969:35). The prosperity of San Luis Rey was attributed to the efforts of Father Peyri (Forbes 1937:142–143), also responsible for the reported misery of his Indians produced by severe enforcement of religious discipline

(Robinson 1969:26). Other priests remarked upon include Father Felipe Arroyo at San Juan Bautista, who learned the Indian language and gained the respect of his charges (Khlebnikov 1940:313), and the drunkard priest at San Juan Capistrano, who was partially credited with this mission's early demise (Pattie 1930:215).

In the San Diego Presidio District, San Gabriel Mission achieved great economic success under Father Jose Zalvidea (1806 to 1827), who at the same time caused the Indians to suffer greatly under his strict edicts. Hugo Reid's eloquent contrast between Zalvidea and his successor, Sanchez, documents dramatic changes observed in both the appearance and attitude of the Indians under a new priest, with no substantial changes in the economy (Reid 1978:270–280).

> The padre [Zalvidea] had an idea that finery led Indians to run away, for which reason he never gave either men or women any other clothing (including shirts and petticoats) than coarse frieze (*xerga*) made by themselves, which kept the poor wretches all the time diseased with the itch. If any handkerchiefs or cotton goods were discovered among them, the same was immediately committed to the flames (Reid 1978:273–274).

Under his successor, Sanchez, however:

> ...the females had their friez (*xerga*) converted into sweat cloths, and more suitable garments provided them. This measure effected a great change, for now of a Sunday might be seen coming out of church, women dressed in petticoats of all patterns and colors, with their clean chemise protruding from the bosom, with a 'kerchief round the neck and *rebozo* round the shoulders; while the men had their pants, jacket, trousers, hat and fancy silk sash. Even the children sported in a white or fancy shirt, with a handkerchief tied around the head (Reid 1978:278).

Idiosyncratic buying is also evident in the previously discussed archaeological remains from San Buenaventura and La Purisima. The paucity of English ceramics at San Buenaventura Mission is in apparent contrast to its documented role as one of the most active trading institutions in California. At La Purisima, in contrast, a low trading profile seems to contradict the remarkably high percentages of imported English and Chinese wares found in the Indian residences. It may have been that at San Buenaventura local pottery production was successful and ceramics were not purchased in large quantities by the padres, as they did not seem necessary; while at La Purisima, there was little local pottery production, and Indian households were therefore supplied primarily with imported wares.

The fathers at Missions Santa Barbara and San Antonio were credited with producing clean and cheerful mission settings from less than abundant resources. At the latter institution, both production statistics and ceramic data suggest that the padres initially refrained from active participation in the hide and tallow trade, apparently only deciding to embrace this economic activity in the late 1820s. At this time, the size of livestock herds fell sharply and the Indians received new, English ceramics for use in their residences.

The living conditions at individual missions apparently had as much to do with the attitudes, dispositions, and talents of the missionaries as with economics.

Conclusions

Several conclusions can be drawn about the evolution of the California Mission economies based on the research outlined above. (1) Following the political and economic changes of the 1810 Mexican War of Independence, the missions became economically more autonomous and began to evidence increasingly divergent trading and buying patterns. (2) Although ecological and geographic factors generally influenced the agricultural success of the missions, local historical factors, particularly the talents of the individual padres, appears to be the primary factor in economic success in the later years. (3) Economic success, as reflected in high per-capita production and the presence of trade goods, did not necessarily equate with "good" living conditions for the Indian labor force.

In light of these conclusions, general statements concerning activities and living conditions throughout the California missions, especially concerning the years ca. 1810 to 1835, should be made with caution. Similarly, as generalizations made about the entire mission system may not be appropriate for particular institutions, conclusions drawn from research on one institution cannot be unreservedly extended to all other missions.

The present study has also provided suggestions of some patterns that may be applicable to colonial institutions in general. (1) Economic diversity increased as a result of increased political autonomy. (2) When institutional economic success depended on the capitalistic efforts of individuals, the ranges of success and failure dramatically enlarged. (3) Opportunities for greater extremes in the treatment of the native residents — both supportive and abusive — increased with the consolidation of power in the hands of individual priests.

The use of both archaeological and documentary data sources in this study, while illustrating the importance of wedding historical and archaeological approaches, more significantly demonstrates the value of using multiple data sources for researching and testing hypotheses. Three distinct avenues of inquiry were used for this study: excavated ceramic collections, agricultural production records, and observations made by foreign visitors. It is doubtful if the conclusions concerning increased mission economic variability could have been reached through one approach alone; observed patterns in any one data set certainly could not have been as fully interpreted without the advantage of the combined analysis.

References

Archibald, R. (1978) *The Economic Aspects of the California Missions.* Academy of American Franciscan History, Washington, D.C.

Bancroft, H. H. (1966) *The History of California, Vol. II, 1825–1840.* The Works of Hubert Howe Bancroft, Vol. XX. Reprinted. Wallace Hebberd, Santa Barbara. Originally published 1886, The History Company, San Francisco.

Bandini, J. (1951) *A Description of California in 1828.* Translated by Doris Marion Wright. Bancroft Library Publications, No. 3. The Friends of the Bancroft Library, Berkeley.

Beechey, F. W. (1831) *A Narrative of a Voyage to the Pacific and Beering's Strait, to Cooperate with the Polar Expeditions: Performed in His Majesty's' Ship Blossom, under the Command of Capt. F. W. Beechey...in 1825, 26, 27, 28.* H. Colburn and R. Bentley, London.

Bowman, J. N. (1958) The Resident Neophytes (Existentes) of the California Missions, 1769–1834. *Historical Society of Southern California Quarterly* 40(2):138–148.

Costello, J. G. (1989a) Variability Among the California Missions: The Economics of Agricultural Production. In *Columbian Consequences, Vol. 1: Archaeological and Historical Perspectives on the Spanish Borderlands West,* D. H. Thomas, Ed. Smithsonian Institution, pp. 345–350.

— (1989b) *Excavations at Santa Ines Mission 1986–1988.* California Historical Archaeology, No. 1. Coyote Press, Salinas, CA.

— (1991a) *Variability and Economic Change in the California Missions: An Historical and Archaeological Study.* Unpublished Ph.D. dissertation, Department of Anthropology, University of California, Santa Barbara.

— (1991b) *Documentary Evidence for the Spanish Missions of Alta California,* Vol. 14, The Spanish Borderlands Sourcebooks, Garland Press, New York, in press.

Coulter, T. (1951) *Notes on Upper California.* Glen Dawson, Los Angeles.

Dana, R. H. (1980) *Two Years Before the Mast.* Macmillan Company, New York. Reprinted. Mayflower Books. Originally printed by Harper and Brothers, New York, in 1840.

Deetz, J. (1978) Archaeological Investigations at La Purisima Mission. In *Historical Archaeology: A Guide to Substantive and Theoretical Contributions,* R. L. Schuyler, Ed. Baywood, Farmingdale, NY, pp. 160–190.

Duhaut-Cilly, A. B. (1929) Duhaut-Cilly's Account of California in the Years 1827–1828. Translated by C. F. Carter. *California Historical Society Quarterly* 8(1,2,3):130–166, 214–250, 306–336.

Engelhardt, Z., O.F.M. (1915) *The Missions and Missionaries of California,* Volume 4. James H. Barry, San Francisco.

— (1920) *San Diego Mission.* James H. Barry, San Francisco.

— (1921) *San Luis Rey Mission.* James H. Barry, San Francisco.

— (1922) *San Juan Capistrano.* The Standard Printing Company, Los Angeles.

— (1923) *Santa Barbara Mission.* James H. Barry, San Francisco.

— (1924) *San Francisco or Mission Dolores.* Franciscan Herald Press, Chicago.

— (1927) *San Gabriel Mission and the Beginnings of Los Angeles.* Mission San Gabriel, San Gabriel.

— (1929a) *San Antonio de Padua: The Mission in the Sierras.* Mission Santa Barbara, Santa Barbara.

— (1929b) *Mission Nuestra Senora de la Soledad.* Santa Barbara Mission, Santa Barbara.

— (1929c) *San Miguel, Archangel: The Mission on the Highway.* Mission Santa Barbara, Santa Barbara.

— (1930) *San Buenaventura: The Mission by the Sea.* Mission Santa Barbara, Santa Barbara.

— (1931) *Mission San Juan Bautista: A School of Church Music.* Mission Santa Barbara, Santa Barbara.

— (1932a) *Mission Santa Ines: Virgen y Martir and its Ecclesiastical Seminary.* Mission Santa Barbara, Santa Barbara.

— (1932b) *Mission La Concepcion Purisima de Maria Santisima.* Mission Santa Barbara, Santa Barbara.

— (1963) *Mission San Luis Obispo in the Valley of the Bears.* W. T. Genns, Santa Barbara.

— (1973a) *San Fernando Rey: The Mission of the Valley.* Ballena Press. Ramona, CA.

— (1973b) *Mission San Carlos Borromeo (Carmelo): The Father of the Missions.* Ballena Press, Ramona, CA.

Farnsworth, P. (1987) The Economics of Acculturation in the California Missions: A Historical and Archaeological Study of Mission Nuestra Senora de la Soledad. Unpublished Ph.D. dissertation, Department of Anthropology, University of California, Los Angeles.

Forbes, A. (1937) *California: A History of Upper and Lower California.* John Henry Nash, San Francisco. Reprinted 1972 by Kraus Reprint, New York.

Green, J. S. (1915) *Journal of a Tour on the North West Coast of America in the Year 1829.* Charles Fred. Heartman, New York City.

Greenwood, R. S. (1975) *3500 Years on One City Block.* Greenwood and Associates. Submitted to Redevelopment Agency, City of Buenaventura, CA.

— (1976) *The Changing Faces of Main Street.* Greenwood and Associates. Submitted to Redevelopment Agency, City of Buenaventura, CA.

Hoover, R. L. and J. G. Costello, Eds. (1985) *Excavations at Mission San Antonio 1976–1978.* Monograph 26, Institute of Archaeology, University of California, Los Angeles.

Hornbeck, D. (1989) Economic Growth and Change at the Missions of Alta California, 1769–1846. In *Columbian Consequences, Vol. I: Archaeological and Historical Perspectives on the Spanish Borderlands West,* D. H. Thomas, Ed. Smithsonian Institution, Washington D.C., pp. 423–433.

Jackson, R. H. (1988) Patterns of Demographic Change in the Missions of Central Alta California. *Journal of California and Great Basin Anthropology* 9(2):251–272.

Khlebnikov, K. T. (1940) *Memoirs of California....* Translated and with introduction by A. G. Mazour. *The Pacific Historical Review* 9:307–336.

Leonard, Z. (1934) *Narrative of the Adventures of Zenas Leonard, Written by Himself,* M. M. Quaife, Ed. The Lakeside Press, R. R. Donnelley and Sons, Chicago.

Meko, D., C. Stockton, and W. Boggess (1980) A Tree-Ring Reconstruction of Drought in Southern California. *Water Resources Bulletin* 16:594–600.

Menzies, A. (1924) Menzies' California Journal. A. Eastwood, Ed. *California Historical Society Quarterly* 2(4):265–340.

Morrell, Capt. B. J. (1832) *A Narrative of Four Voyages to the South Seas, North and South Pacific Ocean, Chinese Sea, Ethiopia and Southern Atlantic Ocean, Indian and Antarctic Ocean, from the Year 1822 to 1831...* J. and J. Harper, New York.

Nye, P. H., and D. J. Greenland (1960) *The Soil Under Shifting Cultivation.* Technical Communication No. 51. Commonwealth Bureau of Soils. H.A.R. Harpenden, Ed. Hollen St. Press, London.

Pattie, J. O. (1930) *The Personal Narrative of James O. Pattie, of Kentucky...* Lakeside Classics, New York.

Peard, G. (1974) The Views of Lieutenant George Peard, R. N., on Alta California, 1826 and 1827. B. M. Gough, Ed. *Southern California Quarterly* 56:213–232.

Reid, H. (1978) Letters on the Los Angeles County Indians. In *A Scotch Paisano in Old Los Angeles*, S. B. Dakin, Ed. University of California Press, Berkeley, pp. 215–286.

Robinson, A. (1944) Journal on the Coast of California by A. Robinson, on Board the Ship Brookline Year 1829; Ogden, A. in Alfred Robinson, New England Merchant. *California Historical Society Quarterly* 23(3):203–213.

— (1969) *Life in California: During a Residence of Several Years in That Territory...* Da Capo Press, New York; originally published 1846, New York.

Rowntree, L. B. (1985a) A Crop-Based Rainfall Chronology for Pre-Instrumental Record Southern California. *Climate Change* 7:327–341.

—(1985b) Drought During California's Mission Period, 1769–1834. *Journal of California and Great Basin Anthropology* 7(1):7–20.

Shaler, W. (1808) Journal of a Voyage Between China and the Northwest Coast of America Made in 1804. *The American Register: or General Repository of History, Politics, and Science.* Part 1 for 1808; Vol. III. C. and A. Conrad, Philadelphia.

Vancouver, G. (1954) *Vancouver in California.* Edited and annotated by Marguerite Eyer Wilber. Glen Dawson, Los Angeles.

7: Documentary and Archaeological Evidence for Household Differentiation in Colonial Soconusco, New Spain

Janine Gasco
Institute for Mesoamerican Studies
State University of New York, Albany, New York

A basic problem that all archaeologists face when trying to assess economic variability among households is how to measure differences in a meaningful way. This is difficult because, first, we must rely on material remains that represent an incomplete record of the goods that once existed in houses, and second, we must in some way evaluate the relative values of the items that we do find. For those of us working on historic period sites, the documentary record is a source of information that can provide details, not only about perishable materials, but also about the absolute and relative values of a wide variety of items.

My basic objectives in this paper are to illustrate how the documentary record can help us to gain a more complete understanding of the total range of goods that might be found in colonial Mesoamerican households and how documents can allow us to better assess the relative values of goods. A secondary objective is to stimulate interest among historical archaeologists working in Mesoamerica to examine certain kinds of documents that are particularly useful for archaeologists. Finally, historical archaeologists working in North America may find the data presented here useful for comparative purposes.

A wealth of information about material culture can be found in colonial documents. General information is contained in documents such as freight records, import/export lists, and tax records. More specific information about household consumption patterns can be found in the household inventories that are often included in wills and sometimes can be found in criminal investigations. In this paper I focus specifically on household inventories.

Probate inventories have become an important part of colonial North American social historical research (Jones 1977; Main 1982). In general, material culture studies have become an important element of the social history and ethnohistory of colonial North America (Schlereth 1983). Similarly, historical archaeologists working in North America have effectively used probate inventories not only to assess wealth, but also to track changing values (Deetz 1977). In addition, freight records have been used to compile price lists for ceramics (Miller 1980). These, in turn, have been used in studies of variable consumption patterns of households and communities (Spencer-Wood 1987).

For colonial Mesoamerica, ethnohistorians and social historians have used information in both Indian and Spanish wills to examine early colonial Aztec inheritance patterns and kinship patterns (Cline 1986, 1984; Kellogg 1986) and to examine the roles and behaviors of women (Lavrin and Couturier 1979). Economic historians also have used shipping records and inventories to examine questions related to material culture (Boyd-Bowman 1973, 1972).

Clearly the potential exists for using documents in innovative ways to examine household differentiation in colonial Mesoamerica, yet, to my knowledge, archaeologists working on historic sites in Mesoamerica so far have not made good use of such documents.

Household inventories frequently appear in wills, but they also appear in cases where the deceased failed to leave a will or an heir, and the estate is either being contested or is in the process of being taken over by the Crown. Less frequently, household inventories appear as part of the investigation of criminal cases. The most obvious use for household inventories is simply to compare the wealth of individuals. Yet for this and many other kinds of questions, one needs a good sample.

Ethnohistorians and social historians, no less than archaeologists, are concerned with the representativeness of their samples (Jones 1977:1809ff.; Lavrin and Couturier 1979). For much of colonial Mesoamerica, this presents an insurmountable problem for those of us interested in the whole spectrum of society. Generally, only wealthier people left wills or estates large enough to become the focus of Crown interest (Lavrin and Couturier 1979). This is not to say that Indians did not leave wills (Cline 1986; Cline and Leon-Portilla 1984), but it is clear that in many regions Indians were much less likely to leave wills than were Spaniards.

Although I have not yet made a concerted effort to seek out wills, during the course of archival research on the colonial Province of Soconusco, New Spain (Figure 1), I have inadvertently located several wills made by Spaniards who lived in the region. At the same time, I have only seen one such document for an Indian. While a more ambitious search will undoubtedly turn up more wills, I am not optimistic that I will ever find a large corpus of wills for the Indian population of Soconusco. Nevertheless, I am convinced that the available documents contain valuable information that can be used profitably.

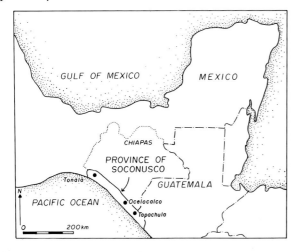

FIG 1. Province of Soconusco, Mexico.

The Colonial Soconusco Documents

During the course of archival research in the Archivo Histórico Diocesano de San Cristóbal de las Casas and the Archivo General de Centroamérica,[1] I had the opportunity to look at a number of documents that contained household inventories. Although these documents were not the focus of the research, when I saw lists of household goods together with prices, I was intrigued, particularly since many of the items on the lists were the very same items I had recovered while excavating at the

colonial Soconusco townsite of Ocelocalco (Gasco 1987, 1989).

Because of time limitations, I was only able to record information in seven documents that date from 1654 to 1833 (see Table 1 for description of documents). Six of the documents pertain to Spaniards, and the seventh lists the belongings of an Indian from the town of Ayutla (modern Tecún Umán, Guatemala). Three of the Spaniards were priests, one was a merchant, one was a deputy to the governor of the Province of Soconusco, and one was a woman. One of the inventories was included as part of a criminal investigation of an alleged theft. In four cases the items were simply assessed, and we are told what a particular item was worth. In two cases, however, the items were auctioned, so we know what someone actually paid for those items. In the seventh case, several items are identified by their prices (e.g., rings that cost 1 real). Some items were used, others were new. All of an individual's possessions were included in the inventories, including personal items (e.g., clothing, jewelry), household goods, tools, property, and livestock.

Large quantities of many of the goods suggest that one of the priests and the governor's deputy must have been acting as merchants, even though this was against the law. For example, hundreds of yards of cloth are included among the possessions of a parish priest in 1740, and dozens of pottery vessels are among the possessions of the deputy to the governor in 1654.

Household Inventories and Questions of Economic Differentiation

Previously I have examined household economic differentiaton within the colonial town of Ocelocalco, relying exclusively on archaeological data (Gasco 1988). In that study, I used what seemed to be straightforward measures of relative wealth based on artifacts recovered from residential structures at the site. I focused on Spanish-introduced pottery, that is, glazed, wheel-thrown pottery (majolica and lead-glazed earthenware), assuming that this pottery was relatively expensive and was therefore a good indicator of wealth. Specifically, I compared houses in terms of total percentages of Spanish-introduced pottery and in terms of diversity of majolica (tin-glazed earthenware) types. Briefly, both in terms of percentages of Spanish-introduced pottery, as well as diversity, the evidence from Ocelocalco suggested that economic disparities among households decreased as the Colonial period progressed.

With the new information from the household inventories, it is possible to review some of the assumptions

[1] Research was partially funded with a Travel Grant from the National Endowment for the Humanities.

Table 1
DOCUMENTS CITED

Date	Description	Citation
1654	Inventory of the house of Antonio Pastrana, Teniente del governador	AGCA A1 127 970
1674	Inventory of possessions of Lázaro Gaspar, Indian of Ayutla	AGCA A1 245 1770
1687	Inventory of possessions of Br. don Miguel Díaz Rubio, priest of Ayutla	AHDSCLC
1692	Inventory of house in Tonalá of Antonio Sanchez Pardillo	AGCA A1 259 1843
1724	Will of doña Petrona de Monjaras, resident of Acapetahua	AHDSCLC
1740	Will of Br. Francisco de Oliver, priest of Escuintla	AHDSCLC
1833	Inventory of possessions of don José Marciot y Ortega, priest of Tuxtla Chico	AHDSCLC

Abbreviations: AGCA: Archivo General de Centroamérica, Guatemala City; AHDSCLC: Archivo Histórico Diocesano de San Cristóbal de las Casas, Chiapas, Mexico

that I (and others) have made about the relative values of objects that are found archaeologically. These assumptions clearly have an effect on our interpretations about economic differentiation. The inventories also allow us to get a glimpse of a wide range of household goods that are not preserved in the archaeological record.

The items in several general categories found in the inventories can be expected to be at least partially preserved in the archaeological record. These categories include arms (Table 2), ceramics (Table 3), a variety of household and kitchen objects (Table 4), glass objects (Table 5), jewelry (Table 6), ground stone implements (Table 7), metal tools (Table 8), horse-related gear (Table 9), religious objects (Table 10), clothing and accessories such as buckles and buttons (Table 11), and furniture (Table 12). Whereas some objects found in excavations correspond exactly to written descriptions (e.g., *manos* and *metates*, machetes, majolica plates), there are other less obvious connections. For example, a brass button could come from one of many items of clothing, most with different monetary values.

Among the objects found in the inventories, ceramics are very much at the lower end of the price scale. Whereas in 1740 *piedras de moler* (grinding stones) were worth 4 pesos each, at the same time majolica from Puebla (of unspecified form) was worth 2 reales and porcelain vessels of unspecified form also were worth 2 reales. There were 8 reales in a peso, so this means that the grinding stones were worth 16 times as much as the glazed and porcelain pottery. Also, it is interesting to note that a *cantaro de Tehuantepec* (an indigenous tradition water jar) was valued at 2 to 3 reales. This means that

a porcelain vessel shipped from China was worth the same or even less than a *cantaro* from a neighboring province. This suggests that we may have to rethink some of our assumptions about "high-cost imported" goods.

Other items that might be recovered during excavations include arms, and these represent a much greater investment than pottery or grinding stones. In the mid-17th to mid-18th centuries they range in value from 3 to 16 pesos (Table 2). I might add that I did not find any arms parts that were recognizable at Ocelocalco. Machetes and knives (which I did find at Ocelocalco) range in value from 1 to 3 reales for knives (Table 4), and from 4 reales for an old machete to 1 peso, 2 reales for a new, large machete (Table 8). Glass goods cover a wide range of items and a similarly wide range of prices (Table 5). At the lower end of the spectrum are *copitas de cristal* and *vidrios de Puebla* at $1\frac{1}{2}$ reales (even cheaper than majolica vessels), and the most expensive item was a *frasquera completa con 6 frascos grandes* and *6 pequeños* (bottle case with 6 large and 6 small bottles or flasks) valued at 16 pesos in 1833. Here, I should add that I found little glass during excavations.

The absolute values of these items are meaningless unless we know a bit more about other apects of the economy. For example, how do these prices compare with wages and the cost of food? The only evidence I have regarding wages in the Soconusco for the time period covered here indicates that agricultural laborers were paid 2 reales per day for their work in the cacao orchards. In Central Mexico, Gibson reports that wages for agricultural workers in the 17th and 18th centuries were 1.5 to 2.5 reales per day (1964:250–251). This means that an

Table 2
ARMS

Item	Translation	Cost		Date
		Pesos	Reales	
Arcabus (bien tratado)	*Harquebuse* (in good condition)	16	4	1654
Carabina	Carbine	12		1654
Polvora/lb	Gunpowder/lb	1		1687
Escopeta (maltratado)	Musket (in poor condition)	8	4	1740
Espada	Sword	4		1740
Pistol (usada)	Pistol (used)	3		1740

Table 3
CERAMIC GOODS

Item	Translation	Cost		Date
		Pesos	Reales	
Apastle	Earthenware tub or basin	1	2.5	1687
Botizuela	Small pitcher or jar		2	1724
Cántaro (nuevo)	Water jar (new)		2	1724
Cántaro de Tehuantepec	Water jar from Tehuantepec		2–3	1740
Losita da Puebla	Small Majolica cups (?) from Puebla		1.5	1740
Paileta azul de loza	Blue Majolica basin		1	1833
Pichel blanco de loza	White Majolica pitcher		4	1833
Pichel de China celeste	Blue porcelain pitcher		4	1833
Plato azul de loza	Blue Majolica plate		2	1833
Plato de orilla azul de loza	Majolica plate with blue rim		2	1833
Plato de talavera o loza	Majolica plate		2.5	1833
Platón grande de orilla azul de loza	Large Majolica plate with blue rim	1		1833
Platón grande de orilla azul de loza	Large Majolica plate with blue rim		6	1833
Pocillo bueno	Good tea cup used for chocolate		2	1833
Pocillo quebrado	Broken tea cup		1	1833
Pocillo con su cajoncito de madera	Tea cup used for chocolate with wooden box		3	1833
Porcelanas	Porcelain (cups or bowls?)		2	1740
Pozuela de loza de China (maltratada)	Porcelain basin (in poor condition)		2	1724
Taza de China	Porcelain cup	1		1740
Tazita caldera	Soup cup?		1	1833

Table 4
MISCELLANEOUS KITCHEN AND HOUSEHOLD ITEMS

Item	Translation	Cost		Date
		Pesos	Reales	
Baul	Chest	5		1724
Caja de cedro con llave	Cedar chest and key	3		1740
Caja sin llave	Chest without key	2		1740
Candela	Candle		2	1654
Candela de cera	Wax candle		4	1687
Candela de cera	Wax candle		1	1654
Candelero de cobre	Copper candleholder		4	1740
Cedazo	Strainer		4	1740
Cofre grande de cedro con su herraje	Large cedar chest with accessories (lock and key)	2		1833
Cofre pequeño forrado con su herraje	Small lined chest with accessories	1	4	1833
Cuchillo de mesa	Table knive		2	1833
Cuchillo (nueva)	Knife (new)		3	1724
Cuchillo pequeña con bayna	Small knife with *bayna?*		1	1654
Embudo	Funnel		1	1833
Jabón de la Puebla (1 cajón)	Soap from Puebla (1 case)	28		1654
Navaja ordinaria con cabo de cuerno	Ordinary folding knife with horn handle		1	1654
Palmatoria de bronza	Small candlestick		4	1833
Pan de Jabón Mexicano	Loaf of Mexican soap		4	1654
Paragua de tafetán (usado)	Taffeta umbrella (used)	4		1833
Perol de cobre (quebrado)	Copper kettle (broken)	4		1833
Petate de Chiapa	Straw mat from Chiapa		2	1687
Petate	Straw mat		2	1740
Plancha de fierro para ropa	Clothes iron made of iron	2		1833
Plancha de plomo	Lead iron		1	1740
Plato de peltre (viejo)	Pewter plate (old)		5	1692
Plato de peltre	Pewter plate	4		1740
Platón de peltre abollado en partes	Large pewter plate partially embossed	1		1692
Tabaquero	Tabacco holder(?)		2	1692
Tintero y salvadera de cristal	Crystal inkwell and sandbox (for writing)		4	1833
Tintero y salvadera de bronze	Bronze inkwell and sandbox	1	4	1740

agricultural laborer was paying the equivalent of one day's wages to buy pots and the equivalent of almost 3 weeks' wages to buy a grinding stone. Much of Soconusco's Indian population actually owned their own cacao trees, and presumably they earned more than unskilled agricultural laborers did, therefore the acquisition of these items may have represented fewer days of work.

Corn prices in the 17th and 18th centuries fluctuated wildly. In Central Mexico, for example, *fanegas*, or bushels of corn, were valued at between 7 and 40 reales (Gibson 1964:453–454). For Soconusco, I do not have enough data to chart this kind of variability. The only evidence currently available indicates that in the late 17th

and 18th centuries, corn cost from 10 to 12 reales per *fanega*.

Other food items appear in the house inventories. In the late seventeenth century *frijoles* (beans) were assessed at 3 pesos per *fanega*, sugar cost 4 1/2 pesos per *arroba* (approx. 25 lbs), *canela* (cinnamon) cost 6 pesos per pound, fish was valued at 4 reales per *arroba* for *pescado podrido* (rotten fish) to 1 peso per *arroba* (for apparently good fish). Salt was worth 3 pesos to 3 pesos 6 reales per *tercio* (1/3 of a mule load) or 6 pesos per *carga*. *Pimienta* (pepper) from Spain was valued at 2 pesos per pound, and *pimienta* from Chiapas was worth only 1 real per pound.

Finally, textiles are the largest general category of items that appears in the inventories, and of course,

Table 5
GLASS

Item	Translation	Cost		Date
		Pesos	Reales	
Botella de vidrio	Glass bottle		2	1833
Copita de cristal	Crystal cup		1.5	1833
Cristales de tomar chocolate	Crystal cups for drinking chocolate		7	1740
Frasco grande de cristal	Large crystal bottle or flask		2	1833
Frasquera completa con 6 frascos grandes y 6 pequeños	Bottle case with 6 large and 6 small bottles		16	1833
Frasquera con 11 frascos	Bottle case with 11 bottles	4		1740
Frasquera con 6 frascos	Bottle case with 6 bottles	2		1740
Frasquito	Small bottle		2	1833
Limetas	Small bottle or vial	2	5	1740
Limetas	Small bottle or vial	3		1740
Pinchel de cristal	Crystal pitcher	1		1740
Salserillas de cristal	Small crystal vessel		4	1833
Vaso grande labrado de cristal	Large etched crystal glass	2	4	1833
Vidrio de Puebla	Glass (bottle?) from Puebla		1.5	1740

Table 6
JEWELRY

Item	Translation	Cost		Date
		Pesos	Reales	
Millares de abalorio, azul y blanco	Blue and white glass beads		4	1654
Anillo de plata sin piedra	Silver ring with no stone		1	1654
Anillo de China	Ring from China		0.5	1740
Zarcillos de cristal/par	Crystal earrings/pair	1		1740
Zarcillos de oro con 34 perlas	Gold earrings with 34 pearls	8		1740

textiles are unlikely to be preserved in the archaeological record. The textiles have been divided into three subgroups: clothing (Table 11), linens/bedding (Table 13), and yard goods (bolts of cloth, trimmings, etc., Table 14).

The assessed values of items of clothing, such as shirts, trousers, *huipiles, naguas,* and stockings, all tend to vary widely. Shirts range from 4 reales for an old *estopilla* (coarse cotton) shirt to a linen shirt valued at 3 pesos to shirts of unspecified fabric worth almost 7 pesos. Similarly, *huipiles* (Indian women's blouses) range from a low of 5 reales for a *huipil* of unspecified age, fabric, and provenience, to Zoquean *huipiles* worth 6 reales to a new silk and cotton *huipil* worth 3 pesos. *Petate* hats are valued between 1.5 and 4 pesos. In terms of wages, an agricultural laborer would have to work approximately 2 weeks to buy a linen shirt or a new silk and cotton *huipil* for his wife.

Suggestions for Future Work

Beyond these general comments regarding relative values of goods and the range of goods that might have existed in colonial Mesoamerican households, an obvious use for data from household inventories is the examination of household differences. At this early stage of the analysis, with only a handful of documents studied, I am reluctant to do this with the Ocelocalco data, but it is clearly a possibility for future work. However, I think that there are broader issues that also can be addressed with these data.

Table 7
GROUND STONE

Item	Translation	Cost		Date
		Pesos	Reales	
Mano de metate (nueva)	*Mano* (for a *metate*) (new)	1		1724
Metate con mano	*Metate* with *mano*	3		1724
Metate sin mano	*Metate* without *mano*	2		1724
Piedra de moler	Grinding stone (*metate?*)	4		1724

Table 8
METAL TOOLS

Item	Translation	Cost		Date
		Pesos	Reales	
Coa	Hoe		4	1687
Coa (nueva)	Hoe (new)	1		1724
Coa (servida)	Hoe (used)		3	1724
Fierro de herrar	Iron brand?	2		1740
Hacha	Axe	1		1687
Hacha (nueva)	Axe (new)	2	4	1724
Hacha (usada)	Axe (used)	1	4	1724
Machete	Machete		4	1687
Machete (vieja)	Machete (old)		4	1740
Machete larga (nueva)	Large *machete* (new)	1	2	1724
Machete larga (viejo)	Large *machete* (old)		6	1724
Machete mediano (nuevo)	Medium-sized *machete* (new)	1	1	1724
Martillo	Hammer		5	1692
Martillo	Hammer		4	1740
Sierra	Saw	1		1740
Tijeras	Scissors		4	1740

Table 9
HORSEGEAR

Item	Translation	Cost		Date
		Pesos	Reales	
Espuela	Spurs		2	1674
Estribos de fierro ordinario	Ordinary iron stirrups	1		1692
Freno	Bridle	1	2	1674
Laso pequeño	Small lariat	3		1654
Silla mediana sin estribos	Medium-sized saddle without stirrups	3		1740
Silla bordada de pita	Saddle, embroidered	12		1740
Silla sin estrivos	Saddle without stirrups	6		1740
Silla (vieja) de andar	Saddle (old)	3		1674
Baqueta	Ramrod	2		1833

Table 10
RELIGIOUS OBJECTS

Item	Translation	Pesos	Reales	Date
		Cost		
Camándula con su cruz	Rosary with a cross		4	1833
Cruzesita de oro (peso 3 ochabas)	Gold cross weighing 3/8 of a peso?	5	3	1740
Cuadro de los corozones sagrados	Painting of the sacred heart	12		1833
Cuadro de Nuestra Señora de la Luz	Painting of Our Lady of Light	12		1833
Imagen de Nuestra Señora de la Luz	Image of Our Lady of Light	2	4	1833
Medalla de latón	Metal medallion		0.5	1724
Medalla pequeña de estaño	Small tin medallion		1	1654
Rosario de ambar	Amber rosary	1	2	1740
Rosario de Chiapa	Rosary from Chiapa		0.5	1740
Rosario de coral	Coral rosary	1		1724

Table 11
CLOTHING

Item	Translation	Pesos	Reales	Date
		Cost		
Bata de zarasa	Chintz dressing gown	8		1740
Botas (usadas)	Boots (used)	1	2	1833
Calzoncillas de royal	Underwear of royal?		4	1833
Calzones cortos de punto negro	Knee breeches with black stitching?	2		1833
Calzones de paño pardo aforrados (viejos)	Dark woolen, lined breeches (old)	1		1674
Camisa	Shirt	2		1740
Camisa	Shirt	6	7	1687
Camisa	Shirt	4		1692
Camisa (maltratada)	Shirt (in poor condition)	1		1740
Camisa de estopilla	Shirt of coarse cotton	2		1833
Camisa de estopilla (vieja)	Shirt of coarse cotton (old)		4	1833
Camisa de lienzo	Shirt of coarse linen	3		1740
Camisa de ruan con balona de bretaña	Shirt of cotton or linen with collar? of Brittany	1		1674
Chaleco de terciopelo labrado con botones	Embroidered velvet waistcoat (or vest) with buttons	2		1833
Chaleco de terciopelo labrado	Embroidered velvet waistcoat	1		1833
Chaleco negro con botones de laton	Black waistcoat with metal buttons		6	1833
Chaqueta de indiana amarillo	Yellow chintz jacket		4	1833
Chaqueta de indiana morada/negro	Purple/black chintz jacket		6	1833
Cuello	Collar		4	1833
Cuello	Collar		6	1833
Gaban	Overcoat or caftan	1	4	1687

Table 11 (continued)
CLOTHING

Item	Translation	Cost		Date
		Pesos	Reales	
Huipil	Indian woman's blouse		5	1687
Huipil	Indian woman's blouse	1	5	1687
Huipil de hilo y seda (nuevo)	Indian woman's blouse of cotton and silk (new)	3		1724
Huipil Zoque	Zoque woman's blouse		6	1687
Medias blancas de hile	White cotton stockings		4	1740
Medias de hilo	Cotton stockings		1.5	1833
Medias de hilo	Cotton stockings		1	1833
Medias de hilo (usadas)	Cotton stockings (used)		1	1833
Medias de lana	Woolen stockings		4	1687
Medias de seda	Silk stockings	3		1740
Medias de seda (maltratadas)	Silk stockings (in poor condition)	1		1692
Medias de seda negra	Black silk stockings		4	1833
Medias de seda pequeñas	Small silk stockings	2		1740
Nagua ordinario/vara	Ordinary petticoat/skirt/*vara*		2	1724
Nagua/vara	Petticoat/skirt/*vara*	3	5	1687
Nagua (1 corte)	Petticoat/skirt	5		1687
Nagua de China (1 corte)	Petticoat/skirt from China (1 cut)	6		
Pantalones de dril celeste	Blue duck-cloth trousers		6	1833
Pantalones de raso blanco (usados)	White satin trousers (used)	1		1833
Solideo	*Calotte* (cap worn by clergy)		3	1833
Sombrero	Hat	3		1687
Sombrero aforrado	Lined hat	3		1687
Sombrero de petate	Straw hat	4		1833
Sombrero de petate forrado de negro	Straw hat lined with black cloth?	1	4	1833
Sombrero fino	Fine hat	3		1687
Sotana de sarga negra	Black serge cassock	4		1833
Vestido	Dress	4		1687
Vestido de gergetilla	Serge dress	3		1687
Zapatos	Shoes		2	1692

Table 12
FURNITURE

Item	Translation	Cost		Date
		Pesos	Reales	
Catre Granadino (nuevo)	Cot from Granada? (new)	25		1833
Catre (viejo)	Cot (old)	6		1833
Escritorio	Desk	8		1740
Escritorio (viejo)	Desk (Old)	4		1740
Mesa grande	Large table	4		1740
Mesa mediana	Medium-sized table	2		1740
Sillas de sentar	Chair	1	4	1740

Table 13
LINENS

Item	Translation	Cost Pesos	Cost Reales	Date
Colcha azul	Blue quilt or bedspread	1	4	1724
Colcha blanca de algodón	White cotton quilt	1		1833
Colcha de hilo blanco	White cotton(?) quilt	1	4	1724
Colcha de lana celeste	Blue wool quilt	2	4	1833
Colchón	Mattress	1	4	1724
Funda de almohada de rúan	Rouen linen pillowcase		4	1833
Funda de almohada	Pillowcase		3	1740
Funda de almohada de royal bordada	Embroidered royal(?) pillowcase		4	1833
Hamaca de brin	Canvass hammock	1		1833
Mantel	Tablecloth	1		1740
Mantel blanco de mesa	White tablecloth	1		1833
Paño de mano de crudo	Hand towel of unbleached cotton?		5	1724
Paño de mano de rúan	Rouen linen hand towel	1	6	1724
Sábana de crea	Dowlas (coarse linen) sheet	3		1740
Sábana de crea (vieja)	Dowlas sheet (old)	1		1833
Sábana de lienzo (usada)	Coarse linen sheet (used)	2	1	1740
Sábana de manta (usada)	Cotton? sheet (used)		4	1724
Sábana de manta (vieja)	Cotton? sheet (old)		2	1833
Sábana de rúan	Rouen linen sheet	2		1833
Servilleta blanca	White napkin		1	1833
Servilleta con cabaceras bordadas	Napkin with embroidered edges		1.5	1833
Servilleta con cabeceras con brillos bordados	Napkin with edges embroidered with lustrous thread?		2	1833
Servilleta de hilo	Cotton(?) napkin		1.5	1833
Sobrecama de Indiana de colores	Chintz bedspread	3		1833

Much has been written about official Spanish colonial trade policies, with the focus on Spain and Mexico, the Manila *galleon*, etc. Whereas many of the items found in the Soconusco house inventories might be found in official import or tax records (e.g., imported items and goods manufactured in Mexico City or Puebla), many other items undoubtedly escaped any official notice. We know very little about the kinds of goods that were produced in the provinces by native craftspeople and how these products were moved from one provincial region to another. A thorough examination of household inventories may be the best (and perhaps only) method for better understanding these aspects of colonial society. Among the goods produced by provincial craftspeople that appear in the Soconusco, house inventories are ceramic water jars from Tehuantepec, straw mats from Chiapa, ground stone objects, and handwoven textiles.

The data presented here represent only a small (and by no means random) sample of the values of certain items (at certain times) and the range of goods that were consumed in colonial households. As an exploratory effort, this is only a first step in what must become a more systematic and comprehensive data collection process. A cooperative effort that would result in the compilation of the values and range of goods found in Mesoamerican colonial households would be extremely useful for a wide range of research topics. To do this it is critical to be able to compare prices of items across time and space.

In conclusion, a major objective in this paper has been to alert Mesoamerican historical archaeologists to the great potential that household inventories have for better understanding household differences, as well as other topics. These inventories are perhaps most frequently viewed as containing detailed information about individuals, and are thus overlooked by problem-oriented archaeologists. However, their unique quality is that they also contain information that can be used to address broader issues.

Table 14
YARDGOODS AND SEWING ACCESSORIES

Item	Translation	Cost Pesos	Cost Reales	Date
Bramante/vara	Twine/vara[a]		6	1740
Bretaña ancha/vara	Cotton from Brittany/vara	1		1724
Bretaña/vara	Cotton from Brittany/vara	1		1740
Cambray bueno/vara	Good cambray/vara	2		1654
Encaje/vara	Lace/vara		1.5	1740
Encaje/vara	Lace/vara		1	1740
Encaje/vara	Lace/vara		5	1740
Estamena/vara	Tammy cloth/vara		4	1687
Floxa de seda/oz.	Loose silk/oz		4	1740
Gaza listada/vara	Ribbon for bows/vara		4	1740
Gerga/vara	Serge/vara		4	1687
Gerga/vara	Serge/vara		3	1687
Gerga/vara	Serge/vara		2.5	1740
Indiana francesa/vara de 3/4	French chintz of 3/4(?)	1		1833
Listón de China/vara	Ribbon from China/vara		1	1740
Listón de terciopelo labrado/vara	Embroidered velvet ribbon/vara		2	1833
Listón/vara	Ribbon/vara		1	1740
Listoncillo/vara	Small (narrow?) ribbon		2	1740
Madeja de hilo	Skein of yarn (thread)		2	1654
Madeja de hilo azul de algodón pequeño	Small skein of blue cotton thread		0.5	1654
Madejita de hilera blanca de Castilla	Small skein of white Castillan thread		0.5	1654
Madejita de pita de Chiapa	Small skein of string from Chiapa		1	1654
Paño de la Puebla/vara	Wool from Puebla/vara	2	4	1687
Puntas de manta/corte	Cotton lace?/cut	3		1740
Puntes de Flandes pequeñas/vara	Small Flemish lace/vara		1.5	1654
Rúan/vara	Rouen linen/vara	1		1724
Tafetán carmesi/vara	Crimson taffeta/vara	1		1740
Tafetán celeste/vara	Blue taffeta/vara	1		1687

[a] A vara is equal to approximately 2.8 ft.

References

Boyd-Bowman, P. (1973) Spanish and European Textiles in Sixteenth Century Mexico. *The Americas* 29(3):334–358.

— (1972) Two Country Stores in XVIIth Century Mexico. *The Americas* 28(3):239–251.

Cline, S. L. (1986) *Colonial Culhuacán, 1580–1600.* University of New Mexico Press, Albuquerque.

— (1984) Land Tenure and Land Inheritance in Late Sixteenth-Century Culhuacán. In *Explorations in Ethnohistory,* H. R. Harvey and H. J. Prem, Eds. University of New Mexico Press, Albuquerque, pp. 277–309.

Cline, S. L. and M. Leon-Portilla (1984) *The Testaments of Culhuacán.* UCLA Latin American Center Publications, Los Angeles.

Deetz, J. (1977) *In Small Things Forgotten.* Anchor Press/Doubleday, Garden City, NY.

Gasco, J. (1989) Material Culture and Indian Society in Southern Mesoamerica: The View from Coastal Chiapas, Mexico. Paper presented at the meetings of the Society for Historical Archaeology, Baltimore.

— (1988) Socioeconomic Change within Native Society in Colonial Soconusco, New Spain. Paper presented at the meetings of the Society for American Archaeology, Phoenix.

— (1987) Cacao and the Economic Integration of Native Society in Colonial Soconusco, New Spain. Ph.D. dissertation, University of California, Santa Barbara, University Microfilms, Ann Arbor.

Gibson, C. (1964) *The Aztecs under Spanish Rule.* Stanford University Press, Stanford.

Jones, A. H. (1977) *American Colonial Wealth*, 3 Vols. Arno Press, New York.

Kellogg, S. (1986) Aztec Inheritance in Sixteenth-Century Mexico City: Colonial Patterns, Prehispanic Influences. *Ethnohistory* 33(3):313–330.

Lavrin, A. and E. Couturier (1979) Dowries and Wills: A View of Women's Socioeconomic Role in Colonial Guadaljara and Puebla, 1640–1790. *Hispanic American Historical Review* 59(2):280–304.

Main, G. L. (1982) *Tobacco Colony Life in Early Maryland 1650–1720*. Princeton University Press, Princeton.

Miller, G. L. (1980) Classification and Economic Scaling of 19th Century Ceramics. *Historical Archaeology* 14:1–40.

Schlereth, T. J. (1983) Material Culture Studies and Social History Research. *Journal of Social History*, Summer 1983, pp. 111–143.

Spencer-Wood, S. M. Ed. (1987) *Consumer Choice in Historical Archaeology*. Plenum Press, New York.

Part C: Hypothesis Formation

8: From Ethnohistory to Archaeology: Ottawa and Ojibwa Band Territories of the Northern Great Lakes

Charles E. Cleland
Michigan State University, East Lansing, Michigan

During the five or six decades that anthropologists and archaeologists have given serious scholarly attention to the cultures and histories of upper Great Lakes people, it has been presumed that profound cultural changes occasioned by Euroamerican contact greatly diminished the usefulness of such studies for our understanding of prehistoric lifeways. Indeed, epidemic disease, consequent depopulation and social destabilization, movement due to war and trade, intense involvement in political struggles, the influence of Christian religions, and especially the adoption of Western material culture are cited as the causes of cultural discontinuity. It is, of course, true that these factors did impact native culture and in many places importantly so. Theories about culture change, which have tended to overemphasize both the impact of technology and the global involvement of Indian societies in mercantilism, have also led us to disregard or to underemphasize discrete local cultures and the continuity of these cultures in time and space. A direct consequence is that historical texts concerning such societies are assumed to have little relevance for the interpretation of archaeological data from prehistoric contexts.

There is, of course, an enormous range in the effects that Euroamerican cultural contact had on Native American societies. On the one extreme, some groups were totally annihilated, while on the other, contact was accompanied by change, which had scant impact on the principles through which culture was organized. It is suggested here that Ottawa, and particularly Ojibwa, represent societies that had not undergone substantive culture change by the end of the first third of the 19th century. If this is true, then these groups represent a very good case study for establishing ethnographic analogy to the proto- and prehistoric groups of the same region.

When the U.S. government began to deal intensively with the Ojibwa and Ottawa people of the upper Great Lakes in the period after the War of 1812, they encountered people who were not only politically organized, but who also maintained social organization based upon traditional principles, provisioned themselves from the land, resided in traditional territories, and maintained systems of reciprocal exchange. A great deal of written data in the form of correspondence, reports, census data, and contemporary maps indicate that this condition persisted though the northern two thirds of Michigan and Wisconsin, most of Minnesota, and in all of Ontario north of the Great Lakes. This is the case despite the presence of powerful external political influences, emerging mixed blood communities, vast change in material culture, and articulation with fur trade capitalists. All of these influences, it is argued here, were accommodated with little substantive cultural change. It is also, therefore, a contention of this paper that the study of 19th-century Indian culture of the upper Great Lakes can provide valuable clues for those who seek a better understanding of prehistoric Woodland culture in the region. Central to this thesis is the notion that both historic and prehistoric territories were conditioned by the same underlying ecological and economic constraints, and were organized on the basis of similar social and political mechanisms.

Specifically this study focuses on the geographic and demographic aspects of mid-19th century Ojibwa and Ottawa life, because this information can be directly applied to questions concerning prehistoric settlement systems and especially the spatial relationship between these people. It is not the goal of this study to test propositions that may emerge, but rather to suggest hypotheses for future study.

In order to show that mid-19th century historical data are useful to the interpretation of Late Woodland data, it is necessary to advance several major assumptions. The first is that the Ojibwa and Ottawa people of the mid-19th century had subsistence requirements very similar to people of the region prior to contact. Central to this assumption is that population distribution, density, and composition were also similar. First, as I have recently argued, the Late Woodland population in the region fluctuated very dramatically during the period after A.D. 800 (Cleland, 1989). For this reason it is impossible to determine a prehistoric population base, since prehistoric populations are likely to have fluctuated almost as dramatically as historic populations. Some may suggest, of course, that historic population levels were drastically depressed as the result of European epidemic diseases. While this may well have been the case in the 17th century, Kay (1984) has convincingly argued that some northern Great Lakes populations recovered from these epidemic losses quite rapidly. By the time of the first reliable Indian census in the upper Great Lakes in 1839, it is probable that population had not only recovered, but was likely higher than the low population levels that seem to have characterized the region in the period shortly prior to contact. Even if 19th-century population size is close to that of the late prehistoric, some historians have argued that historic Indian population was more concentrated, particularly around trading and mission establishments. This proposition is to some degree true, since census data show some large settlements as Wikwemikong on Manitoulin Island, Sault Ste. Marie, Chequamegon, Fond du Lac, Lac Court Oreilles, Lac du Flambeau, and La Abre Croche. Some of these sites are also the location of very large prehistoric sites, raising the question as to whether Indians are flocking to traders or whether traders are flocking to concentrations of Indians. In either case, these large settlements are clearly a summer phenomenon. Certainly the people of these larger towns were not dependent on Euroamericans for provisioning. Instead, the historical records indicate it was the missionaries and traders, the permanent residents of these places, who often suffered hunger during the winter months.

A second necessary assumption is that the subsistence resources garnered by historic Ottawa and Ojibwa were essentially similar to those relied upon in prehistoric times. In fact, archival and other evidence leaves no doubt that deer, moose, wild rice, garden products, and especially fish formed the core of both prehistoric and historic diets. Faunal analysis from sites occupied during both periods indicates very little difference in the kinds and quantities of resources consumed. This is true despite the use of firearms in hunting and the diversion of effort to the production of furs. By and large, the acquisition of fur could be accomplished within preexisting seasonal rounds. Time and effort for the processing of fur was made possible on the energy surplus achieved by the two most important fur trade items, cloth and tailored clothing (Anderson n.d.). An exception in the subsistence-fur trade compatibility occurred at the end of the period of the most intensive trade; that is, the early 1820s when the fur bearer supply was depressed by overtrapping and a new market developed for deer, moose, and caribou hides. The Ottawa and southern Ojibwa were literally forced to begin overkilling their major food to accommodate trader demand. This trend may have as its northern counterpart the fish-hare period suggested by Rodgers and Black (1976). With the demise of the intensive trade in the mid-1830s, subsistence systems soon recovered.

A final assumption is that mid-19th century territorial requirements were similar to those of prehistoric times. Basically this assumption follows those that reflect the quantity and quality of food extracted as a measure of need plus the assumption that ecological components of the environment were similar. In the mid-19th century there were no major ecological disruptions in the Great Lakes region beyond those produced by natural processes.

It is, of course, in the examination of this last assumption that we find the best opportunity to use documentary materials to generate hypotheses of interest to archaeologists. The use and distribution of raw materials, patterns of trade, the definition of style pools, and the recognition of discrete distribution of specific artifacts and artifact styles, as well as seasonal rounds, all presumably are impacted by territorial boundaries. This is so because the behaviors of people in these activities are conditioned by limitations of communication and/or habitual travel imposed by boundaries. It is important to note that in the case of reciprocal exchange systems, boundaries enhance long-distance exchange by focusing exchange between groups through a trade nexus that has both a social and geographic dimension. If it is possible to establish the location of boundaries between historic and protohistoric groups, it is then possible to test the prehistoric reality of these same boundaries. In this sense a historic map becomes a hypothesis to be tested with archaeological data. Methodologically it is important to keep the archival and archaeological data sets distinct so that the same data is not used to both generate and test the hypothesis. The latter is a common fault and is constant temptation for those who use documentary data in archaeological research.

As an aid to making such suggestions in the Ojibwa-Ottawa case, Figure 1 has been prepared, which shows early 19th-century territories of the upper Great Lakes basin. Before drawing observations from this map, it is

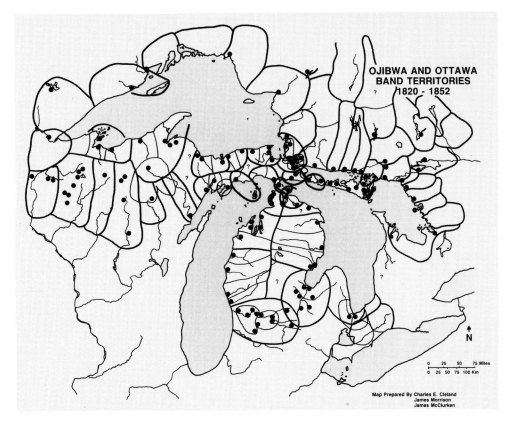

FIG. 1. Ojibwa and Ottawa band territories, 1820–1852.

necessary to note some problems with the data. Band boundaries of Michigan, Wisconsin, and northeastern Minnesota are drawn from divisions of bands and sub-bands from documents relating to treaties between the U.S. and the Ottawa and Chippewa in 1818, 1836, 1837, 1842, and 1854, as well as other documents describing the extent of hunting territories. The interior boundaries are poorly known. To the contrary, the boundaries of band territories north of Lakes Superior and Huron were mapped in 1852 and are quite accurate (Vidal 1849).

Population figures for the U.S. area are the result of a person-by-person family census made by the government in 1832 and 1839. In all cases, major summer villages are mapped according to general location. In some cases it is known that band territories were in fact subdivided into sub-band territory, but it is not known exactly where these were. In regard to the territories east of Georgian Bay, some of the smaller territories are likely to represent sub-band territories. Lighter lines on the map show political subdivisions or sub-band territories.

The actual plotting of Chippewa and Ottawa band territories suggest some interesting points. First, and of little surprise, territories almost always follow river drainage. This is thought to be a reflection of the fact that, in the heavily forested and often swampy upper lakes region, waterways are the only practical means of travel. Secondly, rivers are the most apparent means of de-

marking territory. It is important to remember, however, that Ojibwa and Ottawa territories are more accurately thought of as being impermanent and sociological, rather than permanent and political; that is, the band boundaries exist to circumscribe the resources collectively used on an annual basis by a group of related people. The boundaries between bands and sub-bands, therefore, are only as stable as these groups. Historical evidence suggests that during the 19th century they were quite stable. This seems true despite the fact that resource use patterns may have changed within the territories (Bishop 1986).

Referring to the map, it is apparent that there is considerable variability in the size and shapes of band territories. However, four distinct patterns seem to be recognizable. These patterns are believed to be directly related to ecological and economic variables. In the country both north and south of Lake Superior, as well as inland north of Lake Huron, territories were large, encompassing between 3000 and 4000 square miles. These were occupied by Ojibwa, who were mainly either hunters or fishers. In the latter case, territories are usually rectangular and parallel the lake. The second category of territories range between 2000 and 3000 square miles. These are occupied by peoples with mixed economies. North of Lake Huron and on Georgian Bay, these territories are occupied by Ojibwa who garden, hunt, and fish. The territories are rectangular, providing access to the lake, as well as ample interior hunting space. A similar situation is found among the Ottawa along the western coast of lower Michigan, where a mixed fishing, farming, and hunting economy structured Ottawa territories.

A third and very distinct territorial pattern is found in the eastern part of Michigan's Upper Peninsula, and especially in the Ste. Mary's River and Straits of Mackinac region. Here Ojibwa territories are very small, that is, between 500 and 1000 square miles. The small size is thought to be a reflection of the very rich fishery resources of these regions. These territories show yet another interesting characteristic, that is, the overlapping of band territories. In the case of the Straits and the Ste. Mary's River, the territories of at least six bands overlap in their use of these areas.

Finally we are able to distinguish a still different pattern for the strongly agricultural people of southern Michigan and southwestern Ontario. Here both Ottawa and Ojibwa depended primarily on corn agriculture, but also collected, hunted, and fished. Band territories are about the same size as those used by more northern people with mixed economies, that is, 2000 to 3000 square miles. Within these, however, are many smaller sub-band territories, each organized around the resources regularly exploited by the people of several related villages. During the winter season the whole larger territory is used.

The boundaries separating Ojibwa and Ottawa groups have various degrees of correlation to ecological, geomorphological, ethnic, linguistic, and political realities. As Hickerson (1970) pointed out long ago, the deciduous forest/prairie land margins that formed the southern and western boundary between Sioux and Ojibwa county through Minnesota and Wisconsin has important linguistic, ethnic, and ecological implications. In this case and in others, such boundaries are often contested. Another example is an overlapping boundary between the Ottawa and Saginaw Ojibwa in the northern reaches of the Grand River valley of southern Michigan. Although presumably peaceful, these two ethnic groups came into competition for the same resources when the Ottawa expanded into territory occupied by Ojibwa (Montfort 1990). Another boundary with even more subtle ethnic implications is the boundary between the Lake Superior Ojibwa and the Mississauga Ojibwa in northeast lower Michigan. Though this boundary, which is implicitly codified in the Treaty of 1819, may have an ecological or geomorphological correlate, it is clear that it separates two groups of ethnically distinct Ojibwa.

In some other cases it appears that boundaries may have a purely ecological or geomorphological basis. An example of the latter is the boundary line across the Upper Peninsula of Michigan, which is found in the 1836 and 1842 treaties connecting the mouth of the Chocolay River and Little Bay de Noc. This boundary follows the edge of the Canadian Shield but otherwise seems to separate related Chippewa groups. The Michipicoten

River on Lake Superior shore marks the northernmost extension of the Great Lakes mixed conifer/deciduous forests, and although it marks an abrupt ecological transition, it is not an ethnic boundary. It is, however, a cultural boundary, since it separates two distinct style pools in Lake Woodland ceramics.

Given the assumptions mentioned earlier about the concordance between ecological stability and subsistence type, the documentary record can be helpful in establishing approximate demographic estimates. The first accurate census of the Lake Superior Ojibwa was made in 1832 (Mason 1958). This count includes the Ojibwa residing in interior Wisconsin. While it is considered accurate, it does not provide information on households. In 1839 there was a household-by-household census of the Ottawa and Ojibwa of Michigan, which is very accurate but which does not include the Ojibwa of interior Wisconsin or Minnesota (Schoolcraft 1839). While there are no accurate population figures for the Canadian side of the upper Great Lakes until after the midpoint of the 19th century, there are counts made on Manitoulin Island in 1852, reflecting Indians of various bands who visited in order to receive presents. Obviously visitation counts are not very reliable.

An important question that arises in reviewing these population figures is the relationship between household censuses and household composition. This question is important for two reasons. First, the 1839 census shows only Indian persons, where Indian women are married to non-Indians, only women and children are reported for the household. In these cases, however, households are easy to identify, since Indian women are shown with French or English surnames. This form of partial reporting was only a problem of major proportion in the case of the Mackinac Island band, where only one male head is shown for 34 households. Presumably this Indian community was composed of the wives and children of French Canadian canoemen who were absent during the census period. To this day the Mackinac Island band is known among local Indians as the *biddy band*. Since this band was anomalous, it is entirely deleted in these considerations. Another problem arises in the case of plural marriages. Since the census process did not recognize plural marriages, second wives were shown as heads of households. It was almost always possible, however, to recognize these marriages from the context in which they were listed in the census.

An interesting aspect of the population statistics that are shown in Table 1 is the contrast between the southern Ottawa, who strongly relied on corn agriculture; the northern Ottawa, who had a mixed economy based on agriculture, fishing, and hunting; and the Ojibwa, who were primarily fishermen or hunters. As we have already seen, the size of territories held by bands seems to generally reflect these conditions, with the agricultural and fishing peoples maintaining smaller territories than

Table 1
Population Statistics for the Ottawa and Chippewa Bands of Michigan and Wisconsin[a]

	Northern Ottawa	Southern Ottawa	Total Ottawa	Chippewa 1839	Chippewa 1832
Number of bands	13	10	23	14	19
Households censused	500	285	785	320	597[b]
#/% Est. polygamous households	58/11.6	43/15	101/12.8	19/5.9	—
Est. total households	442	242	684	301	562[c]
Total pop.	2020	1345	3365	1409	2785
Population per band	155.4	134.5	146.3	100.6	146.6
Persons per household	4.57	6.55	4.90	4.68	4.95
Households per band	34	24.2	29.7	21.5	29.5
Range of pop./band	30–349	50–160	30–345	33–172	31–448
Range of households/band	9–73	13–41	—	6–47	—

a   Chippewa data are from 1839 and 1832 census; Ottawa data are from 1839 census.
b   Households were calculated by reducing the number of adult males (746) by 20%.
c   Calculated by reducing estimated households by 5.9% or the percent of polygamous Chippewa households in 1839 census.

hunters. Other than the fact that there seemed to be fewer polygamous households among the Ojibwa, the population figures do not reflect any significant difference in total population size, number of bands, number of households, population per band, people per household, or household per band. In the several statistical categories that would have the most direct implications for archaeological remains — mean population per band, number of people per household, and the number of households per band — the Ottawa aggregate figures are nearly identical with those of the Ojibwa.

The conclusion that seems to emerge is that local group size, as well as household size, is probably determined by sociopolitical and ideological factors, rather than by economic ones. The greatest range of band size occurs among summer population aggregates, which range from a minimum of 30 people to as many as 450 people. The significant figure in terms of population distribution, that is, the mean number of people in each band, is about 150. These people united by close family ties are not only the largest economic unit of Ottawa and Ojibwa society, but also the most meaningful sociopolitical unit. It is also this group that maintains the territorial dimension and, to the extent that they exist, the boundaries between territories. While these boundaries may have occasionally had an ecological or geophysical dimension, they are mainly sociological and are marked by obvious features of the natural environment — usually rivers. Sites of aggregation seem to be on or close to the margins of such territories and in some important cases seem to have been used by people from slightly overlapping band territories. Ottawa and Ojibwa territory size thus seems to be determined by the space needed to contain enough resources to support about 150 people on an annual basis and to provide access to critical resources. In the latter regard, territories also seem to be constructed so as to include certain combinations of resources, for example, high population of deer, wild rice beds, or hunting and fishing territories. This latter dimension is likely quite subtle and probably extends to a range of crucial resources upon which the viability of the economic cycle depends.

Finally, the mapping of Ojibwa and Ottawa territories suggests some immediate implications for Late Woodland and historic era archaeology. First it is apparent that site size and placement is definitely a reflection of territorial criteria. Each territory has a single large site and undoubtedly many smaller ones. In historic times bands claimed resource use prerogatives within these territories; in some cases they had distinctive decorative styles and coherent political systems. In a real sense the major village of each band was the "capital" of the territory. The territory was often identified and named for this village. It is also apparent in some cases that there are regional sites of importance. In historic times Wikwemikong, Chequamegon, and La Abre Croche are examples of villages with regional significance. It is likely that Late Woodland sites, such as the Juntunen site at the Straits of Mackinac and the Whitefish Island site in the Ste. Marys River, are examples of such regional villages in prehistoric times. Parenthetically these two sites are both located in the approximate center of the overlapping territories of six historic bands. In the case of the Ste. Marys River, the regional name *Saulteaur* is applied to the six bands that shared this river valley and its fishery. Other such sites no doubt exist.

For the most part, boundaries between Ojibwa, as well as Ottawa bands and sub-bands, pose no barriers to communication. It is difficult to suggest social or political mechanisms that could account for a break in the flow of people or information between adjoining bands. Yet it is clear that such boundaries existed in Late Woodland times. For example, the Michipicoten River on the north shore of Lake Superior forms a major boundary between early Late Woodland Blackduck and Mackinaw ceramic style types and continues to represent a stylistic boundary through the Late Woodland. The Spanish River on the north shore of Lake Huron is likewise a major boundary between the Juntunen ceramic styles in the west and Iroquoian ceramic traditions to the east. Presumably proto Ojibwa bands inhabited both banks of both rivers.

Barbara Luedtke's (1976) study of the distribution of major chert types on lower Michigan sites is an illustration of the applicability of the present work. It is clear from her maps that the distribution of Late Woodland Bayport chert exactly corresponds with the historic distribution of Missisauga Ojibwa and that the Late Woodland distribution of Norwood chert corresponds with the territory occupied by the northern Ottawa. Since neither of these groups occupied this region until the early 18th century, the historic band structuring of territories must be reflective of the same condition upon which the territories of earlier Late Woodland people were constructed. Obviously, if historic and prehistoric band territories were structured in approximately the same way at two different times and under two sets of historical circumstances, there must be underlying cultural and ecological regularities that are responsible for this condition. The fact that the question is even posed is the result of text-aided archaeology.

References

Anderson, D. (n.d.) Merchandise for the *Pays de Haut:* Indian People and European Trade Goods in the Western Great Lakes Region. Paper presented at the Canadian Archaeological Association, Toronto, 1986. On file at MSU Museum.

Bishop, C. A. (1986) Territoriality among Northeastern Algonquians. *Anthropologica* 28(1–2):37–63.

— (1970) The Emergence of Hunting Territories Among the Northern Ojibwa. *Ethnology* 9:1–15.

Cleland, C. E. (1989) Comment on "A Reconstruction of Aboriginal Fishing Strategies in the Northern Great Lakes Region" by S. R. Martin. *American Antiquity*, 54(3):605–609.

Hickerson, H. (1970) *The Chippewa and their Neighbors: A Study in Ethnohistory.* Holt, Rinehart and Winston, New York.

Kay, J. (1984) The Fur Trade and Native American Population Growth. *Ethnohistory* 31(4):265–287.

Luedtke, B. (1976) Lithic Material Distribution and Interaction Patterns During the Late Woodland Period in Michigan. Unpublished Ph.D. dissertation, University of Michigan, University Microfilms, Ann Arbor, MI.

Mason, P., Ed. (1958) *Schoolcraft's Expedition to Lake Itasca.* Michigan State University Press, East Lansing.

Montfort, M. (1990) Ethnic and Tribal Identity Among the Saginaw Chippewa of Nineteenth Century Michigan. Unpublished M.A. thesis, Michigan State University, Lansing.

Rodgers, E. S. and M. Black (1976) Subsistence Strategy in the Fish Hare Period, Northern Ontario: The Weagonaw Ojibwa 1880–1920. *Journal of Anthropological Research* 32(1):1–43.

Schoolcraft, H. R. (1839) Census of Michigan Indian Population Under the Treaty of Washington 1836. In *The Papers of Henry R. Schoolcraft 1821-1878.* Library of Congress Microfilm R66:41828.

Vidal, A. (1849) Crown Land Department, Surveyors Office West, Montreal, August 1849, Dept. of Indian Affairs, Ottawa.

9: The Harbor Herod Built, the Harbor Josephus Saw

Robert Lindley Vann

School of Architecture, University of Maryland, College Park, Maryland

Archaeologists at Caesarea Maritima, an ancient city on the coast of modern Israel between Haifa and Tel Aviv, can read an eyewitness description of their city with its harbor recorded by Flavius Josephus more than 85 years after its dedication in 10/9 B.C. by Herod the Great. In brief passages from the *Jewish Wars* and *Jewish Antiquities,* this ancient historian provides first-hand observations that have been invaluable for those studying the city and its monuments. Special attention is given the magnificent harbor, the *raison d'être* of this new city. The purpose of this article is to compare the harbor that Herod built with that which Josephus saw and described for us. An understanding of the author's heritage and motives for writing these two works is important, as is a careful reading of the descriptions of the city and its harbor. Comparing the literary evidence to the results of earlier surveys and excavations should offer an opportunity to examine the accuracy of our sources and to determine their importance for a study of ancient Caesarea.[1]

The Site

The site, though poorly preserved, is one of the most important building projects of Herod the Great. Among his many architectural endeavors, he is probably best known for rebuilding the Jewish temple in Jerusalem and his spectacular northern palace at Masada,[2] but he was also responsible for rebuilding several cities including Caesarea, Samaria (Crowfoot et al. 1942–58), and Antipatris, as well as constructing another harbor in Anthedon. This innovative and ambitious king introduced many new ideas of Graeco-Roman architecture into the eastern Mediterranean, and although Rome already had provinces north (Syria) and south (Egypt) of his kingdom, many of the new standard western building

types, such as podium temples, amphitheaters, theaters, and circuses, were first built by this Judaean king, either in his own realm or in cities of neighboring lands. Likewise, Herod introduced new building materials and techniques of construction, the most important of which was *opus caementicium,* or concrete, which was to be a crucial component of his harbor project.[3]

The city became capital of the province of Judaea in the early first century A.D. and continued to be the governor's base through six centuries of Roman and then Byzantine rule. Caesarea grew, expanded, remodeled, and — when necessary after damage either by natural causes or at the hands of enemy troops — rebuilt. Many times new buildings rose at the expense of older ones, employing readily available building stone from nearby structures rather than encumbering the expense of quarrying new blocks. Reuse of *spolia* on a large scale was characteristic of Arab and Crusader construction at the site, and one might expect the same to be true of the earlier Herodian phase. Despite the poor state of preservation, archaeologists at Caesarea enjoy several advantages, in addition to the literary accounts. For example, the deserted nature of the site has also meant that archaeological investigation is not limited to the occasional opportunities of excavating, as one might now find in cities such as Athens, Rome, or Jerusalem, where the ancient site is now covered by later medieval and modern structures.

The fact that Arabs deserted the city at the end of the Crusades meant that the harbor was also clear for archaeological investigation. Some ancient ports, such as Alexandria or Piraeus, were never abandoned and have served the same purpose for hundreds of years. Excavation in those ports today would be hampered not only by the deposition of debris in the bottom of the harbor but also by continuous dredging, necessary to keep the anchorages open, resulting in the removal or disturbance of ancient levels. Other important harbors from the Graeco-Roman world have silted in, leaving once busy ports like Ephesus and Rome (Portus) high and dry. In contrast to those, Sebastos, the port of Caesarea, remains underwater and is easily accessible to archaeologists. In fact, most of the Herodian harbor has subsided and is now 4 to 5 m deeper than in antiquity. The discovery of a fault line parallel to and about 100 m offshore has insured that much of the Herodian structure has been better protected from centuries of Mediterranean storms. Even though the breakwaters themselves are in poor condition, the huge concrete blocks set down as their foundations can still be seen once the sand above has been excavated.

The Author

Josephus was born Joseph ben Matthias in Jerusalem in A.D. 37, the same year as the death of Tiberius and the accession of Caligula.[4] His father was a member of the original list of 24 priestly clans while his mother claimed royal blood of the Maccabee family. In other words, Josephus belonged to the ruling class of priests, who generally supported Roman rule and had the most to lose from a rebellion against the empire. According to Rhoads (1976:5), revolution against Rome was also revolution against the high priests of Israel (*Wars* 4.148, 152), the wealthy (*Wars* 2.427), and those of noble birth (*Wars* 4.139). It is against this background that one must evaluate the actions of Josephus in his later relationship with Rome and his native countrymen.

References in another work of Josephus, entitled the *Life*, state that as a young man he was already counted among the most erudite members of the priesthood, and at the age of 16 he had undertaken a study of the Pharisees, Sadducees, and Essenes. He spent time in the wilderness as a hermit, but 3 years later, at the age of 19, he was living in Jerusalem as a priest of the Pharisee community (*Life* 8–10). Josephus traveled to Rome at age 26 to defend a group of his fellow priests. Although initially unsuccessful, he was able, through a friendship with Poppaea — consort of Nero — to eventually obtain their release. This exposure to the riches and power of Rome had a lasting effect on the young man, and upon his return to Israel in A.D. 66, with the province on the verge of rebellion, he spoke in favor of accommodation rather than armed revolt. Not to be denied, the rebellious Jews defeated Cestius Gallus, the Roman governor of Syria who had been sent south to Jerusalem to bring the situation under control. Josephus and the other moderate Pharisees, who remained optimistic that further warfare might be avoided, found themselves nonetheless part of the struggle. These were the conditions in Israel when Josephus was appointed to organize the defenses of

Upper and Lower Galilee, specifically those areas of Gaulanitis and Galilee — east, north, and west of the Sea of Galilee — with their concentrations of Jewish population in cities such as Tiberias and Taricheae.

As one might expect, the policy of a commanding officer with divided loyalties was, at best, inconsistent. His own accounts of that period in *Life* and *Wars* reveal the dichotomy. For example, he took weapons from the "brigands and revolutionaries" in order to arm "select men of the nation" (*Life* 28–29). There are several other areas where anti-Roman and pro-Roman sentiment seems apparent (Rhoads 1976:7). Josephus' defense of the north finally brought him into armed conflict with Vespasian at Jotapata, and when the city fell in the summer of 67, he and another survivor surrendered to the Romans rather than carry out a suicide pact that had been agreed upon by 40 of the last survivors of that siege.[5] During his surrender to Vespasian, Josephus prophesied that the Roman general would one day become emperor, and when this prediction was realized 2 years later, Josephus was freed (*Wars* 3.351–352, 399ff; 4.646). During the years of captivity and those that followed, he traveled first with Vespasian and then with Titus, serving as both interpreter and spokesman. But Josephus was unable to convince his fellow Jews to surrender, and after the fall of Jerusalem in A.D. 70 he left for Italy, where he spent the remainder of his life.

According to references in the *Life* (364), Titus commissioned the *Jewish Wars*, signed it, and ordered its publication. The text, appearing first in Aramaic between A.D. 75 and 79,[6] was addressed to Jews in the East as a manifesto of Roman power and a warning for others not to follow in rebellion. Although we do not know contemporary reaction to the book, it has since been dismissed by many as a biased justification by Josephus for his actions at Jotapata.[7] But despite the fact that Josephus wrote a text clearly endorsing Roman power in the East, recent scholarship is more generous in recognizing its true value as a serious history (Thackeray 1967:23–50).

The Jewish Antiquities, written some 20 years later, represents a substantially different point of view. By that time, Josephus no longer enjoyed the imperial patronage that had been his under Vespasian and Titus. Domitian, by comparison, was no friend of literature. Laqueur (1920:258) suggests that a reference in the autobiography (*Life* 429) to "Jewish accusers" represented enemies at court who made life less comfortable. Josephus did find another patron, a certain Epaphroditus, perhaps the Greek grammarian Marcus Mettius Epaphroditus, who had been trained in Alexandria but spent the remainder of his life in Rome. Josephus dedicated all his later work to this man. *Jewish Antiquities*, more correctly entitled *Ioudaiki Archaiologia* or *Jewish Archaeology*, was his magnum opus written some 20 years after the *Wars*. It belongs to his late career, took longer to complete, and was often set aside, but was finally finished with the

FIG. 1. Map of Herod's kingdom (Holum, K. G. et al. (1988) *King Herod's Dream: Caesarea on the Sea*. W. W. Norton, New York and London, p. 58. With permission. Drawing by R. Ziek).

encouragement of others (Thackeray 1967:51–74). In this text he has broken both with the imperial house and with Roman political propaganda. His motives for writing a history were most certainly not to ingratiate himself with offended countrymen, as suggested by Laqueur (1920:258), but the result of long, careful, and deliberate planning.

Foundation of the City

Herod built Caesarea on the coast between Joppa and Dor in the northwestern extremities of his territory and on the site of an earlier settlement known as Strato's Tower (Figure 1). Access to the Mediterranean was not easy along this seaboard, although these were the very busy sea-lanes from Egypt that had been traveled for centuries.

> Now this city is located in Phoenicia, on the sea-route to Egypt, between Joppa and Dora. These are small towns on the seashore and are poor harbours because the south-west winds beat on them and always dredge up sand from the sea upon the shore, and thus does not

permit a smooth landing; instead, it is usually necessary for merchants to ride unsteadily at anchor off shore (*Antiquities* 15.333).

> For the whole seaboard from Dora to Joppa, midway between which the city lies, was without a harbour, so that vessels bound for Egypt along the coast of Phoenicia had to ride at anchor in the open when menaced by the south-west wind; for even a moderate breeze from this quarter dashes the waves to such a height against the cliffs, that their reflux spreads a wild commotion far out to sea (*Wars* 410).

The date, extent, and location of that town has been discussed widely in recent literature and remains one of the least understood aspects of the site.[8] Josephus described the settlement as dilapidated, but not deserted or destroyed, and with an advantageous situation on the coast that provided Herod with an excellent opportunity for building. Herod was already an experienced builder who, according to Netzer, was particularly drawn to dramatic and sometimes difficult sites. Witness the precipitous position of the northern palace at Masada, the wadi bed dividing two portions of a winter palace in

Jericho, the dramatic siting of the three towers of Hippicus, Phasael, and Mariamme along a high ridge at Jerusalem, and the monumental treatment of a hilltop at Herodium to serve as his tomb (Netzer 1981).

> And when he observed that there was a place near the sea, formerly called Strato's Tower, which was very well suited to be the site of a city... (*Antiquities* 15.331).

> His notice was attracted by a town on the coast, called Strato's Tower which, though then dilapidated, was, from its advantageous situation, suited for the exercise of his liberality (*Wars* 410).

The new city was an architectural showcase (Figure 2).

> ...he set about making a magnificent plan and put up buildings all over the city, not of ordinary material but of white stone [marble]. He also adorned it with a very costly palace...Herod also built a theater in stone in the city and on the south side of the harbour, farther back, an amphitheater large enough to hold a great crowd of people and conveniently situated for a view of the sea (*Antiquities* 331, 341).

> This [the city] he entirely rebuilt with white stone [marble], and adorned with the most magnificent palaces, displaying here, as nowhere else, the innate grandeur of his character...The city Herod dedicated to the province, the harbour to navigators in these waters, to Caesar the glory of this new foundation, to which he accordingly gave the name of Caesarea. The rest of the buildings — amphitheater, theater, public places — were constructed in a style worthy of the name which the city bore (*Wars* 410, 412–413).

Public buildings provided the architectural setting for requirements of a Graeco-Roman city with the many aspects of public life that might not have been consistent with those of other cities of the kingdom. Caesarea was to be a city of the classical western world and, as such, would have been much different from his capital of Jerusalem, where one would not expect to find such institutions as the gladiatorial events of the amphitheater or a cult temple to a foreign emperor. Foremost among those buildings that could only be built in a "western" city was the principal temple.[9]

> In a circle round the harbour was a continuous line of dwellings constructed of the most polished stones, and in their midst was a mound on which stood a temple of Caesar, visible a great way off to those sailing into the harbour, which had a statue of Rome and also one of Caesar (*Antiquities* 15.339).

> On an eminence facing the harbour-mouth stood Caesar's temple, remarkable for its beauty and grand proportions; it contained a colossal statue of the emperor, not inferior to the Olympian Zeus, which served

for its model, and another of Rome, rivaling that of Hera at Argos (*Wars* 412).

The ambitious nature of this city was not limited to the public monuments.

> But below the city the underground passages and sewers cost no less effort than the structures built above them. Of these some led an equal distance from one another to the harbour and sea, while one diagonal passage connected all of them, so that the rainwater and the refuse of the inhabitants were easily carried off together (*Antiquities* 340).

Description of the Harbor

The focus of the new city was its harbor facility, Sebastos.

> ...what was greatest of all and required the most labor...a well protected harbour, of the size of the Piraeus, with landing places and secondary anchorages inside — Herod laid out a circular harbour enclosing enough space for large fleets to lie at anchor near shore... (*Antiquities* 332, 334).

> However, by dint of expenditure and enterprise, the king triumphed over nature and constructed a harbour larger than the Piraeus, including other deep roadsteads within its recesses (*Wars* 410).

The protected harbor consisted of two breakwaters constructed of enormous blocks.

> The structure which he set in the sea as a barrier was two hundred feet (in width). Half of it was opposed to the surge of the waves and held off the flood of waters breaking there from all sides, and was therefore called a breakwater. The other half — a series of vaulted recesses as shelters for sailors. And before them there was a wide quay which encircled the harbour (*Antiquities* 335–336, 337).

> Notwithstanding the totally recalcitrant nature of the site, he grappled with the difficulties so successfully, that the solidity of his masonry defied the sea, while its beauty was such as if no obstacle had existed. Having determined upon the comparative size of the harbour — he had blocks of stone let down into twenty fathoms of water, most of them measuring fifty feet in length by nine in depth and ten in breadth, some being even larger. Upon the submarine foundation thus laid he constructed above the surface a mole two hundred feet broad; of which one hundred were built out to break the surf while the remainder supported a stone wall encircling the harbour (*Wars* 411).

This central wall divided the landward and seaward portions of the breakwater and might have been part of

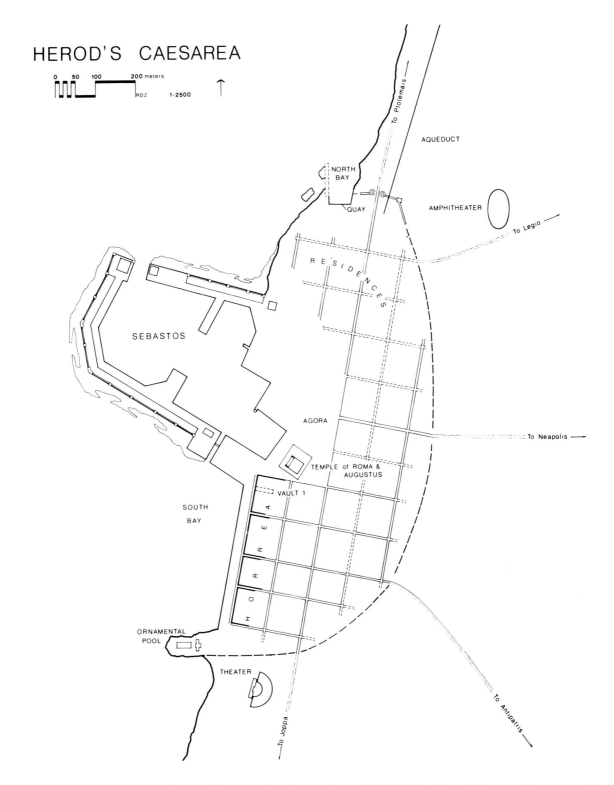

HEROD'S CAESAREA

0 50 100   200 meters

RDZ   1:2500

NORTH BAY

QUAY

AQUEDUCT

AMPHITHEATER

To Ptolemais

To Legio

RESIDENCES

SEBASTOS

AGORA

TEMPLE of ROMA & AUGUSTUS

VAULT 1

HOREA

SOUTH BAY

To Neapolis

ORNAMENTAL POOL

THEATER

To Joppa

To Antipatris

FIG. 2. Plan of Caesarea during the Herodian Period (Holum, K. G. et al. (1988) *King Herod's Dream: Caesarea on the Sea.* W. W. Norton, New York and London, p. 83. With permission. Drawing by R. Ziek).

a system that surrounded the harbor, perhaps connecting to the city fortification system. The largest of the towers along that wall has been suggested as a pharos or lighthouse of the ancient harbor (Vann, in press a).

The other half, supported on a stone wall, was divided at intervals by towers, of which the largest, a very handsome thing, is called Drusus, taking its name from Drusus, the stepson of Caesar, who died young (*Antiquities* 336).

From this wall arose, at intervals, massive towers, the loftiest and most magnificent of which was called the Drusion after the step-son of Caesar (*Wars* 411).

Josephus was very specific concerning the harbor entrance.

> The entrance or mouth of the harbour was made to face north, for this wind always brings the clearest weather. The foundation of the whole circular wall on the left of those sailing into the harbour was a tower resting on piled stones as a broad firm base to withstand pressure (from the water), while on the right were two great stone blocks, larger than the tower on the other side, which were upright and joined together (*Antiquities* 337–338).

> The entrance to the port faced northwards, because in these latitudes the north wind is the most favorable of all. At the harbour mouth stood colossal statues, three on either side, resting on columns; the columns on the left of vessels entering port were supported by a massive tower, those on the right by two upright blocks of stone clamped together, whose height exceeded that of the tower on the opposite side (*Wars* 412).

Josephus continues by proclaiming that no less impressive than the siting and scale of the harbor was the fact that the structure was built of imported materials brought at great expense from places distant from the Levantine coast.

> But what was especially notable about this construction was that he got no material suitable for so great a work from the place itself but completed it with materials brought from outside at great expense (*Antiquities* 332).

Finally, he adds that the project progressed at an amazing rate, dedicating the city in little more than a decade.[10]

> Now the city was completed in the space of twelve years, for the king did not slacken in the undertaking and he had sufficient means for the expenses (*Antiquities* 341).

Results of Early Surveys and Excavations

How does the harbor that Josephus saw and described compare to the harbor that Herod built? At present we are unable to discern with any degree of accuracy the details of the late first century B.C. port facility. First, the harbor itself is mostly destroyed, the breakwaters submerged and badly battered. No complete structure, either on land or in the water, has been preserved intact, and the most we can hope for is a further understanding of the harbor plan through the future discovery of additional portions of the breakwater substructure, or

perhaps by the preservation of diagnostic architectural fragments. But even then, would we be able to recognize differences between original Herodian construction as opposed to later Roman or even Byzantine additions or repairs? As we will see, recent excavations have produced additional data concerning the harbor and its construction, but it is with the limitations mentioned above in mind that we should review the archaeological evidence of Herod's city and its harbor.

The first plan of the site by Richard Pococke appeared in his book entitled *A Description of the East and Some Other Countries,* published in London in 1745 (Figure 3). This prominent European traveler was the first to make detailed observations at the site, and although he correctly identified and placed features such as the late Roman city wall and smaller Crusader circuit, as well as the high- and low-level aqueducts, he incorrectly placed the harbor south of its actual location, in the south bay between the theater promontory and the south breakwater. Although we now believe that the bay provided an anchorage for local traffic, it was entirely outside the protective enclosure of the Herodian harbor. Pococke thus identified the southern breakwater as a northern breakwater and the theater promontory as the southern breakwater. The remains of late Byzantine fortification walls on that promontory were mistaken for the Drusion. Familiar with Josephus and the public buildings mentioned in his account, Pococke placed the temple of Roma and Augustus, the forum, and the theater on the three sand dunes facing his harbor. The theater, unexcavated but identifiable as a major structure, was labeled as the amphitheater.

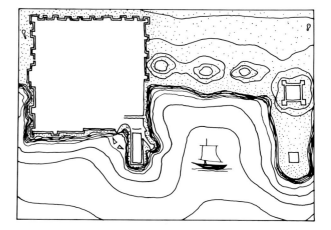

FIG. 3. Plan of harbor according to Pococke (Yuan).

It was more than a century before the Palestine Exploration Fund (PEF), under the direction of Claude R. Conder, produced the first carefully surveyed plan of the site (Conder 1873, 1874, 1879; Conder and Kitchner 1882) (Figure 4). A number of important monuments were first correctly identified by the PEF survey, includ-

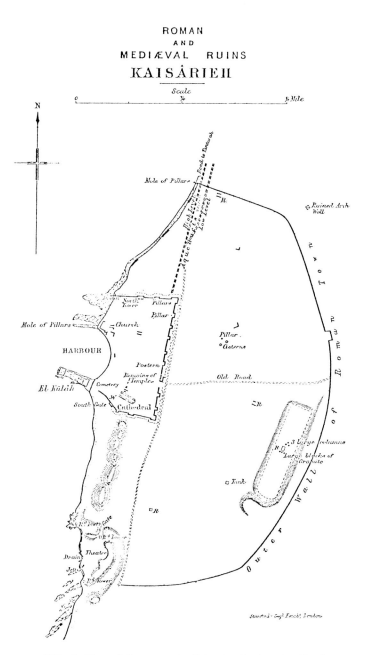

ROMAN
AND
MEDIÆVAL RUINS
KAISÂRIEH

Scale

0   ½   ¾ Mile

FIG. 4. Plan of Caesarea by Palestine Exploration Fund.

ing the theater and circus, as well as the rock-cut basin on the theater promontory that has been variously identified as a public fish market, an ornamental *piscina* (pool), or the palace of Herod (Flinder 1976; Oleson in Raban 1989:160–167; Levine and Netzer 1986:176–182). Lt. Conder identified the present-day anchorage as the Herodian harbor but failed to recognize the full extent, including the dark shadows of submerged breakwaters that extended seaward from that site. This first known study of the harbor included a survey of the southern breakwater.

The harbor of Caesarea measures 180 yards across, and on the south a long reef runs into the sea for 160 yards from the shore. This appears to be the mole

mentioned by Josephus — the general plan, half break-water (*prokumatia*) half occupied by a tower (on the site probably of the ancient Drusus), is still maintained. Under the present tower (el Kulah) two columns of red granite lie fallen — These are possible remains of the stelae which stood on the mole (Conder and Kitchner 1874:16).

Further discussion of the harbor by Conder and his questions concerning the value of Josephus' description will be discussed below in the next section. There were numerous other travelers and early scholars who visited the site during the 19th century, but systematic excavation did not begin until well into the 20th century (Vann, in press b).

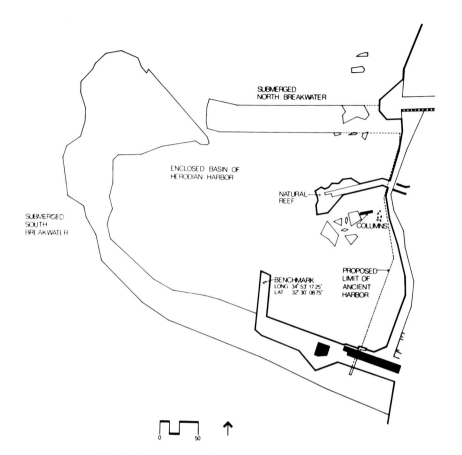

FIG. 5. Plan of Harbor by Link Expedition (Monaldo).

The location of Herod's harbor remained uncertain until 1960, when the first underwater excavations, sponsored by Edwin A. Link with the assistance of project directors Charles T. Fritsch of Princeton Theological Seminary and Immanuel Ben-Dor of Emory University, verified the identification (Ben-Dor 1961; Fritsch and Ben-Dor 1961; Hohlfelder in Raban 1989:65–71, 363–364; Link 1956). After a frustrating summer of very poor sea conditions, Link was able to work for a brief 10-day period in September, during which time his team of professional divers and nondiving archaeologists were able to produce the first rough plan of the breakwaters (Figure 5). The breakwater outlines are very schematic and reflect field sketches produced by divers that, for some reason, were not modified, despite the fact that aerial photographs were available to Link. A full report was never published, although further discussion of the Link expedition will soon appear (Hohlfelder, in press).

There were other early excavations at the site during the same years (Raban 1989:55–63). The Italian Mission (1959–1963) under the direction of Antonio Frova uncovered the theater, verifying its original Herodian date and tracing a series of later additions and repairs (Frova et al. 1965). Josephus had confused its position with that of the amphitheater (Levine 1975:24, n. 161), but this issue was settled with the excavation and partial

reconstruction of the theater and the discovery of the amphitheater in the northeast section of the city. The mission also cleared portions of the triple-channeled high aqueduct system, which, despite numerous brief publications, is yet to be fully studied (Hamburger 1959; Kedar and Ziv 1964; Olami and Peleg 1977; Olami and Ringel 1975; Peleg in Raban 1989:46–49).[11]

Early Mandate and Israeli excavations (Yeivin 1955; Schwabe 1950; Avi-Yonah 1970), the Hebrew University work directed by Michael Avi-Yonah and Avraham Negev (Avi-Yonah 1956), as well as those of the National Park Service led by Negev (Negev 1967), all added to our knowledge of the site, but did not provide significant new information concerning the Herodian period.

The Joint Expedition to Caesarea Maritima (JECM) directed by Robert J. Bull was the next major land excavation (Bull 1982; Holum et al. 1988; Hohlfelder in Raban 1989:63–65). Of the many areas opened by the JECM, that most valuable for our understanding of the Herodian harbor was Field C, immediately south of the Crusader city walls and extending from the shoreline — and a street dubbed the *via maris* by its excavators — to a parallel street lined with colonnades. The major structures uncovered in Field C included a building decorated with mosaic inscriptions describing the activities of tax officials, a small bath suite, an open court with short

CAESAREA MARITIMA
C.A.H.E.P EXCAVATIONS
COMPOSITE PLAN   1:1000   RLV

FIG. 6. Plan of Harbor by CAHEP (Vann).

columns inscribed with the names of provincial governors, a long rectangular apsidal room similar to the audience halls of late Roman governor's palaces, and other rooms (perhaps for dining?) decorated with remains of the finest mosaics found in Caesarea. In short, this very important area of the city appears to have been the location of the governor's palace, at least in the late Byzantine period of the fifth and early sixth centuries. More important for an understanding of the harbor was the fact that the westernmost series of these rooms was built over a lower level of large vaulted *horrea*, which, according to the ceramic evidence (Blakely 1987), served as storehouses for goods coming in and out of the harbor.[12]

Results of CAHEP

The most significant excavations for our understanding of Herod's harbor are those of CAHEP, the Caesarea Ancient Harbour Excavation Project.[13] Research objectives included a full survey of the remains and an understanding of the harbor(s) of the city during all phases of its (their) development. But most important was a focus upon the Herodian harbor, its extent, and the processes by which it was constructed. CAHEP is now in the last year of a second 5-year program of excavation, with the final results of the 1980–1985 seasons now appearing in two of the four projected volumes (Raban 1989; Oleson, in press).[14]

Underwater surveys and the study of a series of aerial photographs provide detailed plans of the two giant breakwaters that create the inner protected basin (Figure 6). The northern breakwater is fairly regular in outline and extends 250 m from the shore. Situated in the lee of the great southern breakwater and being somewhat protected from prevailing southwesterlies, this feature has retained much of its original configuration. The southern breakwater, on the other hand, has been subject to the full force of the waves and is more badly destroyed. The larger of the two is about 750 m long, forms the south and west limits of the harbor, and terminates opposite the western end of the northern breakwater. The entrance, as we heard from Josephus, was to the north. The remains of the harbor clearly indicate that ships entered at the northwest corner.

Plans based upon aerial photographs are highly variable and somewhat schematic. These overhead shots, taken for a number of years in different seasons, clearly indicate that the amount of sand either deposited or scoured away by storms leaves a slightly different configuration of the breakwaters each time the plan is drawn. At a period when there is a high sand level a larger portion of the breakwater might be covered, while after a strong storm that leaves a lower sand level more of the structure might be exposed.[15] One area that varies greatly is within and just beyond the harbor mouth, where a spill of rubble, presumably washed off the main body of the breakwater, has been deposited. This rubble partially blocks the ancient harbor entrance and a direct passage into the protected basin (Figure 6, Area R).

As stated above, the edges of the breakwaters are rather vague and have no apparent finished surfaces. The northern structure, although more regular because of its protected position, might have been restored during the Byzantine period when we know that Anastasius made improvements to the harbor (Hohlfelder 1988). On the other hand, a stretch of large ashlar blocks, set side to side in Areas A, B, and C, appear to be the inner (eastern) side of the southern breakwater (Raban 1989:104–131, 375–384). Another feature that might be an original portion of the Herodian south breakwater is the floor uncovered in Area F (Raban 1989:124–127, 401–403). Excavations carried out in 1983 (Oleson et al. 1984:290, Fig. 7; Raban 1985b:163, Figs. 6, 7) and 1990 have yet to determine whether or not the feature was a part of the main breakwater, or perhaps a pier set into the harbor off the inner edge of that structure. The floor has maximum dimensions of 17 × 4 m, is now 5 m below mean sea level, and consists of kurkar blocks of standard size (ca. 1.05 × 0.50 × 0.45 m) laid without mortar or clamps. The blocks are set in a header pattern along the northern and eastern (perhaps original?) edges, with a more varied pattern elsewhere.

Another candidate for a Herodian pier is Area L, situated between the late-18th-century column jetty and the modern breakwater north of the present harbor (Figure 6). The ashlar paving was first studied by the Center for Maritime Studies for their report to the Israel Electric Company (Raban et al. 1976:33–34, Fig. 24), investigated once more by Levine and Netzer (1986:65), and more recently by CAHEP in 1983 and 1984 (Raban 1989:151–154, 439–445). This feature, preserved in two superimposed courses of header construction, measures 23 × 6.4 m and, near its eastern terminus, has at least one dovetail cutting for a large metal clamp (Vann in Oleson, in press) similar to ones found elsewhere in Area S.[16]

Determining the width of the ancient entrance has been one of the principal objectives of excavation in Area D (Raban and Oleson in Raban 1989:113–119, 385–394). An east-west trench dug into the terminus of the northern breakwater from 1982 until 1988 failed to uncover positive evidence, but a spectacular discovery in Area K in 1990 appears to have provided the answer. If the large concrete blocks found *in situ* in areas K and G are in fact the western and eastern edges of the passage, the width was 75 m, consistent with the entrance to a comparable harbor at Lepcis Magna in Libya, but not as wide as the much larger passages into Ostia or Alexandria.[17]

Josephus provides us a very clear description of the harbor entrance, with twin towers linked together on the starboard side of a ship entering port. On this elevated platform were three columns, which in turn supported three colossal statues. A single, taller tower with a similar number of columns and statues stood to port. Two massive towers remain off the tip of the northern breakwater in Area K (Oleson et al. 1984:293–294; Raban 1983:245–248; Vann in Raban 1989:149–151, 436–438). Excavations in 1981 failed to uncover their bases, but careful surveys of the blocks revealed hollow passages within them. The towers were both built of concrete, and cavities remained where large timbers were employed to stabilize and reinforce the wooden formwork into which the concrete was poured.

The piers are eroded, roughly square in plan, and stand 6 m apart. The eastern tower is the taller of the two and measures 5.10 m north-south, 6.80 m east-west, and rises to within 1.65 m of mean sea level. When the piers were surveyed in 1982, the eastern tower protruded 6.10 m above the seabed. In 1990 that measurement was close to 8 m because of the scouring effect of winter storms and the removal of large amounts of sand. None of the exterior faces were preserved with finished surfaces but, if the account in Josephus is to be followed, the "two upright blocks of stone clamped together," one might imagine that the exterior of these towers were clad with marble revetment. During the 1990 season, a large number of marble revetment fragments and one slab of alabaster revetment appeared in the excavation of Area K-2, some 5 m south of the tower. The western tower is much shorter, standing 3.30 m high, measuring 7.50 m north-south, 7.00 m east-west, and rising to within 3.10 m of mean sea level.

The most important discovery in the Herodian harbor during the first 5-year program was the 1982 excavation of a massive block of concrete in Area G (Oleson in Raban 1989:127–130) (Figures 7 and 8). Aerial photographs reveal a regular, squared corner at the northwest extremity of the northern breakwater. Even prior to excavation divers could recognize the regularity of a vertical surface, which suggested an artificial object that remained in its original position. Excavation around the perimeter of the feature revealed a huge block 11.50 × 15 m, 2.75 m high, with an irregular surface 4.0 to 5.1 m below mean sea level. The vertical faces of the block were well preserved, except for the northeast corner and eastern flank. The wooden formwork into which the concrete was poured remains along portions of the north, east, and west sides.

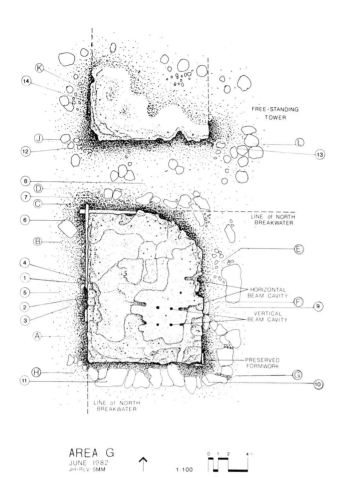

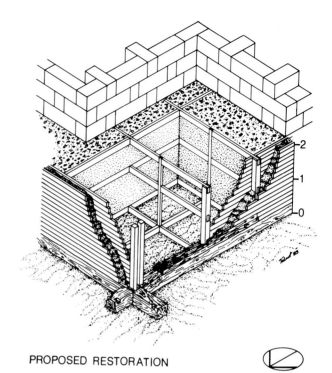

PROPOSED RESTORATION

FIG. 9. Corner detail of formwork (Talaat).

AREA G
JUNE 1982
JH·RLV·SMM

1:100

FIG. 7. Plan of concrete block in Area G (Vann).

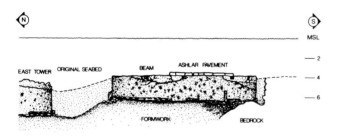

FIG. 8. Section through concrete block in Area G (Vann).

CAESAREA MARITIMA
AREA K2   19 JUNE 90
SITE PLAN   1:50 MRA

FIG. 10. Plan of Area K-2 formwork (Agnew).

The carefully excavated northwest corner of the block provided the best information concerning the formwork construction (Figure 9).[18] The huge sleeper beam was pine (*Pinus*) and fir (*Abies*) (29 cm²), with a series of pine uprights (12–15 × 23 cm) at intervals of 1.60 m carrying inner and outer planking (8 cm thick and 14 cm wide), which, in turn, created a hollow core (13 cm wide). The lowest plank was preserved and fastened into the sleeper beam with mortise-and-tenon joints. The fragments of tenons recovered were of oak (*Quercus*) and poplar (*Populus*). Once again, more extensive remains of mortise-and-tenon joining were discovered during the 1990 season (Figures 10 and 11).[19]

113

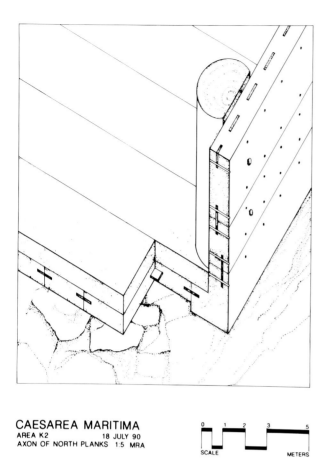

FIG. 11.   Detail of K-2 formwork with mortise-and-tenon construction (Agnew).

A series of horizontal and vertical cavities within the core indicate that a system of wooden braces was used to stabilize the form for transport from the beach into position at the end of the breakwater and to strengthen the caisson during the pouring and curing process. Once the matrix hardened, the block was a monolithic solid and the timbers no longer served a structural purpose. Over years the wood disintegrated, leaving channels 18 cm² at intervals of 1.6 m between east-west beams and (possibly) 1.3 m between uprights. Although no north-south horizontal cavities have been located, it is very likely that they too exist within the core of the block.

A series of three blocks located near the southwest bend of the southern breakwater are also of concrete (Figure 12). They average 3.5 × 4.5 × 1.7 m and on their upper surfaces have clearly preserved cavities left by timbers. There are no other large blocks around them of comparable size, and an explanation of their function is uncertain, although such blocks must have been used to support a heavy structure. Their position toward the center of the breakwater suggests that they might have carried one of the series of towers that Josephus mentioned along the spinal wall that separated the landward and seaward sides of the jetty. We have crisscrossed the

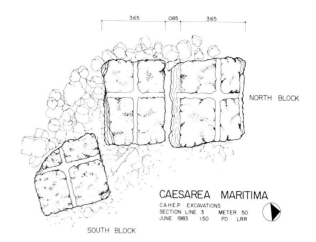

FIG. 12.   Concrete blocks on Section Line 3 (staff).

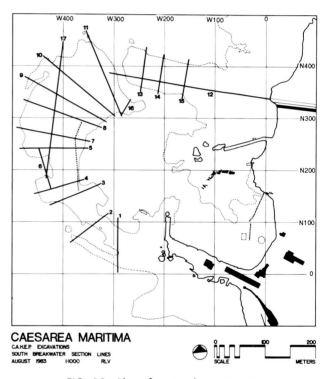

FIG. 13.   Plan of section lines (Vann).

breakwaters on many occasions, searching for additional examples of such blocks, but have found none.

There is little direct evidence for the spinal wall. During the 1983 and 1984 seasons, a series of section lines drawn across the breakwaters revealed a slight rise just seaward of the center (Figure 13). This ridge is off-center, suggesting that the wall above might not have divided the breakwater in two equal halves. Instead, the inner quay side and its structures, described by Josephus as "shelters for sailors," might have been wider than the outer *prokumatia* or breakwater.

There have been a number of other discoveries, both on land and in the water, that might have been parts of the Herodian harbor not included in passages by Josephus. For example, Area E, identified as a subsidiary breakwater (Oleson in Raban 1989:120–124, 397–400), is a well-defined barrier of concrete blocks and kurkar rubble running parallel to the southwestern portion of the southern breakwater (Figure 6). This feature varies from 4 to 8 m wide, can be traced over a length of 130 m, and although today in 6 m of water, would have risen almost to the surface of the ancient mean sea level prior to local subsidence of the breakwaters. What was the purpose of such a structure? Two seasons of excavation in 1980 and 1983 did not provide direct evidence of its function, but it is possible that it served as an initial barrier behind which the major breakwaters were built in calmer seas. Its construction is similar to rubble-mound breakwaters used elsewhere in the Mediterranean and could have been built more rapidly than the larger structures that required either lowering massive concrete blocks into place or towing even larger formwork out to sea. Whether the subsidiary breakwater dates before or after the southern breakwater, it appears to have been of continued importance. As a preliminary barrier it was able to break the waves' power before they crashed into the main structure, thereby providing additional protection for the crucial southwestern section of the harbor that faced the strongest waves. Inevitable structural repairs would have been far less expensive and complex for the smaller rubble-mound subsidiary breakwater than for the principal southern breakwater. According to Quinn (1961:153–154) and Cornick (1959:116, 118–122), similar preliminary breakwaters continue to be employed in contemporary harbor design.

Another interesting discovery was in Area I (Figure 6), the silted inner harbor (Raban 1989:131–143, 415–427). During earlier Israeli excavations in the Crusader city during 1960, Negev excavated a Roman pier covered with marine incrustation and identified it as part of the harbor complex (Negev 1967:27–30; 1975:274). The site was excavated again in 1976 by the Center for Maritime Studies (Raban et al. 1976:36–38; Raban 1989:80–81) and once more in 1983 by CAHEP (Raban 1989:132–137, 416–420). It is about 100 m from shore and situated beneath a large vaulted platform, which presumably supported the Herodian temple. The "pier" mentioned by Negev, actually a wall at least 10 m long, included a very clear erosion notch covered with intertidal marine encrustation. At a level 20 cm below the erosion notch, there was a separate line of Ostrea, a mollusc that lives beneath the tidal zone. The most important discovery of the 1983 season was an intact mooring stone set into this same wall. Additional trenches laid out farther north and south failed to trace the extent of the wall. This area might have been the inner anchor-age that Josephus mentioned (*Antiquities* 15.332), perhaps a cothon of Hellenistic type (Lehmann-Hartleben 1923:65–74) excavated behind the beach and partially landlocked.

Area T might also been part of the inner harbor (Raban 1989:177–184, 374, 478–483). A round tower, 13 m in diameter and now lying in 1 m of water 10 to 20 m off the modern beach, was discovered and first investigated by a Center for Maritime Studies workshop in 1978 (Raban and Linder 1978:243; Raban 1989:89–90) and studied once more in 1984 (Raban 1985b:163–165) and in 1990 by CAHEP. The tower, built in header construction, with blocks averaging $1.5 \times 0.50 \times 0.60$ m radiating from the center, is almost identical in size with those of the north city gate discovered by the Italian Mission during their work in the early 1960s (Frova et al. 1965:247–292). Raban dates the tower to the late Hellenistic period on the basis of comparable material in other sites, notably Samaria (Crowfoot et al. 1942–1958:27, n. 2; Winter 1971:194; Adam 1982:62). What was the function of this tower? On the basis of stylistic comparison with the city gate towers, it is possible that Area T was part of the defensive circuit and, as such, would have been the principal defense for this small basin.[20] Little is known for certain about the identification of an inner harbor, other than the position of the eastern quay wall with its mooring stone remaining *in situ*. There is, to date, no determination of the northern or southern extent of this basin, no clear idea of how the tower at Area T related to it, or, in fact, if the inner harbor was an artificial cothon. Finally, there is little evidence other than stylistic masonry patterns and limited ceramic analysis to provide a date. The basin remains, however, a likely candidate for Josephus' inner basin.

Finally, the great vaulted platform that overlooks the harbor is now being investigated by the Combined Caesarea Expeditions (CCE), a newly formed organization that joins the efforts of CAHEP and the Caesarea Land Excavation Project (CLEP). The work, carried out by Kenneth G. Holum with the assistance of Robin Ziek, focuses upon a major octagonal building that Holum suggests is a principal Christian structure, perhaps the martyrium of St. Procopius (Holum et al. 1988:177). Its vaulted substructure, mentioned above in discussions of Area T, was presumably built by Herod the Great as the vast podium for his temple to Roma and Augustus. No trace of the temple remains *in situ*, nor is there any direct evidence for the mosque of the Arab period, which, according to Crusader sources, had previously been a church. The Franks rededicated the building as the Cathedral of St. Peter, which in the 12th century was replaced with the unfinished structure that stands there today. Although the temple platform has been badly damaged by numerous construction projects that continually displaced and reused earlier building materials, it is hoped that the recently initiated CCE excavations will add greatly to our knowledge of this critical feature of Caesarean topography.

The Value of Josephus as a Literary Source

Eighteenth and 19th century visitors to the site came with the works of Josephus in hand but were very disappointed at what they found. The city had suffered a series of devastating sieges at the hands of Persian, Arab, and Crusader armies. In the years that followed the final battle (February 27, 1265), the Mamluk sultan of Egypt ordered that Caesarea and all other coastal cities be destroyed to deny a port of entry to future European invaders. Following those centuries of turbulence were others during which the site was deserted but, being on the sea, became a convenient quarry for building stone. Surrounded by malarial swamps, the site was not on the itineraries of many early European travelers who would enter the Levant through Beirut, Akko, or Jaffa (Vann, in press b).

What had been the fate of Herod's magnificent harbor? The offshore fault line reported by the Center for Maritime Studies in its study for the Israel Power Company confirmed Byzantine reports that the breakwaters were awash. Procopius of Gaza described the repaired harbor in a letter to the emperor Anastasius.

> Since the port of the city named after Caesar had fallen into bad condition in the course of time and was open to every threat of the sea, and no longer in fact deserved to be classed as a port, but retained from its former fortune merely the name — you did not overlook her need and her constant laments over the ships which frequently, escaping the sea, were wrecked in the harbour. Those who awaited the cargoes suffered pitifully, seeing the destruction of those things of which they were in need, and seeing it without being able to help. But, thanks to your good will, the city is rejuvenated and receives ships with good courage, and is full of the necessities (*De aedificiis* 1.11.18–20 translated by Levine).

The exact nature of Anastasius' harbor restoration remains unclear, but CAHEP excavations in Area H (Oleson in Raban 1989:130; Raban and Steiglitz 1987) on the northern breakwater suggest that the activity might have included that area. Although we cannot provide an accurate date for closing the harbor,[21] it is most likely that the subsidence was gradual. In fact it is very possible that even as Herod was building the massive breakwaters, the process might have been in progress. Whatever the nature and extent of Byzantine repairs, the harbor had once more disappeared by the time of the Crusades. Without its magnificent harbor and substantial remains of public buildings, travelers arriving at Caesarea were indeed disappointed and perhaps had reason to question the accuracy of Josephus' accounts. It is no surprise that the literary evidence of so grand an edifice as the harbor was dismissed as a gross exaggeration.

> Beyond all doubt, much of that description is magniloquent Josephian hyperbole. Who can read of the mole, two hundred feet broad, built of stones more than fifty feet long, eighteen wide, and nine deep, without a smile? Why the whole harbour enclosed by it is not much broader (Thompson 1861:495).

Lt. Conder who was responsible for the first accurate survey of the site was more specific, but no more generous about the value of the sources.

> At Caesarea we are brought face to face with another vexed question — the reliability of Josephus. Some writers have extolled the Jewish historian as a model of almost infallible veracity...That the present text is often corrupt, there is abundant evidence to prove. That Josephus wrote descriptions which he knew to be exaggerated, it is more difficult to show (Conder 1879:206).

Conder describes the harbor:

> Here at Caesarea we have a description of the port and public buildings which contains undoubted inaccuracies. He represents the port as equal in size to the Piraeus, but it measures scarcely two hundred yard across, whilst the famous harbour of Athens was three quarters of a mile long and over 600 yards in breadth. Josephus also speaks of the mole on the south side of the harbour as being "two hundred feet." This can hardly mean in length, for the present measure is more than a hundred and thirty yards, and if he means in breadth, the estimate is exaggerated, for the greatest width at present is eighty-five feet.
>
> Thus, without taking any notice of the great length given for stones sunk to form part of the breakwater, we find that Josephus estimates the harbour as equal to one of twenty times its capacity, and the mole at over double its real width. It must indeed be remembered that he wrote neither at Caesarea nor at Piraeus, and that exact surveys had then no existence. Yet this case is sufficient to prove that the measurements twice given are unreliable, and the descriptions exaggerated (Conder 1879:207–208).

Despite different attitudes reflected in portions of *Jewish Wars* and *Jewish Antiquities*, including references to the crimes of Herod the Great, Josephus seems to be very consistent in his two descriptions of Caesarea. Both passages describe the harbor in almost identical terms, which might have come either from personal observation during a visit to the city or from his principal historical source, Nicolas of Damascus (Wacholder 1962). Each discusses the city in the broader context of Herodian building programs elsewhere in the kingdom. Likewise, they also stress the difficult nature of the site and the problems with good anchorages in the region. What is not said is also of interest; nowhere are we told why Strato's Tower was selected. Presumably the territory was secure and whatever installations served the earlier settlement could also be utilized in the new construction. Judging from the outcroppings of bedrock still to be seen on the present southern breakwater, there was a small promontory behind which the inhabitants of Strato's Tower had already secured their vessels. The inner basin with its mooring stone (Area I-1) in place and round tower protecting its entrance (Area T) might have belonged to that pre-Herodian period or they might represent Herod's remodeling. Both sources mention an inner harbor, secondary anchorages (*Antiquities*), and deep roadsteads (*Wars*).

The broad outlines of the harbor are suggested in each. The circular shape corresponds well with the curved line of the southern breakwater, and the reference to an entrance on the north side has also been confirmed. Josephus states that the barriers were 200 ft wide, a figure difficult to comprehend for earlier travelers who thought that the portion of the breakwater still above water was the limit of the harbor. In fact, measurements taken along the better preserved northern breakwater are very close to those figures. The more badly damaged southern breakwater is broader in most areas, but this increased width can be attributed to the disintegration of a structure about the same size as that mentioned in our source.

Numbers always pose a problem in ancient sources where different manuscripts often reveal irregularities. Centuries of translations and different editions provided many opportunities for corruptions, such as those pointed out by Conder in the above quotation. The numbers describing Herod's harbor were incredible, as long as the submerged breakwaters were hidden from view, but, in fact, discoveries by CAHEP have confirmed many of the site's impressive credentials. The breakwaters were most likely 200 ft wide; the size of the harbor — including its inner and intermediate basins and the anchorages in the north and south bays — are comparable to Piraeus; and the enormous blocks mentioned in both sources have been found. There does remain one problem, the depth of the harbor does not approach the 20 fathoms (37 m) mentioned in *Wars* 1.411.

Both sources mention the white stone, which is generally interpreted as marble, a preferred material for monumental architecture. Because there is no native marble in the region, it is understood that such stone would be imported from elsewhere, probably Greece or Asia Minor. What was more surprising, however, was that the materials found in the Area G formwork — both timbers (Raban 1989:191–192) and cement — were also imported. Most exciting is the evidence that cement used in the concrete matrix can be identified as pozzalana from the region of Vesuvius (Oleson in Vann, in press b). It has been well known that the best concrete construction was built with this superior material from the Bay of Naples region, and although the use of pozzalana has been suggested for structures in other parts of the empire, this is the first archaeological proof that the material was exported. The source of these materials in Italy opens a new line of thinking about Roman participation in the project. We know that concrete was employed on a large scale, and the suggestion is now that imperial patronage, including shipping materials east — perhaps on the same freighters that had taken Egyptian wheat to Rome — might have been much more extensive than suspected earlier. Likewise, the architects and engineers working with these advanced western materials must have been those from Rome who had experience in the field.

Many problems remain with the study of Caesarea's harbor, but none were more difficult than the search for the Drusion. Both sources mention that the breakwater was divided by a wall with towers at intervals, the largest and grandest called the Drusion, in honor of the emperor's stepson. The Drusion was, in fact, mostly likely the lighthouse of the ancient harbor, and the spill of enormous concrete blocks at the harbor entrance (Area K) is the best candidate for this site. Another difficulty is the presence of towers outside the harbor entrance. They stand there, exactly where Josephus told us they would be. Our problem is to explain their function. To decorate the harbor entrance is not unusual, and there is a long line of examples from Rhodes to New York that illustrate this point. But why, if statues were to be displayed, were they not placed on the large structure that has collapsed nearby (whether it be the Drusion or the lighthouse)? We do not know why the towers were placed outside the entrance, where they might be navigational hazards, but the most convincing argument to date is that they in some way served as targets to assist sailors as they entered the port.

In summary, although the political and personal messages within *Jewish Wars* and *Jewish Antiquities* might be open to debate, the passages from both sources that describe the harbor are very similar. Whatever the inconsistencies of *Wars* or *Antiquities*, the texts dedicated to Herod's building programs, and Caesarea in particular, served only to praise the man for his accomplishments in building. Moreover, when comparing the literary evidence with that gathered in the field by travelers and scholars, the descriptions are compatible.

Notes

1 For general account of the city and its recent archaeological activity, see K. Holum et al. (1988) *King Herod's Dream: Caesarea on the Sea*. W. W.

117

Norton, New York. The most comprehensive account of the archaeological remains is L. Levine (1975) *Roman Caesarea: An Archaeological-Topographical Study*. Qedem 2. Monographs of the Institute of Archaeology. Institute of Archaeology, Jerusalem. The two most complete histories of the site are J. Ringel (1975) *Roman Césarée de Palestine: Étude Historique et Archéologique*. Association des Publications Près les Universitiés de Strasbourg, Paris and L. Levine (1975) *A History of Caesarea under Roman Rule*. Brill, Leiden. A summary of early investigation and excavation will appear in my Early Travelers and the First Archaeologists at Caesarea, in *Recent Investigations at Caesarea Maritima*, in press b. Texts for Josephus are from the following: *Autobiographie Flavius Josèphe*, trans A. Pelletier. Sociète d'Edition "Les Belles Lettres," Paris; *Josephus, The Jewish Wars*, trans H. St. J. Thackeray (R. Marcus, A. Wikgren, and L. H. Feldman). Heinemann, London; Harvard, Loeb Classical Library, Cambridge; *Josephus, Jewish Antiquities, Books I–III*, trans. R. Marcus. Heinemann, London; Harvard University, Loeb Classical Library, Cambridge.

2 Archeological reports on the Temple Area include: A. Perrot (1957) *The Temple of Jerusalem*, trans B. E. Hook, in *Studies in Biblical Archeology*, no. 5, (London, pp 76–100; H. Schmidt (1933) *Der heilige Fels in Jerusalem: Eine Archäologische und Religiongschichtliche Studie*, Tübingen pp. 17–39 on the layout of the sanctuary; and for the early drawings of the sanctuary, C. Warren and C. R. Conder (1889) Jerusalem, in *Survey of Western Palestine, Vol. V. London, pp. 97–225, 307–319* and C. Warren (1884) Plans, Elevations, *Sections Shewing the Results of the Excavations at Jerusalem, 1867–1870*, London. More recent investigations of the Temple Mount are reported in B. Mazar (1969) The Excavations in the Old City of Jerusalem: Preliminary Report of the First Season, "1968," *Eretz-Israel* 9:161–174 and item, (1971) Excavations in the Old City of Jerusalem near the Temple Mount: Preliminary Report of the Second and Third Seasons, 1969–1970, *Eretz Israel* 10:1–31. The popular account of excavations at Masada is Y. Yadin (1966) *Masada; The Zealots' Last Stand*. Weidenfeld and Nicolson, London. A general discussion of the Herodian building program is found in J. B. Ward-Perkins (1981) *Roman Imperial Architecture*. Harmondsworth, pp. 309–314.

3 Excellent examples of *opus reticulatum* appear in the Herodian winter palace at Jericho (E. Netzer [1974] The Hasmonean and Herodian Winter Places at Jericho, *Qadmoniot* 7:27–63 [Hebrew]) and item (1977) The Winter Palaces of the Judean Kings at Jericho at the end of the Second Temple Period, *Bulletin of the American Schools of Oriental Research* 228:1–13) and terrace walls at Banias that presumably are part of his palace there (Conder and Kitchner, Vol. II, 388, 392).

4 The principal source in English remains H. St. J. Thackeray (1929) *Josephus the Man and Historian*. New York, repr. New York, 1967. A more popular account is G. A. Williamson (1964) *The World of Josephus*. London. On the disparity of the *Life* and *Jewish Wars*, see Shaye J. D. Cohen (1979) *Josephus in Galilee and Rome: His 'Vitae' and Development as a Historian*. E. J. Brill, Leiden. For Herod and his construction program at Caesarea, see A. Raban (1982) Josephus Flavius and the Herodian Harbor at Caesarea, *Josephus Flavius Historian of Eretz Israel*. Yad Izhak Ben Zvi, Jerusalem (Hebrew).

5 It was after the fall of the fortress of Jotapata and Josephus' surrender that Vespasian returned with his army to Caesarea in order to initiate the second phase of this Galilee campaign. Presumably Josephus had been there before, in A.D. 63, for example, on his first trip to Rome. By that time the city had been dedicated for three quarters of a century, but in fact it must have seemed very new, with gleaming marble buildings that announced that Caesarea was indeed a city of the Roman world. During that brief decade during which Herod built the city and its harbor, there must have been an initial focus upon critical elements such as the water system, an ordered arrangement of city streets, and, for the harbor, the initial phase of constructing its massive southern breakwater. But one can imagine that for decades following the dedication there would have been constant building activity. Even without the continued patronage of Herod, Caesarea prospered. It was this city that Josephus visited in A.D. 63 or 67.

6 The date of publication was after the dedication of the *Templum Pacis* in Rome (commemorating peace in Judaea) and before the death of Vespasian, who was given a copy of the text.

7 For example, Whilhelm Weber, *Josephus und Vespasian: Untersuchungen zu den jüdischen Krieg des Flavius Josephus* (Berlin, 1921) and Helgo Lindner, *Die Geschichtsauffassung des Flavius Josephus im Bellum Judaicum* (Leiden, 1972).

8 Raban 1987. A contrasting point of view is found in D. W. Roller (1982) The Northern Plain of Sharon in the Hellenistic Period, *Bulletin of the American Schools of Oriental Research* 238:35–42; *ibid* (1983) The Problem of the Location of Strato's Tower, *Bulletin of the American Schools of Oriental Research* 252:61–66. Joint Expedition excavations concerning the issue are reported in J. Blakely (1984) A

Stratigraphically Determined Date for the Inner Fortification Wall at Caesarea Maritima, in H. O. Thompson, Ed. (1984) *The Answers Lie Below: Essays in Honor of Lawrence Edmund Toombs.* University Press of America, Lanham, MD, pp. 3–38 and *ibid* (1989), The City Wall of Strato's Tower: A Stratigraphic Rejoinder, *Bulletin of the American Schools of Oriental Research* 273:79–82.

9   Herod rebuilt another city, Samaria Sebaste, along the same lines. It too included Roman architectural types and was the location of another temple dedicated to Rome and the emperor.

10 It is interesting to note that, despite the size of this project and the amazing speed with which it was built, it was not the only building program being undertaken during that decade. The enlargement of the temple platform in Jerusalem was started in 19 B.C. and finished in 10 B.C.

11 Diane Everman, a graduate student in the History Department at the University of Maryland, is presently writing a Ph.D. dissertation on the water systems of Caesarea.

12 One of the largest vaults was remodeled at a later date to serve as a Mithraeum. For results of the Joint Expedition excavations, see Robert J. Bull, The Mithraeum of Caesarea Maritima, *Études Mithraiques, Texts et Mémoires* 4:75–89. The final publication of pottery has also appeared. Jeffrey Blakely, *Caesarea Maritima, Vol. IV. The Pottery and Dating of Vault 1: Horreum, Mithraeum, and Later Uses.* Edwin Mellen, Queenston.

13 Created in 1980 under the direction of Avner Raban of Haifa University, the co-directors are Robert L. Hohlfelder of the University of Colorado, Robert L. Vann of the University of Maryland, and, until 1985, John P. Oleson of the University of Victoria. Robert Stieglitz of Rutgers University at Newark joined as co-director in 1986.

14 For a recent listing of CAHEP publications, see the bibliography in Avner Raban (1898) *The Harbours of Caesarea Maritima: Results of the Caesarea Ancient Harbour Excavation Project, 1980–1985, Vol. I: The Site and the Excavations,* B.A.R. International Series 491. British Archaeological Reports, Oxford.

15 A particularly low level of sand in 1990 provided divers a clear view of huge blocks of wooden formwork for Herodian concrete construction.

16 Locus 225 in Wall 1 of Area S-2 was relaid by the Crusaders, judging from the numerous examples of unmatched cuttings for earlier Herodian dovetail clamps and at least one example of an iron C-clamp of Crusader date that remains *in situ* (Raban 1989:Vol. II, 476).

17 For discussion of the Severan harbor at Lepcis Magna, see R. Bartoccini and A. Zanelli (1960) *Il Porto di Lepcis Magna,* Bollettino del Centro di Studi per la Storia dell' Architettura, 13 (Rome) and M. Squarciapino (1966) *Lepcis Magna.* Raggi, Basel. For Ostia see R. Meiggs (1973) *Roman Ostia.* Clarendon Press, Oxford. O. Testaguzza, The Port of Rome. *Archaeology* 17.3:173–179. An excellent survey of Roman harbors is D. J. Blackman, Ancient Harbors in the Mediterranean. *International Journal of Nautical Archaeology* 11:79–104, 185–211.

18 The illustration, a black-and-white photograph of a National Geographic Society painting, was first published in Robert L. Hohlfelder (1987) King Herod's City on the Sea: Caesarea Maritima, *National Geographic Magazine* 171.2:261–279.

19 Similar techniques for joining wooden formwork underwater have been reported from North Africa and France. R. A. Yorke and D. P. Davidson, Survey of Building Techniques at the Roman Harbours of Carthage and some other North African Ports, pp. 157–164 in Raban 1985a. Xerge Ximénès and Martine Moerman (1989) Le Quai de la Crique est du Port Romain des Laurons (Martigues). *Cahiers d'Archéologique Subaquatique* 8:179ff.

20 According to Raban, another portion of this fortification system, which he dates not to the Herodian period, but to the earlier Hellenistic settlement of Strato's Tower, is the south wall of the vault in Area I-3 (Raban 1989:138–143, 421–423, 425). That wall, laid in a system of alternating stretchers and headers, identical with sections of the city wall adjacent the northern towers, later served as part of the Herodian platform supporting the temple to Rome and Augustus. For references concerning the dating of the wall, see note 8.

21 Hohlfelder (in Raban 1989:69–70) has argued against the catastrophic earthquake theory suggested by Fritsch and Ben-Dor (1961:50–59). There is no direct evidence that the earthquake caused damage in Caesarea, much less that it was serious enough to destroy the harbor. That event would have been an occasion worthy of mention.

References

Adam, J.-P. (1982) *L'Architecture Militaire Grecque.* Picard, Paris.

Avi-Yonah, M. (1956) Caesarea, in "Notes and News." *Israel Exploration Journal* 6:260–261.

— (1970) The Caesarea Porphyry Statue. *Israel Exploration Journal* 20:203–208.

Blakely, J. (1987) *Caesarea Maritima, Vol. IV. The Pottery and Dating of Vault I; Horreum, Mithraeum, and Later Uses.* Edwin Mellen, Queenston.

Ben-Dor, I. (1961) A Marine Expedition to the Holy Land, Summer 1960. *American Journal of Archaeology* 65:186.

Bull, R. J. (1982) Caesarea Maritima: In Search of Herod's City. Biblical *Archaeology Review* 8:24–40.

Conder, C. R. (1873) The Survey of Palestine, Report XII, the South Side of Carmel. *Palestine Exploration Quarterly* 5:82–86.

— (1874) The Survey of Palestine, Report XVI. *Palestine Exploration Quarterly* 6:13–15.

— (1879) *Tent Work in Palestine.* Richard Bentley and Son, London.

Conder, C. R. and H. H. Kitchner (1882) *Survey of Western Palestine, Memoires of the Topography, Orography, Hydrography, and Archaeology.* Palestine Exploration Fund, London. Vol. II, pp. 13–29 and sheets VII–XVI.

Cornick, H. F. (1959) *Dock and Harbour Engineering, II: The Design of Harbours.* C. Griffin, London.

Crowfoot, J. W., K. M. Kenyon, E. L. Sukenik (1942–1958) *Samaria-Sebaste. Reports of the Work of the Joint Expedition in 1931–1933 and of the British Expedition in 1935,* 3 vols. Palestine Exploration Fund, London.

Flinder, A. (1976) A Piscina at Caesarea: A Preliminary Survey. *Israel Exploration Journal* 26:77–80.

Fritsch, C. T. and I. Ben-Dor (1961) The Link Expedition to Israel, 1960. *Biblical Archaeologist* 24:50–59.

Frova, A., D. Adamesteaunu, A. Albricci, G. Belloni, V. Borroni, C. Brusa Gerra, S. Finocchi, and G. Struffolino (1965) *Scavi di Caesarea Maritima.* Istituto Lombardo, Accademia di Scienze e Lettere, Milan.

Hamburger, H. (1959) A New Inscription from the Caesarea Aqueduct. *Israel Exploration Journal* 9:188–189.

Hohlfelder, R. L. (1988) Procopius de Aedificiis 1.11.18–20: Caesarea Maritima and the Building of Harbours in Late Antiquity. In *Mediterranean Cities: Historical Perspectives,* I. Malkin and R. L. Hohlfelder, Eds. Frank Cass, London, pp. 54–62.

— (in press) A Pioneer of Underwater Archaeology: Edwin A. Link at Caesarea Maritima. *Deutsche Hydrographische Zeitschrift.*

Holum, K. G., R. L. Hohlfelder, R. J. Bull, and A. Raban (1988) *King Herod's Dream: Caesarea on the Sea.* W. W. Norton, New York and London.

Kedar, Y. and Y. Ziv (1964) The Water Supply at Ancient Caesarea. *Yedioth* 28:122–131 (Hebrew).

Laqueur, R. (1920) *Der Jüdische Historiker Flavius Josephus.* Giessen, 1920. Repr. Darmstadt, 1970.

Lehmann-Hartleben, K. (1923) *Die Antiken Hafenanlagen des Mittelmeeres.* Klio, Beitrage zur Alten Geschichte, Beiheft 14. Klio, Wiesbaken.

Levine, L. (1975) *Roman Caesarea: An Archaeological-Topographical Study.* Qedem, Monographs of the Institute of Archaeology, Hebrew University, 2. Hebrew University, Jerusalem.

Levine, L. and E. Netzer (1986) *Excavations at Caesarea Maritima, 1975, 1976, 1979 — Final Report.* Qedem, Monographs of the Institute of Archaeology, Hebrew University, 21. Hebrew University, Jerusalem.

Link, E. A. (1956) *Survey Trip to Israel: (a) The Port of Caesarea.* Privately Published, New York.

Negev, A. (1967) *Caesarea.* Lewin-Epstein, Tel-Aviv.

Netzer, E. (1981) Herod's Building Projects: State Necessity or Personal Need? *Jerusalem Cathedra* 1:48–61.

Olami, Y. and R. Peleg (1977) Caesarea's Aqueducts. *Archaeological News* (Department of Antiquities) 46:6–8 (Hebrew).

Olami, Y. and J. Ringel (1975) New Inscriptions of the Tenth Legion Fretensis from the High Level Aqueduct of Caesarea. *Israel Exploration Journal* 25:148–150, pl. 13b.

Oleson, J. P. (in press) *The Harbours of Caesarea Maritima. Results of the Caesarea Ancient Harbour Excavation Project, 1980–1985, Vol. II: The Finds.* British Archaeological Reports, International Series 491. B.A.R., Oxford.

Oleson, J. P., R. L. Hohlfelder, A. Raban, and R. L. Vann (1984) The Caesarea Ancient Harbour Excavation Project (C.A.H.E.P.): Preliminary Report on the 1980–1983 Seasons. *Journal of Field Archaeology* 11:281–305.

Pococke, R. (1745) *A Description of the East and Some Other Countries.* W. Bowyer, London.

Quinn, A. de F. (1961) *Design and Construction of Ports and Marine Structures.* McGraw-Hill, New York.

Raban, A. (1983) Recent Maritime Archaeological Research in Israel. *International Journal of Nautical Archaeology* 12:241–251.

— (1985a) *Harbour Archaeology: Proceedings of the First International Workshop on Ancient Mediterranean Harbours. Caesarea Maritima.* British Archaeological Reports, International Series 257. B.A.R., Oxford.

— (1985b) Caesarea Maritima, 1983–1984. *Journal of Nautical Archaeology* 14.2:155–177.

— (1987) The City Walls of Straton's Tower: Some New Archaeological Data. *Bulletin of the Schools of Oriental Research* 168:71–87.

— (1989) *The Harbours of Caesarea Maritima. Results of the Caesarea Ancient Harbour Excavation Project, 1980–1985, Vol. I: The Site and the Excavations.* British Archaeological Reports, International Series 491. B.A.R., Oxford.

Raban, A. and E. Linder (1978) Underwater Excavations at Akko, Dor and Caesarea. *International Journal of Nautical Archaeology* 7:238–243.

Raban, A. and R. Steiglitz (1987) Caesarea Maritima, C.A.H.E.P. 1986. *Israel Exploration Journal* 37:187–190.

Raban, A., Y. Tur-Kaspa, E. Adler, E. Sivan, and G. Kaplan (1976) *Marine Archaeological Research in Caesarea.* CMS Publication 2/76. Center for Maritime Studies, Haifa.

Rhoads, D. M. (1976) *Israel in Revolution: 6–74 C.E.: A Political History Based on the Writings of Josephus.* Fortress Press, Philadelphia.

Schwabe, M. (1950) The Bourgos Inscription from Caesarea Palaestinae. In J. N. Epstein Jubilee Volume. Jerusalem, pp. 273–283 (Hebrew).

Thackeray, H. St. J. (1967) *Josephus the Man and Historian.* New York, 1929. Repr. New York, 1967.

Thompson, W. M. (1861) *The Land and the Book.* T. Nelson and Sons, London.

Vann, R. L. (in press a) The Search for Herod's Lighthouse. *Proceedings of the II International Congress on Biblical Archaeology.* Jerusalem.

— (in press b) Recent Investigations at Caesarea Maritima. *Journal of Roman Archaeology.* Monograph Series, Ann Arbor, Michigan.

Wacholder, B. Z. (1962) *Nicolaus of Damascus.* University of California Press, Berkeley and Los Angeles.

Winter, F. E. (1971) *Greek Fortifications.* University of Toronto Press, Toronto.

Yeivin, S. (1955) Excavations at Caesarea Maritima. *Archaeology* 8:122–129.

10: Health and Demography in a 16th-Century Southeastern Chiefdom

Dorothy A. Humpf

Department of Anthropology, Pennsylvania State University, University Park, Pennsylvania

Hernando de Soto and his entrada entered the interior southeastern United States in 1540. Four accounts of the expedition have been published. These include eyewitness descriptions by Rodrigo Ranjel, de Soto's secretary (Bourne 1922); Luys Hernandez de Biedma, the factor of the expedition (Smith 1968); and an account by an anonymous author known as the Gentleman of Elvas (Smith 1968). A fourth account contains information from several participants compiled by an Inca Indian, Garcilaso de la Vega (Varner and Varner 1951).

The chroniclers report that the entrada observed numerous aboriginal populations, many organized into complex chiefdoms. The province of Coosa is described as one of the most powerful societies encountered. Recent reconstructions of de Soto's route through the Southeast have allowed archaeologists and historians to link specific 16th-century archaeological sites with named towns visited by de Soto (DePratter et al. 1985; Hudson et al. 1984). In particular, the province of Coosa, centered in northwest Georgia, has been intensively studied (Hudson et al. 1985).

Two decades later, two other Spanish expeditions visited many of the same towns in Coosa contacted by de Soto: the Tristan de Luna expedition in 1560 and the Juan Pardo expedition in 1566. Locations of particular towns and distances between them are fairly consistent between the three expeditions, but descriptions of particular towns and provinces often vary. For example, Ranjel describes the chief of Coosa as powerful with rule over a "wide territory, one of the best and most abundant found in Florida" (Bourne 1922). Later, Augustin Davila Padilla reports that the main town in 1560 "did not have above thirty house, or a few more" and that the town "looked so much worse to the Spaniards for having been depicted so grandly" (Quinn 1979). Padilla also reports that the population of Coosa had decreased and the chief had lost some of his political power (Quinn 1979).

In this sense, these documents provide a unique chronicle of the changing character of southeastern U.S. aboriginal culture. The accounts provide descriptions of towns and societies at particular points in time, and comparisons of documents from the three expeditions provides information about how these towns and provinces changed over time.

This paper presents the results of an analysis of skeletal series from three particular towns visited by early Spanish explorers. All are located within the paramount chiefdom of Coosa (Hudson et al. 1985). They include the Little Egypt site (identified by Hudson et al. [1985] as the main town of Coosa), the Etowah site (de Soto's Itaba), and the King site (the probable site of the town of Piachi) (DePratter et al. 1985).

The research presented here was designed to investigate the variation in community health and mortality at different sites within a unified multilevel chiefdom. The communities in the sample represent two levels of the settlement hierarchy of the paramount chiefdom of Coosa —a mound center (Little Egypt) and outlying nonmound large towns (Etowah and King). It was expected that health would be best and expectation of life longest at the main town of Coosa, because it is the primary center of the chiefdom. Instead, all indices of health and longevity are poorest at the capital. These results cannot be explained by archaeological data alone. The ethnohistoric documents, however, provide provisional explanations for some of the patterns found in the skeletal series. This "ethnohistoric-archaeological approach" (Brain et al. 1974) has played a critical role in allowing a better understanding of Coosa and other prehistoric chiefdom polities in the southeastern United States.

Ethnohistoric and Archaeological Background

Various reconstructions of particular parts of the routes of these expeditions and different locations of specific towns have been proposed (Lankford 1977; Curren et al. 1989; DePratter et al. 1985; Hudson et al. 1984, 1985; Hudson 1988). The identification of the Coosa province presented by Hudson et al. (1985) is utilized here.

Hudson et al. have reconstructed the routes of de Soto (DePratter et al. 1985; Hudson et al. 1984), de Luna (Hudson et al. 1989), and Juan Pardo (DePratter et al. 1983) using accounts of the three expeditions and distributions of known 16th-century archaeological sites. Accounts of all three expeditions discuss the province of Coosa. The de Soto expedition visited numerous towns in the province in 1540 and spent over 90 days traveling through towns subject to the main town, which was also called Coosa (Hudson et al. 1985). They stayed in the principal town for over a month. A detachment of the Luna expedition reached Coosa in 1560 (Hudson 1988; Hudson et al. 1989), and while Pardo never reached the main town of Coosa, apparently at least one of his soldiers did (Hudson et al. 1989).

The chiefdom of Coosa covered a narrow, but very long, area from eastern Tennessee to central Alabama (Figure 1). The reconstruction of the province by Hudson et al. (1985) was based primarily on reported distances and travel times between towns. The distribution also appears to correspond reasonably well with the distribution of certain artifact styles, particularly the Citico-style gorget (Hudson et al. 1985).

It is clear that Coosa was one of the most complex chiefdoms visited by de Soto. Numerous "provinces" are described as being subject to or under the control of the main town. The paramouncy included a minimum of seven clusters of archaeological sites, which represent independent chiefdoms, united at least for a short time, with the main town (Hally et al. 1989). Hudson et al. (1985) further note that Spanish accounts list several named provinces, which correspond to some of these site clusters. These named provinces were separated by unoccupied areas and included provinces called Chiaha, Coste, Coosa, Ulibahali, Talisi, and a province identified with the Napochies (Hally et al. 1989).

The large powerful chiefdom of Coosa of 1540 had apparently undergone significant changes by the time it was visited by Tristan de Luna's men 20 years later. Some members of the Luna party who had been to Coosa with de Soto could explain the difference only by saying that they must have been bewitched to think the land was so good (Hudson et al. 1989). Alternatively, the decline was attributed to the "excesses of a certain captain," de Soto

(Davila Padilla 1596, quoted in Hudson et al. 1989). In particular, the main town was smaller and could no longer rigidly control some of the towns to the north. Hudson et al. (1989) detail one of the most telling incidents of this decline in political power. The Spaniards were asked by the leaders of Coosa to help them raid a nearby group of Indians, the Napochies. The Napochies had recently stopped sending tribute to the main town and had cut off the town's lines of communications to the north (Hudson 1988; Hudson et al. 1989).

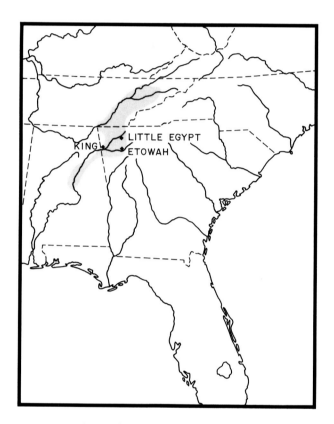

FIG. 1. Boundaries of the Coosa chiefdom and location of sites in the present sample.

These differing descriptions suggest that the main town had, in 20 years time, lost some of its political power. Coosa was not the significant center it had been when de Soto saw it. The reason for this decline is not clear from the documents, although Luna's men implicated de Soto to some degree. Smith (1987) suggests that epidemic disease, reflected by increased numbers of mass and multiple burials, decreased numbers of sites, and decreased site size may be responsible for the decline of Coosa.

A later description of the province is provided in documents from the Pardo expedition. At the town of Satapo, in the northern part of the province, the expedition was informed of an ambush organized by the chief of Coosa. They then left the province without reaching the capital. However, they were told that Coosa was the best town in the entire region, besides Santa Elena, a large town on the coast (DePratter et al. 1983). Pardo was also told that the town had approximately 150 inhabitants. DePratter et al. (1983) suggest that this was an error and that the informant actually meant 150 houses. Coosa apparently had regained some of its former power since 1560.

The Archaeological Sample

The skeletal series studied here were excavated from three Late Mississippian/Protohistoric sites in northwest Georgia. Localized, regional variants of the Late Mississippian and Early Historic periods have been recognized throughout the Southeast. In the Ridge and Valley province of Georgia, the only recognized variant is the Lamar culture, which ranges from A.D. 1350 to A.D. 1540.

The Little Egypt site (9Mu102) is located in Carters, Murray County, Georgia, at the junction of the Coosawattee River and Talking Rock Creek (Hally 1979). It is one of two known Lamar mound and village sites in the Georgia Valley and Ridge province (Hally and Langford 1988). The site has two components — an early Lamar (Little Egypt phase, A.D. 1400–1500) component and a late Lamar (Barnett phase, A.D. 1500–1600) component (Hally 1979). The site appears to have reached its greatest size during the Barnett phase (Hally 1980; Hally and Langford 1989).

The first major archaeological investigation of the site was conducted by Warren K. Moorehead in 1925. Moorehead described the site as having three mounds (the largest 14 feet high and the others "smaller"), in addition to a large village area (Moorehead 1932). During the several weeks he spent at Little Egypt, Moorehead excavated between 35 and 40 burials from the larger mound and the village. The location of these burials is at present unknown. Moorehead presents no inventory of individual burials, but notes that most were flexed and poorly preserved, and that several contained grave goods, including one burial in the village area with over 2000 beads (Moorehead 1932:151) and one (Skeleton H) in the large mound that contained both iron and aboriginal artifacts (Moorehead 1932:153). Moorehead apparently did not excavate in either of the two smaller mounds (Moorehead 1932:152).

David Hally directed University of Georgia excavations at the Little Egypt site between 1969 and 1972 (Hally 1980). The excavations were conducted as part of a mitigation project prior to the construction of Carter's Dam by the U.S. Army Corps of Engineers. The site was inundated in 1976 (Hally 1980). In 1969, only the larger mound (designated Mound A) and one of the smaller mounds (Mound B) could be located. It is thought that the third mound described by Moorehead may have been destroyed by erosion (Hudson et al. 1985).

The two remaining mounds were separated by a plaza (Hally 1980), and a large village was present to the south and west of the mounds. The site covered an area of 50,000 m^2 (Hally and Langford 1988). Fifty-nine burials were excavated by the University of Georgia.

The King site (9Fl5) is located on the Coosa River in Rome, Floyd County, Georgia. It was initially excavated by field crews from Shorter College under the direction of Patrick Garrow and later by field crews from the University of Georgia under the direction of David Hally. The site is a large nonmound village, which includes a central plaza containing at least two public buildings and an outer zone of an estimated 50 domestic buildings (Hally 1975). These were enclosed by a defensive ditch and palisade (Hally et al. 1975). The site dates to the 16th-century Barnett phase and was probably occupied for less than 50 years (Hally 1975). A short occupation is suggested by limited rebuilding of the domestic structures and little evidence of repair of the surrounding palisade. Two hundred and ten burials were excavated (Hally 1975).

Although the King site contains no mounds, burials do appear to be spatially and artifactually segregated. Some interments occur in and around domestic houses, an area designated as "private" (Seckinger 1977). "Public" space includes the plaza and surrounding areas (Seckinger 1977). Smith (1975) suggests the public burials may be high-status individuals, because the plaza is described by Garcilaso, one of the Soto chroniclers, as high-status space. Some high-status burials contain Spanish-introduced metal artifacts (Seckinger 1977) and several types of aboriginal goods (Smith 1987), while a high percentage of private-area burials include only utilitarian items or no grave goods (Seckinger 1977). Burials have not been separated with respect to differential social status in the present analysis; future work, however, will examine the effect of intrasite social status on health and longevity.

The Etowah site (9Br1) is located on the Etowah River in Bartow County near Cartersville, Georgia. Although the Etowah site contains numerous mounds, no mound stages have been assigned to the Lamar period (Larson 1971). The mounds and the defensive ditch and palisade that surround the site date to the earlier Wilbanks phase (Larson 1971).

A large village occupation, however, was present at Etowah during the Lamar period. The village area was excavated by the Georgia Historical Commission under the direction of Lewis Larson, Jr. Seventy-six burials were excavated from the village area and represent a mixture of Lamar-period Brewster phase and earlier Wilbanks phase burials (Larson 1971).

Methodology

AGE AND SEX DETERMINATION

Each skeleton in the sample was assigned an age and sex using standard osteological techniques. Where possible, adult aging focused on age-related changes in the pubic symphyses (Todd 1920; McKern and Stewart 1957; Gilbert and McKern 1973; Meindl et al. 1985). Other measures, such as the degree of endocranial suture closure (Todd and Lyon 1924) and changes in the auricular surface of the ilium (Lovejoy et al. 1985), were used to support ages obtained from the pubis. Where pubic symphyses were not preserved, the iliac auricular surface was used as the primary method of age determination. Only in the absence of both pubic symphyses and the auricular surface was cranial suture closure used as the primary method of age determination. In some cases, preservation was so poor that none of these techniques could be applied and the individual was designated only as "adult."

Subadults were assigned ages on the basis of epiphyseal union (Ubelaker 1978; MacKay n.d.), dental eruption, and development standards (Thoma and Goldman 1960; Ubelaker 1978; Moorrees et al. 1963a,b), and long bone lengths (Ubelaker 1978). Sex was determined only for adults in the sample. Sex was assigned primarily on the basis of pelvic and cranial morphology (Phenice 1969; Ubelaker 1978; Bass 1987; Acsadi and Nemeskeri 1970). Secondary criteria included the maximum size of the head of the femur (Ubelaker 1978) and humerus (Dwight 1904–1905).

HEALTH STATUS

Numerous proximate measures of health have been used by archaeologists to assess the well-being of prehistoric populations. These measures are based on the incidence of various types of bone or dental lesions in skeletal populations. The frequency of pathological processes (disease) reflects the ability of a population to adapt to the environmental and social demands placed upon them. Differential health status is measured by a comparison of the incidence of pathological processes in skeletal series.

In the present sample, each individual bone or bone fragment was macroscopically observed for the presence of bone lesions. The type of lesion (proliferative or resorptive) was noted, as was its condition (active or healed) and its location (anterior or posterior surface, medial or lateral surface, proximal or distal surface). Only those bone lesions indicative of periostitis will be presented here. Enamel hypoplasia, dental caries, stature, and other bone lesions will be discussed at a later date.

Periostitis is an inflammation of the outer membrane (the periosteum) of a bone. It appears as a porous, often irregularly distributed, layer of new bone deposited on the normal bone surface. Periostitis is considered to be useful indicator of nonspecific infectious processes in skeletal series (Goodman et al. 1984).

BURIAL PHASING

All burials from the three sites were initially examined, even though it was known that some may have resulted from an occupation earlier than that of interest in the present study. At the King site, all burials could be confidently assigned to the 16th-century Barnett phase and are included in the present analysis. At Little Egypt and Etowah, however, two occupations were identified, and some burials could not be definitely assigned to 16th-century late Lamar phases. For these two sites, burials were designated Lamar, probable Lamar, or phase unknown using diagnostic ceramic attributes and stratigraphic information. There were 31 burials at Little Egypt and 44 burials at Etowah that were designated definite or probable late Lamar. Many of the remaining burials without diagnostic grave goods may also date to the late Lamar occupation at both sites.

AGE-AT-DEATH DISTRIBUTIONS

Age-at-death distributions were calculated for each site. Six age intervals (0–5, 5–15, 15–25, 25–35, 35–45, and 45+) were used for this analysis. Ten-year age intervals were used to lessen any effects of problematic age determination (Milner et al. 1989). The distributions include adult individuals who could not be assigned ages and individuals whose ages overlapped two intervals. In the latter case, individuals were evenly apportioned between two adjacent age intervals. The apportioning of individuals designated only as "adult" was more problematic. Milner (1982) has suggested that unaged adults be unevenly assigned to age categories based on the proportion of aged individuals in each category. He argues that this results in a more realistic representation of the population than does assigning these individuals equally in the distribution (Milner 1982:130). At the Little Egypt and King sites, individuals were unevenly apportioned.

Due to small sample size at the Etowah site, however, no individual burials aged 25–35 could be definitely assigned to the Lamar period. At this site, the unaged adults were therefore evenly apportioned among the adult age categories.

LIFE TABLE CONSTRUCTION

Life tables were constructed for all three skeletal series, even though sample size was small. In large modern populations, life tables measure mortality levels by combining age-specific mortality rates into a single statistical model (Shyrock and Siegel 1975). The life table statistic most utilized by paleodemographers is life expectancy at birth (e_0). Life expectancy at birth expresses the expected number of years to be lived, on average, by a newborn individual in a particular population (Shyrock and Siegel 1975).

The validity of constructing life tables for archaeological populations has recently been questioned due to problems with sampling, differential bone preservation, and age and sex determination (Angel 1969; Bocquet-Appel and Masset 1982). Nevertheless, as discussed below, life-table statistics in the three groups discussed here parallel untransformed age-at-death distribution data and can be a useful statistic for comparison with other prehistoric populations. A FORTRAN program written by Dr. Steven Whittington, Pennsylvania State University, was used to calculate life tables for each population and for the sample as a whole.

Results

AGE-AT-DEATH DISTRIBUTIONS AND LIFE TABLES

The untransformed age-at-death distributions of Lamar individuals from the three sites are presented in Figure 2. Several observations can be made from these distributions. First, the proportion of infants and young children (<5 years of age) is considerably higher at the Little Egypt site (9Mu102) than at the King (9Fl5) or Etowah sites (9Br1). A number of explanations can be offered for this difference, including sampling error, and these are discussed in more detail below.

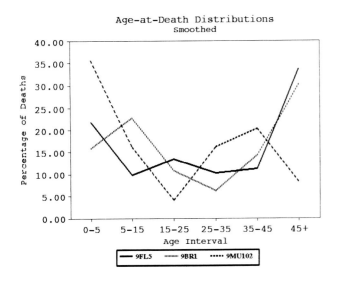

FIG. 2. Age-at-death distributions for the Little Egypt (9Mu102), Etowah (9Br1), and King (9Fl5) skeletal series.

Adult mortality peaks at different ages at the three sites. At Little Egypt, adult mortality is highest in the 35 to 45-year age interval, while at the other sites, mortality peaks in the 45+ age interval. The percentage of individuals

dying in the 45+ interval is much lower at Little Egypt than at the other sites. Most individuals, it appears, did not survive to older ages, as did individuals at King or Etowah.

The cumulative mortality distributions (Figure 3) also show a trend toward younger mortality in the Little Egypt skeletal series. By age 15, 51.6% of all deaths have occurred in the Little Egypt series, compared to 31.7% in the King series, and 38.6% in the Etowah series. Between the ages of 15 and 25, mortality becomes somewhat more even between the three sites, with cumulative mortality by age 25 at 55.6% at Little Egypt, 45.1% at King, and 49.4% at Etowah. In the next interval (25–35), however, mortality again is quite different, with cumulative frequencies of 71.7% at Little Egypt, 55.3% at King, and 55.6% at Etowah. By the end of the 35–45 interval, mortality reaches 91.9% at Little Egypt, 66.4% at King, and 69.8% at Etowah.

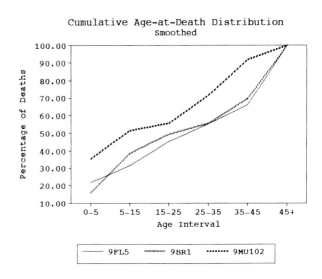

FIG. 3. Cumulative age-at-death distributions for the Little Egypt (9Mu102), Etowah (9Br1), and King (9Fl5) skeletal series.

The life tables presented in Tables 1 to 3 show a similar trend. Life expectancy at birth is lowest in the Little Egypt series ($e_0 = 20.06$), intermediate at Etowah ($e_0 = 27.33$), and highest at King ($e_0 = 28.55$). Life expectancy at age 15 (e_{15}) is 21.74 at Little Egypt, 24.63 at King, and 25.44 at Etowah.

PERIOSTEAL REACTIONS

Periostitis is the most common bone lesion in all three skeletal series. Periostitis is unquestionably more frequent at the Little Egypt site than at the others. Osteomyelitis is present, but rare. Periostitis ranges from a low of 11% in the Etowah series, to 14% in the King series, to a high of 32% in the Little Egypt series. At Etowah, all periosteal reactions were observed in adult

Table 1
ABRIDGED LIFE TABLE FOR LITTLE EGYPT (9Mu102)

x	D_x	d_x	l_x	q_x	L_x	T_x	e_x
0–1	3.00	9.68	100	.097	92.59	2005.63	20.056
1–5	8.00	25.81	90.32	.286	296.77	1913.04	21.180
5–15	5.00	16.13	64.52	.250	564.52	1616.26	25.052
15–25	1.25	4.03	48.39	.083	463.71	1051.75	21.736
25–35	5.00	16.13	44.35	.364	369.62	588.04	13.258
35–45	6.25	20.16	28.23	.714	178.09	218.41	7.738
45+	2.50	8.06	8.06	1.00	40.32	40.32	5.000

Table 2
ABRIDGED LIFE TABLE FOR ETOWAH (9Br2)

x	D_x	d_x	l_x	q_x	L_x	T_x	e_x
0–1	3.00	6.82	100	.068	94.45	2733.04	27.330
1–5	4.00	9.09	93.18	.098	350.00	2638.59	28.317
5–15	10.00	22.73	84.09	.270	727.27	2288.59	27.216
15–25	4.75	10.80	61.36	.176	552.79	1561.31	25.444
25–35	2.75	6.25	50.57	.124	475.85	1008.52	19.944
35–45	6.25	14.20	44.32	.320	382.10	532.67	12.019
45+	13.25	30.11	30.11	1.00	150.57	150.57	5.000

Table 3
LIFE TABLE FOR KING (9Fl5)

x	D_x	d_x	l_x	q_x	L_x	T_x	e_x
0–1	5.00	2.68	100	.027	97.63	2854.97	28.550
1–5	35.50	19.06	97.32	.196	341.62	2757.34	28.334
5–15	18.50	9.93	78.26	.127	732.91	2415.72	30.869
15–25	24.96	13.40	68.33	.196	616.36	1682.81	24.629
25–35	18.96	10.18	54.93	.185	497.44	1066.45	19.416
35–45	20.85	11.19	44.75	.250	401.24	569.01	12.716
45+	62.50	33.55	33.55	1.00	167.77	167.77	5.000

individuals. At the King site, 26 of the 28 occurrences of periostitis were in adults. The remaining two cases of periostitis were observed in individuals in the 1 to 5-year age interval. Ten cases of periostitis were present at Little Egypt (seven in adults, three in children).

The periosteal reactions at the Little Egypt site also involve more bones than at the other sites. In the majority of occurrences at Little Egypt, more than one bone displays periostitis. At the King and Etowah sites, single bone occurrences are more common. In addition, the majority of periosteal reaction at King and Etowah are quite localized — only a small portion of the bone is affected. At Little Egypt, the periosteal reactions are more diffuse.

Discussion

The untransformed age-at-death distributions differ between the three sites. Although sample size is small in the Little Egypt (N = 31) and Etowah (N = 44) skeletal series, the results show several trends. First, the percentage of deaths between birth and 5 years of age is considerably higher at the Little Egypt site than at King or Etowah. It is possible that this is due to problems with infant and child bone preservation and underenumeration, which was noted to be a particular problem at the King site (Tally 1975). In other words, Little Egypt seems to have a higher infant and child mortality, because fewer infants and children were recovered from the other sites.

However, of the three series, bone preservation was poorest at the Little Egypt site.

The cumulative death distributions show that 51.6% of the deaths in the Little Egypt series occur by age 15. This is much higher than at the King site (25%) and higher than at Etowah (35%). Life expectancy at birth and at age 15 is also lower at the Little Egypt site. Periosteal reactions are more frequent at Little Egypt than at the other sites in the present sample. These indices suggest that individuals at Little Egypt experienced higher mortality and more exposure to infectious disease than did those at the King or Etowah sites. Preliminary analysis of other indices of health (e.g., enamel hypoplasias, dental caries, and stature) also indicate that health status was lowest at Little Egypt (Humpf 1989).

Documents from the de Soto expedition suggest two possible factors that may help explain the apparent low health status at the capital city. Biedma describes the area around the capital as "thickly settled in numerous and large towns" (Smith 1968), apparently containing a higher concentration of towns than other areas. Of several clusters of 16th-century archaeological sites in the chiefdom, the cluster that includes the Little Egypt site contains the largest number of large sites and the closest spacing of sites (Hally et al. 1989). Infectious disease might therefore be expected to occur in higher levels. Several stresses appear to produce high frequencies of periosteal reactions, including low resistance to disease (Rose and Santeford 1985), crowding, and unsanitary conditions (Weaver 1981). In the case of a densely settled area, the chance of contact with a pathogen is increased (Boyden 1972). Individuals living at and near the capital core of the chiefdom may have experienced such increased contact with infectious pathogens. Whittington (1989) found a pattern like this at the Maya site of Copan, Honduras. Individuals living in the densely packed "core" area of Copan displayed significantly higher frequencies of periosteal reactions than did noncore individuals (Whittington 1989:376).

However, dense settlement alone may not adequately explain the lower health status observed at Little Egypt. Powell reports that her analysis of the Moundville skeletal series reveals generally good health (Powell 1988:142). At its height, Moundville and its surrounding area contained the second largest prehistoric population in North America (Peebles 1979). Large, densely packed population aggregations may therefore not necessarily lead to poor health.

Second, Ranjel reports that the expedition remained in the capital city for over a month (Bourne 1922), longer than they remained at either Itaba (Etowah) or Piachi (King). This sustained contact with the town of Coosa may have provided a greater chance for the population of that town to be exposed to Spanish-introduced epidemic disease. Unlike at some other towns in La Florida, where the Spaniards camped nearby but outside of the town, at Coosa, Biedma reports that the entrada lodged in the houses of the town's inhabitants (Smith 1968:76). The large, closely spaced towns characteristic of this area may also have increased the possibility of transmission of epidemic diseases.

Additional factors are suggested in descriptions of Coosa provided by the de Luna expedition. As discussed above, Padilla reported that the capital city had recorded some demographic decline, as well as some loss of political control over the Napochies, who had recently (since de Soto's visit) stopped sending required tribute to the main town. This tribute, according to Padilla, was pledged to be restored after the Napochies were defeated by a party of Coosa natives and the Spanish. The tribute was to be paid three times a year and was to be in the form of food: "game, or fruits, chestnuts, and nuts" (Quinn 1979).

It is unclear from the documents how long the withdrawal of tribute had been occurring. It is also impossible to detect how much the loss of this food supply would have affected the diet and health status of Coosa's population. Tribute from this particular group, however, might not have been the only tribute disrupted. Hudson (1988) reports that another result of the Napochie rebellion was the closing to Coosa of trails to towns in the northern reaches of the province. It is possible that tribute from groups further north than the Napochies was also not reaching Coosa. Such loss of tribute may have impacted the diet, and consequently the health status, of individuals at the capital city.

While mortality appears to be higher and health status somewhat lower at Little Egypt, the other sites display mortality statistics similar to other Mississippian populations. Life expectancy at birth and at age 15 for selected Mississippian skeletal series is shown in Table 4. At Moundville, life expectancy at birth is 28.54 (Powell 1988:100), very similar to the values at King (28.55) and Etowah (27.33). These are also similar to the values calculated for the Kane Mounds (24.08) from the American Bottom region in the midwestern U.S. (Milner 1982).

The Little Egypt statistics are most similar to those at the Averbuch site in middle Tennessee and the Toqua site in eastern Tennessee. At Averbuch, life expectancy at birth and at age 15 are 16.61 and 14.79, respectively (Berryman 1981). Paleopathologic analysis at Averbuch shows a high level of infectious disease and chronic nutritional stress (Eisenberg 1986). Berryman (1981) concludes that the Averbuch population was severely stressed (Berryman 1981:185) and that most of the inhabitants of Averbuch experienced some type of biological stress (Berryman 1981:161).

Berryman (1981) suggests that a possible cause of the low expectation of life at Averbuch is soil depletion due to population pressure, which may have resulted in increases in malnutrition, mortality, and morbidity. Unlike at Little Egypt, where Spanish-introduced diseases provide a possible explanation for low health status and low life expectancy, the Averbuch site has been dated between the 13th and 15th centuries, prior to direct contact with Spanish explorers. It is unlikely that epidemic disease is responsible for the vital statistics noted in the Averbuch series.

Table 4
LIFE EXPECTANCIES AT BIRTH (e_0) AND AGE 15 (e_{15}) FOR SELECTED MISSISSIPPIAN SKELETAL SERIES

Site	e_0	e_{15}
King	28.55	24.63
Moundville	28.54	19.08
Etowah	27.33	25.44
Kane Mounds	24.08	19.58
Ledford Island	22.47	19.07
Little Egypt	20.06	21.74
Averbuch	16.61	14.79
Toqua	16.12	12.99

At the Toqua site, life expectancy at birth is 16.12, while life expectancy at age 15 is 12.99 (Parham 1987:446). Parham suggests that the Toqua population experienced "tremendous stress" (Parham 1987:452), with high infant and child mortality and a significant prevalence of nutritional deficiencies and infectious disease.

Like Little Egypt, Toqua is a Late Mississippian site located near the northern boundary of the reconstructed paramount chiefdom of Coosa. Unlike Little Egypt, which is hypothesized to have had direct contact with the Spanish, Toqua is located along a stretch of the Little Tennessee river, which Hudson et al. (1985) suggest was never traversed by the entrada. It is unclear, therefore, whether epidemic disease could be responsible for low expectation of life at Toqua.

The similarities and differences in vital rates discussed above suggests that simple, unicausal explanations of biological stress are inadequate to explain observed health and mortality characteristics of prehistoric populations. Mortality statistics for the Little Egypt, Toqua, and Averbuch series are quite similar, suggesting that these populations may have experienced similar biological and/or environmental stresses. However, a single explanation (e.g., population pressure or epidemic disease) does not explain the similarities in vital rates.

The Spanish encountered many populations as they traveled throughout the interior Southeast. It is clear from Spanish documents that these groups varied in size and power. Environmental and social differences were also noted between different groups. A close examination of the environmental and cultural differences noted in these ethnohistoric accounts may help archaeologists better understand the similarities and differences in many different biological and social aspects of protohistoric Native American populations.

Conclusions and Future Work

Some unexpected results emerged from the analysis of the three skeletal series studied here. It was initially expected that health might be better and mortality lower at the capital city, because Spanish documents and archaeological evidence suggest that elite individuals may have access to a better diet than nonelite individuals. Instead, the reverse was found here. Health status appears lowered and mortality elevated at the Little Egypt site.

Several explanations for this pattern were suggested in documents from 16th-century Spanish expeditions who visited these towns. The core area, including the capital city, may have been relatively more densely settled, creating an environment more favorable for the transmission of infectious disease. The spread of Spanish-introduced diseases may have been faster in this environment, and the possibility of Spanish diseases being introduced may have been elevated due to the sustained contact of the de Soto expedition with the town of Coosa. Because epidemic diseases, such as smallpox, rarely affect bone (Ortner and Putschar 1985), it is not possible to directly determine the frequency of these diseases in each skeletal series.

It is clear from Spanish documents that Coosa had declined politically and demographically after de Soto. At this time, it is impossible to determine whether these trends were also accompanied by a decline in health status, because burials have not yet been separated into pre- and postcontact subsamples. Ongoing research on the King site skeletal series focuses on the division of burials into a pre- and postcontact sample, so that the health status of each may be studied. Other health status indices, e.g., stature, enamel hypoplasias, and traumatic injuries, are currently being tabulated.

To date, analysis has focused on intersite variability in heath and longevity. An examination of intrasite variability, focused on differential social status within each site, is currently being conducted. Future research will also focus on carbon isotope analysis of the Little Egypt and King site series. Dietary differences between the sites may be apparent as this analysis is completed and will provide additional information about the demographic and health status of individuals from these three 16th-century towns in the Coosa province.

Acknowledgments

I would like to thank Dr. David J. Hally for permission to study the Little Egypt and King site skeletal series, and Dr. Lewis H. Larson, Jr. for permission to study the Etowah village series. Dr. James W. Hatch provided valuable comments on an early draft of this paper and has provided encouragement and support throughout my research. I would also like to thank Dr. Stephen Whittington for the use of his life-table program. Partial support for this research was provided by a Hill Fellowship grant from the Pennsylvania State University Department of Anthropology.

References

Acsadi, G. and J. Nemeskeri (1970) *History of Human Life Span and Mortality.* Akademiai Kiado, Budapest.

Angel, J. L. (1969) The Bases of Paleodemography. *American Journal of Physical Anthropology* 30:427–438.

Bass, W. M.(1987) *Human Osteology: A Laboratory and Field Manual of the Human Skeleton,* 3rd ed. Missouri Archaeological Society Special Publications, Columbia, MO.

Berryman, H. E. (1981) The Averbuch Skeletal Series: A Study of Biological and Social Stress at a Late Mississippian Period Site from Middle Tennessee. University Microfilms, Ann Arbor, MI.

Bocquet-Appel, J. P. and C. Masset (1982) Farewell to Paleodemography. *Journal of Human Evolution* 11:321–333.

Bourne, E. G. (1922) *Narratives of the Career of Hernando de Soto.* Barnes, New York.

Boyden, S. (1972) Ecology in Relation to Urban Population Structure. In *The Structure of Human Populations,* G. A. Harrison and A. J. Boyce, Eds. Oxford University Press, London.

Brain, J. P., A. Toth, and A. Rodriguez-Buckingham (1974) Ethnohistoric Archaeology and the de Soto Entrada into the Lower Mississippi Valley. *Conference on Historic Site Archaeology Papers* 7:232–289.

Curren, C., K. J. Little, and H. O. Holstein (1989) Aboriginal Societies Encountered by the Tristan de Luna Expedition. *Florida Anthropologist* 42:381–395.

DePratter, C. B., C. Hudson, and M. T. Smith (1983) The Route of Juan Pardo's Explorations in the Interior Southeast. *Florida Historical Quarterly* 62:125–158.

— (1985) The de Soto Expedition: From Chiaha to Mabila. In *Alabama and the Borderland: From Prehistory to Statehood,* R. Badger and L. Clayton, Eds. University of Alabama Press, Tuscaloosa.

Dwight, T. (1904–1905) The Size of the Articular Surfaces of the Long Bones as Characteristic of Sex: An Anthropological Study. *American Journal of Anatomy* 4:19–31.

Eisenberg, L. E. (1986) Adaptation in a "Marginal" Mississippian Population from Middle Tennessee: Biocultural Insights from Paleopathology. University Microfilms, Ann Arbor, MI.

Gilbert, G. B. and T. E. McKern (1973) A Method for Aging the Female Os Pubis. *American Journal of Physical Anthropology* 38:31–38.

Goodman, A. H., D. L Martin, G. J. Armelagos, and G. Clark (1984) Indications of Stress from Bones and Teeth. In *Paleopathology at the Origins of Agriculture.* M. N. Cohen and G. J. Armelagos, Eds. Academic Press, New York.

Hally, D. J. (1975) Archaeological Investigation of the King Site, Floyd County, Georgia. Report submitted to the National Endowment for the Humanities.

— (1979) *Archaeological Investigation of the Little Egypt Site (9Mu102) Murray County, Ga., 1969 Season.* University of Georgia, Laboratory of Archaeology Series Report No. 18, Athens, GA.

— (1980) *Archaeological Investigation of the Little Egypt Site (9Mu102) Murray County, Georgia, 1970–72 Seasons.* Report submitted to the Heritage Conservation and Recreation Service, U.S. Department of the Interior.

Hally, D. J. and J. B. Langford, Jr. (1988) *Mississippi Period Archaeology of the Georgia Valley and Ridge Province.* University of Georgia, Laboratory of Archaeology Series Report No. 25, Athens.

Hally, D. J., P. H. Garrow, and W. Trotti (1975) Preliminary Analysis of the King Site Settlement Plan. *Southeastern Archaeological Conference Bulletin* 18:55–62.

Hally, D. J., M. T. Smith, and J. B. Langford, Jr. (1989) The Archaeological Reality of de Soto's Coosa. Paper presented at the 54th Annual Meeting of the Society for American Archaeology, Atlanta, GA.

Hudson, C. (1988) A Spanish-Coosa Alliance in Sixteenth-Century North Georgia. *Georgia Historical Quarterly* 72:599–626.

Hudson, C., M. T. Smith, and C. B. DePratter, (1984) The Route of the de Soto Expedition from Apalachee to Chiaha. *Southeastern Archaeology* 3:65–77.

Hudson, C., M. T. Smith, D. J. Hally, R. Polhemus, and C. B. DePratter, (1985) Coosa: A Chiefdom in the Sixteenth-Century Southeastern United States. *American Antiquity* 50:723–737.

Hudson, C., M. T. Smith, C. B. DePratter, and E. Kelly (1989) The Tristan de Luna Expedition, 1559–1561. *Southeastern Archaeology* 8:31–45.

Humpf, D. A. (1989) Health, Demography, and Status in the Sixteenth-Century Coosa Chiefdom. Paper presented at the 54th Annual Meeting of the Society for American Archaeology, Atlanta, GA.

Lankford, G. E., III (1977) A New Look at de Soto's Route through Alabama. *Journal of Alabama Archaeology* 23:11–36.

Larson, L. H., Jr. (1971) Archaeological Implications of Social Stratification at the Etowah site, Georgia. In *Approaches to the Social Dimensions of Mortuary Practices,* J. A. Brown, Ed. *Society for American Archaeology Memoirs* 25:58–67.

Lovejoy, C. O., R. S. Meindl, T. H. Pryzbeck, and R. P. Mensforth (1985) Chronological Metamorphosis of the Auricular Surface of the Ilium: A New Method for the Determination of Adult Skeletal Age at Death. *American Journal of Physical Anthropology* 68:29–45.

MacKay, R. H. (n.d.) Skeletal Maturation Chart. Eastman Kodak Co., Rochester.

McKern, T. W. and T. D. Stewart (1957) *Skeletal Age Changes in Young American Males, Analyzed from the Standpoint of Identification*. U.S. Army Quartermaster Research and Development Command, Technical Report EP-45.

Meindl, R. S., C. O. Lovejoy, R. P. Mensforth, and R. A. Walker (1985) A Revised Method of Age Determination Using the Os Pubis, with a Review and Tests of Accuracy of Other Current Methods of Pubic Symphyseal Aging. *American Journal of Physical Anthropology* 68:29–45.

Milner, G. R. (1982) Measuring Prehistoric Levels of Health: A Study of Mississippian Period Skeletal Remains from the American Bottom. University Microfilms, Ann Arbor, MI.

Milner, G. R., D. A. Humpf, and H. C. Harpending (1989) Pattern Matching of Age-At-Death Distributions in Paleodemographic Analysis. *American Journal of Physical Anthropology* 80:49–58.

Moorehead, W. K. (1932) *Etowah Papers*. Department of Archaeology, Phillips Academy, New Haven, CT.

Moorrees, C. F. A, E. A. Fanning, and E. E. Hunt (1963a) Age Variation of Formation Stages for Ten Permanent Teeth. *Journal Dental Research* 42:1490–1502.

Moorrees, C. F. A, E. A. Fanning, and E. E. Hunt (1963b) Formation and Resorption of Three Deciduous Teeth in Children. *American Journal of Physical Anthropology* 21:205–213.

Ortner, D. J. and W. G. Putschar (1985) *Identification of Pathological Conditions in Human Skeletal Remains*. Reprinted. Smithsonian Contributions to Anthropology No. 28, Smithsonian Institution, Washington, D.C. Originally published 1981.

Parham, K. (1987) Toqua Skeletal Biology: A Biocultural Approach. In *The Toqua Site: A Late Mississippian Dallas Phase Town, Vol. I*. R. Polhemus, Ed. University of Tennessee Department of Anthropology Report of Investigations No. 41, Knoxville.

Peebles, C. S. (1979) Excavations at Moundville: 1905–1951. University of Michigan Press, Ann Arbor, MI.

Phenice, T. W. (1969) A Newly Developed Visual Method of Sexing the Os Pubis. *American Journal of Physical Anthropology* 30:297–301.

Powell, M. L. (1988) *Status and Health in Prehistory: A Case Study of the Moundville Chiefdom*. Smithsonian Institution Press, Washington, D.C.

Quinn, D. B. (1979) *New American World, Vol. II, Major Spanish Searches in Eastern North America, Franco-Spanish Clash in Florida, The Beginnings of Spanish Florida*. Arno Press, New York.

Rose, J. C. and L. G. Santeford (1985) Burial Interpretation. In *Gone To a Better Land*. J. C. Rose, Ed. Research Series No. 25, Arkansas Archaeological Survey, Fayetteville, AK.

Seckinger, E. W. (1977) Social Complexity during the Mississippian Period in Northwest Georgia. Unpublished Master's Thesis, University of Georgia, Athens.

Shyrock, H. S. and J. S. Siegel (1975) *The Methods and Materials of Demography*, 3rd revised printing. Government Printing Office, Washington, D.C.

Smith, B. (1968) *Narratives of de Soto*. Palmetto Books, Gainesville, FL.

Smith, M. T. (1975) European Materials from the King Site. *Southeastern Archaeology Conference Bulletin* 18:63–66.

— (1987) *Archaeology of Aboriginal Culture Change in the Interior Southeast: Depopulation During the Early Historic Period*. University of Florida Press, Gainesville, FL.

Tally, L. (1975) Preliminary Analysis of the King Site Burial Population. *Southeastern Archaeology Conference Bulletin* 18:74–75.

Thoma, K. and H. Goldman (1960) *Oral Pathology*. C. V. Mosby, St. Louis.

Todd, T. W. (1920) Age Changes in the Pubic Bone: Part I, The White Male Pubis. *American Journal of Physical Anthropology* 3:285–334.

Todd, T. W. and D. W. Lyon, Jr. (1924) Endocranial Suture Closure: Its Progress and Age Relationship. Part I, Adult Males of White Stock. *American Journal of Physical Anthropology* 7:325–384.

Ubelaker, D. H. (1978) *Human Skeletal Remains, Excavation, Analysis, Interpretation*, Aldine Press, Chicago.

Varner, J. G. and J. Varner (1951) *The Florida of the Inca*. University of Texas Press, Austin.

Weaver, D. S. (1981) An Osteological Test of Changes in Subsistence and Settlement Patterns at Casas Grandes, Chihuahua, Mexico. *American Antiquity* 46:361–364.

Whittington, S. L. (1989) Characteristics of Demography and Disease in Low Status Maya from Classic Period Copan, Honduras. Unpublished Ph.D. Dissertation, University Microfilms, Ann Arbor, MI.

Section II. Documentary Myths and Archaeology

11: Text Aided or Text Misled? Reflections on the Uses of Archaeology in Medieval History

Bailey K. Young
Assumption College, Worcester, Massachusetts

For the medieval historian, "text-aided archaeology" ought to be considered one type of source useful in the writing of history, as one side of an equation whose other term would be "archaeologically-aided historical reflection." I shall argue in this paper that for most of the time since medieval archaeology began to emerge as a discipline about the middle of the 19th century, the nature of this interdependency has been too often misunderstood. Archaeologists untrained in the intricate problems of textual criticism have allowed text-generated preconceptions to define their discoveries, and historians untrained in the complexities and ambiguities of archaeological research have been happy to accept these discoveries as illustrating the truth of what they already believe they know from the written sources. In the specific field of monumental archaeology, which has long been central to research on the Middle Ages, the tendency to put one's faith first in written sources can combine with a faith in what one can *see* standing as ruins to dangerously prejudice the archaeologist's approach to a site. Before texts can *aid* the archaeologist to carry out and interpret his or her fieldwork, a critical wariness is necessary.

There are two examples offered to illustrate the problem. The first is the problem of the "barbarian invasions" said to have brought down the Roman Empire in the fifth century, especially as it was formulated in the work of Edouard Salin, an excavator who was considered at midcentury to be *the* authority on this period of archaeology in France. The second concerns the study of religious monuments.

The Barbarian Invasions

M. Salin began his work before the First World War and published a four-volume work between 1951 and 1959, called *La Civilization Mérovingienne,* which he presented and which was received as a global overview of archaeology's contribution to early medieval history in France (Salin 1950–1959). If we leave aside one volume devoted to technology and laboratory analysis, we quickly note that the archaeology is almost entirely funerary, and that it is dominated by the theme of the "Great Invasions." The role of excavation is mostly to open "barbarian graves" and to recover the artifacts therein in order to identify the tribe buried in a particular place and to study their material culture and burial rites. Salin is very explicit about the extent to which this enterprise is "text aided": at the end of each volume he assembles an array of excerpts from the literary sources to remind the reader just what the archaeology is supposed to illustrate. Volume 1 presents a narrative summary of the historical events drawing on these excerpts, as well as on standard narrative treatments: it tells the story of warlike "barbarian" (mostly Germanic) tribes — the Visigoths, Burgundians, and Franks are most important in the light of future events — who break into the Roman Empire, raid and plunder, and finally carve out new kingdoms for themselves in the old Western provinces. Salin assumes that each of these "barbarian tribes" arrives on the scene as a distinctive culture whose characteristic artifacts and traditions — funerary, at any rate — can be deciphered from their cemeteries. By plotting where these cemeteries are located, he also hopes that the process of conquest and settlement can be mapped more precisely and accurately than the rather scanty references in the written sources permit. A closely related problem suggested by the literary sources concerns the relationships established with the Gallo-Romans. Salin, therefore, seeks to define their burial practices and tries to show how on certain sites the two traditions gradually mingle until a "progressive fusion" shows that assimilation has taken place.

Salin did not invent this approach, which makes archaeology the uncritical handmaiden of a particular historical narrative: it underlies all the work done in Merovingian archaeology before him. Nor was this approach limited to France. Between about 1840 and 1860 excavators deriving from the old antiquarian traditions in England, Germany, Belgium, Switzerland, and France created a new field in archaeology by correctly identifying the grave-goods in a series of cemeteries (a burial facies) with the period when the Roman Empire in the West was replaced by the barbarian successor-states (Périn 1980:14–28). The Romantic movement had created in the educated public a heightened fascination with the question of "national origins," and it is not surprising that the archaeology was called upon to help fill in the blanks left by the very incomplete written sources. These sources had been shaped into a narrative by historians like Edward Gibbon, whose persuasive essay, *The Decline and Fall of the Roman Empire*, was enormously influential in defining both learned and popular conceptions of the period (Gibbon, Ed. Bury, 1897–1900). Therefore the first generations of French scholars who attempted to make historical sense of the new information archaeology was providing sought to identify a material culture distinctive of the Franks in the regions that this people were known to have controlled by the sixth century. Similarly, they sought a Burgundian material culture in that part of France that still bears the name of this group of Germanic invaders, and a Visigothic material culture in the old Roman province of Aquitaine (now southwest France), which this barbarian people controlled from 418 to 507 A.D. (Figure 1). The historical sources also dictated a second area of concern. The barbarian peoples were at some point transformed from pagan hordes to good Christians: could archaeology illustrate this process?

Let us take the example of the warrior graves excavated at Lavoye (Meuse), near Nancy in eastern France (Figure 2), to illustrate the reasoning of Salin and his predecessors (Joffroy 1974). The panoply of weapons seems to leave no doubt that we are dealing with "barbarian" warriors. The richly decorated sword (gold leaf and semiprecious stones set into the hilt) and such high-status items as the belt buckle and purse lid made with the *cloisonée* technique (garnets individually cut and inserted into "cells" underlain by gold foil) identify grave 319 at the "chief" (Figure 2B); the distinctive throwing-axe, or *francisca*, of grave 194 would confirm that these men were, as we would expect, Franks, known for their skill with this weapon (Figure 2C). The cemetery to which these graves belong was dug partly into the ruins of a Roman villa: what more convincing evidence is needed of the "smoking gun" of invasion and take-over? Grave 319 also enclosed an unusual item, of undoubtedly Christian origin: the "*buire*," a wooden pitcher decorated with repoussé bronze plates that depict such scenes as Christ calling Lazarus from the grave (Figure 2C). This was undoubtedly a liturgical vessel that had belonged to some church; thus it was thought to represent an item of plunder taken proudly by this pagan chieftain into the grave with him. Beside him were buried a young woman (grave 307) and a young girl (grave 307bis) whose high-quality jewelry (pairs of silver brooches, silver bracelet, necklace of gold coins) and glass-and-bronze vessel deposit confirm both their relationship to the chief, and the prevalence of these "barbarian" burial customs that the invaders had brought from their Germanic homeland.

FIG. 1. Map of Gaul around A.D. 500 designed to show the regions controlled by the different "barbarian peoples" mentioned in the written sources. A: Francs (Franks) in the north; B: Wisigoths (Visigoths) in the southwest; C: Burgondes (Burgundians) in the southeast. (From Feffer, L.-C. and P. Périn (1987) *Les Francs,* vol. 1. Armand Colin, Paris, p. 144. With permission.)

The fit of the archaeological data to the previously known historical narrative thus seems to work extremely well, so well that it lulled the critical sense of scholars for a century and more. Over the last 30 years, however, its plausibility has been weakened by new work by historians and archaeologists alike. One line of research, largely pursued by German scholars, focused on the origin of the furnished-burial traditions, such as those we have just illustrated at Lavoye, and demonstrated that they did not derive from ancestral Germanic practices, but rather evolved in the new militarized environment of the Late Roman frontier (Böhme 1974). Other scholars, analyzing more closely the chronology, typology, and distribution of the artifacts in Merovingian cemeteries in France, further weakened the argument for an "ethnic" basis to burial practices by showing that neither the

FIG. 2. A: Map of the Merovingian cemetery of Lavoye (near Nancy, France) showing the typical row-grave alignments. The chieftain's grave #319 (B: detail) is set off by itself on the eastern edge of the cemetery, but the two closest graves are those of a woman and a young girl (307 and 307bis), which by their high-status grave goods are contemporary with the chief and associated with him in a privileged burial concession reserved for the leading family. Grave 194 lies to the west (south of grave 196) and is one of a number of weapons and female-ornament graves attesting to the popularity of this burial practice among the Frankish "military elite" around A.D. 500. C: Material from graves 319 and 194. Small diamonds represent weapons graves (group A). Large diamonds represent female ornament graves (group B). (From Young, B. K. (1984) *Quatre Cimetières Mérovingiennes de l'Est de la France. Etude Quantitative et Qualitative des Pratiques Funéraires.* B.A.R., Int. Series 208, Oxford.)

137

Burgundians nor the Visigoths had a distinctive "funerary culture" during the period (fifth and earlier sixth centuries) when they controlled independent kingdoms in Gaul (Gaillard de Sémainville 1987; James 1977). My own work on comparative burial practices, analyzed in a quantitative perspective, suggests that the so-called "barbarian funerary" facies derives from Gallo-Roman funerary traditions adapted to the taste and self-affirmation of a *parvenu* military elite of largely Germanic background (Young 1977:36–44). P. Périn has come independently to a similar conclusion (Périn 1981:125–145). Let us take another look at the grave-groups from Lavoye in the light of these new perspectives.

We can distinguish two classes of objects included in the grave. The first consists of personal possessions of the deceased, which clearly point to a specific individual identity. These consist essentially of the man's weapons and the woman's jewelry; German scholars have identified these with a legal category of personal possessions (*Heergewäte* and *Gerade*, respectively) considered to be uninheritable (J. Werner 1968:96–98). I group with these such other personal items as belt buckles and everyday accessories, such as combs, flint strike-a-lights, tweezers, or even old bronze coins, which seem to have been carried with the other items in a leather purse for good luck, and designate this the *dressed burial* element of the grave group (Young 1977:43–45). The other major element I call the *funerary deposit*: this consists essentially of vessels placed in the grave as an offering to accompany the deceased (represented, for example, by the glass cups in the two warrior graves and the glass, bronze, and ceramic vessels in the young child's grave). A survey of hundreds of grave groups dating between the late third and the early eighth centuries A.D. throughout Merovingian Gaul (Young 1977:73–81, Figs 1–9) plus a more narrowly focused study of over a thousand grave groups in four cemeteries in the same region (including Lavoye) (Young 1984) have provided me with a data base broad enough to argue that the funerary practices observed at Lavoye and elsewhere do not derive from the ancient religious traditions of German "invaders," as Salin and his predecessors thought. The *funerary deposit* element derives from burial traditions prevalent in Roman Gaul long before there were significant Germanic intrusions; indeed, it can be shown that this particular tradition was imitated by some privileged Germans living outside the Empire, although by far the most common "ancestral" Germanic burial practice was cremation, with few, if any, accompanying objects. The *dressed burial* element (and particularly the inclusion of weapons and jewelry) is very exceptional in Gallo-Roman traditions, but it is not "ancestral" to the Germans either: it was a *new invention* by a powerful new social group who appear in the late Roman west, the professional military elite. As Böhme rightly argues, they were no doubt predomi-

nantly Germans, but they were Germans working in some capacity for the vastly expanded and complex "Roman" military machine of the fourth and fifth centuries: we find the first "chieftain's graves" in late Roman cemeteries outside garrison towns, such as Vermand, or rural defensive posts, such as Monceau-le-Neuf (Figures 3 and 4) (Böhme 1974). The so-called barbarian invasions of the fifth century now look more like episodes in a complex series of civil wars and power struggles during which certain barbarian groups, such as the Burgundians and the Visigoths, succeeded in settling in parts of Gaul because they became useful allies of the Roman authorities; their military organization was quite "Roman" in character (Bachrach 1972). There is little or no evidence that they followed the type of funerary practice we have seen at Lavoye at this time; indeed, I think we can now conclude that they (and most if not all other barbarian peoples mentioned *as invaders* in the literary sources, such as the Vandals, Sueves, Alans, etc.) had no "ethnically" distinctive funerary traditions at all. The "Germanic" burial practices of the late Roman military elite were maintained during the disruptions of the fifth century by the one "barbarian" people who did not have to "invade" the Empire then, because they had already been settled within it for over a century. From the days of Constantine the Great (A.D. 306–338), who reestablished the security of the Roman frontier in the Lower Rhine, where the Franks lived, significant groups of these Germans had been allowed to live within the frontiers and provide military support to the Romans. The view that the Frankish king Clovis, who seized power in Northern Gaul after a victory over the Roman general Syagrius at Soissons in 486, was an uncouth "invader" long held sway in the learned and popular imagination, but is thoroughly discredited today. Clovis is more accurately seen as a successful *putchist*, a kind of Bonaparte, whose victory was the sign and symbol of the rise to power of a new social group, the military elite (K.-F. Werner 1984:297–310; Périn 1981). A link can be established between the expansion of Frankish military power under Clovis and the spread of weapons in graves in certain regions of Gaul (Young 1986b). Looked at from this perspective, the archaeological evidence of funerary practices, no longer distorted by a false historical vision, has a significant, independent role to play in the reinterpretation of the birth of the Middle Ages, which is now taking place.

If Merovingian funerary practices do not derive, then, from ethnic tribal traditions, do they reflect Germanic paganism, as the other key assumption of Salin ran? The archaeological evidence supports two statements that challenge such an assumption. The first is the striking contrast between the *funerary deposit* as it was practiced in Roman Gaul and later, during the Merovingian period (Young 1977:36–40, 46–47) (Figures 5 and 6).

of the community. It is precisely this aspect of funerary practice that has been modified or has entirely disappeared in Merovingian cemeteries. The vessel deposit, when it survives, has been reduced in the vast majority of cases to a single biconic vase (a new form that did not figure in the earlier assemblages of tableware) more likely to have held water in some kind of a purification rite than a food offering (Figure 5). There is, at any rate, very little reliable evidence of the food offering after the fifth century. Although Roman coins do continue to turn up much less often than in Roman times (Figure 6B), they do not unambiguously reflect the "Charon's obol" ritual so much; often they turn up with everyday items in the purse as a kind of bric-a-brac, or they have been transformed into jewelry, as in the case of the young girl at Lavoye (grave 307bis), whose necklace incorporates a series of gold coins. The grave group is now dominated by objects deriving from dressed burial, as is the case at Lavoye and in the Merovingian funerary series as a whole (Figure 6A). I think we can conclude that the Franks and others who revived and redefined furnished burial customs in the fifth century were less interested in the aspects that pointed to particular beliefs in the afterlife and more

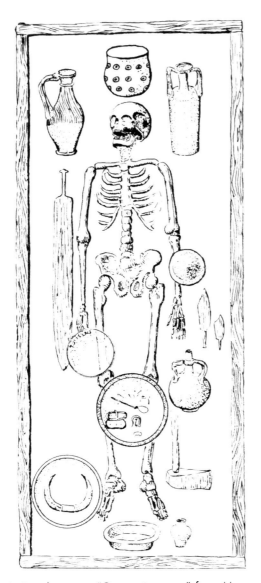

FIG. 3. Fourth-century "Germanic grave" from Monceau-le-Neuf, illustrating the genesis of new burial practices by the new military elite within the late Roman Empire. The array of weapons indicates that the subject was no doubt a German soldier serving Rome; the vessel deposit derives from the Roman funeral practices, but he has underlined his high status by supplementing the ceramics with expensive glassware. (From Pilloy, J. (1899) *Etudes sur d'Anciens Lieux de Sépulture dans l'Aisne*, vol. 3, Saint-Quentin.)

The Gallo-Romans often placed a variety of cups and plates and bottles with the deceased (6 to 12 items are common in the fourth century) and often included a food offering and a small coin placed ritually in the hand, the mouth, or the eye as a penny to "pay the infernal boatman Charon," a pagan superstition attested in literary sources (Young 1977:40–43) (Figures 5A, 5B, and 6B). Most or all of the items in a typical Gallo-Roman grave group can usually be included as part of this funerary offering to the deceased, in what I would term an *impersonal ritual gesture*, not to an individual, but to a departing member

FIG. 4. Artist's reconstruction of a "chieftain's grave" from the earlier Merovingian period: the subject was buried fully dressed in a carefully constructed "wooden-chamber grave"; along with his weapons, horsegear and a vessel deposit were included in the funerary deposit. (From Feffer, L.-C. and P. Périn (1987) *Les Francs*, vol. 1. Armand Colin, Paris, p. 216. With permission.)

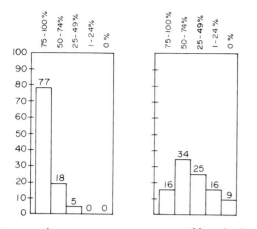

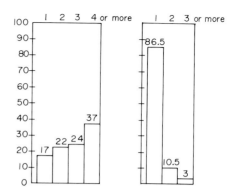

A: Graves with ceramics as a percentage of furnished graves (by site): (left) late Roman (22 sites); (right) Merovingian (56 sites).

B: Number of ceramic vessels in furnished graves (by grave): (left) late Roman (659 graves); (right) Merovingian (974 graves).

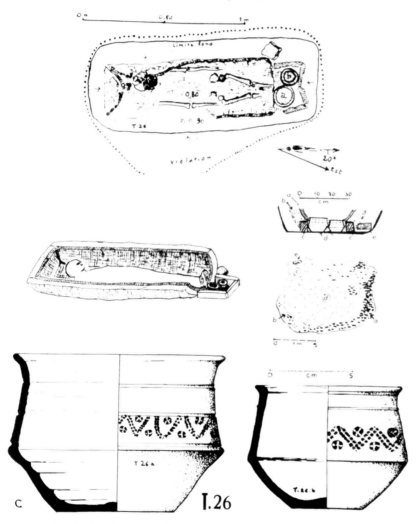

FIG. 5. Vessel deposit compared in the late Roman and Merovingian cemeteries. A compares the incidence of ceramics within graves with the grave groups, including ceramics expressed as a percentage of the total number of graves with material. In the late Roman period this is very high (in 77% of the sites surveyed, 75% or more of the graves included ceramics), but it falls off sharply in Merovingian times. Similarly, the number of ceramics placed in the grave diminishes (B), reflecting a fundamental change in the meaning of the practice. Instead of the tableware set common in Roman times, the single clay pot that appears in the vast majority of Merovingian graves that do contain ceramics (86.5%) is a new type of biconic vessel (C), which may have held water used for purification, rather than a food offering. (A and B from Young, B. K. (1977) in *Archéologie Medievale* VII: 5. C from Périn, P. (1980) *La Datation des Tombes Mérovingiennes*. Librarie Droz, Geneva. With permission.)

140

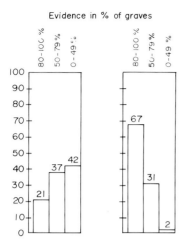

Evidence in % of graves

Coins in % of graves

A: Graves with dressed burial as a percentage of furnished graves (by site): (left) late Roman (19 sites); (right) Merovingian (52 sites).

B: Incidence of coin deposits in cemeteries (by site): (left) Late Roman (22 sites); (right) Merovingian (56 sites).

FIG. 6. Dressed burial and coin deposit in late Roman and Merovingian burial horizons. A shows that evidence of dressed burial is much rarer during late Roman times than the vessel deposit (in fewer than half of the graves on 42% of the sites surveyed) but has become the norm during the Merovingian period (in 80 to 100% of the graves in 67% of the sites surveyed). B establishes that the coin deposit occurred with some regularity in late Roman cemeteries, but has declined sharply in later times (no coins at all in 36.5% of the sites surveyed; coins in only 1 to 10% of the graves in another 36% of the sites. (From Young, B. K. (1977) in *Archéologie Medievale* VII:5.)

FIG. 7. The Christianization of rural cemeteries under aristocratic domination. Artist's reconstruction of the enclosed cemetery and funerary church of Hordain, near Douai, France. The original cemetery gravitated around the tumulus to the left of the chapel, which set off the cremation burial of the founding chieftain; around A.D. 550 the chapel was built to house the inhumation graves of the leading family, who practiced richly dressed burial; the surrounding graves then adopted the new west-east orientation of the building. (From Demolon, P. in Feffer, L.-C. and P. Périn (1987) *Les Francs*, vol. 1, Armand Colin, Paris, p. 75. With permission.)

interested in status display of personal possessions. The burial practices were more a cultural statement than an expression of any particular religious beliefs, in other words.

The second statement that the archaeological evidence allows is that the furnished burial practices described above often took place in unambiguously Christian contexts. Merovingian royalty began seeking — or constructing — *ad sanctos* Christian burial chapels from the time of Clovis himself, who converted from paganism to Catholicism around A.D. 500. Although few of these richly furnished royal burials have survived, recently

excavated cases associated with the monastery of Saint-Denis north of Paris (France-Lanord and Fleury 1962) and with the cathedral of Cologne (Doppelfeld and Pirling 1966) prove that lavish dressed burial, with weapons and jewelry and much beside, did not appear to be "un-Christian" in ruling circles during the sixth century. The aristocracy followed suit by building its own private burial chapels, where it continued to practice "barbaric funerary display" in a Christian context (Young 1986a); there are unambiguous examples at Arlon in Belgium (Roosens and Alenus-Lecerf 1965) and Hordain, near Douai (Figure 7) (Demolon 1974). More alert and

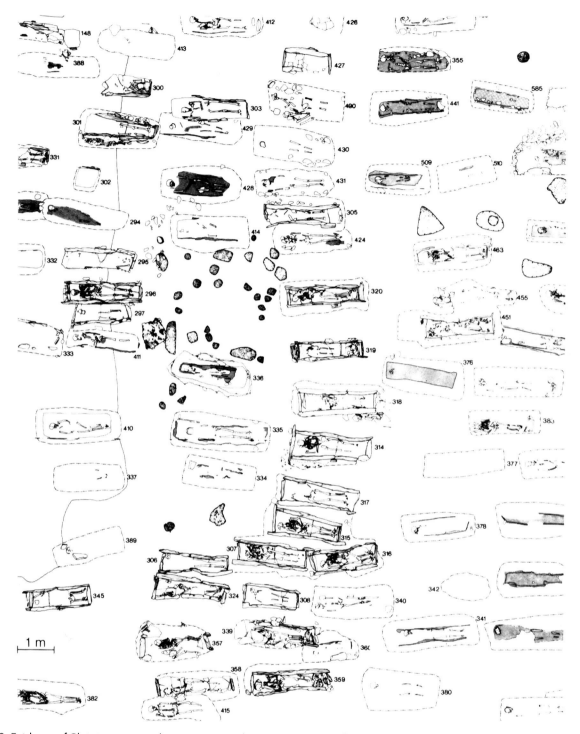

FIG. 8. Evidence of Christian memorial structures in rural cemeteries previously considered as "pagan." Ground plan of a proposed wooden-post structure with three associated graves from the center of the cemetery of Sézegnin (near Geneva). On urban sites, similar monuments of stone construction have been identified as Christian "memoria" attested in written sources; evidence of such flimsy, posthole constructions was no doubt overlooked by earlier generations of archaeologists, whose chief concern was the contents of individual graves. (From Privati, B. (1983) *La Nécropole de Sézegnin (IVe–VIIe Siecle).* Societé d'Histoire et d'Archéologie de Genève, Geneva. With permission.)

sensitive excavation also suggests that the country cemeteries that Salin and his predecessors had regarded as "pagan" sometimes included Christian chapels or memorial structures in wood (Figure 8) (Privati 1983:61–64). Once again, if the prior conviction that the cemeter-

ies must be barbarian and the burial customs must be pagan is discarded, the archaeology suggests a much more complex picture of social and religious structures during the Merovingian period. Instead of a model of invaders seeking to impose already defined traditions, a more dynamic model of cultural creation is suggested. Recent regional studies show how much the overall historical vision can be enhanced by funerary archaeology freed of the old preconceptions and integrated with other types of evidence (Colardelle 1983).

Religious Monuments

My second example concerns what is arguably one of the oldest specific branches of medieval archaeology, the study of religious monuments (Hubert 1961). In France this achieved official recognition as early as 1830, when the first legislation on historical monuments created a commission under Prosper Mérimée, which began scheduling, restoring, and maintaining monuments. Medieval churches were among the first to draw attention and were a particular concern of the architect Viollet le Duc, who worked on some of France's most celebrated cathedrals and abbey-churches and published the enormously influential *Dictionnaire Raisoné d'Architecture Francaise du XIe au XVIe Siècles* between 1854 and 1868. Although we owe the very survival of many priceless monuments to Viollet le Duc and his successors, he created a tradition that defined medieval archaeology as the study of *standing monuments* removed from their diachronic context that has impeded the development of a modern archaeological site analysis until recent years. In the terms of this book, the "text" that serves to define the research parameters refers not only to written records concerning a given church building, but to *the building itself*. Even the building itself was seen in terms of its dominant stylistic characteristics, with a view to deciding the nature of the restorations to be undertaken: Romanesque? Early Gothic? High Gothic? The notions that the building fabric contained evidence of other phases, or that excavation could reveal phases of site history that the standing remains did not even suggest, were not taken into consideration. Since the visible aspects of the vast majority of medieval religious buildings in France date from the High or the Late Middle Ages (ca. A.D. 1000 to 1500), this means that any Early Medieval constructions have been lost. The experience of recent research indicates that much can be recovered, if the archaeologist is careful not to let the "texts" create misleading assumptions and develops a methodology sensitive enough to recover information about very badly damaged and mostly "lost" phases of activity. Charles Bonnet has furnished a remarkable example of how alert and judicious excavation can recover unsuspected phases of site development in his study of the former church of the Madeleine in Geneva (Bonnet 1977).

The former Benedictine abbey of Psalmodi lies in the marshy region known as the Camargue, east of Montpellier, in southern France (Dodds et al. 1989). Abandoned in the 1530s and turned into a farm, it fell into ruins; during the 1960s the imposing monumental vestiges of the south wall of the choir of the abbey church attracted the attention of professors Whitney and Brooks Stoddard, American art historians. Such stylistic criteria as the type of masonry in regularly cut and snugly jointed ashlar blocks betrayed the skill of professional High-Medieval masons, and the half-engaged columns from the top of which arches sprang allowed them to "read" a choir vaulted in the new Gothic style pioneered far away, in northern France. There is a rich collection of written sources that confirm the importance of the abbey in the High and Late Middle Ages; these sources also indicate that the monastery was founded during the eighth century, destroyed and abandoned during a politically unstable period, then refounded around A.D. 1000. When excavations began in 1970, the objectives included a thorough study of the great Gothic church (still partially standing) and of the two previous churches whose existence was attested in these sources: one Romanesque and one Carolingian. Evidence of the Romanesque phase turned up right away in the form of sculptural fragments, like the fragment of a cloister capital depicting the Massacre of the Innocents found propping open a door on the farm (Figure 9A). The little monk's head (Figure 9B) was a clue that the cloister was transformed during the Gothic period, but only a careful study of the relation between burials and construction phases led to the hypothesis that the Romanesque cloister was replaced by a much larger one, as part of an extensive Gothic building program (Figure 10). Not until 1974 was evidence found of an older church, whose foundations are partially preserved under the Gothic structure. These older vestiges gave evidence of different masonry styles, which supported the view that the rebuilt church of ca. 1000 largely reused the foundations of the church of ca. 800 (Dodds 1986). So archaeology and texts seemed to support one another once again.

The excavation began turning up evidence, however, that indicated the occupation of the site began well before A.D. 800. These included fragments of Roman architecture, some of them found lying about the farm without archaeological context, and some reused in the foundations of the Gothic and pre-Gothic church structures on the site. There was a temptation to see these as evidence of an earlier Roman villa, and when pieces of red-slip pottery that seemed to fit within the traditions of the Roman period terra sigilata began to appear, the hypothesis that the Christian monastery was built in Charlemagne's day on the site of a ruined villa was advanced in preliminary field reports. The presence of significant quantities of broken Roman roof tile in certain parts of the site also seemed to support this hypothesis. After the removal of the tons of unstratified material that had covered the whole site after the collapse of the last church building allowed extensive and careful area excavation, it was found that these tiles had been used to construct a type of grave: the flat tiles were leaned up against one another like the two sides of a pup tent, and the joints were covered by the curved tile — an adaptation of the standard roofing technique to burial. Con-

A

B

FIG. 9. The archaeology of medieval Christian monuments. This mutilated capital (A) depicting the Massacre of the Innocents was found during preliminary site-survey at Psalmodi (near Montpellier, France), propping open a farmhouse door. It derives from a cloister of the Romanesque period. Subsequent excavation turned up many other sculptural elements, attesting to several major phases of rebuilding and redecoration during the Middle Ages: B, for example, is a monk's head that decorated the much larger Gothic cloister which replaced the Romanesque one. (Photo courtesy of Stoddard. With permission.)

sultation with French colleagues established that this type of burial had been recognized as typical of the late-Roman period (fourth to seventh centuries A.D.) in the area (Gagnière 1960) and beyond (Colardelle 1983:345–348, Figures 125, 126); it also showed that most of the *sigilata*-tradition ware fit into this time period, and not earlier. Translated into broader historical terms, this meant that the original hypothesis of a villa dating to the heyday of the Roman Empire had to be abandoned. The earlier occupation of the site of Psalmodi had taken place during the centuries where the later Roman Empire overlapped with the early Middle Ages, a period also known as "Early Christian," since it corresponds to the first spread of Christianity in Western Europe after the Emperor Constantine began to encourage Christianity throughout the Roman Empire. Other artifactual proof of this occupation continued to turn up in the part of the site where the tile graves had been identified: a gold coin datable to the middle of the sixth century, for example, and a bone fitting decorated with an incised human face of a distinctively early medieval appearance.

But what was the nature of this occupation? The Roman villa hypothesis does not seem tenable: Roman

villas were extensive, solidly built structures whose foundations are always recognizable, and their sites abound in the ceramics produced and consumed on a large scale. At Psalmodi the Roman vestiges amount to a few architectural blocks reused in medieval foundations; they could easily have been brought in for this purpose during the Middle Ages. The ceramics are post-Roman: could they indicate a new settlement built on this island in the marshes with the onset of the "Dark Ages," when the relative inaccessibility of the site could be seen as an advantage? This hypothesis was tentatively advanced in field reports. But I was troubled by the absence of positive structural evidence for a village: what the evidence does indicate is the presence of a cemetery during this period. In 1987 I advanced another hypothesis: that Psalmodi was in fact founded *as a monastery* during the early Christian period and that the tile graves we had found belonged to the cemetery surrounding the first church on the site (Young and Carter-Young 1987). This hypothesis, discussed by the research team and with colleagues working on early medieval religious sites elsewhere, led us to reexamine the surviving remains of the earliest vestiges of the church. It was clear from a study of

FIG. 10. The relationship between burials and construction phases is an important key to deciphering the chronology of medieval Christian religious monuments. The location and position of these three burials indicate they took place in the gallery of a much expanded cloister, which in the Gothic phase invaded the space previously reserved for the nave: the anomalous north-south orientation of one of the burials can only be explained by its relation to the cloister wall. Artifacts confirmed this chronology. (Photo courtesy of Stoddard. With permission.)

the masonry that different construction phases could be distinguished. The best-preserved fragment of the nave wall, for example (Figure 11), shows marked differences between the lower courses, made up of irregular stones without mortar and the well-mortared upper courses; these we had always suggested reflected the rebuilding of the church around A.D. 1000 on the vestiges of the church built around A.D. 800 — the two phases that the written sources had led us to expect. But could there be an earlier phase, ca. A.D. 400–600, whose existence was not hinted at in those sources, but was suggested by the funerary and the ceramic evidence? To answer this question, we studied the plans of churches from this period recovered from excavations elsewhere and applied them to Psalmodi, in order to generate a hypothetical plan that would fit the structural evidence we had and that could be tested by new excavation. This hypothetical plan led us, in 1989, to remove part of a paved medieval floor, to look for evidence of an earlier wall. What we found was not a wall, but a filled-in trench of the right dimensions, and in the right place, to correspond to our model. A look at the stratigraphy (Figure 12) shows that the trench is

filled with a type of destruction rubble, which includes artifacts that fit into the late or post-Roman context. The hypothesis that this filled-in trench can be interpreted as the ghost wall of an early Christian basilica thus becomes plausible.

The Psalmodi excavations are incomplete, and the hypothesis thus advanced should not be taken as a solid conclusion. But the example does illustrate that the relationship between written sources and archaeological research in medieval Europe is not a simple one and is fraught with dangers for the unwary. Without the evidence of the late antique ceramics and burial practices, the temptation would have been great to interpret the architectural evidence as confirming the building sequence suggested both by the monumental remains standing on the site and by the written sources. The lesson here seems to be that the later medieval building campaigns almost obliterated the physical evidence of early medieval site occupation, while the medieval written sources show that the pre-Carolingian history of Psalmodi had been forgotten by that time.

The lesson of the "barbarian graves" has suggested

FIG. 11. The evidence of relative chronology in building phases and the problems of interpretation. This nave wall at Psalmodi shows at least two very distinct types of masonry, which presumably correspond to different building periods. Do we have the carefully mortared walls of the rebuilt (Romanesque?) church atop the cruder, unmortared foundations of the earlier (Carolingian?) building? (Photo courtesy of Stoddard. With permission.)

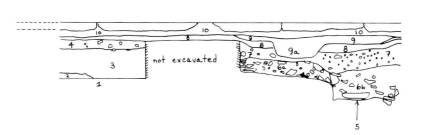

FIG. 12. Psalmodi. Stratigraphic section showing the paved choir floor of the Gothic church (10) covering over footing levels for one or more earlier church floors (9, 8, 7), and sealing the rubble debris of a destroyed structure (6a: the Carolingian church?), which spills into (6b) the negative of an East-West trench (5: a "ghost wall" of the Early Christian church?). The level of clay with construction debris to the north (4) might be associated with either of the two earliest construction periods. Under it is a level of dense clay (3), which contains (here and elsewhere on the site) the earliest coherent group of datable artifacts on the site (late Antique ceramics). This lies on the geological substratum, or *poudinge* (1,2). (Plan: From B. K. Young.)

another way in which archaeological evidence can be made to fit into the mold of historical preconceptions. Both examples prove that if these preconceptions are reexamined critically, archaeology is better able to fulfill its potential as a source of history, and our overall vision of the early Middle Ages is vastly enriched.

References

Bachrach, B. (1972) *Merovingian Military Organization.* University of Minnesota, Minneapolis.

Böhme, H. (1974) *Germanische Grabfunde des 4. bis 5. Jahrhunderts zwischen unteren Elbe und Loire,* 2 vols. Muncher Beitrage zur Vor-und Frühgeschichte, 19. Munich.

Bonnet, C. (1977) *Les Premiers Édifices Chrétiens de la Madeleine à Genève.* Mémoires et Documents Publiés par la Société d'Histoire et d'Archéologie de Genève, t. VIII, Geneva.

Colardelle, M. (1983) *Sépulture et Traditions Funéraires du Ve au XIIIe Siècle ap. J.-C. dans les Campagnes des Alpes Francaises du Nord.* Société Alpine de Documentation et de Recherche en Archéologie, Grenoble.

Demolon, P. (1974) Cimetière et Chapelle Rurale Mérovingienne à Hordain (Nord). *Septentrion* 4:71.

Dodds, J. (1986) The Carolingian Abbey Church of Psalmodi: Formal History and Historical Context. *Gesta* XXVI/1:9.

Dodds, J., B. W. Stoddard, W. S. Stoddard, B. K. Young, and K. Carter-Young (1989) L'Ancienne Abbaye de Psalmodi (Saint-Laurent-d'Aigouze, Gard). Premier Bilan des Fouilles (1970–1988). *Archéologie Médiévale* 19:7.

Doppelfeld, O. and R. Pirling (1966) *Frankische Fürsten im Rheinland. Die Graber aus den Kölner Dom, von Krefeld-Gellep und Morken.* Schriften des Rheinischen Landesmuseum, 2, Bonn.

France-Lanord, A. and M. Fleury (1962) Das Grab der Arnegundis in Saint-Denis. *Germania* 40/2:341.

Gagnière, S. (1960) Les Sépultures à Inhumation du IIIe au XIIIe Siècle de Notre Ère dans la Basse Vallée du Rhone. Essai de Chronologie Typologique. *Cahiers Rhodaniens* 7:34.

Gaillard de Sémainville, H. (1987) Aux origines de la Bourgogne: Burgondes, Francs et Gallo-Romains. In *Bourgogne Médiévale, la Mémoire du Sol. 20 Ans de Recherches Archéologiques.* Association Générale des Conservateurs des Collections Publiques de France pour la Région Bourgogne, Dijon.

Gibbon, E. (1897–1900) *The Decline and Fall of the Roman Empire,* 7 vols., J. B. Bury, Ed. London.

Hubert, J. (1961) Archéologie Médiévale. In *L'Histoire et ses Méthodes,* Ch. Sammaran, Ed. Encyclopédie de la Pléiade, Paris, pp. 275–328.

James, E. (1977) *The Merovingian Archaeology of South-West Gaul,* 2 vols. B.A.R., Int. Ser. 25, Oxford.

Joffroy, R. (1974) *Le Cimetière de Lavoye (Meuse). Nécropole Mérovingienne.* Picard, Paris.

Périn, P. (1980) *La Datation des Tombes Mérovingiennes. Historique, Méthodes, Applications.* Droz, Geneva.

— (1981) A Propos de Publications Récentes Concernant le Peuplement en Gaule à l'Époque Mérovingienne: La "Question Franque." *Archéologie Médiévale* 11:125.

Privati, B. (1983) *La Nécropole de Sézegnin (IVe–VIIe Siecle).* Société d'Histoire et d'Archéologie de Genève, Geneva.

Roosens, H. and J. Alenus-Lecerf (1965) Sépultures Mérovingiennes au "Vieux Cimetiere" d'Arlon. *Archaeologica Belgica* 88:1.

Salin, E. (1950–1959) *La Civilisation Mérovingienne,* 4 vols. Picard, Paris.

Viollet le Duc, E. (1854–1868) *Dictionnaire Raisoné d'Architecture Francaise du XIe au XVIe Siecles,* 10 vols. Paris.

Werner, J. (1968) Bewaffnung und Waffenbeigabe in der Merowingerzeit. In *Ordinamenti Militari in Occidente nell' alto Medioevo, Settimane de Studio del Centro Italiano di Studi Sull'alto Medioevo (Spoleto 1967),* Spoleto.

Werner, K.-F. (1984) Les Origines. In *Histoire de la France,* t. 1. Fayard, Paris.

Young, B. K. (1977) Paganisme, Christianisation et Rites Funéraires Mérovingiennes. *Archéologie Médiévale* VII:5.

— (1984) *Quatre Cimetières Mérovingiennes de l'Est de la France. Etude Quantitative et Qualitative des Pratiques Funéraires.* British Archaeological Reports, Int. Series 208, Oxford.

— (1986a) Exemple aristocratique et mode funéraire dans la Gaule mérovingienne. *Annales E.S.C.* 2:379.

— (1986b) Quelques Réflexions sur les Sépultures Privilégiées, leur Contexte et leur Évolution, Surtout dans la Gaule de l'Est. In *L'Inhumation Privilégiée du IVe au VIIIe siècle en Occident,* Y. Duval and J.-C. Picard, Eds. Université de Paris-Val de Marne, de Boccard, Paris, pp. 69–89.

Young, B. K. and K. Carter-Young (1987) Psalmodi, un Site Paleochrétien sur le Littoral de Septimanie. *Gaule Mérovingienne et Monde Méditerranée. Les Derniers Romains en Septimanie. IVe–VIIe siècles.* C. Landes, Ed. Musée Archéologique de Lattes, Lattes.

147

12: Documentary Archaeology in Sardinia

Robert J. Rowland, Jr.
Loyola University, New Orleans, Louisiana

Although there exist for the classical world of ancient Greece and Rome almost no texts and documents of the sorts that are available in great profusion for an archaeologist or historian of more recent periods (cf. Beaudry 1988), there are, of course, some texts and documents that have often been employed by archaeologists both in designing and, more often, in interpreting their research, not infrequently to the detriment of the results (cf. Snodgrass 1987). For my own work in Sardinia, surviving texts (literary, legal, and epigraphical) are so few and so spotty that, valuable as they may be and happy as we are to have them, they leave vast areas and periods of time uncovered. One form of documentation I have attempted to integrate with archaeological data for both the prehistoric and the Roman periods is that provided by 19th-century writers who provide information about rural life, agricultural productivity, and the like (Rowland, in press a and 1990). In the following two parts of this paper I shall illustrate how these texts may assist in analyzing archaeological data. In the final part, I shall turn to the medieval period, for at least part of which documents do exist.

Evidence for Copper and Bronze Age Contadini-Guerrieri

Although numerous now-dried swamps and lagoons in Sardinia should provide abundant evidence for that island's paleoecology and paleoclimate, nobody has yet taken the initiative to drill cores and analyze the results. In anticipation of such research and in view of the fact that the climate through much of the third and midsecond millenium B.C., as well as during the time of the Roman Empire, was sufficiently similar to that of the 19th century (cf. Greene 1986:83), 19th-century documents have been indispensable for my analysis of the evolution of society through the chalcolithic and early bronze ages

to suggest that that society was dominated not by the fierce, combative *pastori-guerrieri* (shepherd-warriors) of the prevailing model (Lilliu 1984, 1988) but by *contadini-guerrieri* (peasant-warriors), more precisely, barley farmers (Rowland, in press a).

The prevailing model is based largely on two facts — one archaeological, the other historical — and on a myth. The archaeological fact is that the stone towers (known as nuraghi) built and inhabited by the indigenous Sardinian population are most particularly visible in upland, pastoral areas (Lilliu 1961); documentary evidence from the last century, as well as more recent studies of the utilization of the soil (Mori 1972), show that pastoralism was not and is not the exclusive or even dominant economic strategy in most of these zones. The historical fact is that native Sardinians, aided by their often rugged terrain, vigorously resisted the Roman conquest of their island (Rowland 1985a), and this gave rise to the myth of unyielding indigenous resistence to intrusive exploiters. This myth has in turn informed the current semimythical model of prehistoric development in which, during the bronze age, the *pastori-guerrieri* spilled out of their mountain fastnesses, back to which they subsequently retreated in the face first of Carthaginian, and then of Roman invaders (Lilliu 1984, 1988).

Surely, it is the existence of the myth that created the prehistory, and the two have fed upon one another since the resurgence of Sardinian patriotism in the 1830s (Sotgiu 1986:43–46). The reality might be something quite different, and it is time to examine the extant remains in the absence of aprioristic reasoning. Vague references to "harshness of the terrain" or to "fertile plains" are no substitute for examination of sites and their environments. That the low-lying Campidano *is* fertile and intensively cultivated does not necessarily mean that it was so in prehistory, surely not before the arrival of a cash- (or tax-) crop economy; nor does the fact that stockraising is historically the dominant (but certainly not the exclusive) economic strategy in the uplands translate into an *exclusively* pastoral economy in the past.

For town after town in the now fertile Campidano, Vittorio Angius, writing in the period of the 1830s to 1850s, speaks of the bad air, the bad water, the terrible heat, and the swamps and marshes. Of Sestu, for example, he tells us that in the summer one feels great heat because the sea breeze cannot move the air at such a low altitude; the air was harmful to health and to vegetation; springs are very rare, and one must drink well water that is often salty and "heavy on the stomach"; the river carried no water in summer and too much in the rainy months, when bogs and swamps formed, whence came in the summer months "the pestilence of miasms" (Angius 20.12). At Serramanna the heat was worse in the low-lying areas, where moisture was an affliction not only in the wet seasons, but even in the summer; the air was unhealthy in all seasons because miasms came "from many places where there are quagmires"; the well water in town was not very good, but there were some good springs in the territory, one at Muntonali (where there is a nuraghe), and the water of the Leni (next to the nuraghe of S. Maria di Monserrato) was also good (Angius 19.919–923). Except for his figures on crop yields, Angius' descriptions of the Campidano very much resemble those of marginal land that would have had very little attractions for most prehistoric settlers of the island.

La Marmora makes similar observations in the 19th century regarding Trexenta and Marmilla, at present two of Sardinia's most important agricultural zones. "The basin of Trexenta, despite its renowned fertility in cereals, is striking to the traveler for its 'nudità' caused by the lack of water; even drinking water was lacking; what one drank was scarce and brackish: the wealthy have it transported from afar" (La Marmora 1874:179). The equally renowned Marmilla suffered from the same "almost total lack of trees and what is worse, the dearth and bad quality of drinking water ... the inhabitants of the zone were required to drink rain water either collected on the roofs of their houses or percolated through saltiferous deposits, rendering it brackish" (La Marmora 1874:255).

By contrast, in the zones where one finds nuraghi or remains of nuraghi in abundance, one also finds (in the pages of Angius and La Marmora) good water in ample supply, numerous huntable animals, wood and forest products (including acorns and, at least in modern times if not in prehistory, chestnuts), and crop yields that are comparable with and sometimes even higher than those of the Campidano, particularly for barley. Angius calls Sedilo, to take one example, the most suitable place in the island for a fortress because of its healthiness; he noted that there were more than 35 springs in its territory. In 1846 the town had 450 farmers and 218 shepherds, some of whom also engaged in cultivation (Angius 19.730–732, 737); at about the same time, Sestu had 330 farmers, 60 shepherds (Angius 20.15), and Serramanna had 650 and 80, respectively (Angius 19.296).

At Sedilo, each year there were sown 7000 *starelli* of grain (1 *starello* = 49.2 liters), 2000 of barley, 1000 of beans, plus chickpeas and flax, with an ordinary and average yield overall of 12-fold (Angius 19.754–759). At Serramanna, "one of the principal agricultural towns of Sardinia," were sown 3500 *starelli* of grain, 300 of barley, 700 of beans, 200 of other legumes, and 100 of flax, with an average yield of 12- to 15-fold (Angius 19.927). The annual crop yield at Sestu was abundant "if the rains come at the right time," ranging from 12-fold for grain to 18-fold for beans (Angius 20.16). However, still in the Campidano, at San Sperato, where cereals prospered and fructified abundantly "if the rains do not fail," the average yield of grain and barley was only 10-fold (Angius 18.755–756). The "pastoral" territory of Bono included some 300 gardens and about 20 square miles of oak trees, which could have fed some 30,000 pigs instead of the 6500 that were being raised in 1833; other stock included 15,000 sheep, 2000 cows, 2500 goats, and 450 horses, as well as abundant wild animals. Here, Angius enumerated 368 farmers and 568 shepherds (Angius 2.426–429). At Sorgono, where there were 330 farmers and 240 shepherds, crop yields ranged from 7-fold for grain (900 *starelli* sown) to 14-fold for barley (1200 *starelli*). There were about 12,000 nut trees and a variety of animals:120 horses, 1050 cows, 2300 pigs, 3500 goats, and 16,000 sheep (Angius 20.287–289). Even at Tonara, 910 m above sea level on the western slopes of the Gennargentu, were sown 700 *starelli* of grain, 500 of barley, and 70 of legumes, with an average yield of 7-fold; there were perhaps more than 200,000 "fruit" trees (chestnut being most common), along with 1250 cows, 1600 pigs, 7000 goats, and 14,000 sheep (Angius 20.992–997). Recently, with specific reference to Austis, Benedetto Meloni described the traditional upland practices, before changes during the last 30 years:

> What is important to note is that itinerant pastoralism accompanies agriculture and that the two activities exchange resources, which guarantees a complete ecological equilibrium. The practice of cereal culture on arable lands, associated with a system of rotation, guarantees that the soil will be cleared of weeds and other infestations, consequently improving the quality of the pastures (Meloni 1989:123).

So, in the upland areas, particularly at the highland-lowland interface, natural resources allowed at least the possibility of a reasonably secure existence for the prehistoric inhabitants. Water from springs, streams, and rainfall is both more abundant and more potable than in the now more heavily populated and cultivated lowland zones; agricultural potential, albeit on less acreage, was comparable with that of the lowland and, if we think of barley as the staple crop and think in terms of subsistence rather than (anachronistically) of a cash or tax crop, agricultural potential was even greater; wild animals (deer, boar, hare) were more abundant, while fish and eels should have been ample, however much they are missing from the archaeological record (cf. Rowland 1987); nuts would have produced food for humans and fodder for animals; and domesticated animals would have been raised in relatively larger numbers than in the plains, perhaps (but not inevitably) migrating from late fall to early spring. Winters would have been harsher in the uplands then as now: there is a fairly close correlation between those regions of Sardinia that have rainfall on more than 70 days per year and those regions that have more than 10 days during which the temperature falls below 0°C. This was not a golden age when the earth produced abundantly of its own accord, certainly; but the areas of midrange altitudes were much more conducive to the establishment and development of settled life based on polyculture (barley mostly, with legumes and garden crops) and stockraising supplemented by hunting, fishing, and gathering.

One measure to test this hypothesis on existing evidence is the relative affluence of nuragic sites, and one manifestation of affluence — in addition to the complexity and extent of the structure itself — is the existence of metal, particularly bronze, a detailed or even summary presentation of all the details of which is out of place here (cf. Rowland, in press a). On the basis of the summaries provided for each town and its territory (comune) in the *Dizionario della Sardegna* (Boscolo et al. n.d.), 135 of the comunes where bronze has been found at one or more sites are chiefly agricultural, producing grain, cereals, or the like (in many cases, along with stockraising); only 16 could be said to be largely pastoral. Of those 16, however, Arzachena produces wine; Bono, vegetables; Gadoni, garden crops; Olmedo (where in 1843 the principal occupation was agriculture) (Angius 13.92), *crine vegetale*; Orgosolo, vines and *carbone vegetale*; Tempio, legumes and potatoes (cf. Angius 20. 787–795). Thus, on this testimony, only 10, or less than 7%, can be seen as truly pastoral; these are Ala, Aritzo, Belvi, Budduso, Burgos, Ollolai, Orune, Teti, Thiesi, and Urzulei. But there is more to it than that.

Of the land of Ala, Angius says it was

> ...more suitable for pasturage than for raising crops; nonetheless, in many sites, especially towards the southern part [i.e., precisely where bronze has been found] they grow grain and barley, the produce of which can scarcely suffice for the subsistence of the inhabitants [i.e., 950 persons].... Grain renders ordinarily 6-fold, barley 8-fold (Angius 1.110).

At Belvi in 1833, of a population of 816, no more than 30 persons were shepherds (Angius 2.222). Of the land of Budduso, Angius observed that it was "more conve-

nient for pasture than for cultivation"; nonetheless, 300 *starelli* of grain and 800 of barley were sown annually, with an ordinary return of 6- and 8-fold, respectively: "from barley they make the bread with which the major part [of the inhabitants, which, in 1833 numbered 2200] take their nourishment" (Angius 2.686–687). At Burgos, although the majority of the males were shepherds, many were farmers; grain yielded 8-fold, barley 20-fold (Angius 2.703–704). At Ollolai in 1843, there were 130 farmers, 160 shepherds; grain produced 7-fold, barley 10-fold (Angius 13.88–89). At Orune, 200 persons applied themselves to the "agrarian art," 400 to pastoralism; grain produced 7-fold, barley 10-fold, and here, as at Ollolai, most people ate barley bread (Angius 13.583–584). At Teti, in the 1846 census, there were 74 farmers and an equal number (*altrettanti*) of shepherds; here, "they sow less grain than barley, because it is believed that the climate is less propitious to the former than to the latter species, and this must be considered true since grain usually renders no more than 3-fold, barley ordinarily 8-fold" (Angius 20.868–869). At Thiesi, *agricoltori* outnumbered *pastori* 650 to 130; grain and barley produced 7- and 12-fold, respectively, and "if the farmers weren't so stupid, they would not have to be jealous of other regions which are most fertile in cereals" (Angius 20.936–938). At Urzulei, "despite the absence of care, grain ordinarily renders tenfold, barley even twentyfold" (Angius 23.420).

Thus, of the 152 comunes where bronze artifacts from the nuragic period have been found, Aritzo alone can be regarded as truly pastoral; yet, some of the bronze found there was discovered during agricultural work. All the other regions are either largely agricultural or at least sufficiently agricultural as to have supported a relatively small population in nuragic times. Indeed, more than supporting the nuragic population, these places were able to produce a surplus, and it is this surplus that is (in part) represented by the accumulation of metal and metallic objects, not just the relatively large hoards, but the small accumulations of ingots, fragments, pins, and other items.

Although most findspots of bronze artifacts can be related to the agricultural potential of the zone, not all regions where bronze has been found have the best quality soils. The hoard at Su Tempiesu-Oliena (along with Lula, the only other identifiable findspot apparently at class 5 soil [cf. Pietracaprina 1971]) is surely a consequence of cult, but its associated nuragic complex Santa Lulla commands a fertile river valley. Similarly, the enormous size of the hoard at Abini-Teti may be explained more as a theological surplus than an agricultural one. It is of course impossible to ascribe causes to any individual find, whether of a single item or of a large hoard; how could one distinguish between bronze that is the result of agricultural (and, yes, pastoral) prosperity, bronze that is the result of commercial activity, and bronze that is the result of a successful attack on a neighboring or distant tribe? What is striking about the evidence is the frequent close relationship between surplus wealth, as reflected in the accumulation of metal, and the agricultural potentiality of the zone. With two exceptions, it would seem that all findspots in the 10 so-called pastoral comunes are located in areas of class 4 soil. It needs to be stressed that, save for the religious sites, the finds of metallic objects in these areas are relatively exiguous.

Conversely, only a dozen of the relevant comunes are situated, in whole or in part, on class 1 soil (Pietracaprina 1971). Here, too, with the exception of the hoard at Uta, the amount of metal is relatively small, confirming the hypothesis that what are now the best and most productive lands were not necessarily such in prehistory.

The vast majority of the findspots and the bulk of the material found are located in the optimum zone for nuragic development, where soil, climate, and water all combine to support a society based on polyculture, the prime crop of which was barley. Not only is barley more productive than grain in the areas of high nuragic-metallic density, but it has a shorter growing season. According to Giulio Angioni's analysis of traditional agriculture in Sardinia, "Grain is sown in mid-November...around mid-December are sown...barley (and others)... In February...the fields of barley are weeded... Around the end of April and up to late May the most difficult and important work is weeding the grain fields... Barley is harvested around the end of June" while the harvesting of grain continues through July "and sometimes even early August" (Angioni 1976:221–224).

In other words, a community of barley farmers could complete their harvest by the end of June and, if they were so minded, attack the grain farmers before the latters' harvest was in. At the end of the summer-fall fighting season, the grain farmers would have had to return to sow next year's crop a full month before the barley farmers would have had to do likewise. All other factors being equal, barley farmers therefore had a full 2 months' advantage over any of their counterparts who grew grain, and their potentiality for producing a surplus would have been greater. I have suggested, therefore, that the prime movers of the evolution of nuragic society in the third and second millenia B.C. were the fierce combative *contadini-guerrieri*, the barley farmers of the lowland-upland interfaces, midrange uplands, and well-watered upland river valleys, whose prosperity resulted in part from their agricultural success and is in part reflected in their accumulated wealth manifested partly in metallic objects.

Sardinian Productivity in the Roman Period

In solving what I somewhat whimsically called The Case of the Missing Sardinian Grain (Rowland 1984a), I demonstrated, contrary to what text-based interpretations had held, that Sardinia was important to the Roman grain supply, not only during the Republican (238 to 44 B.C.) and late Imperial (3rd to 5th centuries A.D.) periods, when it looms large in our written sources, but throughout the High Empire (44 B.C. to 3rd century A.D.) as well. Although common sense ought to have cautioned us that such should have been the case, common sense is not proof; scholars for whom an off-the-cuff remark in the text of Pliny the Elder is a more valuable witness than are hundreds of pages of archaeological reports may not yet be persuaded, but Geoffrey Rickman, whose inadequately informed interpretation (1980:106–107) was my original point of departure, quickly agreed with my conclusion derived from an analysis of the available archaeological material (personal communication).

Briefly put, the Sardinian countryside, particularly in the most fertile areas, was indeed heavily studded with villages, the pottery remains of which demonstrate that they flourished during the High Empire. In many areas, these Roman period villages show an exploitation of an arable vastly more extensive than that exploited by previous populations (Rowland and Dyson, 1991). Survey work conducted between 1987 and 1989 by myself and Stephen L. Dyson in the Tirso River valley provided some refinements to what all too frequently is called in the literature simply *Roman period* settlements, without more precise chronological indications, and expanded enormously the number of known Roman sites (Rowland and Dyson 1988, 1989).

Early modern writers familiar with ancient sources were struck by the contrast between Sardinia's reputed fertility in antiquity, particularly during the Roman period, and its evident poverty during their own age and, in ignorance of the real reasons for the difference, encouraged inappropriate, in truth impossible, reforms: a Spanish ecclesiastic in 1611 wrote "all writers, ancient as well as modern, who mention Sardinia call it fertile and abundant; experience shows this to be so, and if it were all cultivated (most of it is not), it would provide grain for all the nearby realms" (Plaisant 1970:80). In 1776, another priest, Francesco Gemelli, "Professor Emeritus of Latin Eloquence at the Royal University of Sassari," wrote a three-volume work (Gemelli 1776; cf. Da Passano; Sotgiu 1986:153–171, 435) perpetuating what Marco Tangheroni has called "the myth of Sardinia-granary" (Tangheroni 1981:33–49).

In recent years, many scholars have attempted to replace that so-called myth with another, namely, that Sardinia, far from being a productive granary, was precisely the opposite. These scholars, having read Braudel, know that Mediterranean lands, no matter how well endowed with fertile soil, are subject to periodic droughts and inadequate crop yields. There are, of course, texts to be quoted that contradict the classic view of "Sardinia-granary;" and these texts, because they are historical documents more often than products of the literary imagination, seem to carry more weight. Because they often convey vivid testimony of human suffering, they seem to be more convincing (Manconi 1982).

One such text is in fact a poem, from the early 19th century, written by Melchiorre Murenu, "The Homer of the Poor," entitled "*S'istadu de Sardigna*," (the Condition of Sardinia) (Pira 1975:194):

> *Mira sas istagiones cambiadas*
> *C'affligint su coro in sas intragnas.*
> *Fritturas, in s'atunzu, antecipadas.*
> *Isteriles, patidas sas campagnas.*
> *Abbas, in s'ilgerru, illimitadas.*
> *Beranos oppremidos cun siccagnas.*
> *E in sos istios, arias superbas*
> *pro cunvertire in pruer' sas erbas.*

> See the seasons' changes,
> How they afflict the heart in one's intestines.
> In autumn, early cold,
> Sterile, suffering fields.
> In winter, water without limits.
> Spring oppressed by dryness.
> And in the summer, air splendid
> For transforming vegetation to dust.

The records of the Jesuits in Cagliari, the chief city, who provided food for the hungry, document years of famine in the late 1500s, years "of such hunger and so sterile that the majority of the people could sustain life only by eating wild ferns and other weeds." The years 1570 to 1572 were particularly disastrous, and the famine at that time was compounded by the enormous loss of animals caused by unusually cold winters (Manconi 1982:56). Later, in the terrible famine of 1680, some 80,000 persons, out of a total population of 250,000, are said to have died, and entire villages were devastated (Manconi 1982:61). Sometimes, severe drought was local, rather than island-wide: in 1645, the villages of Furtei, Segariu, and Nureci had to beg grain from the capitol; and in 1775, two of these same villages plus Mandas had crop yields ranging from 1:1 to $2\frac{1}{2}$:1. An official report states that the plants grew to only one-third their normal height (Manconi 1982:65–66). In 1843 in the fertile fields around Oristano, even beans and chickpeas yielded only $2\frac{1}{2}$:1 and 2:1, respectively (Angius 13.277).

Historians who emphasize these and other similar data do so with the specific intention of contradicting what they call the myth, believing that a grain-rich Sardinia and a poverty stricken, agriculturally depressed Sardinia are mutually exclusive. In fact, both views are true; they are just not true simultaneously. In order to use more modern data to support or contradict hypotheses or statements about the ancient world, it is essential to compare comparables, and the history of climate suggests that data from the early modern period are simply incomparable with those of the Roman period (Greene 1986:81–86). It is only at about the middle of the 19th century that we can legitimately begin to utilize modern comparanda in an attempt to analyze the situation in the Roman period, an important point that has rarely been attended to by scholars (Greene 1986:83; Lamb 1977:chap. 17–18; Lamb 1981).

Certainly, in the mid-19th century, even in the 20th, there were sporadic widespread or local famines; that is to be expected, and I would be the last person to minimize the human suffering that results from famine. But the comparability of the Roman and 19th-century climates allows us, for the first time, to expect that crop-yield data might be comparable. Further, all available evidence about agricultural production in that period suggests that, for the most part, 19th-century Sardinian agriculture was essentially still Roman (Le Lannou 1979:275; Angioni 1976; Wagner 1982); indeed, in some aspects and in some places, it seems to have been even more primitive. At Monti, for example, not a particularly fertile zone, grain yielded eight-fold and barley 10-fold with methods described by Angius (11.317) as follows: "they sow and they harvest, and these two acts comprise the sum of their agricultural work." Nuragugume also yielded 8-fold; here "the men labor with very little diligence in cultivating the fields" (Angius 12.735). At Semestene the yield was 10-fold, and Angius (19.832) explains that it is so low because of the "very little diligence in their work and because animals often enter the areas that have been sown and trample them." In the territory of Sassari, which formed the basis of the grain export from Turris Libyssonis (modern Porto Torres), one of the two Sardinian cities recorded on mosaics in the Piazzale delle Corporazioni at Ostia (Becati 1961:4.71–73; Meiggs 1960:286–287 with Plate XIIIc), the 20-fold yield could be doubled, we are told (Angius 19.137–138), except that "they work following the traditional methods and generally without understanding the quality of the soil or the proper time to sow, and without diligence."

In contrast both with the modernists' gloomy portrayal of Sardinian productivity and with the widespread opinion that the mountainous interior of the island was exclusively pastoral, consider Gavoi, well up in the hills of the interior, which regularly produced a 7-fold grain and 10-fold barley crop, while the subregion S'Eremu produced 16- to 30-fold, and Narboni, another subregion of Gavoi, often produced a barley crop of more than 150-fold: in 1833 it came in at 208:1 (Angius 7.287)! In the Sulcis region of the southwest, 10-fold grain crops were common, 16-fold was frequent; in the year of jubilation some regions produced 100-fold, and in the harvest of "the sacred year" (presumably so-called because of its extraordinary abundance), a few reached as much as 260:1 (Angius 8.351).

During the 19th century, many towns in the interior produced surplus grain and barley, or wine produced from grapes that, arguably, might have been grown on land that in the Roman period had been devoted to cereal crops. These surpluses were carted sometimes over long distances: grain from Laconi (Angius 9.46) for example, was much valued at Cagliari, distant 75 km in a straight line. On the average, Laconi produced a surplus sufficent for a year's supply of grain and/or barley to 1380 persons more than the town's population (assuming 5 *starelli* per person) (Angius 19.66). Gesturi produced, on the average, grain and barley for some 3800 persons against a population of 1779, plus 900,000 l of wine (Angius 8.23); even allowing a liter a day per person, women and children included, the surplus vineyards, if converted to grain, could have fed an additional 324 persons. Isili produced grain and barley for about 5200 persons against a population of 2196 (Angius 8.532); here too surplus wine was produced. Osilo regularly sold as *surplus* enough grain to feed 3960 persons (Angius 13.625).

Therefore, since we cannot, or at least should not, confine ourselves simply to the coastal areas, we must consider the agricultural potential of the entire island. In his comprehensive accounts of Sardinian towns in the 19th century, Angius provides average crop yields for 264 villages. Confining ourselves simply to the wheat yield, the average of these average yields is 9.8-fold. How much grain did Roman Sardinia produce? It is obviously impossible to know for certain, but informed guesswork can at least produce an order of magnitude. In modern times, 300,000 hectares devoted to grain in 1910 is that crop's peak (Mori 1972:147): at an effective yield of 8.8:1, a year's supply of grain would have been provided for 1,324,445 persons; but the population of the island in that year was 850,000 (Pracchi 1980:163). If we assume a Roman-period population of 350,000 (a plausible enough guess) (Pardi 1926:39) and a production reduced proportionately (that is, to 42% of the above figure), Sardinia in the High Empire could have produced grain to provide subsistence levels to 556,267 persons; because a greater percentage of the Roman-period population would have been engaged in agriculture, we might be justified in increasing this amount by 10% to 611,894 persons. Deducting the hypothetical 350,000 inhabitants of Sardinia, we are left with 261,894 additional persons who could have been provided subsistence levels of grain from Sardinia's surplus. Of course, these figures give a specious appearance of precision; however, the order of magnitude — surplus grain for about a quarter of a million persons — seems reasonable enough as an absolute minimum.

Medieval Sardinia

In a very real and very lamentable sense, we, near the

end of the 20th century, know very little more about the history of the events of late Roman and early Medieval Sardinia than what was already available to Fara in the 16th century (Fara 1835/1838); nor are we in a very secure position regarding questions of continuity and transformation in the underlying structures of society, economy, agrarian history, and so forth. Archaeologically, for this period, we are adrift on a vast uncharted sea, with ignorance on every side as far as the eye can see; even where excavations have occurred, as for example at Tharros (Pesce 1966; Zucca 1984) and Nora (Pesce 1972; Tronchetti 1984a), the Byzantine layers (like the Arab levels at biblical sites) have simply been discarded and unrecorded. Subsequent work at Nora (Tronchetti 1984b) has shown that the second-century Baths by the Sea were converted into a fortification in the fourth or fifth century (actually, it would seem, the mid fifth century) and destroyed by a fire in the seventh or eighth. Against whom and by whom it was fortified and whether the fire was an isolated accident or accompanied by widespread devastation and, if the latter, who the perpetrators were, are unknown. Some medieval materials, of course, have been preserved and published over the years: my own research on the spread of Christianity in the island to about A.D. 600 was based largely on an examination of archaeological materials (Rowland 1978a, 1984b), which, when marshaled together, forced a radical revision of accounts deriving from the written record alone. The relatively large number of published finds of coins of Leo I and Anthemius provide archaeological confirmation of Procopius' account of an East Roman invasion of the now Vandal island in 468 (Rowland 1978b).

There are certain indications that medieval archaeology in Sardinia might receive greater attention in the future than in the past, although pressing, possibly even deteriorating, financial problems will unquestionably impede progress. The three most significant of these indications are as follows. First, the late Alberto Boscolo, dean of traditional, text-based medievalists, speaking on the current state of research on Sardinia in the Byzantine and Giudical periods (Boscolo 1982), notes that "some archaeological discoveries and some consideration of the (written) sources can even now offer new data for the reconstruction of society in that period" (i.e., the period of domination by the Vandals); little is to be gained by observing either that these new lines of research are essentially similar to what Alfons Dopsch preached more than half a century ago (Dopsch 1923/24, 1937) or that Boscolo seems to have been unaware of the concept of programatic archaeological research. Boscolo continues with two examples, the first "a tomb in the territory of Quartuccio, an example of a Vandal burial in a latifundium...(which) merits careful study" (which it has not yet received); he knows that it was a *latifundium* (a large slave- or tenant-operated estate) because conven-

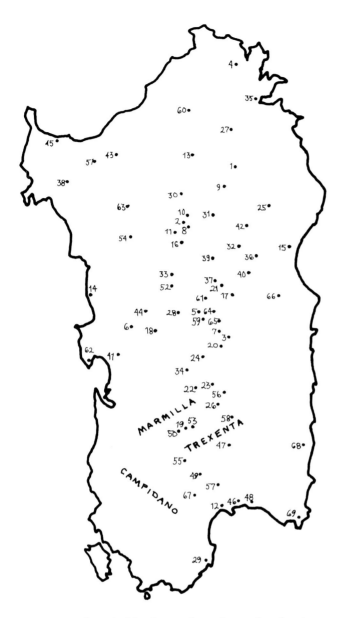

FIG. 1. Sites mentioned in text.

1. Ala	11. Burgos	21. Gavoi
2. Anela	12. Cagliari	22. Gesturi
3. Artizo	13. Castro	23. Isili
4. Arzachena	14. Cornus	24. Laconi
5. Austis	15. Dorgali	25. Lula
6. Bauladu	16. Esporlatu	26. Mandas
7. Belvi	17. Fonni	27. Monti
8. Bono	18. Fordongianus	28. Neoneli
9. Budduso	19. Furtei	29. Nora
10. Bultei	20. Gadoni	30. Nughedu

31. Nule	41. Oristano	51. Sassari
32. Nuoro	42. Orune	52. Sedilo
33. Nuragugume	43. Osilo	53. Segariu
34. Nureci	44. Paulilatino	54. Semestene
35. Olbia	45. Porto Torres	55. Serramanna
36. Oliena	46. Quartuccio	56. Serri
37. Ollolai	47. S. Andrea Frius	57. Sestu
38. Olmedo	48. San Gregorio	58. Siurgus
39. Oniferi	49. San Sperato	59. Sorgono
40. Orgosolo	50. Sanluri	60. Tempio

61. Teti
62. Tharros
63. Thiesi
64. Tiana
65. Tonara
66. Urzulei
67. Uta
68. Villaputzu
69. Villasimius

tional wisdom holds that to have been the dominant mode of production at the time, a conclusion that remains to be demonstrated. Further, speaking of the Arab period, Boscolo states that

> ...sooner or later there will come to light in our fields discoveries such as those at Olbia, *that got lost and were never studied* [emphasis added], and it will be possible to say something new. Recently there appeared the remains of the fortification of Mughahid not far from San Gregorio, a fortification that had beside it a bath that was produced by the Arabs' transformation of a Roman bath (Boscolo 1976, Tangheroni 1976).

When we recall that only a minuscule fraction of surviving nuraghi has been excavated and even fewer have received anything resembling a proper publication, we should not be surprised that this so-called fortification of Mughahid remains inadequately published.

Our second indication that the situation might improve is an essay by Giovanni Lilliu, remarkably up to date in its outlook, "Towards an Interdisciplinary Research in Archaeology and History" (Lilliu 1981). Lilliu gives no indications of being aware of Dopsch's major work, but his conclusions, *mutatis mutandis*, are similar. For example, Pais followed Procopius in characterizing the Vandals as "destructive harassers" (Pais 1923:193–216). Lilliu observes that "archaeology presents quite a different picture than that offered by written sources concerning the character of Vandal civilization both in Sardinia and in the provinces of their empire." On the Lombards, too, "archaeology orients us quite differently, indeed, precisely the opposite." Summarizing the work of Delogu (1953) and Renata Serra (1971a, b) for the seventh and eighth centuries, Lilliu concludes

> ...from this collection of art-historical and object oriented data, one can reconstruct, almost independent

155

of narrative history, a picture of Sardinia not closed in on itself culturally or withdrawn from the vital activities of the Mediterranean, but thoroughly involved in a vast network of relationships, production and exchanges which also involved the great Byzantine and Arab civilizations of the east and the civic structures of the Western Mediterranean and barbarian and Roman Europe.

It is indeed the Byzantine and sub-Byzantine periods in Sardinia that can profit the most from extensive archaeological research, not only because these periods encompass more than half a millenium in time (from the 6th to the 12th century) and extended, as we shall see shortly, over the entire island, but also because they are of supreme importance and because there should be masses of evidence available, particularly in the countryside, at the village level. It is here that Lilliu is at his most withering:

> ...but everything that deals with objects is considered banal and vulgar, while at the same time it nonetheless signifies the realities of life of individuals and of society; yet has interested none of these scholars. And this is not because there are no traces (quite the contrary, there are many traces buried in destroyed castles and villages), but because for the exquisite palates of the 'signori' of source-based history, material culture is something disgusting to be removed: in short, it is not history. Because of this logic, nobody in the educational and scientific structures of history has ever attempted to convince a group of experts to take soundings in the buried layers of castles or within the habitations of the hundreds of villages that have been abandoned and destroyed for centuries. Nor (save for a few feeble thoughts directed towards royal tombs, without any practical result) has anyone ever attempted to explore communal cemeteries in which one will certainly find skeletons and grave goods, apart from the interest in individuating types, forms, and structures of the burials themselves.

Given the substantial contributions that archaeology can make to historical understanding and vice versa, one hopes that Lilliu's final words on the subject will prove prophetic (1981:186): "Hence there is the need to develop as soon as possible interdisciplinary research in these directions if we wish to be competitive in the fields of medieval archaeology and history."

Our third source of optimism is the publication a few years ago of a catalogue of the paleochristian and medieval materials in the National Museum in Cagliari, largely the work of Letizia Pani Ermini (1981), who was subsequently appointed the first medieval archaeologist in a Sardinian university. She has been reexcavating the paleochristian site at Is Columbaris outside of the city of Cornus (Giuntella and Pani Ermini 1981; Giuntella et al. 1985; Pani Ermini et al. 1986; cf. Mastino 1979:85–106) and the Basilica of S. Saturno in Cagliari (Pani

Ermini 1982/83) and has begun work, with an Italian-French team, at the church of Nostra Signora di Castro (Pani Ermini 1989). However, at the University of Sassari, bureaucratic wrangling has so far blocked a proposal made years ago by Ercole Contu and Marco Tangheroni to have medieval archaeology approved as a field of study in the Faculty of Magistero (Tangheroni 1985:12–13); one hopes for an eventually successful outcome. In any event, the need is urgent: every year more material vanishes from the countryside, much of it without even being recorded much less analyzed in detail. Lilliu's 25-year old observation remains equally true today: "one cannot today speak of Byzantine archaeology (sc. in Sardinia) true and proper" (Lilliu 1964/65:30; cf. Paulis 1983:9–10, 21).

Notwithstanding numerous difficulties, progress is being made. In recent years, Cagliari has seen some brilliant, cooperative research, most notably the multiperiod, multidisciplinary study of the zone around S. Igia (Santa Cecilia) (Fois et al.1986); the important reexamination of both the old excavations in the area around the church of S. Saturno and the relevant documents (Mureddu et al.1988); and the multidisciplinary examination of the church of S. Restituta (Lilliu et al.1988) — all of which (and others besides) augur well for future developments.

It seems safe to predict that even some very limited campaigns of field work will go a long way toward revising some of the conventional wisdom about medieval, particularly Byzantine, Sardinia, namely, that the Byzantine civilization was urban and military, profoundly influencing the church, civic and military institutions, and art, but with little or no influence in the countryside. Paulis has recently summarized the situation thus (Paulis 1983:10; cf. Piras 1966):

> By limiting Byzantine culture for all practical purposes to churches with cupolas and to inscriptions in medieval Greek, it has been maintained that the Byzantine influence in Sardinia was singularly limited and courtly, that is, reduced to the exclusive ambit of the high functionaries of the imperial administration and ecclesiastical hierarchy. Its geographic extent would have thus been confined to those areas where the inscriptions have been found and where those churches are located; in particular, on this view, the Byzantines would have never penetrated into the interior, mountainous zones of the island.

Some years ago, on the evidence of coin hoards and stray finds, I observed (1) that the circulation of money in early Byzantine Sardinia was extremely limited and (2) that for all practical purposes, "Roman" (i.e., Byzantine) Sardinia was now limited to a few cities and their plains, an area not much greater than was Phoenician Sardinia, certainly smaller even than Punic Sardinia (Rowland

1978b:96). I now subscribe only to the first of those statements. Seventh-century *fibulae* in Pani Ermini's collection, for example, were found at S. Andrea Frius, Serri, Fordongianus, Fonni, Siurgus, and Tiana in the interior (Pani Ermini 1981: nos. 133, 135–139, 141–142, 144, 146, 148, 150, 153, 156, 159, 160, 176, 181, 189–190, 193, 197–198); and a whole host of "medieval discoveries" has been reported at such places as Esporlatu, Anela, Bultei, Nule, Oliena, Nuoro, Oniferi, Neoneli, Nughedu, Austis, Teti, Urzulei, etc. (Paulis 1983:246–247). I give only one specific, recent example: in the territory of Fonni, in a region called *Sa Idda 'e sos Gregos* (the village of the Greeks) were found "numerous archaeological materials of the medieval period (basalt mill-stones, bricks, cups, amphoras, plates deriving from late Roman models, etc.)." The site is particularly paradigmatic, for it has so far been published only in the local newspaper (Paulis 1983:83, citing Lilliu in *L'Unione Sarda*). Similarly, in a recent notice a single sentence in length records "numerous fragments of large storage vessels (at Dorgali), probably locally made, the stamped decorations of which recall Lombard vessels of the 7th and 8th centuries" (Manunza 1984:556). Survey, particularly around Bauladu, Paulilatino, and Fordongianus, has added much to our knowledge of late Roman and early Medieval settlement (Rowland and Dyson 1988, 1989), but not much can yet be made by way of generalization from what remain, for the most part, isolated bits and pieces of inadequately published data.

What, then, of the countryside, the fertile grain growing areas of the Roman period, the Campidano in particular? Here, too, we are confronted with an archaeology in search of archaeologists. In the plain between Oristano and Cagliari, some 300 Roman sites are known (Rowland 1984c:296–297), a figure that surely understates reality by 50% or more; survey at Bauladu has increased the number of known sites by 600% (Rowland and Dyson 1988). Many of these Roman sites are also medieval ones (cf. Rowland 1982:32–34), but in the present state of our knowledge it is impossible to state with confidence that any or all of them continued to be inhabited or if there was a break in settlement and, if there was a hiatus, when it occurred and how long it endured. It was only in 1980, at Dorgali, that archaeologists first recognized that certain hand-made, poorly fired pottery that had seemed prehistoric, not to say neolithic, was actually Medieval (Caprara 1980); and Angela Terrosu Asole complained more than two decades ago about the impossibility of recognizing and dating remains of Medieval structures (Terrosu Asole 1965:207–211). One would like to see some thermoluminescence dates for a sample of materials from rural sites. One would also like to see more excavations, if only test trenches, at sites where both Roman and Medieval presences are attested, as, for example, almost anywhere in the countryside or in

the interior where remains (perhaps only a toponym) of a rustic church, particularly of a Greek saint, stand as mute testimony to a deserted village (cf. Terrosu Asole 1975:37–40). Roberto Ledda (1989:374–390) has recently published the preliminary results of some useful research along these lines in one area, and I have prepared a database and distribution maps of such churches (some of them already in ruins at the time of Angius) and toponyms; the patterns thus revealed suggest a number of interesting lines for future research.

Recently published finds from Sanluri and Villasimius indicate how much can be expected to be found and, in the former zone, indicate at least one of the questions that require an answer. At S. Maria in Villasimius, a Roman bath complex yielded material dating from the second century B.C. to the seventh century A.D. (Tronchetti and Fanni 1982). In the territory of Sanluri, a probable villa yielded a fragment of Hayes 335 (mid-sixth century), while tombs at Giliadiri and Bidd 'e Cresia, at least on the basis of coin finds, continued only to the late third and fourth centuries (Paderi 1982; cf. Rowland 1985b). Did these cemeteries, in fact, go out of use? If they did, was there a reduction in population? If there was, is it to be connected with a reduction in the amount of arable under cultivation? And if this be so, what are the further ramifications?

Given (1) the absolute lack of documentary evidence for the period between Gregory the Great (in the late 6th century) and the native cartularies, called Condaghi (commencing in the 11th century), and (2) the extreme lack of utility of such texts as we possess for epochs prior to the Condaghi, our only hope for comprehending the historical process most broadly defined in late Roman and early medieval Sardinia lies in archaeological research.

The Congaghi themselves and other, briefer documents could be of inestimable value, both in choosing sites and in interpreting them. To the best of my knowledge, only one excavation can be directly related to the evidence of these documents, and that is inadvertent, namely, the still ongoing excavation by Lenore Gallin (1989 a, b; Gallin and Sebis 1989) at the nuraghe S. Barbara-Bauladu, which is most likely the village S. Barbara de Turre mentioned a dozen times in the Condaghe of S. Maria di Bonarcado (Dettori 1955–1956:101–126). Several generations of archaeologists and historians could profitably collaborate on research projects deriving from these and other texts (cf. Borghini 1979/80). To cite only one other such example, in commenting on an 11th-century document, Tola says of the village called Crucca (between Sassari and Porto Torres): "there still exists a small part of the ancient castle, and one can see all around the ruins of many habitations" (Tola 1861:151, n. 9). Crucca was also the site of a Roman villa (Rowland 1981:119). It may be that there is nothing still extant at the site; but, unless someone looks for it, we will never know for certain. There also exist excellent inventories of deserted villages (Day 1973; Terrosu Asole 1974), which could serve as the starting points for multiperiod, multidisciplinary research involving survey, excavation, and examination of surviving documents and records.

References

Angioni, G. (1976) Sa Laurera: Il Lavoro Contadino in Sardegna. EDES, Cagliari.

Angius, V. (1833–1856) Articles on Sardinia. In *Dizionario Geografico-Storico-Statistico ecc*, G. Casalis, Ed. G. Maspero, Turin.

Beaudry, M. Ed. (1988) *Documentary Archaeology in the New World*. Cambridge University Press, Cambridge.

Becatti, G. (1961) *Scavi di Ostia*, Vol. 4. Liberia dello Stato, Rome.

Borghini, G. (1979/80) *I Condaghi Sardi e la Storia Agraria della Sardegna Giudicale*. Tesi di Laurea, Universita degli Studi di Pisa.

— (n.d.) Boscolo, A., M. Pintor, and G. Loi Puddu, Eds. In *Dizionario della Sardegna*. Regione Autonoma, Cagliari.

Boscolo, A. (1976) Gli scavi di Piscina Nuxedda in Sardegna. *Atti del Colloquio Internazionale di Archeologia Medievale, Palermo-Erice, 20–22 Settembre 1974*, Vol. 1. Istituto di Storia Medievale, Palermo, pp. 251–254.

Boscolo, A. (1982) Stato Attuale della Ricerca Sulla Sardegna Bizantina e Giudicale. *Archivio Storico Sardo* 33:141–160.

Caprara, R. (1980) Documenti Archeologici Medievali. In *Dorgali: Documenti Archeologici*. Chiarella, Sassari, pp. 247–268.

Da Passano, M. (1982) L'agricoltura Sarda nella Legislazione Sabauda. In *Le Opere e i Giorni: Contadini e Pastori nella Sardegna Tradizionale*, F. Manconi and G. Angioni, Eds. Silvana, Milan, pp. 76–81.

Day, J. (1973) *Villaggi Abbandonati in Sardegna dal Trecento al Settecento: Inventario*. CNR, Paris.

Delogu, R. (1953) *L'Architettura del Medioevo in Sardegna*. Libreria dello Stato, Rome.

Dettori, I. (1955–1956) *Bauladu Villa Monastica*. Tesi di Laurea, Universita degli Studi di Cagliari.

Dopsch, A. (1923/24) *Wirtschaftliche und Soziale Grundlagen der Europäischen Kulturentwicklung aus der Zeit von Caesar bis auf Karl den Grossen*, 2nd ed. L.W. Seidel & Sohn, Vienna.

— (1937) *The Economic and Social Foundations of Europaean Civilization*. K. Paul, Trench, Trubner & Co., London.

Fara, G. F. (1835/1838) *De Chorographia Sardiniae Libri Duo, De Rebus Sardois Libri Quatuor*, A. Cibrario, Ed. Turin /V. Angius, Ed. Cagliari.

Fois, B., G. Pecorini, E. Atzeni, V. Santoni, F. Barreca, G. Tore, M. A. Mongiu, E. Usai, R. Zucca, L. Pani Ermini, I. Lai, S. Petrucci, P. F. Simbula, P. Fabbricatore, G. Cossu Pinna, A. M. Oliva, M. Marceddu, G. Spiga, E. Gessa, M. Vincis, M. Valdes, G. Todde, F. Segni Pulvirenti, A. Ingegno, and G.

Tola (1986) *S. Igia Capitale Giudicale. Contributi all'Incontro di Studio "Storia, Ambiente Fisico e Insediamenti Umani nel Territorio di S. Gilla (Cagliari)" 3–5 Novembre 1983*. ETS, Pisa.

Gallin, L. (1989a) New Metallurgical Finds in Bronze Age Sardinia. Paper presented at *First Joint Archaeological Congress*, Jan. 1989, Baltimore, MD.

— (1989b) Excavations at Nuraghe Santa Barbara: Village Life in Prehistoric Sardinia. Paper presented at *Archaeological Institute of America, Ninety-first General Meeting*, Baltimore, MD.

Gallin, L. and S. Sebis (1989) BAULADU (Oristano) — Villaggio Nuragico di S. Barbara. *Nuovo Bollettino Archeologico Sardo* 2:271–275.

Gemelli, F. (1776) *Rifiorimento della Sardegna Proposto nel Miglioramento di sua Agricoltura*. G. Briolo, Turin.

Giuntella, A. M. and L. Pani Ermini (1981) Cornus. Indagini nell' Area Paleocristiana. Relazione Preliminare della Campagna 1978. *Notizie degli Scavi* 106:541–591.

Giuntella, A. M., G. Borghetti, and D. Stiaffini (1985) *Mensae e Riti Funerari in Sardegna*. Scorpione, Taranto.

Greene, K. (1986) *The Archaeology of the Roman Economy*. University of California, Berkeley and Los Angeles.

Lamb, H. H. (1977) *Climate, Present, Past and Future*, Vol. 2, Climatic History and the Future. Methuen, London.

Lamb, H. H. (1981) An Approach to the Study of the Development of Climate and its Impact in Human Affairs. In *Climate and History*, T. M. L. Wigley et al. Eds. Cambridge University Press, Cambridge, pp. 291–309.

Le Lannou, M. (1979) *Pastori e Contadini di Sardegna*, Italian translation from the French by M. Brigaglia. Della Torre, Cagliari.

Ledda, R. (1989) *Censimento Archeologico nel Territorio del Comune di Villaputzu*. Edizioni Castello, Cagliari.

Lilliu, G. (1961) *I Nuraghi: Torri Preistoriche della Sardegna*. La Zattera, Cagliari.

— (1964/65) Sviluppo e Prospettive dell'Archeologia in Sardegna. Studi Sardi 19:3–35.

— (1981) Per una Ricerca Interdisciplinare di Archeologia e di Storia. *Quaderni Sardi di Storia* 2:181–186.

— (1984) *La Civilta Nuragica*. Carlo Delfino, Sassari.

— (1988) *La Civilta dei Sardi dal Paleolitico all'eta dei Nuraghi*, 3rd ed. Nuova ERI, Turin.

Lilliu, O., A. Saiu Deidda, M. Bonello Lai, E. Usai, and M. F. Porcella (1988) *Domus et Carcer Sanctae Restitutae: Storia di un Santuario Supestre a Cagliari*. Pisano, Cagliari.

Manconi, F. (1982) La Fame, la Poverta e la Morte. In *Le Opere e i Giorni: Contadini e Pastori nella Sardegna Tradizionale*, F. Manconi and G. Angioni, Eds. Silvana, Milan, pp. 50–68.

Manunza, M. R. (1984) La Collina di Marras — Dorgali (Nuoro). In *The Deya Conference of Prehistory: Early Settlement in the Western Mediterranean Islands and their Peripheral Areas*, W. H. Waldren et al. Eds. B.A.R. Int. Series 229(ii), Oxford, pp. 553–565.

Marmora, A. D. (1874) *Itinerario dell'isola di Sardegna*, Italian translation from the French. Cagliari.

Mastino, A. (1979) *Cornus nella Storia degli Studi*. Ettore Gasperini, Cagliari.

Meiggs, R. (1960) *Roman Ostia*. University Press, Oxford.

Meloni, B. (1989) Mutamento Sociale e Alcune Cause di Conflitto nella Sardegna Centrale. *Quaderni Bolotanesi* 15:121–128.

Mori, A. (1972) *Memoria Illustrativa della Carta della Utilizzazione del Suolo della Sardegna*. CNR, Rome.

Mureddu, D., D. Salvi, and G. Stefani, (1988) *Sancti Innumerabiles. Scavi nella Cagliari del Seicento: Testimonianze e Verifiche*. S'Alvure, Cagliari.

Paderi, M. C. (1982). L'Insediamento di Fundabi de Andria Peis-Padru Jossu e la Necropoli di Giliadiri. Reperti Punici e Romani and Bidd'e Cresia. Sepolture e Corredi di eta Romana. In *Ricerche Archeologiche nel Territorio di Sanluri*, Amministrazione Provinciale, Cagliari, pp. 63–68.

Pais, E. (1923) *Storia della Sardegna e della Corsica durante il Dominio Romano*. Rome.

Pani Ermini, L. (1981) *Museo Archeologico Nazionale di Cagliari. Catalogo dei Materiali Paleocristiani e Altomedievali* (with M. Marinone). Libreria dello Stato, Rome.

— (1982/83) Ricerche nel Complesso di S. Saturno a Cagliari. *Rendiconti della Pontificia Accademia Romana di Archeologia* 55:101–118.

— (1989) Gli Scavi a N. S. di Castro. In *VI Convegno su l'Archeologia Tardo Romana e Medievale in Sardegna 23–25 Giugno 1989*.

Pani Ermini, L. et al. (1986) Cultura, Materiali e fasi Storiche del Complesso Archeologico di Cornus: Primi Risultati di una Ricerca. In *L'archeologia Romana e Altomedievale nell'Oristanese*. Scorpione, Taranto.

Pardi, G. (1926) *La Sardegna e la sua Popolazione Attraverso i Secoli*. Societa Editoriale Italiana, Cagliari.

Paulis, G. (1983) *Lingua e Cultura nella Sardegna Bizantina: Testimonianze Linguistiche dell'Influsso Greco*. L'Asfodelo, Sassari.

Pesce, G. (1966) *Tharros*. Fossataro, Cagliari.

— (1972) *Nora: Guida Agli Scavi*, 2nd ed. Fossataro, Cagliari.

Pietracaprina, A. (1971) Limitazione d'Uso dei Suoli, p. 13 and tavola 6. R. Pracchi and A. Terrosu Asole, *Atlante della Sardegna*, fasc. 1. Edizioni Kappa, Rome.

Pira, M., Ed. (1975) *Il Meglio della Grande Poesia in Lingua Sarda*. Della Torre, Cagliari.

Piras, P. G. (1966) *Aspetti della Sardegna bizantina*. T.E.F., Cagliari.

Plaisant, M. L. (1970) *Martin Carillo e le sue Relazioni sulla Sardegna*. Cagliari.

Pracchi, R. (1980) Variazioni della Popolazione tra il 1861 e il 1971, p. 163. R. Pracchi and A. Terrosu Asole, Eds. *Atlante della Sardegna*, fasc. 2. Edizioni Kappa, Rome.

Rickman, G. (1980) *The Corn Supply of Ancient Rome*. University Press, Oxford.

— (personal communication) Department of Classical Studies, University of St. Andrews, Scotland.

Rowland, R. J., Jr. (1978a) The Christianization of Sardinia. *Bulletin of the Institute of Mediterranean Archaeology* 2:31–36.

— (1978b) Numismatics and the Military History of Sardinia. In *Akten des XI. Internationalen Limes-Kongresses*, Akadémiai Kiado, Budapest, pp. 87–112.

— (1981) *I Ritrovamenti Romani in Sardegna*. L'Erma di Bretschneider, Rome.

— (1982) Beyond the frontier in Punic Sardinia. *American Journal of Ancient History* 7:20–39.

— (1984a) The Case of the Missing Sardinian Grain. *The Ancient World* 10:45–48.

— (1984b) La Cristianizzazione della Sardegna fino al 600 circa dopo Cristo. *Quaderni Bolotanesi* 10:117–128.

— (1984c) The Countryside of Roman Sardinia. In Studies in Sardinian Archaeology, M. S. Balmuth and R. J. Rowland, Jr., Eds. University of Michigan, Ann Arbor, MI, pp. 284–300.

— (1985a), The Roman Invasion of Sardinia. In *Papers in Italian Archaeology IV, The Cambridge Conference*, Vol. 4, C. Malone and S. Stoddard, Eds. B.A.R. Int. Series 246, Oxford, pp. 99–117.

— (1985b) Archeologia Giovenale. *Old World Archaeology Newsletter* 9(2):17–20.

— (1987) Faunal Remains of Prehistoric Sardinia: The Current State of the Evidence. In *Studies in Nuragic Archaeology*, J. W. Michels and G. S. Webster, Eds. B.A.R. Int. Series 373, Oxford, pp. 147–161.

— (in press a) Contadini-Guerrieri: An Alternative Hypothesis on the Evolution of Nuragic Society. In *Acts of the Symposium on Nuragic Archaeology, 7–9 December 1989*. Swedish Institute in Rome.

— (1990) The Production of Grain in Sardinia during the Empire. *Mediterranean Historical Review* 5:14–20.

Rowland, R. J., Jr. and S. L. Dyson (1988) Survey Archaeology in the Territory of Bauladu: Preliminary Notice. *Quaderni della Soprintendenza Archeologica per le Provincie di Cagliari e Oristano* 5:129–139.

— (1989) Survey Archeology in the Territories of Paulilatino and Fordongianus: Preliminary Notice. *Quaderni della Soprintendenza Archeologica per le Provincie di Cagliari e Oristano* 6:157–185.

— (1991) Survey Archaeology in Sardinia. In *La Struttura Agricola Romana nel Mediterraneo: il Contributo della Ricognizione Archeologica*, G. Barker, Ed. British School, Rome, pp. 54–61.

Serra, R. (1971a) La Chiesa Quadrifida di S. Elia a Nuxis. *Studi Sardi* 21:30–64.

— (1971b) L'Oratorio delle Anime a Massama. *Annali delle Facolta di Lettere Filosofia e Magistero di Cagliari* 34:33–56.

Snodgrass, A. (1987) *An Archaeology of Greece: The Present State and Future Scope of a Discipline*. University of California, Berkeley and Los Angeles.

Sotgiu, G. (1986) *Storia della Sardegna dopo l'Unita*. Edizioni Laterza, Bari.

Tangheroni, M. (1976) Archeologia e Storia in Sardegna: Topografia e Tipologia. Alcune Riflessioni. In *Atti del Colloquio Internazionale di Archeologia Medievale, Palermo-Erice, 20–22 Settembre 1974*, Vol. 1. Istituto di Storia Medievale, Palermo, pp. 243–250.

— (1981) *Aspetti del Commercio dei Cereali nei Paesi della Corona d'Aragona*, Vol. 1. La Sardegna. CNR, Cagliari.

— (1985) Prospettive dell'Archeologia Medievale in Sardegna. *Sardigna Antiga* 3:12–13.

Terrosu Asole, A. (1965) Note sulla Dimora Rurale in Sardegna. In *Fra il Passato e l'Avvenire. Saggi Storici sull'Agricoltura Sarda in Onore di Antonio Segni*. CEDAM, Padova, pp. 197–228.

— (1974) *L'Insediamento Umano Medioevale e i Centri Abbandonati tra il Secolo XIV ed il Secolo XVII.* Edizioni Kappa, Rome.

— (1975) *Le Sedi Umane Medioevali nella Curatoria di Gippi.* Leo S. Olschki, Firenze.

Tola, P. (1861) *Codex Diplomaticus Sardiniae,* Vol. 1. Turin.

Tronchetti, C. (1984a) *Nora.* Carlo Delfino, Sassari.

— (1984b) Scavi a Nora. *Fasti Archeologici* 32–33:764, nr. 10894.

Tronchetti, C. and A. Fanni (1982), Santa Maria: Situazione e Problemi; lo Scavo. *Villasimius. Prime Testimonianze Archeologiche nel Territorio,* Amministrazione Provinciale, Cagliari.

Wagner, M. L. (1983) *La Vita Rustica della Sardegna Rispecchiata nella sua Lingua,* Italian translation from the German by V. Martelli. COSMA, Quartu S. Elena.

Zucca, R. (1984) *Tharros.* Corrias, Oristano.

13: Reinterpreting the Construction History of the Service Area of the Hermitage Mansion

Larry McKee, Staff Archaeologist
Victor P. Hood, Deputy Director for Buildings and Grounds
Sharon Macpherson, Deputy Director for Programs
The Hermitage: Home of Andrew Jackson, Hermitage, Tennessee

Those dealing with the past have to one degree or another always surrounded the written record with a "cult of authority." Consequently, historical archaeologists have had to contend with the notion that any particular segment of history can only be dependably known if some applicable documentary evidence survives. Even rich and pristine archaeological sites are considered disappointingly incomplete without some connected assemblage of letters, deeds, diaries, maps, tax records, and account books. But the mere presence of an abundant collection of documents does not in and of itself guarantee secure knowledge. Like the archaeological record, documents require a careful and thorough analysis in order to make the best use of them in reconstructing the past.

The Hermitage, the plantation home of Andrew Jackson located near Nashville, Tennessee is graced with an extensive set of documents pertaining to its history. Those with an interest in studying and preserving this site have until recently taken it for granted that the available sources provide enough data to reconstruct the details of the Jackson family's life on the property. This is especially the case with the sources concerning the interesting architectural evolution of the Hermitage mansion.

Historians have read and interpreted the documentary sources on the Hermitage mansion in the most simple and straightforward way possible. Authors of the standard texts on the house have depended on the authority of the written record, even in its sometimes incomplete, indirect, and contradictory forms, to present a clear, unambiguous picture of the changes to the mansion's floorplan and facade. In this paper, we present a new look at these changes, using new sources, a new emphasis on "reading" the building itself, and a new perspective on the usually cited documents. Our work shows that the building is not as simple or well understood as was previously thought, and that previous histories of the house missed an entire building phase involving the seemingly unnecessary destruction of one kitchen and building of an entirely new one.

This paper untangles and reviews the evidence, both physical and documentary, for this forgotten episode in the mansion's evolution, and examines both why it was done, and why it was obscured in the record and missed by those studying Jackson and his home. Part of the reason this episode was missed involves the desire to believe that the written record provides a seamless picture of the past. An additional reason for the change, and for forgetting it, involves the desire to gloss over the details and realities of tensions within plantation communities.

The reinterpretation of the Hermitage mansion's history presented in this paper was stimulated by a fairly routine preservation-maintenance project at the site. During the winter of 1988 and 1989, the structure underwent a major renovation of its environmental control and fire suppression systems. In the course of the renovation activity, the site's research, archaeological, and preservation staff monitored the work in an attempt to minimize its impact on the historic integrity of the structure and related archaeological deposits. The project also provided the staff with an opportunity to examine some usually inaccessible areas of the mansion, allowing study of portions of it in a detailed fashion for the first time ever. A descriptive report (McKee 1990), on file at The Hermitage, provides a complete account of the project.

161

At the beginning of the project there were no strong expectations that the research would result in any major new findings about the mansion's history. The voluminous secondary literature on Andrew Jackson consistently provides a clear-cut presentation on the Hermitage mansion, chronicling its original construction from 1819 to 1821, its renovation and expansion in 1831, and its reconstruction, completed in 1836, after a disastrous fire in 1834. The only formal architectural analysis of the structure, a manuscript report by Jerry Trescott written in the early 1980s, details the changes that went on in these construction phases. But in the course of the 1988–1989 renovation, converging lines of evidence began to accumulate that pointed to some major undocumented changes in the dining room-pantry-kitchen area of the house. Evidence from both above, in the attic, and below, from a trench dug across the covered passage between the kitchen and the house, began to cast doubt on the currently accepted date of 1831 for the kitchen's construction. The new data suggests that during the postfire reconstruction major restructuring and reorganization occurred in the service areas of the house, involving the demolition of one kitchen and the construction of an entirely new one. These findings have encouraged a full reassessment of both the documentary and standing physical evidence on the use and construction of the mansion.

The mansion service area is made up of the detached kitchen, a separate room commonly known as the storage pantry, and another room known as the service pantry (Figures 1 to 3). All three lie behind the dining room in the west wing of the mansion. The kitchen is fully separate from the house, but is linked to it by means of a covered passageway. The pantry storage room is within the "outline" of the mansion, but both it and the kitchen are 2.2 ft below the house floor level. The storage pantry has only one door, communicating out to the open-ended passage leading to the steps and door into an enclosed entry room. This vestibule has doorways leading into the dining room, the service pantry, and the back parlor.

The service pantry was presumably used both for shelving tableware and for assembling table-ready meals from large portions transported from the kitchen. It has a second door opening directly into the dining room. The storage pantry probably served to store foodstuffs in large quantities and the larger and less frequently used kitchen and table equipment.

The service area's different rooms, doors, steps, and passages present a complicated set of barriers and pathways. From hearth to table, the food, and those moving the food, would have traveled up to 70 ft through four doorways. In addition to these main service rooms, the basement beneath the main house, a large stone-lined root cellar beneath the kitchen floor, and an attic above the pantry storage room served as additional, less-acces-

sible storage spaces. The new evidence gathered during the renovation project suggests that much of this service area, and especially the kitchen itself, was constructed not in 1831, as generally accepted, but after the 1834 fire. The true 1831 kitchen had been attached directly to the back end of the dining wing, and had a short set of steps and a door leading directly to the dining room vestibule. Any attempt to determine the actual sequence and nature of the remodeling of this area must also attempt to determine the reasons such a complicated new plan, with its distances, enclosures, and indirect routes, was used.

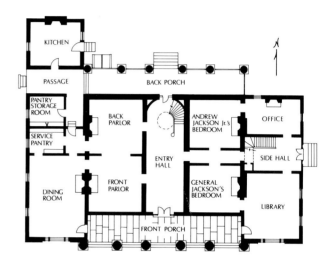

FIG. 1. Hermitage mansion, plan of current ground floor. (Drawing by Sarah Prescott-Sautter and Hannah McKee.)

FIG. 2. Hermitage mansion, elevation of west wing, kitchen, and smoke house. (Drawing by Hannah McKee.)

The Hermitage Mansion's Architectural Evolution

Andrew Jackson and his family moved to the property named The Hermitage in 1804. For the next 17 years the Jacksons lived in a number of log buildings arranged in a cluster near a steadily running spring (Smith 1976:13; Remini 1988:55). In 1819 Jackson commenced the erection of a new home, located approximately 200 yd south of the original "station" of cabins. Completed in 1821, the new house was constructed of brick, with a plain Federal-style facade ornamented only by a fan light above the front door (Figure 4, and see Trescott 1981:14–16). The floor plan of the two-story house followed a

FIG. 3. Ca. 1880 view of the west side of the Hermitage mansion. (Archival Collection, The Hermitage.)

standard central hall double-pile I-house plan (Kniffen 1986:8–10), with two rooms flanking the central hallway on either side both upstairs and down. The house had a combination kitchen and dining room in the basement under its western half, as well as a separate kitchen in the side yard.

The timing of the construction of the 1819 Hermitage mansion has usually been interpreted as a reflection of Andrew Jackson's emerging role as a national leader and celebrity (Remini 1977:379–380). Jackson's victory as the general at the Battle of New Orleans in 1815 and his subsequent service in the Seminole War ensured his position as a man of national prominence and possibly of presidential timber. Although his log home had been two stories tall and was comfortably furnished (Smith 1976:34–43, 135–236), its appearance was clearly not suited to a potential presidential contender. It is impossible to say whose idea and decision it was to build the 1819 house — Jackson's own, or his wife's, or his aggressive group of friends and advisers. The architectural shift may have been encouraged by Jackson's high salary and attendant perquisites during his service as a major general in the army, and by the financial success of the farm during the 1815–1818 boom market in cotton (Horn 1950:18). Rachel and Andrew Jackson were moving into their late middle age at this time, and the new construction may well have been motivated by a desire for more comfortable surroundings during their expected retirement years, as much as by any attempt to display a higher social position. Even with the enormous transition from a relatively informal collection of log cabins to a tall brick building, those who viewed the new house considered it to have been a plain dwelling, with few of the pretensions of most grand plantation mansions (Caldwell 1949:49; Horn 1950:21; Trescott 1981:14–20).

The next major change to the house came in 1831, when flanking wings were added and its facade was given a more ornamented Palladian-style appearance. Figure 4 provides a reasonably accurate artist's reconstruction of the facade of the 1831 house. At the time of the building's construction, Jackson was in the middle of the first of his two terms as president. His wife, Rachel Jackson, had died in December of 1828, and Andrew Jackson, Jr. and his new bride, Sarah Yorke Jackson, were the primary occupants of the house. Jackson only made four short visits home during his 8 years as President, and he left most of the decisions about the 1831 redesign to his son, his local advisers, and the local builders working on the house (Trescott 1981:30–34). It is clear from his limited correspondence that his main concern was with the costs of the construction. Most of his attention focused on the erection of the small temple-like tomb in the garden, the burial spot of Rachel, with an empty vault beside her reserved for himself. Along with the additions and architectural changes, a new kitchen and smokehouse were added at the rear of the house at this time. The literature and guidebooks discussing the site have never questioned the idea that the currently standing smokehouse and kitchen are the ones built in 1831 (Horn 1950:23; Trescott 1981:84; Ladies' Hermitage Association 1987:34–35).

On October 13, 1834, a fire gutted much of the main

163

mansion structure. As part of the 2-year reconstruction, the building underwent extensive changes in appearance (Figure 4) and was transformed into a grand Greek Revival "temple-form" house (Trescott 1981:41–93; Remini 1984:179–191). Again, Jackson, still in Washington, left most of the design decisions to his son and his associates in Tennessee, but it is clear the house's new appearance was intended to reflect the glory of its best known, albeit absent, occupant. Jackson returned to The Hermitage following his retirement from the presidency in 1837, and lived in the house until his death in June of 1845.

The dramatic changes in the architecture of Andrew Jackson's home life, from pioneer cabin to the 1836 plantation big house with its grand porticos, have been interpreted as physical representations of the parallel changes in his political career (Horn 1950:22; Remini 1981:354, 1984:189–191). In keeping with what Henry Glassie has defined as the element of "frontality" in U.S. vernacular architecture (Glassie 1975:166), the building's three different incarnations presented a clearly interpretable face to Hermitage visitors. This paper will not add specifically to this line of historical interpretation, but will look into some of the less apparent, if not less significant, changes in the mansion's architecture.

Evidence of the Undocumented Remodeling

THE PASSAGE TRENCH

The primary source of archaeological data pointing towards undocumented mansion alterations comes from a trench excavated across the passage separating the kitchen from the mansion proper. The trench ranged from 1.8 to 4.2 ft wide and was aligned perpendicular to the 9-ft-wide passage (Figure 5).

The trench, dug in January of 1989 in order to lay a return air duct between the mansion and the kitchen, was a late addition to the 1988–1989 systems-renovation project. Because of time constraints and scheduling problems, the trench excavation was carried out primarily by construction laborers rather than archaeological technicians. The digging was directly monitored by Hermitage staff archaeologists, and much of the deposit was screened through $1/4$ in. mesh. At times the work was halted so staff members could take a closer look at the deposits uncovered in the trench. Ideally the excavation should have been performed by archaeologists working well ahead of the construction crews. Nonetheless, the findings from the trench do allow some detailed analysis of the complicated stratigraphy and related construction sequences revealed in the work.

The basic function of the passage cut by the trench is to provide protected access from the detached kitchen to

the main portion of the mansion, and from the back porch of the mansion out to the yard to the west. Like the kitchen and storage pantry beside it, the passage is raised about 2.5 ft above the surrounding ground surface. Preexcavation expectations were for significant amounts of fill to be present beneath the brick floor of the passage and for this fill to be a rich source of information on the construction history of both the mansion and the kitchen. These expectations were completely fulfilled. The lack of any recent disturbances or intrusions into the material was especially good news, since it allowed a relatively undisturbed view of the building sequence.

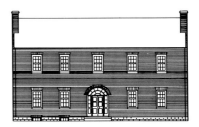

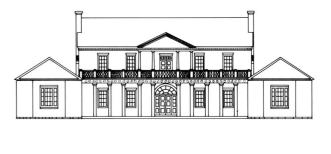

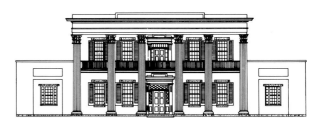

FIG. 4. Hermitage Mansion, showing changes in facade from original construction in 1819 to 1821 through the postfire reconstruction completed in 1836. The top two drawings are artist's renderings developed from contemporary descriptions and illustrations. (Drawings by Sarah Prescott-Sautter.)

The presence of an abandoned stone foundation running across the trench (Figure 5, Feature A in Figures 6 and 7) and some anomalous aspects of the kitchen wall's stone foundation (Feature B in Figure 6) provide the most tangible evidence for some extensive, but forgotten changes in this part of the house. There is a discontinuity in the exposed limestone block foundation along the west edge of the passage area, which seems to be the remnant of the corner end of the abandoned foundation (Figures 2 and 8).

The trench wall profile (Figure 7), showing the relationships of the buried foundation, the prefire ground surface, the subsequent fill layers, and the builder's trenches associated with the kitchen and mansion-side brick walls, allows a close analysis of the construction and fill sequences of this area of the house. Stratum IX, at the base of the trench excavation, is a relatively compact layer of stiff clay flecked with bits of limestone and containing a light scatter of undiagnostic artifacts, including cut nails, plaster, and window glass. This may be the 1831 construction surface or pad, prepared as part of the original construction of the dining wing. This surface is more or less at the same level as the ground surface on the passage's west side. The stratum was only partially excavated, and culturally sterile soil was not reached anywhere in the trench. The top of this stratum is even with the top of the remainder of the stone foundation, Feature A, adjacent to the north.

FIG. 5. Passage trench excavation, showing buried foundation, facing west. (Photograph by Larry McKee.)

Stratum VI is a jumbled deposit of large angular chunks of limestone, with the voids between the rocks filled with loose silt. The large quantity of bone from this stratum was apparently dragged into unfilled pockets by rats (also represented in the faunal assemblage) feeding off kitchen scraps. This rock appears to be trim and rejected pieces discarded during the cutting of foundation stones. Although appearing haphazard, its sharply defined south edge indicates that it was deposited in a purposeful, regular fashion. Stratum VI continues down below the kitchen wall foundation, and appears to form a rubble course base for it. The excavation did not reach the bottom of this deposit.

Stratum VII, the main layer of trench fill, lies south of VI. Stratum VII is made up of loose silt and burned, broken brick. Although the bricks are shattered, scorched,

and have a "shaley" texture, indicating exposure to fire, presumably the 1834 blaze, this is not a classic destruction deposit. It lacks the matrix of ash and charcoal seen in the fire-related stratum under the library in the east wing of the mansion (McKee 1990), and there were virtually no nails or any other artifacts in the layer. This may have been deposited sometime after the initial fire cleanup. The bricks may have come from some of the central mansion walls, which were partially razed after the fire. The lack of limestone chippage and wasted nails indicates that this layer is also not related to reconstruction activity. The layer was apparently put in to raise the passage floor level up approximately 1.9 ft. The burned nature of the material dates this filling to after the 1834 fire, a chronological placement critical in using the stratigraphic sequence to reconstruct service-area building activities.

Stratum V, a patchy, thin layer of almost pure white ash, overlays VII. Probably this originated from periodic cleanouts of the kitchen and mansion fireplaces. Its presence as lenses on top of both Stratum VI and VII suggests that there was an exposed surface at this level for some length of time. It may have been that originally the area had been covered with a plank floor, leaving an open crawl space beneath. A brick shelf projecting from the outside of the kitchen wall, uncovered in the trench excavation, may have played a role in this flooring system. The ashes making up Stratum V may have either filtered down between the planks or, more likely, were dumped beneath the floor through a trap door or loose floor board.

Stratum III is a silty clay fill, very homogenous, with few inclusions or artifacts. This may represent the final leveling of the passage, sealing the "dirty" fill below. It is possibly related to a change from a raised plank flooring across the area to a brick paving. The layer has a complex, difficult-to-interpret relationship with the builder's trenches, related to the brick walls bordering the passageway. Stratum III covers the distinctive builder's trench along its southern, mansion side, but is cut by the builder's trench at the north end of the profile. This would suggest the placement of this final layer of fill postdates the construction of the storage pantry, but predates the construction (or perhaps later alterations) of the kitchen wall. The two builder's trenches are filled with quite distinct material, again strongly suggesting the two associated walls were built at different times. Stratum IV, the profile designation for the deposit along the mansion-side wall, is made up of silt and limestone chippage. Strata I and II, designations for the builder's trench associated with the kitchen wall, is a two-layer deposit with compact ashy silt below and broken (but unburned) bricks in a loose silt matrix above.

The trench features and stratigraphy revealed some complicated fill and construction sequences, completely unexpected from what was casually observable from the

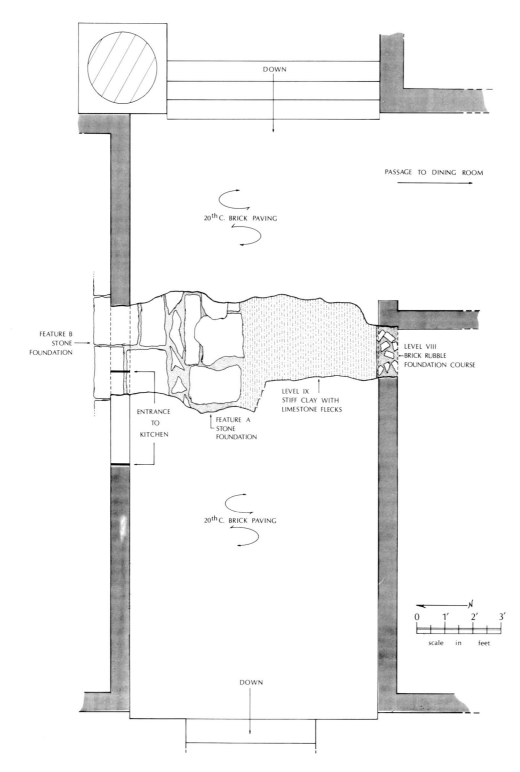

DOWN

PASSAGE TO DINING ROOM

20th C. BRICK PAVING

FEATURE B
STONE
FOUNDATION

LEVEL VIII
BRICK RUBBLE
FOUNDATION COURSE

LEVEL IX
STIFF CLAY WITH
LIMESTONE FLECKS

ENTRANCE
TO
KITCHEN

FEATURE A
STONE
FOUNDATION

20th C. BRICK PAVING

N

0   1'   2'   3'

scale   in   feet

DOWN

FIG. 6. Plan view of passage between the kitchen and mansion, showing the position of the trench. (Drawing by Hannah McKee.)

visible portions of the mansion and what is presented in the standard accounts in the secondary literature. A close look at the foundation beneath the kitchen wall at the north end of the trench provided evidence that began to clarify the situation. The foundation is a little more than 2.5 ft wide, much wider than necessary to support the

wall upon it. Examination of the north, interior side of the wall, visible from the crawl space beneath the kitchen floor, shows that the foundation has discontinuous segments (Figure 9). The segment cut by the trench is smoothly finished, indicating it was once exposed to outside view. The easiest explanation for these observa-

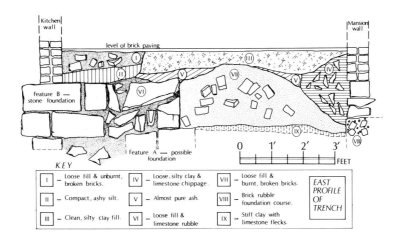

FIG. 7. Profile of east wall of trench excavated across the passage between the kitchen and mansion. (Drawing by Hannah McKee.)

FIG. 8. Shift in the foundation line along the west side of the passage between the kitchen and mansion. (Photograph by Larry McKee.)

FIG. 9. Segmented foundation beneath the south wall of the kitchen, with passage trench excavation at right. (Photograph by Larry McKee.)

tions about this portion of the kitchen foundation — its thickness, its discontinuity with the foundation as a whole, and the precise cut of its facing, now only visible from beneath the kitchen floor — is that it represents the base of a chimney stack projecting out slightly from the rest of the structure it was originally built into. Stratum VI, the rubble lying alongside the foundation in the trench, can thus be interpreted as the fill beneath the hearth floor, and Feature A, the foundation exposed in the floor of the trench, is the "core" foundation into which the hearth and chimney were built.

The archaeological work has revealed that things around the kitchen are clearly not what they should be in terms of the accepted history of the mansion; but no ready explanations or acceptable interpretations could be generated solely from the excavated data. Fortunately, observations made during the course of the systems-renovation project in other parts, and at other levels, of the mansion added data complementing what was discovered in the passage trench.

ATTIC EVIDENCE

The next set of clues on the undocumented changes to the service area came from above, in the attic space over the storage pantry adjacent to the passageway. Entrance to this attic is restricted to a single-hinged window facing the covered passage, accessible only by ladder. The finished floor in the space indicates it was intended for use, probably for storage of seldom-needed items. In this attic, on the upward extension of the brick partition wall between the storage pantry and the service pantry, there is an inverted V-shaped stain or "ghost" (Figure 10). The feature was "discovered" in January of 1989 during a trip into the attic in conjunction with the monitoring of the systems-renovation project. The presence of this remnant of a gable roof abutting the wall is crucial to the argument for forgotten changes to the mansion, as it provides important evidence supporting the interpretation that the current detached kitchen was built after the 1834 fire and the kitchen constructed in 1831 had been appended directly to the rear of the dining room wing.

167

FIG. 10. Gable-end roofline shadow in west wing attic. (Photograph by Larry McKee.)

The presence and visibility of the V-shaped line on the wall is a result of several factors. The first is that the wall above it has been "penciled," a technique whereby the mortar joints between the bricks are highlighted with white paint. There is a tan line staining the wall below this penciling, with "drips" running down from it, probably the result of the mortar being washed before the application of the white paint lines. All the bricks above the line are exterior-grade hard-fired "burgundies," whereas many of the bricks below the line are low-fired "salmons," used by brick masons in wall faces not meant to be exposed to the weather (Noel Hume 1969:174; Smith et al. 1977:75; Gurcke 1987:35–38).

The addition of several roughly finished courses above the penciling shows where the wall was expanded up after the fire to accommodate the change in the wing roof from peaked, gable-ended to shed form. The penciling on the wall above the roof shadow represents the shift in elevation from the peaked roof covering the main, front portion of the dining room down to the roof over the rear portion, presumably the 1831 kitchen. This change is matched by a corresponding drop in the stone foundation line along the west side of the house, at the point where the shadowed wall intersects the outside wall. There is also a "seam," or pattern break in the bond, at the top of the exterior wall at this point (Figures 2, 11, and 12). This is a result of the adding of approximately 10 courses of bricks needed to bring the wall up high enough to support the edge of the new shed roof. The window in this rear section of wall was also adjusted upward, in order to put it at the same level as the other windows along this side of the house. The added brick work below the window also has discontinuities in the bonding pattern. The upward relocation in the window took place despite the unchanged presence of the original structure's ceiling plate and joists, visible running across the window's top row of lights.

The combined evidence from the excavation of the passage trench and the examination of the dining wing

FIG. 11. Exterior west wall of storage pantry, showing the seam in the brick work at the top of the wall to right, the foundation shift at the bottom of the wall to right, the seams in the brick work below the window, and the ceiling plate visible running across the top row of window panes. (Photograph by Larry McKee.)

FIG. 12. Rear portion of west wing of the Hermitage mansion. (Photograph by Larry McKee.)

attic allows the construction of some specific conclusions about the building sequence in this area. There was a room, presumably the 1831 kitchen, attached to the back end of the dining wing, which was apparently demolished as part of the postfire changes to the mansion. It had a gable-ended roof, although its roof peak and floor level was approximately 2 ft lower than that of the front portion of the wing. At its north end, it had a hearth and chimney, which projected out from the rest of the wall. After its removal, the current kitchen was constructed, and the space between the new kitchen and the dining room wing was reconfigured as an open L-shaped passageway and a storage room. The current kitchen's 21 × 19 ft size closely matches the size of the demolished and forgotten kitchen, and the relative positioning of the chimney base is, and was, the same in both. Thus it would seem that the reasons for the replacement of one kitchen with another cannot be explained by a desire for a new design, but rather with a desire for a new, completely separate placement for the facility.

The idea that the current kitchen is not the one built in 1831 runs counter to the established and accepted interpretation of the mansion's construction history. Why is there no clear evidence in the primary sources for such a seemingly major change? Why has the secondary literature on The Hermitage been so insistent on fitting the documents and the house into simple, unambiguous interpretations? Why were such changes, minor in some ways but major in others, made to the house?

REEXAMINING THE DOCUMENTS

The next step in solving the architectural puzzle of the service area involved a reconsideration of the documentary sources on the mansion construction. Histories of Jackson and his home, based on these sources, make no mention of alterations in the mansion service area after the major renovations of the 1831 period. But a close reevaluation of the letters, contracts, and plans involved reveals some definite clues and hints about the details of, as well as the motivations for, the modifications.

Documentary-based analysis of the evolution of the mansion has always used its 20th-century state as the starting point. Narrative histories of the building have sometimes forced and misused unclear and fragmentary texts in order to present a clear-cut, unambiguous construction chronology. Up to now, all such works have been based on the idea that, beyond a change in roof form, little alteration of the service area took place during the 1834 to 1836 rebuilding. Nothing in the secondary literature has ever questioned the idea that the present-day kitchen is the one built in 1831. The current layout of the facilities at the back end of the dining wing has always been used as a guide and anchoring point for piecing together the problematical documentation on both the 1831 and 1836 construction.

Andrew Jackson had little of the keen personal interest in architecture so common among other members of the early American elite. Jackson left few personal writings beyond his correspondence, and his letters from the White House mentioning the 1831 and 1836 changes to the Hermitage mansion mostly concentrate on financial concerns. During the rebuilding after the fire, Jackson specifically abdicated his role in the redesign of the house to his son and daughter-in-law: "...you may exercise your own discretion provided it does not add too much to the expense of the repairs" (Jackson 1834a; all quotes appear as in original). "...make such changes as you may believe will be best for you and Sarah and family hereafter — All I want is a good room to which I can retire if I am spared to live out my irksome term here, and I am sure I shall not want that room long..." (Jackson 1834b).

The primary sources give an incomplete and inconclusive account of the changes to the Hermitage mansion after the fire. Most of the decisions about its redesign were obviously made "on the ground" by Jackson's local advisers, his son, and the builders doing the work. One letter, reporting proposed changes to Jackson, exists only in a fragmentary form, with the extant portion ending precisely at the start of the discussion of design details (Armstrong 1834c). Andrew Jackson, Jr.'s letters have been lost, evidently destroyed by the same hand that wrote them, and his father's half of the interchange is mostly short comments on the proposed specifics.

There are only four specific references to the kitchen area of the Hermitage mansion in documents from the 1830s. The first comes in 1831, in connection with the major additions and changes to the mansion concluded in that year. In December 1831, the builder in charge, David Morison, wrote a long letter to Jackson detailing all the work that had been performed. He makes a quick reference to the destruction of the old kitchen and the construction of a new one. "The old kitchen is removed and the materials employed in the erection of a large and comodeus smoke house which is placed on a line with the new kitchen" (Morison 1831). Archaeological testing done during the laying of a new water line on the west side of the mansion in 1981 uncovered the probable site of this "old kitchen" (Hinshaw 1981). Presumably built along with the house in 1819 to 1821, it was situated to the west and slightly behind it.

The next references to the kitchen area come during the period after the 1834 fire, and are found within the flurry of correspondence going back and forth between Jackson in Washington and his family and agents at The Hermitage. Along with the general reconstruction following the fire, there was apparently some desire either to build a new kitchen, or drastically alter the existing one in some way. In one letter, Jackson apparently replies to the specifics of his son's plans: "As it regards the improvement of the kitchen I leave it entirely to your direction, observing as much oeconomy as you can so as to have it convenient and well done" (Jackson 1835). Almost a year later, a friend of Jackson's, overseeing the repairs, wrote him to explain some additional expenses: "...I was forced...to employ a Bricklayer to finish the kitchen and Wall which I have paid and indorsed" (Armstrong 1836). In the final accounting of the costs for rebuilding the mansion, dated August 2, 1836, there is an entry for $186.00 for "...work done on west wing and New Kitchen..." (Reiff and Hume 1836).

Formal and informal efforts to interpret these limited references have, again, used as a starting point the current configuration of the kitchen-mansion area. In their present state, the kitchen and smokehouse are more or less in line, which would seem to be in keeping with the 1831 reference to their mutual construction. The kitchen's south wall, nearest the mansion, extends up to serve as the terminus point of the shed roof running the length of the dining room wing and extending over the open passage between the wing and the kitchen. The wing's roof changed from a gable-ended peaked style to its present shed form after the fire. Thus, if the current kitchen is the one built in 1831 its south wall, now supporting this roof, would have had to have been changed as well in the 1835–1836 rebuilding.

Jerry Trescott's manuscript report on the evolution of the mansion interprets the above April 1836 "kitchen and wall" reference as documentation for this new construction, saying "...brick masons...[were] still at work completing the new kitchen wall connecting it to the shed roof of the dining room wing in order to create a covered passageway..." (Trescott 1981:63). Although the interpretation seems to read a bit too much into the skimpy and not entirely clear text, it does fit the current connection between mansion and kitchen.

The improvements to the kitchen, of which Jackson approves in his letter to Andrew Jackson, Jr., are more difficult to fit into the visible evidence. If the present kitchen is the one built in 1831, which is the standard, accepted interpretation, and the only postfire alteration to it was a parapet extension of one of its end walls, then what became of the changes recommended by Andrew Jackson, Jr.? With the younger Jackson's correspondence unavailable, the specifics of these recommendations are lost. Trescott concludes that Andrew Jackson, Jr. had second thoughts. "Junior, obviously feeling more economic pressure from his father than confidence in his ability to adequately solve this question, opted to retain the 1831 kitchen" (Trescott 1981:85).

This would seem to be an overinterpretation of the documentation. No analyst looking into the evolution of the mansion has chosen to comment on the entry in the final August 1836 accounting of the expenses for the "New Kitchen." One important piece of documentary evidence, largely ignored by students of Jackson and his home, is a sheet showing a floor plan, side elevation, and cross-section of the mansion (Figures 13 and 14). The drawing, titled "Designs For The Hermitage, The Mansion of Genl Jackson President of the U States" has some inconsistencies with the current mansion layout, which make it an intriguing, but difficult, source (compare Figures 1 and 14). The drawing would seem to be more along the lines of a prospectus, rather than a set of true builder's blueprints, as it has no scale, and no measurement notation.

Marsha Mullin, curator of collections at The Hermitage, has pointed out that it may also be the only surviving sheet of an original set of two or more. Other pieces may have shown front and rear elevations, and the second-story floor plan. The work is well executed, and was done by someone with formal training. In several spots, slight alterations have been made in both pencil and ink to the drawing, seemingly done in the same hand responsible for the initial version (Figure 14). This suggests the plan was used as a working drawing, with changes made to it as new decisions were made. A number of these changes, especially the transformation of several windows into doors, do reflect details of the current mansion. The Ladies' Hermitage Association, which has administered the state-owned site since 1889, has had the document in its collection for a lengthy, but unfortunately undocumented, period of time. There are no specific references to such a plan in the limited documentation on the postfire rebuilding of the mansion. A watermark on the plan's paper may provide at least some rough dating for the document, and research on this clue is currently underway.

Both major and minor discrepancies between the drawing and the present mansion floorplan make it a tantalizing source of clues on the undocumented changes around the kitchen area. There is no question that the plan was drawn in connection with the postfire rebuilding. The accompanying elevation shows the new columns of the front portico and the changes in the wing roofs from pitched to shed forms. Jerry Trescott concluded that it represents a working drawing made during the early stages of planning for the reconstruction, prior to the writing of the January 1835 contract for the work, and that many of its details were altered or not executed as construction took place. Trescott attributes the drawing to Joseph Reiff and William C. Hume (Trescott 1981:81). These two builders, working on the mansion at nearby Tulip Grove plantation at the time, took on the rebuilding of the fire-damaged Hermitage mansion.

Another possible explanation for the plan's origin is that it was drawn as a study by someone with no connection to the project, perhaps for publication in the popular press, with the discrepancies due to a limited viewing of the house by the artist. There would seem to be too much accuracy in the drawing for acceptance of this interpretation. The most glaring errors, or more accurately, discrepancies, in the plan involve the lack of a rear portico, the presence of a conventional "angled" main staircase,

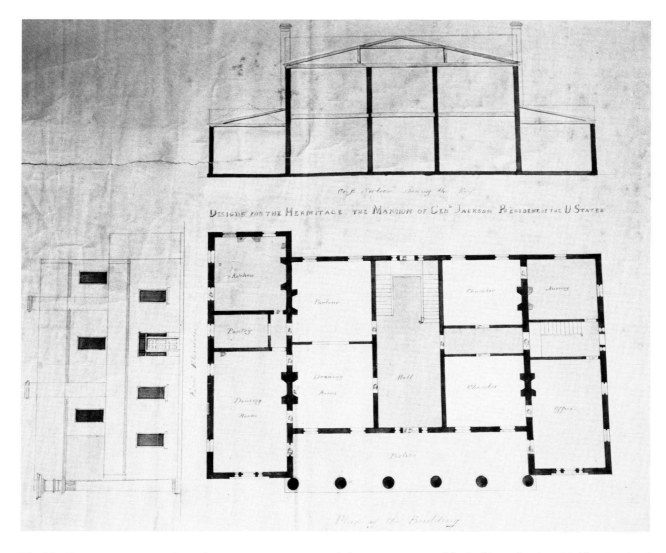

FIG. 13. Hermitage mansion plans, drawn up in conjunction with the reconstruction of the building after the 1834 fire. (Archival Collection, The Hermitage.)

rather than the actual elliptical form, the presence of a room, labeled "Kitchen," appended directly on to the rear of the dining room wing, and the absence of the current detached kitchen. The other rooms are all labeled accurately, in so far as the specific use of each has been documented, except for the back room of the east wing. On the plan this is denoted as "Nursery," while in the letters making reference to the rebuilding plans, this is always referred to as the office or steward's room. This room had been used as the farm office since its construction, presumably in 1831. Until the postfire reconstruction, its only door was to an open entry vestibule between it and the library situated at the front end of the wing. The confusion over the room nomenclature between this plan and the eventual actual room function may reflect the differences between the way Andrew Jackson, Jr., in residence at The Hermitage with his young family, saw its new form, and the way his father, then in Washington, ultimately defined it.

Other problems with the plan are more subtle. Some are likely to be simple problems of measurement and scale, but still reveal some piquantly interesting details. Although the plan shows the mansion facade's length very accurately, it shows the building to be a little more than 3 ft deeper than it actually is. The error seems to have come in the measurements for the back rooms of the building, which are all shown to be about 3 ft deeper on the plan than in actuality. Importantly, the service pantry behind the dining room is shown on the plan in its precise location and size. This suggests the draftsman actually measured the room by hand, and that it was kept unaltered in its prefire incarnation, except for the addition of a doorway communicating directly with the dining room. The presence of the "kitchen" on the drawing immediately adjacent to this accurately represented pantry thus has an even greater need for explanation.

Perhaps the most curious aspect of the plan is the fact that it does not show the detached kitchen now standing behind the mansion. This would seem more than just an oversight, or its dismissal as a separate entity not shown because it had no bearing on the mansion revisions. The end wall of the plan's kitchen, if built as shown, would have overlapped the present kitchen's southern end by several feet. Correcting the plan's apparent scaling error, which shows the mansion as several feet too wide, puts the kitchen end wall precisely on the position of the buried foundation uncovered in the passage trench. Although an elegant link between documentary and archaeological evidence, this makes the absence of the now-standing kitchen from the plan even more difficult to explain. Separated only by inches, and sharing duty in the functioning of the busy Jackson household, it would be unlikely that the two would have had separate end walls and no communicating doorway, if both stood at the same time.

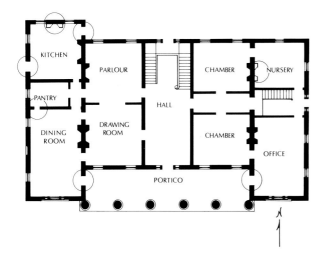

FIG. 14. Proposed postfire reconstruction of the first floor of the Hermitage mansion, taken from Figure 13. Circles indicate additions and alterations made to the plan. (Drawing by Hannah McKee.)

In attempting to reconcile the evidence with the puzzle of the two kitchens, two alternatives emerge. The first is that the now-standing kitchen truly is the kitchen built in 1831, and its absence from the drawing reflects a later-rejected plan to demolish it after the fire and to replace it with an attached kitchen. Jerry Trescott chose to interpret the documentary and physical evidence in this way (Trescott 1981:84–85). But the newer evidence, from the attic and the passage trench, proves that the attached kitchen shown on the plan did actually stand at one time. The second alternative is that the kitchen that now stands behind the mansion was built during the postfire reconstruction. This undocumented construction phase would have also involved the demolition of the attached kitchen shown on the plan drawing, the extension of the shed roof back from the dining room all the way to the new kitchen, and the enclosure of the pantry storage room. The physical evidence from below and above in the mansion both explains and corroborates the existence of the drawing's attached kitchen.

Interpretation

WHY A NEW KITCHEN?

This paper demonstrates that the present kitchen associated with the Hermitage mansion was built in 1836, not 1831, as generally accepted. The actual 1831 kitchen had been appended directly onto the back end of the dining wing, as shown on the circa 1834 reconstruction plan of the mansion. It was apparently demolished during the reconstruction after the fire, and the space it had occupied was redesigned as an open passageway and storage room. At this point, these new findings have generated some specific questions. Why was the old kitchen removed, and an entirely new one added? Why is there such limited record of this extensive, and expensive, work?

Damage from the 1834 fire cannot be posited as the reason for the demolition of one kitchen and rebuilding of another. Extensive accounts of the fire and its effects on the mansion exist in letters written to Jackson, then in residence at the White House. Most of the damage was to the upstairs and the eastern side of the house, opposite from the dining room wing and service area. The roof of the west wing was damaged, but the scorched rafters of the old roof were still in good enough shape to use as "nailers" between the rafters in the new shed roof, where they can still be seen. There is no destruction deposit of charcoal, nails, and burned plaster beneath the dining room, as there is in the crawl space below the library in the east wing of the house, strong evidence backing up the accepted story that the dining room wing was largely spared in the blaze.

In one of the initial letters about the damage to the house, a friend of Jackson's specifically mentions that the kitchen was "safe" (Armstrong 1834b). Even if the kitchen, directly behind the dining room, was damaged, it would have been more practical and financially reasonable to refurbish it than to construct an entirely new building. The shift cannot be explained simply by the need to repair the fire's effects. The reasons that an entirely new kitchen was built probably have to do with Andrew Jackson, Jr.'s particular vision of the new mansion, which was apparently quite different from that of his absent father.

The final form of the 1836 reconstruction, the letters back and forth discussing the progress of the work, and even the plan drawing of the mansion all reveal the tensions between father and son. Although Jackson had written to his son and daughter-in-law that the decisions about the design and layout of the reconstructed mansion were in their hands, the tone of his letters, and his constant mention of the need for "oeconomy" served as a direct reminder that he expected their independent decisions to comply with his own desires and vision of the reconstruction.

Proposed changes to the mansion following the fire can be interpreted as a reflection of Andrew Jackson, Jr.'s own vision of it as a domain of private family life, with a sharp separation of living space from the hubbub of constant visitors, the farm operation, and the slave community. His failures as a planter are well documented (Galloway 1950; Remini 1984:237), and can no doubt be linked in part to a deep lack of interest in the task. His father, in residence at the White House, wrote frequent letters to him full of advice and detailed questions about its operation. The senior Jackson complained loudly and frequently about not receiving responses to his queries about production figures, prices, and scheduling. The plan drawing for the house reconstruction labels what had been the plantation office as a "nursery" and calls for a new door between this room and the adjacent bedroom. This change can be read as the wish on the part of Andrew Jackson, Jr. to separate the center of farm activities from such a close proximity to his personal life and an apparent desire to have the children's quarters more at hand. Trescott's analysis of the 1836 changes notes how, with new doorways and an added back staircase, the east half of the house made the family quarters more private and further "compartmentalized" the mansion (Trescott 1981:78).

In correspondence about the changes to the house, there is continued mention of the use of this room as a steward's, or overseer's, office. Other than the 1830s plan drawing, there is no specific evidence of this room ever being used as a nursery, although in its 20th-century museum interpretation it has been furnished as the children's room. The close proximity and communicating door between this room and the bedroom of Andrew Jr. and his wife would seem to run counter to a common perception of "big house" layouts in which children, and their slave attendants, were kept quite separate from their parent's chambers. Conversely, if this corner room was used as a farm office, its connection to the bedroom mirrors the situation across the hall, where the elder Jackson's bedroom has a door directly into his library. Again, the ambiguity and indecision about the room's actual function reflect the unsettled and tense relationship between father and son.

Jackson's historians have provided ample documentation of the growing precariousness of the family's financial situation during the 1830s (Remini 1984:188). It would seem the costs involved should have been enough to override any desire or reasons to build an entirely new kitchen. In an account of the fire damage written to Jackson in October of 1834, the estimate of the cost of rebuilding is put at about $2500 (Armstrong 1834a).

The contract for the work, written by Joseph Reiff and William Hume in January of 1835, included an estimate of $3950 (Reiff and Hume 1835). By the time the work had been completed more than a year and a half later, the final figure had reached $5125 (Reiff and Hume 1836). This upward spiral came despite the fact that Jackson, writing from Washington, had repeatedly called for monetary prudence in the course of rebuilding.

The motivations for erecting the new kitchen must have been stronger than the impetus for financial caution. There is no single explanation for the erection of the 1836 kitchen. Even though it was at a slightly separate elevation from the rest of the house, the attached 1831 kitchen may have brought the noise, odor, and heat of the busy food preparation activities into the rest of the house at a level intolerable to the mansion residents. The desire to diminish the risk of another fire would also have been a concern, and is reflected not only by the separation of the kitchen from the house but also by the wide stone paving covering half the floor at its hearth end. Jackson specifically called for an expensive metal roof for the reconstructed mansion, another indication of a desire to reduce the threat of fire.

"Functional" reasons for detached kitchens are commonly cited in the interpretation of plantation architecture (cf. Trescott 1981:84), but such listings ignore the social context of plantation life. Plantation kitchens served a wide variety of functions beyond meal preparation, and were busy and almost constantly occupied throughout the day. These facilities, of course, were staffed by slaves, who would have had direct and active control over the lively activities surrounding food preparation and the other domestic chores required by the master's family. The clatter, odor, and heat of kitchens encouraged their isolation from the planter's living quarters, but the close and ever-present proximity of the slaves may have been equally bothersome. Keeping these places separate from the living quarters of the planter and his family provided another layer of social insulation between owners and the owned (Carson 1976). The separateness of the 1836 kitchen, and the complex pathway from it to the dining room, is a very specific example of what Henry Glassie has referred to as an architectural "social lock" (Glassie 1982:398). Visitors to the mansion experienced a similarly complicated and programmed trail through the mansion's public areas, an almost textbook case of what Dell Upton defines as the "articulated and processional landscape" created in many plantation settings (Upton 1988:363–368).

The separateness and partitioning of the facilities at The Hermitage speak of efforts made to structure solutions to the usual tensions, and common mistrust and dislike, between master and slaves. The new storage pantry built in the space previously occupied by the 1831 kitchen would have eased one specific problem of this social situation. In June of 1832, Jackson had written to his daughter-in-law and commented on the loss of table-ware from the kitchen and pantry. "At my dr. Mrs. Jackson's death our table was well furnished with those articles, but where there are no attention but servants, everthing gets destroyed...when you leave the house [you] will have to see that all the furniture for the table is locked up, but what may be necessary, for such company as may be passing, and for the overseer + make a memorandum of that left out" (Jackson 1832).

The pantry storage room, built after the fire, was no doubt intended to prevent theft of both furnishings and food. Similar "solutions," meant to lessen contact and to ease friction between master and slave, may be seen in other aspects of the layout around Jackson's plantation: the fenceline, recently discovered during excavations near the garden, separating the backyard of the mansion from the house servants' quarters; the distance out to the quarters of the field hands and the separate water sources for the mansion and this quarter (Smith et al. 1977:46–57); and even the location of the privy within the fenced boundaries of the large formal garden next to the mansion, no doubt off-limits to black members of the plantation community. The original version of the Hermitage mansion, built in 1819, did have a completely disconnected kitchen, behind the house and to the west. The attachment of the 1831 kitchen directly to the house is in keeping with a trend seen at other local plantation mansions at this time. At least three other "big houses" in the immediate area (at Tulip Grove, the Shute farm, and Cleveland Hall) actually had fully attached "ells," which included kitchens as the main component (Clements 1987 II:148–153).

The construction of a detached kitchen in 1836 actually went against the grain of local contemporary architectural form. The Hermitage's 1831 attached kitchen may have been seen as a failed experiment, with enough shortcomings to warrant its demolition in the course of the rest of the work to the damaged house. From another perspective, those responsible for the change of the mansion into a grandiose example of a Greek Revival plantation big house may have seen it as necessary to complete the transition by severing the service activities from the house's core (see Chappell 1986:38 for discussion of this point). The Hermitage's postfire kitchen may have served, along with other elements of the house, to make a statement about the social distinctiveness of the Jackson family. This message would have been meant for both those within the plantation community and those visiting from the outside.

DOCUMENTARY SILENCE

Two questions remain. Why was the new kitchen construction not discussed more directly in the primary sources? Why has all the secondary literature concerning the mansion's history always accepted the present kitchen as being, without question, the one built in 1831? The question of "documentary silence" in the primary sources is the easier to answer. Andrew Jackson, who never had the opportunity to return to Tennessee during the entire course of the rebuilding, had given his son provisional control of the operation. Letters written by the younger Jackson are no longer extant, and so any written directions to the builders or notes on the project sent to his father are not available for historical scrutiny. The letter from Jackson dating to May of 1835 concerning the kitchen "improvement" may be referring to a complete rebuilding, but without Jackson Jr.'s preceding letter, it is impossible to say.

The reference to the costs of the "New Kitchen" on the final August 1836 accounting of the reconstruction expenditures is too lacking in context to stand on its own as solid evidence for such a seemingly major change. Like most of the dozens of other outbuildings at The Hermitage, ranging from the slaves' housing to the stables and barns to the overseer's quarters, the kitchens never received much written attention. Even the two prefire manifestations of the mansion facade, the most public and visible aspect of The Hermitage's architecture, are imperfectly recorded in surviving descriptive texts and illustrations.

Much of the significance of this paper's reinterpretation of the present kitchen's construction lies in the very fact that it was undocumented, forgotten, and undiscovered by Andrew Jackson's, and The Hermitage's, historians. This does not only reflect the sometimes sloppy scholarship of those looking at this historically important figure, but also a desire to accept evidence on face value, and to simplify, smooth over, and solidify the sometimes contentious and contradictory details of the life of a very complicated man. If a clear understanding of something as "simple" as a man's house cannot be produced, how can people be expected to accept and depend on the accuracy of the rest of the story? Andrew Jackson still awaits a competent, truly analytical historian willing and able to place the man in proper context.

The many biographies of Jackson written over the last 160 years have always had a definite hagiographic tone. The approach taken by the authors of these works bears a striking resemblance to that of archaeological pot hunters, gathering documentary gems and curiosities but leaving behind the harder-to-interpret evidence that would provide a more complete interpretation. The situation is changing for the better, especially through the work of the Andrew Jackson Papers Project at the University of Tennessee, which over the last two decades has pulled together all the scattered primary sources on Jackson for the first time. The next researcher taking on the task of probing the life of this complicated man should have sufficient evidence, both on paper and in physical form, to produce a more rigorous, more question-oriented work.

Up to this point, researchers looked on the absence of clear-cut comments in the documents about alterations to the house as adequate justification to look no further. Their attitude seems to have been that if there was no written record of it, either it never took place, or it was beneath the need for comment. The kitchen's true history may be invisible in the documentary record, but it is quite visible to those willing to read the standing structure of the mansion and kitchen. Although the excavation of the passage trench provided much of the interpretive spark leading to the new interpretation of the service area's evolution, the critical corroborating evidence was gathered with no more effort than looking at brick walls and stone foundations, climbing a ladder, and shining a flashlight. Some specialized skills were required to interpret this evidence, but the main skill needed for noticing the anomalies and inconsistencies in the building involved an open mind and a sharp eye.

Another reason that the 1836 changes to the kitchen area have been overlooked is that the work goes against common sense. The 1831 kitchen was less than 5 years old, and as Trescott pointed out, it "...had yet to see a second coat of paint" (Trescott 1981:84). It had not been damaged in the fire, and Jackson's constant emphasis on economy would seem to have precluded such unnecessary work. The fact that the changes do not make "sense," at least within the framework of conventional Jackson historiography, encourages and requires a deeper look at the motivations behind the work.

In a recent article, Anne Yentsch has looked into the interesting question of why dates traditionally assigned to historic houses are so rarely accurate (Yentsch 1988:6). Her conclusions involve the role houses play in becoming the embodiment and proof of the success of distant ancestors, legitimizing a family's, or in this case a national hero's, place in an area's deep historical foundation. The chronological error involved with the kitchen at The Hermitage falls within this pattern, as it is an attempt to explain the house in a simple, straightforward, rational progression, with an avoidance of any evidence complicating its understanding.

Yentsch also notes that houses bear information on both the "world-as-lived" and the "world-as-thought," and that house layout incorporates "both real space and imaginary space expressing social order" (Yentsch 1988:17). This approach guided the interpretation of the change in the service area as being an attempt to restructure the relationship between the living and working aspects of the house and as a way to restrict the day-to-day contact between white and black members of the plantation community. Examining the house as-thought, versus the house as-lived and the house as-reconstructed, does make the changes seem sensible and, furthermore, explains some of the harder-to-interpret primary sources. It is doubtful that the lost documents recounting the construction details, such as in Andrew Jackson, Jr.'s papers, would present clearly expressed reasons for the changes. The service area, with its separated and distanced facilities, locked rooms, doors, and complicated passage routes, does provide analytically powerful evidence about motivations for those who care to look at it.

The reluctance of "traditional," document-dependent historians to look to the evidence provided by the built environment and the physical remains of the past is slowly fading away. There may remain a few who would say that the fact that the mansion kitchen was built in 1836 rather than 1831 does not matter in the great scheme of things. But most, attune to the work of such scholars as the folklorist Henry Glassie, the archaeologists Jim Deetz and Mark Leone, the architectural historian Dell Upton, and historians such as Rhys Isaac and Cary Carson, who work with more "conventional" sources, know that what remains of the physical world of the past contains too much meaning to ignore. Jackson's historians have most frequently presented his home as his retreat from the travails of public life, as a place of legendary hospitality accorded to a constant stream of visitors (Parton 1860 III:597; Remini 1977:380), and possessing a form "...totally appropriate to the manner, style, and presence of its master" (Remini 1984:191). Unfortunately, in another volume, in the course of two consecutive paragraphs, this same author makes five errors about the house's size and construction history (Remini 1977:379–380).

Now, as attention shifts toward studying The Hermitage within the social context of southern U.S. plantation life, focus on the mansion is moving towards a consideration of its place as a setting for daily social dramas large and small, public and private, and white and black. It is unlikely that future studies of Andrew Jackson and his milieu will ignore the details of his mansion home.

This paper has reported on one aspect of what started as a relatively routine task — the monitoring of a renovation project at a historic house. Findings from the work quickly began to present a scenario contradictory to the established understanding of the house's construction history. In solving the puzzle that emerged from the work, it became not only necessary to document the evidence for the demolition of the true 1831 kitchen and the 1836 construction of the present kitchen, but also to explain the changes and explain why they had escaped notice by other researchers. The interpretations presented here do not ignore the documents, and in fact would have been impossible to construct without constant reference to both primary sources and the secondary literature. Documents are not enough, and artifacts and archaeology are not enough either. Combining what is left on the page and on, and below, the ground provides a powerful way to understand what happened in the past, and why it happened as well.

References

Armstrong, R. (1834a) Letter to Andrew Jackson, October 14, 1834. In Bassett V:295.

— (1834b) Letter to Andrew Jackson, October 20, 1834. In Bassett V:298.

— (1834c) Letter to Andrew Jackson, November 4, 1834. Andrew Jackson Papers, Library of Congress, Washington, D.C.

— (1836) Letter to Andrew Jackson, April 25, 1836. In Bassett V:399.

Bassett, J. S. (1926–1935) *Correspondence of Andrew Jackson (seven volumes)*. The Carnegie Institution of Washington, Washington, D.C.

Caldwell, M. F. (1949) *Andrew Jackson's Hermitage*. The Ladies' Hermitage Association, Nashville, TN.

Carson, C. (1976) Segregation in Vernacular Buildings. *Vernacular Architecture 7*.

Chappell, E. A. (1986) Acculturation in the Shenandoah Valley: Rhenish Houses of the Massanutten Settlement. In *Common Places: Readings in American Vernacular Architecture*, D. Upton and J. M. Vlach, Eds. The University of Georgia Press, Athens, GA.

Clements, P. (1987) *A Past Remembered: A Collection Of Antebellum Houses In Davidson County*. Clearview Press, Nashville, TN.

Galloway, L. B. (1950) Andrew Jackson, Junior. *Tennessee Historical Quarterly* 9:195–216, 306–343.

Glassie, H. (1975) *Folk Housing in Middle Virginia: A Structural Analysis of Historic Artifacts*. University of Tennessee Press, Knoxville, TN.

— (1982) *Passing the Time in Ballymenone: Culture and History of an Ulster Community*. University of Pennsylvania Press, Philadelphia.

Gurcke, C. (1987) *Bricks and Brickmaking: A Handbook for Historical Archaeology*. The University of Idaho Press, Moscow, ID.

Hinshaw, J. (1981) The Hermitage Waterline Excavations. Report on file with the Ladies' Hermitage Association, Hermitage, TN.

Horn, S. F. (1950) *The Hermitage: Home of Old Hickory*. The Ladies' Hermitage Association. Nashville, TN.

Jackson, A. (1832) Letter to Sarah Yorke Jackson, June 21, 1832. Manuscript Collection, The Hermitage, Hermitage, TN.

— (1834a) Letter to Andrew Jackson Jr., November 12, 1834. In Bassett V:307.

— (1834b) Letter to Andrew Jackson Jr., December 7, 1834. Jackson Papers, Huntington Library, San Marino, CA.

— (1835) Letter to Andrew Jackson Jr., May 16, 1835. In Bassett V:295.

Kniffen, F. (1986) Folk Housing: Key to Diffusion. In *Common Places: Readings in American Vernacular Architecture*, D. Upton and J. M. Vlach, Eds. University of Georgia Press, Athens.

Ladies' Hermitage Association (1987) *Andrew Jackson's Hermitage* [visitor's guidebook]. The Ladies' Hermitage Association, Hermitage, TN.

McKee, L. (1990) Archaeological Testing and Monitoring Done in Conjunction with the Hermitage Mansion HVAC Systems Renovation Project, 1988–1989. Report on file with the Ladies' Hermitage Association, Hermitage, TN.

Morison, D. (1831) Letter to Andrew Jackson, December 6, 1831. Manuscript Collection, The Hermitage, Hermitage, TN.

Noel Hume, I. (1969) *Historical Archaeology*. Alfred A. Knopf, New York.

Parton, J. (1860) *Life of Andrew Jackson*. Mason Brothers, New York.

Reiff, J. and W. Hume (1835) Memorandum of Agreement for Rebuilding the Hermitage, January 1, 1835. In Bassett V:315.

— (1836) Estimates for Rebuilding the Hermitage, August 2, 1836. In Bassett V:414–415.

Remini, R. (1977) *Andrew Jackson and the Course of American Empire, 1767–1821*. Harper and Row, New York.

— (1981) *Andrew Jackson and the Course of American Freedom, 1822–1832*. Harper and Row, New York.

— (1984) *Andrew Jackson and the Course of American Democracy, 1833–1845*. Harper and Row, New York.

— (1988) *The Life of Andrew Jackson*. Harper and Row, New York.

Smith, S. D., Ed. (1976) An Archaeological and Historical Assessment of the First Hermitage. Research Series No. 2, Division of Archaeology, Tennessee Department of Conservation, Nashville, TN.

Smith, S. D., F. W. Brigance, E. Breitburg, S. D. Cox, and M. Martin (1977) Results of the 1976 Season of the Hermitage Archaeology Project. Report prepared for the Ladies' Hermitage Association and the Tennessee American Revolution Bicentennial Commission.

Trescott, J. (1981) Architectural Analysis of the Hermitage Mansion. Report on file with the Ladies' Hermitage Association, Hermitage, TN.

Upton, D. (1988) White and Black Landscapes in Eighteenth-Century Virginia. In *Material Life in America, 1600–1860*, R. B. St. George, Ed. Northeastern University Press, Boston.

Yentsch, A. E. (1988) Legends, Houses, Families, and Myths: Relationships Between Material Culture and American Ideology. In *Documentary Archaeology in The New World*, M. C. Beaudry, Ed. Cambridge University Press, Cambridge.

Section III. Text and Context

14: Defining the Boundaries of Change: The Records of an Industrializing Potter

Paul R. Mullins
Department of Anthropology, University of Massachusetts, Amherst, Massachusetts

From the mid-18th to 20th centuries, industrialization produced a complex range of transformations in American social, labor, and economic relations. Analysis of industrialization has tended to conceive of these changes in terms of causal relationships that existed between loosely linked industrial and social contexts. However, transformations or conditions such as emerging labor and social formations, technological introductions, and a profusion of mass-produced material goods did not simply alter the nature and experience of work or social relations; instead, industrial society was a radical reorganization of the *perception* of mutually dependent labor, consumption, and social structures. By reorganizing the ways in which people experienced the relations of work, self, and community, industrial production and consumption transformed how producers and consumers understood those relations. This social disorientation was a process of pervasive defamiliarization in which individuals were forced to define new ways of perceiving and understanding the emerging social order of industrial capitalism.

This study examines how one potter in Virginia's Shenandoah Valley, Emanuel Suter, used text as an essential means to organize his understandings of industrial change during the second half of the 19th century, when industrialization most rapidly and thoroughly penetrated the region. Emanuel Suter was trained in traditional handcraft potting techniques in the early 1850s, and in 1855 he married, established a farm, and built a pottery kiln in his barnyard. He produced redware and some stoneware, and, after receiving an exemption from service in the Confederate military, he continued potting through the Civil War. His small kiln, production of apparently modest amounts of pottery, and his barter exchange in the community were all typical of the many seasonal potteries throughout this and other rural regions.

In October, 1864 Suter's family fled their farm near Harrisonburg, Virginia as the Union Army advanced up the Shenandoah Valley. As Suter went north into Pennsylvania, he began to keep a daily diary, a practice he continued until his death in 1902. When Suter and his family returned to their farm in June 1865, he used the diary to record the daily operations of his pottery, as well as his farming, church, and social activities. In addition to his diaries, most of Suter's ledgers, which record the nature of transactions, the transactors, and the goods exchanged, have been preserved, and a large amount of correspondence received by Suter has been saved with these records. A considerable amount of pottery vessels have also been preserved, and waster sherds have been recovered from both of the Suter production sites.

Industrial changes in American ceramic production and consumption are quite clear in the archaeological record, which became progressively more standardized and dominated by mass-produced goods after the middle of the 18th century (Leone 1988:245). However, most archaeological analysis has suggested that ceramic industrialization was primarily a detached technological or organizational change in which machinery, new economic formations, and labor organizations themselves transformed the domestic ceramic industry, as well as American society. It is clear, though, that the 18th-century emergence of rules that directed personal behavior (Shackel 1987) and subsequent efforts to structure the emerging industrial society (Kasson 1988:69) reflect pervasive changes in the ordering of *both* material labor organization and social behavior in incipient industrial America. The reorganizations of industrialization clearly impelled a dramatic new understanding of production and consumption relations that penetrated social structures on every scale. From this perspective, the production and consumption of industrial ceramics was not simply the manufacture and purchase of refined wares rather than coarse wares; it was instead the consumption, reproduction, and representation of a new *system* of labor and social relations (Baudrillard 1981:5). Consequently, the industrial transformations reflected in archaeological ceramics were clearly transformations in both capitalist labor *and* the social world (Paynter 1988:407). It is not that changes in labor organization changed social structure or vice versa, rather they were mutually dependent transformations, each of which was necessary to give industrialism such a distinct and pervasive meaning.

Historical interpretation has recognized that labor and social change together created a dramatically new society; however, there has still been a tendency to condense and clarify interpretation of the considerable complexity of industrialization. Distinct factors that seem essential to the manner in which industrial change was given social meaning are commonly conceived in interpretation as part of a monolithic societal change. For example, emerging rules directing personal discipline (Shackel 1987; Kasson 1984) were critical to the manner in which labor relations were extended outside the workplace. The dramatically new social structure that emerged during the 18th and 19th centuries also relied on individuals having distinct identities that classified them socially and personally: delinquents, the insane, the poor, ethnic and gender identities, and so on (Foucault 1979). Archaeological interpretation, though, has emphasized the *mechanisms* of industrial changes (e.g., machines and business strategies) and the monolithic effects of this change on domestic consumption (e.g., increased quantities of cheaper goods). Interpretation has typically explained social factors as either detached from or in a cause-and-effect relationship with industrial production, obscuring the complex character of industrial change and the manner in which it was perceived. Such an approach essentially gives human agency to the numerous mechanisms of industrial manufacture; i.e., social change is posed as separate from these "active" mechanisms and reliant on the circumstances that they create. More significantly, this perspective obscures how a diverse range of producers and consumers actively perceived and directed the many changes that are historically lumped together as "industrialization." The changes collectively clearly involve both a material and social defamiliarization in which machines, business strategies, and labor organizations are simply elements of a pervasive transformation with distinct impacts in every community and social group.

One approach taken to examining industrial change in the American ceramic trade has been to contrast preindustrial to industrial production and consumption (e.g., Smith and Rogers 1979:7–9). However, the in-terpretive contrasting of preindustrial/handcraft to industrial/factory production and consumption obscures the impacts industrial organization had for particular social groups, regions, and socioeconomic groups over a relatively long time. While this interpretive contrast has heuristic value, it also has had a tendency to absolutize historical interpretations of preindustrial and industrial organization, suggesting unrealistically clear and extreme differences in their respective forms of production, exchange, and consumption. Industrialization in American ceramic manufacture was pervasive in its ability to impose a dominant organization that restructured the relations of producers and consumers, yet it was actively impeded, embraced, directed, and given meaning by a complex range of producers and consumers over a century and a half. Indeed, many traditional potters clearly integrated elements of industrial organization into their operations (cf. Faulkner 1982), and many industrial potteries manufactured products that were indistinguishable from those of traditional potteries (cf. Zug 1986:266–267). Consequently, it would seem that a more sophisticated understanding of industrialization would not homogenize a broad range of changes and responses; instead, it would be more productive to examine how particular producers and consumers perceived, organized, and gave distinct meanings to the mechanisms and character of industrial change. Using this approach, interpretation of industrialization will reflect how individuals and groups actively gave unique meanings to the mechanisms of industrialization and produced dramatic changes in their individual and collective lives.

The manner in which individuals actively perceived, understood, and responded to industrialization is central to interpreting industrial society. The use of written records in American potteries was certainly uncommon before the advent of industrial capitalism, when producers and consumers of ceramics and other goods became participants in this pervasive reorganization of production and exchange relations. At that point, some potters, such as Emanuel Suter, chose to use text as one means to establish their role within these rapidly changing social structures.

Emanuel Suter's texts are a valuable record, first, because few traditional potters kept written records of their operation, and few industrial potters documented more than their pottery's business transactions or technical administration. Second, they document the postwar period during which Suter expanded his barnyard pottery, selectively embraced industrial technologies and business strategies, and eventually established his own small pottery factory. Consequently, these resources provide a rich foundation for examining how one potter perceived industrialization, defined its organizations, and accommodated its structures to his own concepts of pottery organization. Although this is a rare resource base, both the changes that occurred in the region and Suter's perceptions, organization, and direction of change were distinctive yet not wholly unique. Industrialization as it affected Emanuel Suter was quite comparable to the effects that other American potters actively resisted, responded to, and embraced on various levels in other regions from the late-18th to early-20th centuries.

From an archaeological perspective, these texts provide a rich insight into factors beyond the simple attribution of wares to a particular potter. Instead, these records provide an active understanding of the process of industrial change that the archaeological record documents quite clearly in another form. The diaries, ledgers, and business letters suggest how one potter negotiated his role in industrial society by changing his technical production, the range of products, his distribution, and his complete lifestyle. These were changes that all traditional potters confronted, and their active negotiations are reflected in the transformation of the pottery that fills the archaeological record. Emanuel Suter's texts offer the opportunity to critically examine how consciousness of industrialization was organized and directed, an insight that can significantly enrich archaeological interpretations of the social and material changes attendant to industrialization.

Traditional Craft Production and Consumption

Throughout the Shenandoah Valley and most of rural America, traditional crafts people were typically farmers who produced goods on a seasonal basis using handcraft techniques. The production and consumption of traditional potteries, like that of most crafts, was usually family oriented; i.e., a kin-based group produced wares at their farm for local, household consumption in exchange for other craft goods or services. Traditional production, organization, and stylistic techniques, which responded to a community's specific ceramic consumption needs and natural resources, were transmitted relatively unchanged from one generation to the next (Burrison 1983:3). Consequently, communities tended to share distinctive product styles, forms, and production characteristics. This production and consumption process was structured by the cycles of the seasons, natural resources, and the length of the day.

In the Shenandoah Valley, as in virtually all rural areas, interaction was overwhelmingly with individuals in the community who shared kinship or social bonds. Agrarian craft networks in these communities linked producers of a diverse range of specialized handmade products, skilled services, and labor, which were usually exchanged in barter transactions. These transactions often involved multiple parties, each with unique skills or goods, and exchange could involve several transactions over an extended period of time. This exchange structure created

relationships of interdependence and provided virtually all of the goods most essential to farm families.

These apparently egalitarian relationships masked agrarian social hierarchies, which have little historical visibility. Between 1730 and 1770, the Shenandoah Valley was a major route for settlement expansion southwestward from Pennsylvania and westward from the densely populated Tidewater region of Virginia (Mitchell 1977:16). Before 1760, virtually all of these settlers to the Shenandoah Valley obtained substantial tracts of prime farmland, which could yield far more than any family required, although their personal wealth was quite modest (Mitchell 1977:238). Between 1775 and 1800, however, the valley's population doubled, and by 1800 half of the valley's population did not own land (Mitchell 1977:238). Access to good farmland rapidly decreased, land acquisition became a very profitable investment, and a social hierarchy based on inequalities in land distribution emerged.

These social hierarchies promoted thriving craft exchange networks, which were maintained by restricted socioeconomic mobility and the economic diversification of the region. Although landless settlers could readily find tenant properties and seasonal labor, and eventual ownership of at least marginal farmland was likely for most laborers, craft skills provided necessary resources to ensure subsistence. Craft production, however, was at best only marginally profitable, and very few crafts people in the Shenandoah Valley were socioeconomically mobile as a result of their trade. Higher status landed farmers supported these networks, in part, because they relied on local laborers to maintain their own farms and diverse commercial activities. The exchange networks also defined and maintained the visibility of social hierarchies. Consequently, exchange networks created interdependent relationships, which bound socioeconomic groups together; yet, since they were fostered by and made visible the social inequalities promoted by unequal resource distribution, the craft networks also maintained social distance between groups.

Local potters began production in the southern Shenandoah Valley in the late-18th century, and a handful of potteries operated in the valley before the middle of the 19th century (Rice and Stoudt 1974; Russ and McDaniel 1987; Mullins 1986). Craft production, however, was diversified and household oriented in the region until the late-19th century. While areas such as the urban northeast rapidly became participants during the late-18th century in American industrial production and consumption, the valley did not emerge as an industrial production center. Instead during the 18th century the valley became a decentralized producer of raw goods, rather than a specialized preparation and manufacturing region (Mitchell 1977). The region produced an abundance and extensive range of raw goods, such as leather, cloth, and hemp, but substantial profits were made only by the small minority controlling distribution of those goods, rather than the numerous household producers. Consequently, economic mobility was relatively restricted and marginal farmers maintained general craft skills to ensure subsistence. This social structure persisted with little change from the late-18th century until the Civil War.

Emanuel Suter

Emanuel Suter was just one of the many craft producers in the Shenandoah Valley. Born in 1833, Suter learned to pot from his cousin, John Heatwole. Under Heatwole's tutelage, Suter was producing dated vessels by 1851, and after his marriage in 1855 Suter settled on his father-in-law's farm and apparently built his first kiln there. The record of Suter's pottery production prior to the Civil War is restricted to material artifacts and contains no textual references to pottery-making. The diaries, ledgers, and correspondence that survive from his postwar pottery begin in 1864. Some textual records prior to 1864 have survived, such as personal letters and records, but none refer to Suter's ceramic production. Government records (e.g., the federal census), newspapers, and other text sources also fail to mention Suter as a potter.

This documentary invisibility is not unusual for traditional crafts people. Like most part-time crafts people, potters wanted to be considered landed farmers, the highest social status in an agrarian community (Worrell 1982:164). There was no particular status in being an artisan, and generally only the most specialized or full-time producers appeared in records as crafts people. For instance, the only extant pre-Civil War occupational record for Suter appears in the 1850 and 1860 federal censuses, where he was listed as a farmer. Even in the 1870 and 1880 federal censuses, at times when Suter clearly had a quite prosperous pottery trade, he was listed as a "farmer and potter," refusing to relinquish the title of farmer.

The complete organization of Suter's pottery, and the social world attendant to it, changed dramatically when the Civil War broke out. Both Suter and Heatwole were members of the large Mennonite community in Rockingham County, and the Mennonites' nonresistance doctrine, which was unique in the South, was met with considerable incredulity by the newly established Confederate government (Brunk 1959). At the outbreak of the war, some Mennonites went into hiding to avoid military service and others attempted to gain exemptions from service, but many served and simply refused to fire at Union troops. John Heatwole was one of the Mennonites who served a year and was allowed to temporarily return to his farm to tend his crops, but Heatwole refused to return to the army when his leave ended in the summer of 1862 (Carr 1967:3). He spent the rest of the war hiding from Confederate bounty hunters, and much of his time in hiding was spent in West Virginia, where he is credited with spreading the Mennonite faith (Kaufman 1978:6).

Emanuel Suter did not enlist for military service, instead paying the army for a temporary exemption in June, 1860. In March, 1862 he extended his exemption by supplying "a substitute for the war in the person of Ebenezer Nicely," making Suter permanently exempt from service under 1862 Confederate policy. During the war Suter produced coarseware table vessels, a staple product of the wartime southern potter, in addition to his standard utilitarian wares, and he continued to produce some of these table wares after the war. Suter also figured prominently in wartime church politics; in 1862, for instance, he went to Richmond on behalf of the church to pay the indemnity fines of a group of Mennonites who were being held in Libby Prison (Heatwole 1906:31).

In October, 1864 Union General Phillip Sheridan began to advance northward up the Shenandoah Valley, destroying everything in his path, and the already desperate Confederates rescinded their exemptions. In the face of Sheridan's wholesale destruction and the threat of military service, the Suters fled to Lancaster County, Pennsylvania, the home of a large Mennonite community. Suter began his extant diary on the trip north; his comments do not indicate that there were previous diaries that are now destroyed, rather this apparently was a new practice. A eulogy written after his death in 1902 commented that "later in life Brother Suter became a profound student and reader" (Heatwole 1906:32), but Suter's initial reasons for beginning the text are not explicitly articulated in the diaries. The sudden emergence of this daily textual record and Suter's lengthy diary entries and correspondence commenting on his forced flight suggest that the social instability of the war and this migration, in particular, prompted him to reorganize his perceptions of society. This reorganization of Suter's understandings of his world directly relate to the total social destabilization of the war: Suter and members of his family and church were threatened with military service, military action in the region physically imperiled his farm, and social relationships within the community and church were permanently fragmented by death, migration, financial and property losses, and conflicting convictions. The flight itself was socially and spatially disorienting; the diaries and personal correspondence were a form of representation intended to reorient himself to an unstable social structure and to accommodate his values to an unfamiliar culture.

In March, 1865, while in refuge in Pennsylvania, Suter wrote to a friend of the instability of "this troublesome world" and his flight north.

> ...Dear Brother, my mind is sometimes unconsciously carried back to those blue mountains of Virginia — to

that beautiful valley, the place of my birth, where I spent my boyhood's days in innocent glee, and grew up to years of maturity; yes, all these beautiful scenes, friends, relations, brothers and sisters, have won in my heart the warmest affections, and it is hard to forget them. Never did I appreciate my earthly home as I now do: yet when my heart is burdened with the gloomy thought of being absent from all that is so near and dear to me, there is a thought again that gladdens my heart — the thought of a home in heaven for all the children of God.

The inhabitants of that home are secure — there is no power in existence that can scatter them or drive them from it, for they are protected by the arms of an omnipotent God, yea, they are safely folded in the arms of the good Shepherd Jesus Christ — gathered into his sheepfold where no evil can reach them... (Suter 1865).

The instability of the war certainly affected all potters in the region, so it is not surprising that they initially reestablished most of their former organizations, whose familiarity they perceived as stable. Few, if any, of these potters rapidly transformed their operation following the war. However Suter's previously ordered social world of active participation in a stable church, relatively equitable exchange among a close circle of neighbors, and comparable social convictions was devastated by the war: Suter's religious convictions were challenged, the Mennonite community was oppressed, and major schisms developed within the church itself (Brunk 1959:164–167); and Suter's texts reflect his anxiety over the likelihood of losing family, friends, and his farmland and property. The stability provided by these elements had been essential to the manner in which Suter ordered his world, but the postwar instability in these key organizational elements transformed the community social structure. Consequently, Suter rapidly adopted many new technologies and organizations after the war that dramatically changed the character of his pottery; along with these reorganizations, text represented one active approach to organizing his perceptions and coherently establishing the form of the new social structure, where he was situated in it, and what his roles were as a father, church member, farmer, and potter.

One measure Suter used to immediately reestablish a social role, even in refuge, was to continue potting. On January 5, 1865, while in refuge in Harrisburg, Pennsylvania, Suter "went to Wilcox the potter to see about work" and secured a job at the Cowden and Wilcox Pottery Company in February. In the previously cited letter, Suter emphasized that he considered his stay and work in Pennsylvania temporary, writing "I am here working at my trade, which is that of a potter. How long I will remain here I am not able to say. I do not bind myself for any time, as I expect to return home just as soon as an opportunity affords itself." Suter only worked at the factory until April 15, glazing and decorating vessels, and records such as this letter suggest that he did

not intend the industrial pottery to provide him a model for new approaches to ceramic production and consumption. Nevertheless, the large coarseware pottery obviously exposed Suter to the newest technologies, organizational strategies, and marketing practices of industrial potteries. The around-the-clock production schedules, extensive marketing and shipping networks, and division of labor using mechanized equipment were just a few of the characteristics of the factory pottery that were unfamiliar concepts to a barnyard potter from Virginia.

His exposure to the efficient mass-production pottery and the wartime social instability together promoted Suter's modification of his farm pottery by incorporating what he saw as the most effective elements of both industrial and traditional techniques. When he returned to Virginia in June, 1865, Suter immediately began to design a larger kiln and technically improved barnyard pottery. Suter burned (i.e., fired) his old kiln for the first time after the war on August 1, 1865, but he was soon purchasing and constructing new equipment for the pottery. In September, 1866 Suter "commenced working on the kiln," a new 12-ft-diameter rock and brick structure, and he outfitted his new pottery with much of the equipment he had seen in the Pennsylvania factory. In 1866 alone Suter purchased a machine for pressing tile, he began to use "jigger" molds, and he adapted other equipment from the much larger Cowden and Wilcox operation. His glazing machine, for instance, was a hand pump connected by hose to a wooden bucket. Suter's machine used the nozzled hose to spray glaze from the bucket onto vessels, a rudimentary adaptation of equipment he had seen in the Pennsylvania factory. Prior to 1866, vessels had been turned on the wheel, rather than by molds, and glaze had been applied by dipping each vessel in a glaze suspension. Suter's neighboring Rockingham County potters were still continuing these practices after the war; some such as John Heatwole never made these new technologies more than a peripheral part of their operation, but most appear to have made at least limited changes by 1880. Within the region Suter was unusual for his rapid and pervasive adoption of these technologies; however, most of the region's largest potteries made similar changes during the 1870s.

Superficially, these were all simply technological modifications of Suter's pottery; i.e., Suter's texts do not suggest that he saw these changes as reorganizations of the social relations of production and consumption. Despite the increased social fragmentation historically associated with industrialization, Suter desired the potential socioeconomic betterment and increased efficiency, which he believed industrial technologies could provide. He and other valley farmers apparently saw technology and the social disruption of the factory as separate phenomena and gave independent contextual meanings to industrial technologies as they were applied in the agrarian community and as they were applied in the factory (Marx

1964:146). These farmers distinguished between the social organizations structuring mass production and those that ordered the agrarian community, and many believed technology could be accommodated in different ways to either social structure. In this sense, they certainly did not perceive themselves as overwhelmed or constrained by industrialization; they instead explicitly encouraged many of its material changes and implicitly promoted its social transformations. For Emanuel Suter and other Rockingham County potters, these changes together necessitated a dramatically new form of representation.

Like Suter, many farmers and crafts people adopted more efficient and productive agrarian or manufacturing technologies but retained what they perceived as the fundamental production and marketing elements of traditional farm and craft organizations. For Suter, perhaps the most essential element of the pottery's organization was its kin-based production control. Suter rapidly began to use mechanized equipment and other industrial strategies after the war, but he and his family continued to manage the complete operation from production to marketing until the early 1890s. Suter was intent on retaining control of the pottery in his family, rather than sharing control with an external resource base, introducing many unrelated laborers to the operation, or becoming a detached manager of the pottery. The skilled positions in Suter's potteries (i.e., the turners and technical administrators) were members of Suter's immediate and extended family, which included 13 children, numerous relatives by marriage, and a few close neighbors. Before his operation moved in 1892, extremely few individuals employed in the pottery did more than menial tasks if they were not part of this extended kin structure.

The laborers outside this kin network had considerably different manager-worker relations with Suter than he had with his relatives and close neighbors. Suter would commonly record an agreement over the length of time, job duties, and the rate of pay for which these detached laborers would work. In December 1870, for example, "Joseph Ganes set in to work for me for another year at nine Dollars per month and is to Board himself for which I am to furnish two hundred weight of Bacon and three Barrels of flour." Ganes performed relatively unskilled pottery labor, such as digging clay and cutting firewood, as well as working on Suter's farm, and records were made of all of these mundane tasks. Such a systematic record was never made of the labor of Suter's relatives, reflecting a clearly different system of valuing the labor of his kin. The labor of extended kin was assumed as part of their expected social role, and Suter understood himself to have obligations to these individuals as well. In contrast, the obligations to workers outside the kin network were made explicit. Suter's obligations to his kin were tangible because they had a shared sense of roles and responsibilities within the kin network, but the obligations between other individuals and Suter were groundless in what

Suter perceived as a tangible social relationship. Such tangible relationships were assumed progressively less during the time Suter produced his diaries, a reflection that the relationship between Suter and his workers became more abstract; progressively fewer obligations to individuals outside Suter's immediate family were assumed, and the texts were a means of explicitly defining the nature of these relationships.

At the same time that new technologies began to be adopted after the war, the social and economic foundations of the neighborhood exchange networks had been extensively fragmented. Exchange in craft networks had previously functioned primarily in maintaining social structure, by delineating transactors' roles. However, as hierarchical relations intensified the emphasis on the economic nature of exchange, exchange clearly was not economically profitable to many transactors. Suter and other crafts people modified the economic resource potential of this relationship by changing the nature of exchange. Suter attempted to stabilize the foundations of social exchange by maintaining close social links through relations other than craft exchange.

In the rebuilding community structure of postwar Rockingham County, Suter's diaries and his community roles clearly reflect an intention to reestablish a social position that was not explicitly connected to his trade. For example, Suter had a prominent role in the Mennonite church, in which he served as Secretary of the Virginia Mennonite Conference; after 1870 Suter lobbied extensively for Mennonite Sunday schools and won their approval, despite church opposition; and he served as a school board member and clerk of the Rockingham County Central School District (Steiner 1977:1). Suter regularly attended court day in Harrisonburg, he constantly visited neighbors and attended funerals, and he wrote wills and letters for illiterate neighbors, ensuring that he maintained a prominent role in the community's social structure. His diaries are filled with references to his constant visitations, attendance at funerals and weddings, and comparable events that fashioned social relations.

Standardization

As a potter, Suter's exchange relationship dramatically shifted after the war. In the traditional exchange relationship of barter and extended transaction, exchange was a tangible transaction in which the process of production and consumption was jointly defined and controlled by the transactors. Transactors were known individuals or individuals from within a "known" socio-geographical community; transactors exchanged goods personally, and they exchanged goods or labor with concrete meaning, rather than currency. The value of a good or service was fluid (i.e., it was set in transaction) and in a barter exchange liability could extend to any transactor. Consequently, there was little need to organize business transactions outside interpersonal compacts, because exchange was itself a tangible, shared, and active social transaction. In this sense, a written record would have been superfluous because it would simply replace what these transactors saw as a tangible verbal agreement with an abstract, comparatively intangible form. The process of traditional craft exchange itself was also controlled by transactors who perceived little or no way to control fundamental production and consumption factors (e.g., weather, time, or availability of resources), which dictated both their consumption needs and their ability to produce goods. Individual producers and consumers could actively contain and define the process of traditional craft exchange and saw little or no means to further control or delineate production or consumption. In this sense, exchange was not simply a social or economic relationship, it was the act that gave meaning to the complete process of manufacturing, exchanging, and consuming pottery.

In the Shenandoah Valley, this changed after the Civil War, when traditional production and exchange organizations were destabilized. Material manufacture, exchange, and consumption became standardized as producers and consumers reestablished the production and consumption process by attaching new meanings to exchange and social roles and embracing many new technologies. These meanings and technologies gave producers greater control over production, exchange, and consumption.

Suter did not adopt the labor organizations of the factory pottery after the war, but he rapidly embraced product standardization and industrial exchange organizations to establish new meanings for the social relationships of exchange. As part of his postwar changes, Suter introduced price lists sometime after 1866, a common sales technique in mass-production potteries. In price standardization, as opposed to barter, usually only the purchaser could incur debt, and a good's value was not negotiable. At the same time, the focus of the Suter pottery rapidly shifted over the late 1860s as the operation turned its emphasis to a local commercial market, rather than a barter network. Suter continued to barter wares in the community until the 1890s, but, in terms of volume, the vast majority of his postwar ware was sold by merchants in the region. Although Suter was financially more successful in this transition than any other county potter, he was not alone in his interest in courting local merchants. Several other potters, including John Heatwole, also began to market their wares in general stores by 1870. By 1878, a merchant complained to Suter that "Mr. Heatwool [sic] is around Retailing Gallon Crocks at 10 c...he has hurt the sale of your crocks."

The social interdependence of the traditional craft network was not promoted by this second-person commercial exchange, deemphasizing the potter's social role;

exchange had previously been a social as well as economic transaction, which affirmed the community roles of both producers and consumers. Traditional exchange had been a shared transaction between parties with mutually understood roles and obligations. In contrast, the introduction of extensive second-person exchange using standard pricing was simply one change that shifted control over and the definition of exchange to the producer (and eventually the merchant). For the consumer, exchange itself became abstract, less active, and antisocial, which gave consumers little foundation for defining exchange or the social roles that had previously been intertwined with it.

Traditional craft exchange, on the other hand, was a stable stage, which gave meaning to production and consumption; in contrast to exchange itself, traditional production and consumption were in many ways uncontrolled by traditional transactors. However, with the introduction of second-person standardized exchange and the technical capability to exert greater technological control over production, the industrializing potter had increasingly more control over the definition of production and exchange. The introduction of standardized products would eventually lead to greater control over consumption as well.

One of the factors affecting production and consumption that Suter could never control was nature's seasonal cycles and constant meteorological variation. Seasonal food preparation (e.g., fall fruit-butter preservation) dictated consumer demand for pottery; during certain times of the year it was not possible to produce wares because of either the cold or pressing farm labor needs, and the farm and pottery's production schedule revolved around the day-to-day weather (e.g., on June 16, 1880 "...we worked in the pottery...until it quit raining then we cut wheat until night"). Consequently, Suter was absorbed in and gave close attention to seasonal change; each entry from 1864 until 1902 includes a record of the day's weather and an original prayer, a good indication of what was important to a Mennonite farmer. This weather entry was as long as both his account of the day's activities and his daily devotional, reflecting Suter's recognition of the extent to which nature structured his life activities. Seasonal change and holy authority were significant influences on Suter's life that he could not control, and the diaries gave him one forum in which he could organize his consciousness of both.

A sensitive reflection of the postwar erosion of exchange networks is that Suter named his previously unnamed pottery the New Erection Pottery, after the nearby town. The 1855 to 1864 Suter pottery, on the other hand, had primarily been represented by Suter himself. Before 1864, representation of the pottery had been a social interaction that confirmed the production and consumption roles of transactors, but his postwar separation from consumers was mirrored in Suter's choice to represent the pottery with a firm name not related to Suter in any obvious way. He later referred to the farm pottery as the New Erection Steam Pottery when he installed steam-powered equipment, emphasizing the technological sophistication of the pottery. This decision to name and later rename the pottery suggests that Suter chose to stress his product and operation, rather than his own place in a social network. He maintained a degree of social cohesion with local consumers by using the town's name in the pottery's new moniker; the new name established the operation as local, but the absence of Suter's name suggests that he did not see his own personal identity as crucial to the new exchange relationship or he perhaps had lost his identity as a producer.

Standardization and segmentation were perhaps most clear in the product itself. After the war Suter initially began to increase the number of vessel forms his shop was producing, manufacturing a range of standard vessel forms that were not commonly produced by traditional potters. Suter's diaries and ledgers mention what he identifies as over 75 distinct vessel forms (Steiner 1977:6). By the late 1870s Suter was producing large quantities of flower pots, drain pipe, and previously uncommon food preservation and preparation vessels, such as large-capacity jars (e.g., 10 gallon), cake bakers, and churns, and in 1871 Suter built what he called a "small kiln" primarily for burning flower pots, tile, and occasional miniature pieces. His 1865 diary includes a list of vessel heights, diameters, and clay weights used to manufacture vessels marketed as distinct by form and capacity, and these wares were part of his postwar price lists. The adoption of vessel molds, new mechanical equipment, and improved kiln technologies made the extent of this variation and standardization considerably greater than it would have been with exclusively handcraft technologies.

Despite the initial increased variation in vessel form types, the general trend was toward producing large quantities of a few vessel types of standard form and capacity. The major product of the pottery was always the common crock or jar. The crock was most often sold in standard capacities between a half-gallon and a gallon and a half, and it could serve a great variety of everyday food-preservation needs: despite standardization of vessel height, diameter, and capacity, it was a functionally versatile product. Other goods, however, such as flower pots, stove flues, and tile, were essentially useless for any function other than that for which they were created, and cake molds and very large jars were among the forms that were not particularly adaptable to many uses.

In the case of all these vessels, Suter used a consistent terminology to segment wares into standard vessel forms and capacities. Despite the functional adaptability of some forms and the individual variation between each vessel, Suter understood every vessel type as having a specific identity. The minor differences between indi-

vidual vessels were because of inconsistent clay sources, variations in kiln atmosphere, or wheel-turned vs. molded vessels, and as the pottery steadily standardized its technical and stylistic production, these variations gradually decreased.

After the war, Suter also began impressing vessel capacities on many of his wares, particularly his food preservation vessels. This practice had been uncommon by Suter before 1864, although other county potters had occasionally stamped wares since the 1830s. After the war, this became a common practice throughout the region, and Suter and Heatwole used many almost indistinguishable stamps to mark vessel capacities. In 1878, one merchant commented that consumers were "much pleased with [the vessels] the way they are numbered," suggesting that consumers were readily adopting the concept of product segmentation. The practice reflected Suter's intent to communicate his perception of his products' identities to his consumers: he gave vessels distinctive functions as well as values in price lists, he technologically standardized vessel manufacture, and he gave one element of this distinct vessel identity, the capacity, a prominent position on the product itself. In this sense, then, standardization and segmentation of production, consumption, and exchange were apparently readily embraced by both consumers and producers. Suter also began to mark some wares with his name and (in some instances) the pottery's location, but these were less common than capacity stamps and in general were a later occurrence. The appearance of stamped names and locations later in the potteries' operation may reflect Suter's intent to establish tangible identities as production-consumption relations became progressively more abstract.

New forms of economic exchange became more abstract for the producer as well as the consumer, particularly as the need for currency transaction emerged. Suter began to require currency as he purchased increasingly more industrial supplies, including shop machinery and professionally prepared resources (e.g., clays). In small-scale community trade, though, currency was not often exchanged, and in the wake of the war, currency was not a medium many southerners saw as representing tangible value. Suter instead used merchants to generate progressively more currency, although he continued to informally barter small amounts of ware in his neighborhood. In 1869 an irate Augusta County retailer complained about a letter from Suter informing the merchant that the pottery "cannot furnish me ware for goods." The retailer insisted that "I represent two stores and the quantity of crocks we will buy certainly ought to induce you to take some goods or I will try to make arrangements with some other kiln." In 1877 another merchant echoed these sentiments when Suter requested currency exchange; the retailer threatened that his stores had never dealt with another pottery, "although we have been frequently urged to do so by other manufacturers." Retailers such as these saw themselves as part of the community exchange system, despite their sporadic use of currency. Retailers bartered mass-produced and specialized goods for local products, and they preferred to reserve their own limited currency for transactions with wholesalers.

Perhaps one of the most unusual aspects of Suter's operation was his extensive production of redware long after virtually every other county potter had abandoned it. After 1850, most county potters produced stoneware, a change that occurred over most of the region. Stoneware, which was more durable than redware, was perceived as being of superior quality, and a major criticism of redware was the danger of lead glazing. Suter was certainly aware of the dangers of lead-glazed earthenwares, which had been recognized since the 18th century, and at least one local stoneware potter, Joseph Silber, publicized these dangers. Silber met Suter in Harrisburg, came to Rockingham County after the war, and in 1875 had a short partnership with Suter, but Silber actively advertised the dangers of lead glazes and the inferiority of earthenware. Over several months in 1866, Silber advertised 5000 gallons of stoneware priced at

> ...a small advance above that of Earthenware, to which it is so greatly superior in beauty, finish and utility, besides being warranted perfectly free from all those noxious and poisonous mineral compounds necessarily used in the manufacturing of Earthenware, rendering it not only deleterious and pernicious to health, but in many cases known fatal to human life itself (Rockingham Register and Virginia Advertizer July, 1866).

In 1876 a merchant complained to Suter about such advertising and the sentiments they stirred, commenting that he "could have sold three times as many if it had not been for some of *your* friends who get up a predudice [sic] against your Crocks."

Despite such sentiments, Suter clearly produced progressively more redware from the end of the war until 1892. This change probably relates to the increased production of nontraditional vessel forms, the availability of stoneware clays, and the volume of ware produced by Suter's operation. In the 1866 to 1869 period, Suter recorded the burning of a relatively modest 23 kiln loads, of which 13 were earthenware and 10 were stoneware, which would not appear to be a substantial difference. The exact number of gallons in a given kiln burn were never specified, and the capacity of the kilns increased over time, so a kiln load in 1866 was not comparable in capacity to one in 1881. However, the ratios of earthenware to stoneware are a sensitive way of evaluating output by ware type. In 1878 to 1881, Suter burned 54 kiln loads, of which 33 were earthenware and 21 were stoneware; six of the earthenware kilns were exclusively flower pots. This earthenware-to-stoneware ratio contin-

ued to increase by the period 1887 to 1890, when Suter burned 39 kilns, of which only 9 were stoneware; by this time the farm pottery had embraced large-scale earthenware production in which flower pots and tile had become a major product of the operation. The demand for flower pots, in particular, reached its peak in the late 1880s; in September 1886, for example, Suter received an order for 20,000 flower pots, a request that took 2 months of work to finish.

Stoneware clays were available throughout the region, and Suter shipped most of his from two locations, which were each about 25 miles from his farm. John Heatwole and Lyndsey Morris exclusively produced stoneware after the war and lived a few miles from Suter. These two potters dug their stoneware clays along the Dry River, which they farmed from opposite sides, but they clearly produced a much smaller amount of ware than Suter. Waster sherds surface-collected from each of their potteries also indicate that both Heatwole and Morris blended redware and stoneware clays to extend the life of their clay sources. These scattered Dry River clay sources were probably not productive enough to consistently supply Suter. Suter's farm, in contrast, had abundant supplies of red clays, like most land in the region.

But this availability of clay was only one factor in Suter's production of redware. By relying on the clay sources on his farm, Suter maintained both a social and economic independence from businesses that provided professionally prepared clays. Besides saving the money necessary to purchase professionally prepared clay, the reliance on his own farm clay and community sources maintained the boundaries of production and consumption: clay was dug in the community, prepared by a member of the (fragmenting) social-exchange networks, vessels were consumed by households in the immediate region, and transaction still involved the exchange of locally made goods (although this rapidly decreased). Only in 1892, when he moved his pottery to nearby Harrisonburg, did Suter cease virtually all redware production. Using professionally prepared clays and glaze materials that he imported from the North, Suter began to almost exclusively produce slip-glazed stoneware and molded Rockingham-glazed earthenwares.

These social and production boundaries were maintained in Suter's spatial definition of his exchange community. Suter never traded extensively outside Rockingham or Augusta Counties, and his infrequent sales outside the region did not occur until the 1880s, when the railroad was reliable enough to be a viable shipping alternative for Suter. However, even when Suter began to use the trains (which were only used to ship wares to merchants), the vast majority of the ware was shipped to destinations in Rockingham County and Augusta County, which bordered Rockingham to the south. In 1881, of 38 "loads" of ware Suter recorded as shipped by train, 27 were to destinations in Rockingham or Augusta, and the remaining 11 destinations were simply unspecified. In 1889, of 25 "loads" of ware shipped from the Harrisonburg depot, 18 went to merchants in Rockingham and Augusta and 7 went to unspecified destinations. The trains probably contributed to more efficient shipping, but there is no indication that Suter aggressively increased his market area by rail or expanded his market beyond the region's general stores. Suter's diaries and ledgers also apparently record only the wagon transport of ware to merchants, not the trading that went on in transit or at the pottery shop yard. The individuals who drove the wagons, however, certainly bartered ware along the trip; on May 31, 1881, for example, Suter took a herd of cattle to Pendleton County, West Virginia and "I Sold a Load of crocks we had along with us." Pottery was also sometimes exchanged at the shop, but the extent or economic gain of this haphazard trading is not clear. Suter did not record these transactions with the systematicity with which he inventoried most of his transactions with merchants. It would seem that both this scattered bartering and regional exchange were organizations of his traditional operation that Suter did not abandon until the 1890s.

Factory Production

In 1890, land grant companies were formed in Harrisonburg, about 7 miles east of Suter's farm, and Broadway, a town about 20 miles north of Harrisonburg. The land grant companies were intended to promote economic growth in the valley by purchasing farmland and offering it to industrial investors free of charge. The land grant properties, which were located along rail lines at the edge of the towns, became home to two potteries in Harrisonburg and another in Broadway. In October 1890, investors from Trenton, New Jersey obtained a Harrisonburg charter for an industrial pottery known as the Virginia Pottery Company. The new pottery was described by the local newspaper as a "$20,000 concern" that primarily produced molded Rockingham-glazed earthenwares. The New Jersey-owned pottery was established on an adjoining lot to the future location of Emanuel Suter's Harrisonburg Steam Pottery, chartered in June 1890. Although Suter apparently had no interest in moving his farm pottery, he was persuaded by other investors to relocate to a lot on the rail lines. In addition to the two Harrisonburg potteries, the Broadway Porcelain Manufacturing Company was established in Broadway in 1891. Formed by Albert Radford, a potter who had previously worked in factories in New Jersey and Baltimore, the Broadway pottery produced refined white earthenware and art pottery (Radford n.d.:2).

The new Suter pottery was primarily administered by his family, but the Harrisonburg operation was quite different from the farm pottery. Although Suter continued to farm, the new pottery consumed much more of his time than the farm pottery had, primarily because it was more complex technically and administratively and it was not located on the farm. Suter was often forced to have extended kin manage the farm while he supervised at the pottery. Previously, he had been able to perform both of these administrative roles. Suter also became involved in very different manager-worker relationships that emphasized contractual obligations rather than the social obligations that Suter had with his sons and farmhands. Although Suter's relationship with consumers had distanced after the war, within his work force of extended kin and neighbors relations had generally remained quite cohesive. In the new pottery, however, Suter became distanced from his work force as well as consumers. For example, Suter had a neighbor, Adam Linhoss, sign an agreement on February 2, 1891 to build the Harrisonburg pottery shop that month; on the 11th, however, Suter noted that he "had expected that A Linhoss would be [at the pottery site] with his hands to commence work on our shop but for Some Cause failed to be there I came home this evening I confess not very well pleased."

Manager-laborer agreements such as this one were unstable in the new pottery, a reflection of an emerging conception of distinct social and labor identities. In barter exchange networks, in contrast, an individual's identity as a laborer and a social actor could not be detached as separate identities. Suter, like most members of his community, perceived individual identity as a complex interplay of labor and social roles. John Heatwole, for example, was known as "Potter John" throughout his life; his identity as a laborer was fundamental to his social identity and naming. In an agrarian community, individuals wished to be seen as farmers, but Suter was not simply concerned that he be represented as a farmer; his deeper concern was instead to fulfill expected social roles, both as a laborer and community member. Work, from this perspective, was crucial to defining identity in an agrarian exchange network, and this identity carried with it social obligations between individuals who perceived themselves as both social actors and laborers. But as laborers in Suter's pottery became abstractly defined workers with no tangible social relation to the administrator, the social obligations attendant to labor became insubstantial; the obligations between administrator and laborer became oriented to relations in the workplace alone, and the absence of social obligations demanded quite explicit codification of labor obligations.

Prior to his move to Harrisonburg, Suter had conceived of the exchange of his labor as a transaction that involved both his identity as a social actor and a laborer (i.e., his pottery). In July 1879, for instance, Suter wrote to his son Reuben to deduct the cost of 20 gallons of ware from a merchant's bill. The merchant had been unsatisfied with the ware, and Suter instructed his son to "make the best settlement you can so as not to give hard thoughts would rather loos a little than to give offence...do not give offence [sic]."

In the Harrisonburg factory individuals became more closely valued with the time that they supplied in the production process. The individual as a distinctly skilled laborer was no longer prominent in the operation; instead, a few skilled workers trained and administered semiskilled laborers, who were paid by their time on a task. These laborers had significantly less socially invested in their identities as kiln-setters or glazers. They also were involved in manager-laborer relations, which were made explicitly hierarchical by contractual obligation. Barter exchange, on the other hand, had been a less explicit interaction of dominance, because each transactor had a distinctive skill or product whose value was recognized by each transactor. Because social relationships had become less tangible by the 1890s, the relationships between managers and laborers were perceived as needing explicit organization. Transactor relationships and their mutual obligations became more intangible over time, and the socially based verbal agreements of barter exchange were replaced by the "concrete" relationships defined by contracts.

The Harrisonburg pottery clearly had less reliance on both the local population and local resources than the farm pottery had. Several of the skilled potters from Suter's farm pottery joined Suter at his new operation, but much of the labor and technical base for the operation came from outside the community. Suter contracted with a kiln engineer from New Jersey, John Hawthorn, to direct the kiln construction, the same engineer who had directed construction of the Virginia Pottery Company's kiln. The kilns that Hawthorn engineered for both potteries were certainly downdraft rather than updraft kilns, a design with more consistent temperature control and economic fuel consumption than an updraft kiln (Olsen 1973:54). Suter was aware of such technical advances in ceramic production and incorporated many of them into his Harrisonburg operation. During an 1890 visit to potteries in West Virginia and Ohio that Suter reported to his sons, Suter was astonished that "the A.P. Donagho and Sons Pottery" in Parkersburg, West Virginia was "still grinding clay with horse useing the common pug mill...turning ware with kicking wheel...useing up draft kilns...[and] set ware in the old Style," technologies that Suter himself had abandoned in the Harrisonburg pottery. Suter also hired several turners from Harrisburg, Pennsylvania on the advice of F. H. Cowden, and Cowden recommended wage rates, kiln technologies, and equipment and clay sources. Along with this technical counsel came business advice; in April 1891, for example, Cowden cautioned Suter in regard to testing new clays that "you have a new enterprise and should take no more risks than is absolutely necessary at the start." In April 1891 Suter went to Pennsylvania and

New Jersey and visited several suppliers of clay, machinery, and supplies, and he was using many of these supplies at the new pottery within a few months. Some of the technical changes at the Harrisonburg pottery produced considerable trouble, though; for example, the shift to coal as kiln fuel was standard in industrial potteries (Faulkner 1982:231), but for Suter it proved less predictable than wood fuel. The first kiln load at the pottery, which was removed from the kiln on June 29, 1891, was "an earthen ware kiln it turned out pretty well burned most too hard."

The degree of family control over the new pottery as a business was significantly diminished by nonpotters who were either members of the pottery's board of directors or stockholders in the company, and several of these individuals were not from the community. The control of the family and extended kin network was also diminished by the pottery's location outside both the immediate neighborhood of the labor force and the backyard of the principal administrator. Suter's records reflect that under this direction the pottery more aggressively became a business interested in attracting a clientele outside the region. In 1894, for example, Suter recorded sales in New York, New Jersey, Pennsylvania, and Maryland.

In the short run, the organization was apparently quite profitable; by September 1891, Suter already noted "quite a demand for ware," and the capital stock in the company rose to $20,000 in 1892. The cost of shipping long distance via rail, however, required that Suter sell large amounts of ware to realize a reasonable profit. The same rail lines that opened up markets for Suter's relatively small pottery were opening up the local market for industrial goods as well. The impact of rail shipping had been delayed through much of the South by the Civil War, but industry was soon able to ship an abundance of products throughout most of the country. Industrial potteries were able to ship cheap coarsewares to a rapidly expanding area; in 1885, for example, a local retailer complained to Suter that the price of flower pots from the Baltimore factory of Edwin Bennett was "significantly decreased from yours." An administrator of the new Broadway Pottery commented that the only drawback of that operation was "some enormous freight bills," freight bills that made it extremely difficult for the valley potteries to be price competitive with northern potteries.

Industry's greater impact on potting, however, was the profusion of material goods it made available to consumers. In place of coarseware storage vessels, glassworks began to offer cheap glass jars, tin-contained goods were becoming more common, and finer ceramic bodies, such as yellow ware, were steadily decreasing in cost. The introduction of refrigerated rail cars also increased the market availability of many perishable goods that had previously been stored in coarsewares. But the

189

market also became an increasingly rich source of a wide range of mass-produced goods; these goods functioned as symbolic status markers in a population that had been socially unstable and economically impoverished since at least the Civil War. Before the Civil War, the restricted hierarchies, great distance between social groups, and limited access to mass-produced material goods had minimized the manipulation of material goods as symbolic status markers; instead, property had functioned in that role. But as farming gradually decreased in significance and industrial products became quite common and inexpensive in the region, the possession of material status markers became progressively more ordinary in Rockingham County. This significantly affected the demand for coarsewares and other utilitarian craft products. Those goods became explicitly peripheral to mass-produced products, which at that time had a richer range of symbolical meanings than craft goods.

In part, the pottery did not become a more vigorous economic force because of the fortunes of the community's other industrial institutions; the land grant boom was short lived, and many of the land grant investors had already filed for bankruptcy in 1891. The Broadway Porcelain Manufacturing Company closed in the mid-1890s, and the Virginia Pottery Company would also close in the late 1890s (Mullins 1986). Suter's pottery continued to be profitable into the late 1890s, but it never became a major economic force in either the community or region.

Suter began to withdraw from the day-to-day operation of the pottery quite soon after it opened. His 223 diary entries in 1891 mentioning the pottery sharply decreased to 90 in 1892 and 103 in 1893. For reasons that he did not explicitly articulate, after 1891 Suter rapidly relinquished much of his control in the operation to his sons. Rather than being a day-to-day administrator, Suter redefined his role and became a visitor who participated in board meetings and occasionally participated in production. Suter's participation also became more specialized; instead of turning crocks all day, Suter would balance ledgers, turn specialized vessel forms (such as large jars), or perform skilled tasks, such as evaluating clay or administering the kiln. The diary entries referring to the operation of the pottery were most often passive commentaries on the maintenance of the operation, not references to his active technical or organizational administration of the pottery. Initially, Suter apparently perceived the control of the pottery as shifting from him to his sons. When mentioning the pottery in his diary after 1891, Suter most commonly referred to what his sons were doing in the pottery, not his own active participation. In July 1896, for example, a Suter diary entry noted that "Swope is with us tonight, he brought with him Several very Small Jars with his white glaze on, they are just fine." In this instance, the vessels were referred to as Swope's, not as that of Suter or *his* pottery.

Previously, Suter had referred to the pottery and its products as either his or his family's; e.g., in September 1866 he noted that "This forenoon we laid off my potter kiln." From Suter's perspective, control of the operation apparently was intended to shift from Suter, to Suter and his sons together, to his sons alone.

Between 1893 and 1897, Suter's commentaries on the pottery decreased dramatically, and he began to use the diary to record his revitalized social interaction, particularly in the church community. What appears in his diaries as an effort to establish closer social ties within the community was comparable to his post-Civil War redefinition of social relations and the prominent social profile Suter maintained after the war. Apparently each instance represented a dramatic change in social relations as Suter perceived them; after the war, Suter significantly changed the exchange relationship yet maintained community cohesion through prominent social roles; in the mid-1890s Suter withdrew from a wide community and most of the production and consumption process to establish a restricted range of closer social relations. The pottery apparently became his sons' operation, so the diary ceased to function as a mechanism for organizing Suter's own understandings of the operation. For Suter this essentially signaled the end of his participation in the pottery, because he could no longer give the operation a coherent meaning. The fundamental elements that had defined Suter's operation were gone: e.g., administrative control, the pottery's role as a family operation, his relationship with workers, and consumer demand had all shifted dramatically and irrevocably.

In January 1897 Suter and his sons met in Harrisonburg to balance the pottery's books for the year, but they found major inconsistencies with their ledgers and those of the company's secretary, John Roller. The books had apparently been tampered with by Roller, who had disrupted the business and technical operation of the pottery from the outset. This incident would rapidly lead to the financial collapse of Suter's pottery; however, his diary contains no reference to any of the events leading up to his withdrawal from the business later that year. Interpersonal conflict, such as that between the Suters and Roller, was a topic that virtually never appeared in the diaries, because Suter used his diary to give the community social coherence. From Suter's perspective, this coherence was a shared understanding of the implicit obligations in social relationships, such as those he had with his extended kin, members of his church, and neighbors. Consequently, the diaries are full of references to activities between Suter and these people with whom he had a clear sense of social obligations. Other relationships could be made explicit, such as those he had with his laborers or merchants, because of a shared understanding of the possible sets of obligations that could be agreed upon between them. The ledgers and letters were the primary forum in which Suter ordered these relationships.

But Roller's deception was irreconcilable with this order of mutual social obligations. When Suter could not give coherence to an incompatible set of social values, he apparently did not comment on them in the diary; when he did, he attempted to translate them into values to which he could give meaning. For example, Suter commented on January 19, 1891 that he and his son John were at the new pottery "Seeing where it would be best to locate our cistern...great many people in town...many I noticed were intoxicated O Lord when will this evil be Staid [emphasis in original]." In this instance, the drunk people in the crowd were not fulfilling their obligation within a disciplined social order, whereas Suter and his sons were working, which they saw as the expected social role. Events and moralities such as this were incompatible with Suter's understanding of social order, so they typically occurred outside his text, which bounded that social world.

Suter sold his share of the pottery to Roller on April 10, 1897 for $2000, a significant financial loss, simply commenting in his diary that "This releves me of further trouble whit that works [sic]." In May, 1897 Suter commented in the diary that his sons Reuben and Swope had been contracted to run the operation, but the pottery rapidly declined and closed before the turn of the century. Roller and his brother John, who had served as a member of the pottery's board, later purchased the abandoned Virginia Pottery Company and Broadway pottery, and converted each to the production of industrial porcelains. This venture, the Adamant Porcelain Company, ended its operation before 1910 (Mullins 1986:21), essentially drawing to a close the county's ceramic industry.

Suter dictated diary entries up until a few days before his death in 1902. On December 16, 1902 Suter died of Bright's Disease, an affliction that may have been promoted by his long-term exposure to lead. The obituary in the local newspaper did not mention Suter's career as a potter, and a thorough obituary in the Mennonite yearbook remarked only that "In connection with active farm work here, he was, also for many years, engaged in operating on an extensive scale the pottery plant established on his farm" (Heatwole 1906:31). Although he is today best known as an artisan, contemporary obituaries instead focused on Suter as he represented himself in his diary and wished to be seen in his community — as a farmer and a devoted church member.

Summary

Emanuel Suter's diaries and business records represent industrialization as an active process that involved continual definition of a complex social structure and his roles in it. From this perspective, industrialization was a process in which Suter understood the society of the 19th-century Shenandoah Valley through *active* nego-tiation within a *bounded* production and consumption process. Suter actively assessed industrial organization and incorporated what he perceived as its most beneficial elements into a coherent local labor and social structure. This continual negotiation involved both Suter's direction and rejection of structures of industrial culture, and it was this negotiation that defined how he perceived his world. Text was a prominent means by which Suter organized his conscious perceptions of how this social structure was bounded.

Despite the extensive changes he made in his pottery after the Civil War, Suter's potteries do not fit well into the typical interpretive definitions of industry, i.e., mass-production factories that dominated organizations of economic exchange, labor and class relations, and material culture. Nevertheless, Suter's comparably restricted potteries accommodated a wide range of the characteristic elements of industrial organization. The labor and social organization of Suter's operation reflects that he was not simply a consumer of industrial technology, rather he was also a consumer of industrial social organizations. The segmentation promoted by industrialization was embraced by Suter in the standardization of the exchange relationship by price lists and second-person transaction; the production of standardized vessel forms and labor tasks with discrete functions and identifications; and a division of roles based on kin relations and explicitly articulated obligations between laborer and employer.

The reproduction of these organizations in Suter's pottery represent ways in which he actively probed how his farm pottery could be modified. This continual evaluation illustrates that Suter was not simply overwhelmed by industrialization, rather he made labor, technical, and organizational modifications that he felt would not violate the coherence of the operation. Text functioned at the boundaries of this coherence by identifying those very boundaries and defining them in terms coherent to Suter (e.g., space, time, social groups).

Suter clearly embraced industrial organizations quite rapidly following the war, particularly the machinery of industry, but he did not see technology or these organizational strategies as themselves divisive. Suter instead saw organizations such as the standardization that accompanied technology as distinct elements in the total structure of production, exchange, and consumption. In this sense, he considered the relations of the mechanisms of industry (e.g., machines and marketing strategies) as only giving the production and consumption process an identity when taken as a whole. From this perspective, the "jigger" mold, price lists, and mass shipping strategies could be accommodated within many different labor and social organizations of production and consumption, from mass-production factories to barnyard potteries, and they clearly were.

The crucial element of Suter's organization was that social, geographical, and technological borders confined production and consumption and gave potting a coherent meaning for Suter despite change. For example, Suter accommodated technological change to the operation by situating new machinery within his own production organization; Suter's family administration of the pottery secured it as a supplemental resource base and gave it a vital role in the life of his family until the 1890s; geographically as well as socially, exchange and consumption of Suter products was confined within space and social groups. These organizations were all boundaries within which the roles of the potter were well defined.

Suter violated these boundaries in the 1890s by marketing ware over a wide area, adopting unfamiliar technologies, and relinquishing total administrative and technical control of the pottery, and he was forced to dramatically redefine his role in the pottery and the role of the pottery itself. The redefinition after the Civil War had also been quite dramatic, but it had not been a complete reorganization of the system that regulated pottery production, exchange, and consumption; in contrast, the redefinition had been coherent because Suter had accommodated elements of industrial organization to his farm pottery's clearly defined organization of production and consumption relations. During the 1890s, the role of the pottery became difficult for Suter to define, since it dramatically violated the limitations of multiple boundaries that framed Suter's understandings of his world.

The extension of the operation and the related reorganization of production and consumption relations was as fragmenting for Suter as it was for any factory worker leaving cottage industries or subsistence farming. These potters were not simply unable to economically compete with northern factory potteries, rather the rapidity of change left producers and consumers so disoriented that they were defamiliarized to both new and old labor and social organizations. Suter himself responded to this 1890s defamiliarization by withdrawing into a social circle with very well-defined boundaries (i.e., the local Mennonite community), in which social roles and relationships were well defined.

Consequently, Suter withdrew from the pottery trade because he could no longer give pottery production and consumption meaning. The administrative control he had over the pottery was gone; the operation's crucial role as a family operation was shattered; his relationships with workers and merchants were tenuous; and the consumer demand for pottery and other material goods had shifted dramatically. The crucial elements that had given coherence to the pottery for Suter were given a completely new meaning by the Harrisonburg operation and its industrial organization.

The archaeological record of industrialization is quite comparable to the textual record. Each reflects how Suter perceived and responded to imperatives to change his production and distribution process. Taken together, the two resources reflect that Suter responded to a wide range of factors: technological change, social fragmentation, and so on. The influences Suter faced were distinctively regional, social, and temporal, making his understanding of industrialization itself distinctive. Nevertheless, the process by which Suter tried to understand and direct this change was quite comparable to the manner in which other traditional craft producers and consumers responded to pervasive social changes. The changes that confronted Emanuel Suter in rural Virginia in the 1860s were not at all unlike the changes faced by traditional potters in the urban Northeast after the Revolution or in early 20th-century Georgia (Burrison 1983). These producers and consumers actively constructed distinct yet comparable understandings of industrialization, stimulating the expansion of the industrial market into other aspects of their daily social lives and material culture.

Text was used not simply to organize the mechanics of Emanuel Suter's pottery, rather it was a stable forum in which he bound and defined his community's social structure, his social role, and his role as a potter. These records reflect that Suter actively directed, rejected, and subsequently gave meaning to the mechanisms and effects of industrialization, not that he was either overwhelmed by industrial change or that he passively adapted to those changes. Instead, he constructed a distinctive and active response to industrial change, just as countless other traditional crafts people did from the mid-18th to late-19th centuries. It is from both the distinctiveness and the active nature of these responses that increasingly sophisticated understandings of industrialization will emerge.

Acknowledgments

The Emanuel Suter papers, housed in Eastern Mennonite College's Menno Simons Library, were made available by Mary E. Suter. This paper grew out of a project by the Massanuten Chapter of the Archeological Society of Virginia; the research assistance of Eleanor Parslow and Janice Biller has contributed significantly to this work. Janice Bailey Goldschmidt, Mary Corbin Sies, Paul A. Shackel, and Barbara J. Little made helpful edits of various versions of this paper. Stan Kaufman and Kurt Russ shared much of their own research; many parts of this work would not be possible without their contributions.

References

Baudrillard, J. (1981) *For a Critique of the Political Economy of the Sign.* Telos Press, St. Louis, MO.

Brunk, H. A. (1959) *History of Mennonites in Virginia 1727–1900,* Vol. I. McClure Printing Company, Staunton, VA.

Burrison, J. (1983) *Brothers in Clay: The Story of Georgia Folk Pottery.* University of Georgia Press, Athens, GA.

Carr, M. R. (1967) "Potter" John Heatwole. *The Valley Mennonite Messenger.* January 5, 1967:1,4.

Faulkner, C. H. (1982) The Weaver Pottery: A Late Nineteenth-Century Family Industry in a Southeastern Urban Setting. In *The Archaeology of Urban America: The Search for Pattern and Process,* R. S. Dickens, Jr., Ed. Academic Press, New York, pp. 209–235.

Foucault, M. (1979) *Discipline and Punish: The Birth of the Prison.* Vintage Books, New York.

Heatwole, L. J. (1906) A sketch of the life and work of Emanuel Suter. *Mennonite Year-Book and Directory, A.D. 1906,* J. S. Shoemaker, Ed. Mennonite Board of Charitable Homes and Missions, pp. 31–32.

Kasson, J. F. (1984) Civility and Rudeness: Urban Etiquette and the Bourgeois Social Order in Nineteenth-Century America. *Prospects* 9:143–168.

— (1988) *Civilizing the Machine.* Penguin Books, New York.

Kaufman, S. A. (1978) *Heatwole and Suter Pottery.* Good Printers, Harrisonburg, VA.

Leone, M. P. (1988) The Georgian Order as the Order of Merchant Capitalism in Annapolis, Maryland. In *The Recovery of Meaning: Historical Archaeology in the Eastern United States,* M. P. Leone and P. B. Potter, Jr., Eds. Smithsonian Institution Press, Washington, D.C., pp. 235–261.

Marx, L. (1964) *The Machine in the Garden.* Oxford University Press, New York.

Mitchell, R. D. (1977) *Commercialism and Frontier: Perspectives on the Early Shenandoah Valley.* University of Virginia Press, Charlottesville, VA.

Mullins, P. R. (1986) Historic Pottery-Making in Rockingham County, Virginia. Paper presented at the Archeological Society of Virginia Spring Symposium, Charlottesville, VA.

Olsen, F. L. (1973) *The Kiln Book.* Keramos Books, Bassett, CA.

Paynter, R. (1988) Steps to an Archaeology of Capitalism: Material Change and Class Analysis. In *The Recovery of Meaning: Historical Archaeology in the Eastern United States,* M. P. Leone and P. B. Potter, Jr., Eds. Smithsonian Institution Press, Washington, D.C., pp. 407–433.

Radford, F. W. (n.d.) Family History. Unpublished manuscript in possession of author.

Rice, A. H. and J. B. Stoudt (1974) *The Shenandoah Pottery.* Reprinted. Originally published 1929, Virginia Book Company, Berryville, VA.

Russ, K. C. and J. McDaniel (1987) The Traditional Pottery Manufacturing Industry in Virginia: Examples from Botetourt and Rockbridge Counties, 1775–1894. Paper presented at the February 1987 meeting of the Rockbridge Historical Society, Lexington, VA.

Shackel, P. A. (1987) A Historical Archaeology of Personal Discipline. Ph.D. dissertation, State University of New York at Buffalo. University Microfilms, Ann Arbor, MI.

Smith, S. D. and S. T. Rogers (1979) *A Survey of Historic Pottery Making in Tennessee.* Research Series No. 3, Division of Archaeology. Tennessee Department of Conservation, Nashville, TN.

Steiner, K. (1977) A Study of the Business Letters Written to Emanuel Suter. Unpublished manuscript in possession of author.

Suter, E. (1865) Personal communication to unknown recipient, March 19, 1865. Manuscript, in possession of Stanley A. Kaufman.

Suter, M. E. (1959) *Memories of Yesteryear.* Charles F. McClung, Waynesboro, VA.

Worrell, J. (1982) Ceramic production in the exchange network of an agricultural neighborhood. In *Domestic Pottery of the Northeastern United States, 1625–1850,* S. P. Turnbaugh, Ed. Academic Press, Orlando, FL, pp. 153–169.

Zug, C. G. III (1986) *Turners and Burners: The Folk Potters of North Carolina.* University of North Carolina Press, Chapel Hill, NC.

15: Alternative Visions and Landscapes: Archaeology of the Shaker Social Order and Built Environment

Ellen-Rose Savulis

Department of Anthropology, University of Massachusetts, Amherst, Massachusetts

A growing number of archaeologists (e.g., Beaudry 1986, 1989; Harrington 1989; Leone 1984; Paynter et al., 1987; Praetzellis and Praetzellis 1989; Rubertone 1986, 1989) note that the built environment is much more than just the conscious manipulation of landscape and architectural designs. Historical landscapes are dynamic cultural artifacts that can legitimize or challenge social order (Gamble 1986; Rapaport 1982). One dimension of landscapes is the reflection of social power (Harvey 1976). In most contemporary societies the physical world, in conjunction with an ideology of inequality, serves to constrain women's access to goods, services, and spaces (McDowell 1983; Hayden 1981). Restriction of women to the "domestic sphere" and men to the "public sphere" intensified during the privatization of family life that coincided with capitalist industrialization in the 19th century (Cott 1977; Hayden 1981). Understanding how the built environment created and reflected a variety of local-level responses to this ideology of gender inequality remains an important challenge for historical archaeologists.

The public/private dichotomization of male and female space is also reflected in the ways past symbolic systems are depicted. Documents archaeologists use, such as maps, account books, and legal records, are neither gender nor value neutral. These traditional sources of documentation can be used in conjunction with alternative media, such as poetry and art, produced by women. The context of a 19th century utopian community illustrates both the diversity of perspectives and the utility of incorporating alternative media in interpretations of historic landscapes.

The Shakers: Historical Background

The formation of alternative communities played an important role in political theory and action in the 19th century. Religious groups, utopian and agrarian socialists, anarchists, as well as industrial capitalists, considered community-level social and economic relationships the most effective arena for social change (Bestor 1950; Cross 1950; Kanter 1972; Kern 1981; Loubere 1974). Hundreds of communities were designed and implemented in the U.S. and Europe to variously foster, or offer an alternative to, industrial capitalism. Their efforts centered on redesigning property, work, family, power, and gender relations. In many such communities, the behavior of members was controlled through a combination of distinct architectural designs and community plans, regulated work routines, and common religious tenets (Garner 1984:6, 10; Hayden 1976).

The most successful alternative community effort in the 19th-century U.S. was The Society of Believers in Christ's Second Appearing, or Shakers, who had their spiritual roots in the 18th-century European Pietist tradition, which professed separatism, equation of conversion with purification, and distinct spiritual and social laws for members. During their formative years, the Shakers were led by a female charismatic leader, Mother Ann Lee, who advocated withdrawal from the world, public confession, celibacy, gender equality, and the sacredness of labor (Schiffer 1979:5). Ann Lee and a small group of Dissenting Quaker followers moved from

Manchester, England to New York City in 1774. The group leased a farm near Albany, New York in 1776 and actively proselytized throughout New England during the Second Great Awakening of the 1780s (Marini 1982:77; Schiffer 1979:5).

Mother Ann's death in 1784 marked the beginning of Shakerism as a national communal society. Her successors — James Whittaker (lead elder, 1785 to 1787), Joseph Meacham (lead elder, 1787 to 1796), and Lucy Wright (lead eldress, 1796 to 1821) — were responsible for shaping a cohesive Shaker doctrine and introducing discipline and central organization to the movement (Brewer 1986:13). Their effective planning led to the formation of 19 communities extending from Maine to Kentucky and a membership of over 6000 by the 1850s (Schiffer 1979:7).

Joseph Meacham, a former New Light Baptist minister from New Lebanon, New York, is credited with formalizing Mother Ann's teachings on gender, family, work, and property relations, as well as designing a Shaker spiritual hierarchy. Mother Ann's view that the sexes were separate but equal was reflected in his vision of a universal kingdom of spiritual beings ruled jointly by Jesus and Mother Ann. This spirit community was divided into male and female hierarchies of faith (Marini 1982:153).

Meacham's design of the Shaker spiritual world was mirrored in the physical and socioeconomic organization of their communities. He designed a model community divided into three orders separated by age and length of membership. These orders formed a hierarchy based on spiritual merit. The Gospel Order included the most recent converts — those most encumbered by worldly experiences. The Novitiate Order, one step up the spiritual ladder, was followed by the Church Order, which consisted of the members of greatest faith (Marini 1982:128).

Each order was conceptualized as a metaphorical "family," and served as the basic unit of social reproduction. (By the mid-19th century each family group generally consisted of 30 to 100 "brothers" and "sisters," who pooled resources and worked collectively.) Families were physically distinct in terms of their dwellings, shops, and fields, but were dependent on each other for spiritual guidance and material assistance. Each family kept their own accounts and conducted their own business, but all communally owned property was held in the name of the Church Family trustees (Nordhoff 1875:140).

Each family in a Shaker village had a gender-balanced power hierarchy. Specialized officers included elders and eldresses, who dealt with spiritual concerns, and deacons and deaconesses, who managed industrial and craft production. Both groups answered to the Church Family ministers, who visited the head community at New Lebanon each year in order to receive economic advice and notice of ritual and doctrinal changes (Marini 1982:133; Nordhoff 1875:139).

In a demographic study of the New Lebanon Church Family, Priscilla Brewer (1986:210) notes that the adult male/female ratio dramatically changed throughout the 19th century. In 1791 there were 101 men and 86 women in the household. By 1800 the ratio was reversed with 88 women and 61 men. In 1865 women began to outnumber men 2:1. In the first half of the 19th century, Brewer (1986:115) also documents a growing number of children and young adults, accompanied by a decrease in the pool of candidates qualified to be spiritual leaders. This pattern was present in all 19th-century Shaker communities. These demographic changes had profound effects on Shaker social and economic organization, spiritual concerns, as well as power and gender relations.

By the late 1830s an economic, spiritual, and social crisis existed in the Shaker movement (Brewer 1986:115). This was a period marked by high apostasy rates, and legal cases involving former members seeking portions of the communal property as payment for their labor, as well as custody of their children living in Shaker communities. A religious revival known as "Mother's Work" began in 1837 when a group of young girls at the Watervliet, New York community started receiving spiritual visitations from Mother Ann, and it quickly spread to other villages. By 1841 communities were performing elaborate cleaning and fasting rituals for the visitations of Holy Mother Wisdom. During the revival, Shaker women produced an elaborate series of drawings depicting spiritual landscapes (Andrews 1969; Patterson 1983).

The Mother's Work revival represented a potential challenge to the legitimacy of the Shaker status quo, because the "instruments" (e.g., those receiving spiritual messages) and the lead ministry both saw themselves sanctified by divine inspiration (Stein 1988). The lead ministry responded by seeking to control the content and legitimacy of the spiritual messages. They prohibited public access to meetings, edited spiritual texts, and enforced tougher regulations on behavior. This control created divisions between the old and the young, male and female, and spiritual leaders and followers (Stein 1988).

By the 1860s the revival had died out, marking the beginning of the end for the Shaker movement. Recruitment dwindled, vast landholdings were sold, outside male laborers and farm managers were hired, and eventually most communities closed. By 1925 only 6 of the 19 original communities remained active (Emlen 1987:182). Today, only two Shaker villages remain, with a handful of members, at Sabbathday Lake, Maine and Canterbury, New Hampshire.

Shaker Gender Ideology

The Shakers professed gender equality in their communities by challenging the traditional male hierarchical structure of the family with a system of dual male/female leadership in both temporal and spiritual affairs. Interpretations of this duality led to extreme efforts to create separate physical worlds for men and women. *A List of Rules and Orders for the Protection of Believers in Christ Second Appearing* states "when any of the brethren or sisters go abroad, it must (be) by permission of the Elders, and without such permission they ought not to go off of the farm; nor sisters many rods from the dwellings" (Anonymous n.d.:3) A 19th-century visitor to the New Lebanon, New York community observed the following:

> Shaker men and women do not shake hands with each other; their lives have almost no privacy; even to the elders, of whom two always room together; the sexes even eat apart; they worship standing and marching apart; they visit each other only at stated intervals and according to a prescribed order; and in all things the sexes maintain a certain distance and reserve toward each other (Nordhoff 1875:66).

Brethren were allowed to "range at pleasure" in areas designated as male spaces (Nordhoff 1875:176), whereas women were more confined to the private realm and the responsibilities of providing food, clothing, health care, and child care. For example, by 1800 at the Canterbury, New Hampshire Church Family, areas closest to Shaker road, and hence the outside world, were reserved for male and secular activities. Female areas and those of religious significance, such as the meeting house, were furthest away. The areas controlled by Shaker brethren included their shop, where small-scale craft production occurred, a wheel shop, tan house, blacksmith shop, herb garden, agricultural fields, and outlying mills. Female work areas consisted of a spin shop, wash house, vegetable garden (if the produce was for Shaker consumption), seed garden, and dwelling houses. Women's activities appear to have been monitored or protected by the placement of these spaces near the meeting house and ministry work shop. Such differential treatment of male and female space suggests that men's work often articulated with the outside world, and women's consisted primarily of daily reproducing the "family" inside the boundaries of the community.

Symbolic Representations

The Shakers went to great lengths to create separate physical worlds for men and women. The ways in which each gender depicted familiar landscapes differed in content and media presentation. Men produced detailed maps of communities, whereas women wrote poetry describing building interiors and painted spiritual landscapes and dwellings.

MAPS

A unique series of village plans were compiled by Shaker male cartographers during the first half of the 19th century. These maps served as planning tools for new communities (Emlen 1987). They ensured conformity of architectural design and village layout, and thus facilitated the reproduction of orthodox Shaker spiritual and economic values across space and through time. These maps also kept the central ministry at New Lebanon, New York informed about the growth of other communities (Emlen 1987:33)

A lot of architectural information can be obtained from such maps, but they provide little information on the careful land-use practices for which the Shakers are best known. For example, a map of the Church Family at Hancock, Massachussetts dating to 1820 only identifies structures, specifically those where rituals were held, children socialized, and manufacturing and craft production took place (Figure 1). When the map is closely examined, minute architectural details are visible, including the shapes of roofs, fenestration, and the placement of chimneys and doorways. The map does not identify outlying fields, gardens, activity areas outside of buildings, pathways, or natural landscape features.

No complete sequence of maps was ever compiled for even a single community. Many were altered by unknown censors at later dates. These modifications included the erasure of colorful embellishments and evidence of sacred spaces created during the Mother's Work revival.

POETRY

In contrast to the public domain of the men, Shaker women's spaces included places where they foraged for or grew food stuffs or dyeing materials, and the interiors of dwelling houses where daily reproductive activities took place. *A Journal of Domestic Events and Transactions* (Anonymous 1868) recorded by the deaconesses of the Second Order at the New Lebanon, New York community records minute, yet apparently critical, alterations to interiors, including new storage areas, additions, maintenance activities, and changes in the function of rooms over time. Deaconesses also used poetry to discuss women's spaces and the labor they performed there. For example, in January of 1851, an unnamed deaconess from the Second Order wrote the following poem illustrated in Figure 2.

> The new year hath already witnessed the industry of our little circle, and thus doth she explain, while tripping from room to room, beaming with energy, life and enterprise. The Elder Sisters first we view, Plying their needles thro' and thro' Forming the Shirts and shoes anew And mending *old ones* weekly. Physicians next, with fingers light, Crimping the paper day and night, That those fine jars be done just right, to *heal*, not *kill* the sickly. Sometimes they've more than they can do, to pack the snuff and powders too, Then others go and help them thro' Thus keep the business stirring. But stop! we've missed an important door, Which should have grac'd our

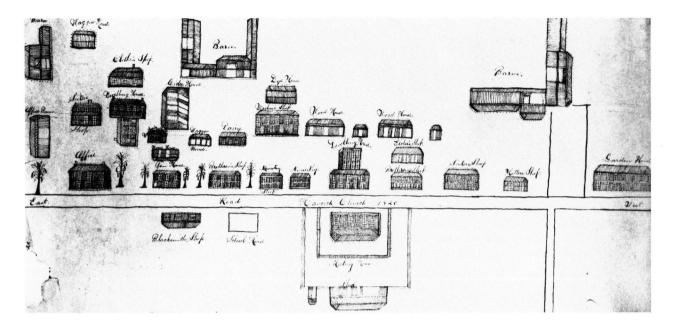

FIG. 1. The Church Family at Hancock (Anonymous 1820). Courtesy of Hancock Shaker Village, Inc., Pittsfield, MA.

lines before The industrious, well known clothing store, A very useful calling. Now to the south we'll take a trip, And if you choose just take a sip In Mary's pantry, well equipt, With much that is refreshing. Here cheese and butter we are told, Is made in scores of many fold. And when preserved from must and mold, Is most delicious eating. Then up the stairs we'll hasten on, Where sewing, spinning both are done. And ragged boys with garments warm, are *here* both made and mended. Now to the north we will proceed, And bless the cooks in very deed, For they have many mouths to feed, Or *some* will be offended. Next up the hill, to the left we'll turn, And enter in the first south room. Here spinning, weaving both are done, With linen wheel and ginny. Now to the north room we'll repair, which might be termed a yearly fair Where all may come and claim a share, With neither price or money. Upstairs we see the little ones, Spinning with zeal their trimming looms. While knitting fills the vacant room, That none be slack or lazy. Next to the wood house, last of all, Upstairs before you make a call, Here you will find a spacious hall. With inmates bright and merry, glowing with money'd enterprise, The loom and needle nimbly flies, This makes the Deacon's spirit rise, with liberal approbation.

Phrases such as "to the south," "to the north," and "up the hill" suggest traveling over a much larger landscape that just the dwelling house described where the women lived and worked (Figure 3). This poem provides information on the location and function of rooms within the dwelling house, distribution of clothing and other personal items, as well as the importance of cooperative work arrangements. It informs us that the sisters, with the help of young girls, manufactured cloth and clothing, put up medicinal herbs, and produced food for the family. The poem also suggests that the sisters were involved in the production of goods for sale to the outside world (possibly rag rugs).

Deaconesses' journals were secular, public documents that were reviewed, and occasionally edited, by superiors. Controversial events, if mentioned at all, were cryptically recorded or written in code (Brewer 1986:84). This poem can be considered a sanctioned, verbal map of the interior of the Second Order's dwelling house. The sisters' use of space and their reproductive activities conformed to Shaker order, and thus the poem may have served a planning function for other households.

SPIRIT DRAWINGS

In contrast to the maps of Shaker villages produced by men throughout the 19th century, Shaker women produced drawings and paintings during the Mother's Work revival between 1837 and the 1850s. These drawings were received from the spirit world through dreams or while in trances or states of possession (Patterson 1983:xi–xii) and depicted images of spiritual instead of physical landscapes. They were carefully planned and contained central symbols with accompanying texts. They ranged from cutouts of leaves and hearts to large colored drawings that incorporated visual motifs from the outside world, such as quilt patterns (Patterson 1983:21; Procter-Smith 1985:202). This art form was very private in nature. Spirit drawings were never circulated or displayed (Andrews 1969:56).

Spiritual homes were a common theme in their illustrations. The Shakers considered working and worshiping as interchangeable activities. This enabled Shaker women to treat dwelling houses as both places to reproduce their households, and also as sacred spaces. For example, a drawing entitled *A Present from Mother Lucy to Eliza Ann Taylor* (Reed 1849) depicts a spiritual

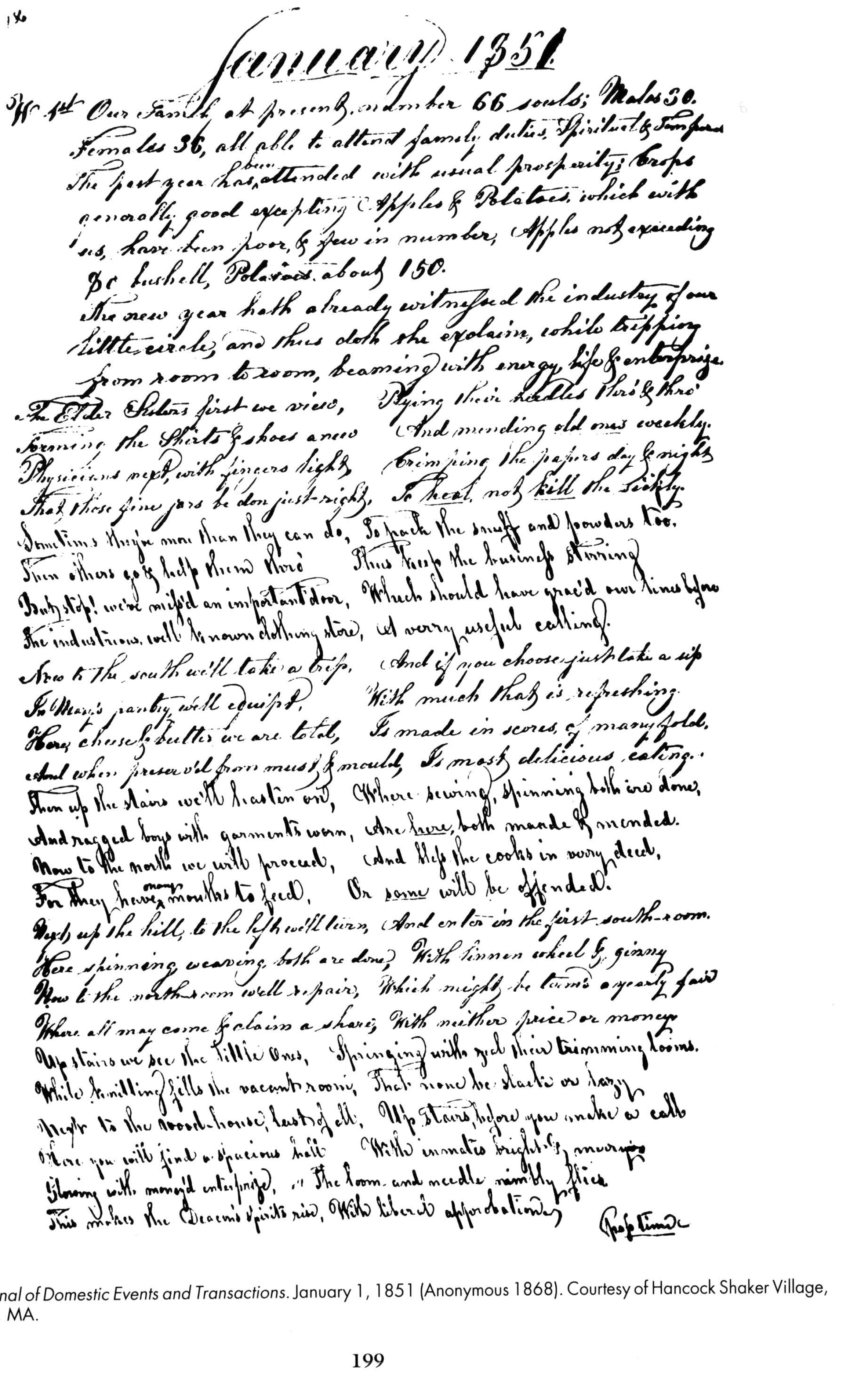

January 1851

Jan 1st Our Family at present, number 66 souls; Males 30.
Females 36, all able to attend family duties, Spiritual & Temporal
The past year has been attended with usual prosperity; Crops
generally good excepting Apples & Potatoes, which with
us, have been poor, & few in number; Apples not exceeding
80 bushell, Potatoes about 150.
The new year hath already witnessed the industry of our
little circle; and thus doth she explain, while tripping
from room to room, beaming with energy, life & enterprize.

The Elder Sisters first we view,   Plying their needles thro' & thro'
Forming the Shirts & shoes anew   And mending old ones weekly.
Physicians next, with fingers slight,   Crimping the papers day & night,
That these fine jobs be don just-right,   To heal, not kill the Sickly.
Sometimes they're more than they can do, To pack the snuff and powders too.
Then others go & help them thro'   Thus keep the business stirring
But stop! we've missed an important door, Which should have grac'd our lines before
The industrious, well known clothing store, A very useful calling.
Now to the south we'll take a trip,   And if you choose, just take a sip
To Mary's pantry well equip't,   With much that is refreshing.
Here, cheese & butter we are told,   Is made in scores, of many fold,
And when preserv'd from must & mould,   Is most delicious eating.
Then up the stairs we'll hasten on,   Where sewing, spinning both are done,
And ragged boys with garments worn,   Are here, both made & mended.
Now to the north we will proceed,   And bless the cooks in very deed,
For they have many mouths to feed,   Or some will be offended.
Next up the hill, to the left we'll turn, And enter in the first south-room,
Here spinning weaving, both are done,   With linnen wheel & jinny
Now to the north room well repair,   Which might be term'd a yearly fair
Where all may come & claim a share,   With neither price or money
Up stairs we see the little Ones,   Springing with yet their trimming looms.
While knitting fills the vacant room,   That none be slack or lazy
Next to the wood-house, last of all,   Up stairs, before you make a call
There you will find a spacious hall   With inmates brightly moving
Glowing with moral enterprize,   The loom and needle nimbly flies,
This makes the Deacons spirits rise,   With liberal approbation.

FIG. 2. *A Journal of Domestic Events and Transactions.* January 1, 1851 (Anonymous 1868). Courtesy of Hancock Shaker Village, Inc., Pittsfield, MA.

FIG. 3. The Second Order Dwelling House, Mount Lebanon (New Lebanon), NY. Courtesy of Hancock Shaker Village, Inc., Pittsfield, MA.

dwelling surrounded by such things as a sprig from an olive tree, the trumpet of wisdom, and a flower of love and purity (Figure 4) (Andrews 1969:109). The accompanying text at the center bottom reads:

> Come saith Wisdom, for I have formed thee a dwelling; and placed thine eye upon it. And from thee sequestered shades of death, my ministering Angels shall gather many souls, whom I shall call upon thee to feed and clothe, and give them where to lay their heads in peace. I shall call upon thee to feed them with Wisdom & understanding, and truth shall blossom in their souls, & they shall bring forth good fruits in abundance. You shall be their Shepard & they shall be my people saith WISDOM.

Discussion

The Shaker movement produced a wide variety of historical texts that document daily and seasonal communal activities. These range from periodicals sanctioned by the lead ministry at New Lebanon, New York to ministerial correspondence, legal and disciplinary accounts, work journals, account books, and personal diaries. These texts can be grouped into two general categories: public documents, those generally available to the membership at large; and private records, such as ministerial journals and diaries. Numerous voices and concerns are heard in these texts. The ministry was concerned with intracommunity economic and spiritual issues and maintaining the Shaker order. Elders and eldresses emphasized spiritual and behavioral matters at the level of the household. Deacons and deaconesses recorded daily and seasonal productive and reproductive activities. Individuals discussed how events in their communities affected them on a personal level.

All of these documents have significant limitations for interpreting the historical landscape of the Shakers. For example, in the early 19th century, the Shakers prohibited the keeping of personal journals. Many of those that were kept in later years were burned when the owner died to prevent them from falling into the hands of outsiders. Thus, serious gaps exist in personal records of daily activities and events. Daybooks and work journals emphasize particular gender-specific activities, such as farming or dyeing cloth. Those compiled by sisters limit their discussion of brethren's work and vice versa.

Hidden within these texts are distinct male and female voices that record the extensive efforts taken to enforce celibacy among the membership. In their efforts to create a world in which the sexes were separate but equal, the Shakers created villages in which men and women had differential access to resources and spaces. Ironically, this system mirrored the social and economic relationships in the outside world that the Shakers tried to challenge.

Shaker men and women depicted landscapes that differed in scale and content. Shaker brethren, when drawing maps of communities, illustrated the variety of spaces to which they had access. They also communicated the symbolic system of the movement's hierarchy. This suggests that, in spite of efforts to maintain a gender-balanced power structure, the movement was dominated by male leadership. These maps convey specific community planning strategies. The dichotomy between the secular, outside world and the sacred, Shaker world was

FIG. 4. A *Present from Mother Lucy to Eliza Ann Taylor* (Reed 1849). Courtesy of Hancock Shaker Village, Inc., Pittsfield, MA.

reinforced by defining specific buildings as mediating spaces (Hayden 1976). The spiritual hierarchy of cooperative families was maintained by the distribution of buildings across space. Those on the outskirts of villages housed the least powerful members.

The poetry and drawings produced by Shaker sisters indicate that their accessible landscapes were confined to the spaces of the domestic realm. Their visions are smaller in scale, yet go beyond the earthly sphere. They incorporated metaphors derived from women's work to describe ideal sacred dwellings. This suggests that Shaker women generally had little input in community design, and only controlled spaces within and surrounding dwelling houses and female craft production areas. Interior architectural details, such as the location of closet space and shelving and the functions of rooms and their contents, may have been determined by the women of the household.

A comparison of alternative media produced by Shaker sisters with traditional documents produced by Shaker brethren illustrates that Shaker men and women had strikingly different worlds, and hence, landscapes. The contrast between male and female visions subverts the unified face conveyed to the public by Shaker society and at Shaker village museums today. Alternative media can depict the daily realities of people without voices in traditional documents. The visions and actions of women, children, the elderly, hired laborers, and outsiders contribute to our understanding of historical landscapes in this and other community contexts.

Acknowledgments

The author wishes to thank Robert F. W. Meader and Magda Gabor-Hotchkiss of Hancock Shaker Village, Inc., for assistance in researching and preparing this study. Robert W. Paynter and David Glyn Nixon of the Department of Anthropology, University of Massachusetts, Amherst and Barbara J. Little of the Department of Anthropology, University of Maryland, College Park provided encouragement and editorial assistance on this paper. This research was funded in part by a grant-in-aid of research from Sigma Xi.

References

Anonymous (n.d.) *A List of Rules and Orders for the Protection of Believers in Christ, Second Appearing.* Western Reserve Historical Society Shaker Collection, Cleveland, OH, Series I B, Vols. 26–27.

— (1820) *The Church Family at Hancock, Massachusetts.* Collection of the Hancock Shaker Village, Pittsfield, MA.

— (1868) *A Journal of Domestic Events and Transactions.* Manuscript on file at the Hancock Shaker Village, Pittsfield, MA.

Andrews, E. D. (1969) *Visions of the Heavenly Sphere.* The University Press of Virginia, Charlottesville, VA.

Beaudry, M. C. (1986) The Archaeology of Historic Land Use in Massachusetts. *Historical Archaeology* 20(2):38.

— (1989) The Lowell Boott Mills Complex and its Housing: Material Expressions of Corporate Ideology. *Historical Archaeology* 23(1):19.

Bestor, A. E. (1950) *Backwoods Utopias: The Sectarian and Owenite Phases of Communitarian Socialism in America, 1663–1829.* The University of Pennsylvania Press, Philadelphia, PA.

Brewer, P. J. (1986) *Shaker Communities, Shaker Lives.* The University Press of New England, Hanover, NH.

Cott, N. F. (1977) The Bonds of Womanhood. Yale University Press, New Haven, CT.

Cross, W. (1950) *The Burned-Over District: The Social and Intellectual History of Enthusiastic Religion in Western New York.* Cornell University Press, Ithaca, NY.

Emlen, R. P. (1987) *Shaker Village Views: Illustrated Maps and Landscape Drawings by Shaker Artists of the Nineteenth Century.* The University Press of New England, Hanover, NH.

Gamble, C. (1986) Archaeology, Geography and Time. *Progress in Human Geography* 11(2):227.

Garner, J. S. (1984) *The Model Company Town: Urban Design through Private Enterprise in Nineteenth Century New England.* University of Massachusetts Press, Amherst, MA.

Hardy, D. (1979) *Alternative Communities in Nineteenth Century England.* Longman, London.

Harrington, F. (1989) The Emergent Elite in Early 18th Century Portsmouth Society: The Archaeology of the Joseph Sherburne Houselot. *Historical Archaeology* 23(1):2.

Harvey, D. (1976) Labor, Capital, and Class Struggle around the Built Environment in Advanced Capitalist Societies. *Politics and Society* 6(3):265.

Hayden, D. (1976) *Seven American Utopias: The Architecture of Communitarian Socialism, 1790–1975.* Massachusetts Institute of Technology Press, Cambridge, MA.

— (1981) *The Grand Domestic Revolution.* Massachusetts Institute of Technology Press, Cambridge, MA.

Kanter, R. M. (1972) *Commitment and Community: Communes and Utopias in Sociological Perspective.* Harvard University Press, Cambridge, MA.

Kern, L. J. (1981) *An Ordered Love, Sex Roles and Sexuality in Victorian Utopias — the Shakers, the Mormons, and the Oneida Community.* University of North Carolina Press, Chapel Hill, NC.

Leone, M. (1984) Interpreting Ideology in Historical Archaeology: Using the Rules of Perspective in the William Paca Garden in Annapolis, Maryland. In *Ideology, Power and Prehistory,* D. Miller and C. Tilley, Eds. Cambridge University Press, Cambridge, MA, pp. 25–36.

Loubere, L. (1974) *Utopian Socialism: Its History Since 1800.* Schenkman Press, Cambridge, MA.

Marini, S. T. (1982) *Radical Sects of Revolutionary New England.* Harvard University Press, Cambridge, MA.

McDowell, L. (1983) Towards an Understanding of the Gender Division of Urban Space. *Environment and Planning: Society and Space* 1:59.

Nordhoff, C. (1875) *The Communistic Societies of the United States.* Harper Brothers, New York.

Patterson, D. W. (1983) *Gift Drawing and Gift Song: a Study of Two Forms of Shaker Inspiration*. The United Society of Shakers, Sabbathday Lake, ME.

Paynter, R., R. Reinke, and J. R. Garrison (1987) Vernacular Landscapes in Western Massachusetts. Paper presented at the 1987 Meeting of the Society for Historical Archaeology Conference on Historic and Underwater Archaeology, Savannah, Georgia.

Procter-Smith, M. (1985) *Women in Shaker Community and Worship, a Feminist Analysis of the Uses of Religious Symbolism*. The Edwin Mellen Press, Lewiston, NY.

Praetzellis, A. and M. Praetzellis (1989) "Utility and Beauty Should be One": The Landscape of Jack London's Ranch of Good Intentions. *Historical Archaeology* 23(1):33.

Rapaport, A. (1982) Sacred Places, Sacred Occasions and Sacred Environments. *Architectural Design* 52(9–10):75.

Reed, P. A. (1849) *A Present from Mother Lucy to Eliza Ann Taylor*. Collection of Hancock Shaker Village, Inc., Pittsfield, MA.

Rubertone, P. (1986) Historical Landscapes: Archaeology of Place and Space. *Man in the Northeast* 31:123.

— (1989) Historical Landscapes as Artifact: Comments on the Archaeological Use of Landscape Treatment in Social, Economic and Ideological Analysis. *Historical Archaeology* 23(1):50.

Schiffer, H. (1979) *Shaker Architecture*. Schiffer Publishing, Exton, PA.

Stein, S. (1988) Shaker Gift and Shaker Order: A Study of Religious Tension in the 19th Century. Paper presented at a symposium, Shaker Religion in Context: Theory and Practice. Center for Research and Education, the Shaker Museum, Old Chaltham, New York.

16: Probate Inventories in Historical Archaeology: A Review and Alternatives

Paul A. Shackel
Harpers Ferry National Historical Park, Harpers Ferry, West Virginia

Probate records are a rich source of data for studying colonial and early American material culture. Probate records include wills, inventories, and accounts of administration. Inventories and accounts of administration have been relied upon by some social historians, architectural historians, archaeologists, and those involved in decorative arts studies for analyses of 17th- and 18th-century American material culture. Although much of this work is placed in site-specific, local, regional, and international contexts, the questions have often been limited to addressing functional use of space, identifying house furnishings, and listing material goods that indicate changing lifestyles. Such work is important and necessary but does not always pursue the extent of information available in probate records. Only a few scholars have analyzed the material goods found in probate inventories from an anthropological perspective that takes into account the symbolic and active meanings of material culture.

This essay is divided into three sections. First, I provide a description of probate inventories and examine the types of approaches that have been pursued with these documents. Representative approaches will be discussed, with the understanding that this chapter does not intend to provide an inclusive review of all probate inventory scholarship. Second, I discuss research goals and the social context of goods. Third, I provide an analysis of probate inventories that is placed in the context of the use and meaning of goods. I demonstrate that objects can be more than indices of wealth, they can be used as active agents in structuring social relationships. Meanings are socially created by constant negotiations and manipulation of symbols between individuals and objects. I use probate inventory data from 18th-century Annapolis, Maryland to demonstrate how a socially dominant group manipulated material culture and the rules

and accoutrements of a new personal discipline to create inequalities and to justify those actions as inevitable and natural. The applicability of this approach to archaeological data is then discussed.

Probate Inventories

In 18th-century Maryland, as in all British colonies of the period, when a person died the court appointed an administrator to settle the estate unless a specific person was designated as executor by the will of the deceased. Whether administrator or executor, this individual cared for the estate, collected from debtors and paid creditors, and divided the remainder of the estate among the heirs, reserving a set proportion as payment for his or her trouble. Appointing an administrator was usually "...avoided because the fees could be substantial, but it protected both heirs and creditors and was especially desirable if the heirs...were minor children" (Carr and Walsh 1977:2). After the appointment of the administrator, the judge of a Commission of Probate chose two or three appraisers familiar with the occupation of the deceased. These individuals inventoried and assessed the value of the estate and determined the value of the belongings in the current market (Main 1975).

To record an inventory one was to:

> ...proceed to the valuation of all and singular the deceased's goods, chattels, wares and merchandises, such as ready money, household furniture, clothing, negroes, stock of cattle, corn, the crop on hand begun...as also of all leases for years (Vallette 1774:13).

The goods appraised varied among the British North American colonies. In Maryland and Virginia only chattel property was inventoried. Chattels are movable property,

205

which could be removed from the estate and hidden from heirs and creditors if not listed in a public document. The listing of these goods and their market value was the probate inventory (Carr and Walsh 1977:3). In New England colonies, such as Massachusetts, real property, i.e., land, was also listed.

Although considered a true and accurate accounting of the estate, an inventory usually omitted items that had no market value. These goods included fruits and vegetables, which were grown by the colonists but were probably considered either perishable or too insignificant to record. Inventories often omitted clothing items as they were probably in the possession of heirs by the time the accounting process began (Carr and Walsh 1977:4). Other items without market value may have also been omitted. Exact numbers and descriptions of goods may be difficult to discern. Sometimes not every individual item was listed but rather lumped and described as "parcel of forks" or "in small things forgotten" (cf. Deetz 1977). Prior to 1715 a wife was allowed to keep a pot and bed from her husband's creditors. Whether inventories included these items is not known (Carr and Walsh 1980:82; Smith 1975). After 1715, English law passed a "statute of distribution" that required one third of a man's estate to be conveyed to his wife, while the children could receive the remainder (Vallette 1774:107).

Data regarding the decedent's estate are greatly improved if an account of administration was recorded. This record provides a final accounting of an estate, including such information as the value of the crops in the field at the time of death and an accounting of debts receivable that were unidentified at the time of appraisal (Carr and Walsh 1977:4). Also recorded were funeral expenses, an allowance of 10% of the estate for the executor or administrator, and 5% for extraordinary trouble in collecting debts (Vallette 1774:40–41). All of these added expenses were usually subtracted from the final estate value. In spite of high administration fees, the executor, who was usually related to the deceased, would not hinder the inventory, since the money would stay in the family. Fees were not taken from paupers (usually with estate values of £10 or less) and would therefore not be a reason for biasing the recording of inventories. The Chesapeake colonial era had a 65 to 70% recording rate and is considered to be a viable sample for analyses (Carr 1983).

There are several biases associated with probate inventories. First, estates of males accounted for the majority of the inventories. Women lost their right to own property when they married and therefore did not often appear in the probate records unless single or widowed. Children also did not have legal status to own property. Second, wealth in the form of goods tends to increase with age, and there is usually a greater proportion of older and relatively richer men who die and are subsequently probated (Carr and Walsh 1980:83). Therefore the probate inventories may be skewed toward an older and wealthier population rather than the average population (Smith 1975:105).

Probate inventories were taken for Euroamerican estates since the early settlement of the New World. They provide a detailed listings of goods possessed by an estate. Despite the many biases related to probate records, they are a useful document in the study of particular objects as well as for broad questions relating to material culture.

PROBATE INVENTORY STUDIES: HISTORY, ARCHITECTURE AND THE DECORATIVE ARTS

Probate inventories are used by various scholars of different disciplines to answer questions specific to their needs. Since the late 19th century some researchers have examined probate inventories to recreate period rooms. Others use larger sets of data to recreate lifestyles on the household, community, and regional levels.

The tradition of using probate inventories continues to be used by museum professionals. For instance, Baumgarten (1975) uses 485 household inventories to determine the types of fabrics most often used in New England interior furnishings. Teller (1968) uses inventories to demonstrate the occurrence of ceramic types among Providence, Rhode Island, households. Other items analyzed include clothing (Trauman 1987) and fireplace equipment (Candee 1987).

Historians use probate inventories to examine changing lifestyles. Main (1977) demonstrates the use of probate inventories to decipher structures of wealth holdings. Her analysis indicates that inequalities in wealth dramatically increased in the New World in the 1830s, prior to any large-scale industrial movement in the New World. In a regional analysis, Carr and Walsh (1977:32, 1980) use an "Amenities Index" to measure the penetration of 11 items into various wealth groups in the Chesapeake. Around 1716, the mean score among the wealthy rose dramatically and continued to rise until the 1770s. All wealth groups increased their amenities scores, but the distance between the rich and poor remained vast (Carr and Walsh 1977). Carr and Walsh (1986:7–8) also use a "Modern Index" with items that they consider basic household equipment for comfort and cleanliness, such as mattresses, bedsteads, bed linens, tables, chairs, pots, coarse ceramics, table forks, and interior lighting. They find that the poor showed only a modest increase of these goods by 1770, while the largest acquisition occurred in the middle and upper groups (Carr and Walsh n.d.:44). Shammas (1980) uses inventories from England to determine the changing lifestyles from Tudor to Stuart England. She incorporates New World data and specific classes of artifacts, such as furnishings, musical instruments, and books, to indicate a change in colonial standards of living by the mid 18th century. Sweeney (1988) studies comparative furniture forms as a means of measuring change in standards of living in Connecticut. He notices a dramatic change in consumer consciousness by the mid 18th century and by the late 18th century "fashionable" objects diffused to the lower groups.

Cummings (1986 [1964]) notices the importance of probate data to complement his vernacular architecture studies. In particular he uses inventories to determine function of space in a household. St. George (1986) also looks for changing functional uses of space and relates this change to broad societal changes in the 17th century. Goods became increasingly important to define the specific functional uses of rooms, for the inhabitants themselves, and for the outside world.

PROBATE INVENTORY STUDIES: ARCHAEOLOGY

Archaeologists have also realized the importance of using probate inventories in material culture studies. Gary Wheeler Stone (1970) performed an early probate analysis and called for the integration of probate data with archaeological analyses. In 1977 James Deetz (1977, 1970) argued that historical archaeology is the study of material culture and should not be limited to archaeologically recovered artifacts. Because historical archaeologists in the U.S. investigate relatively recent data (no more than several hundred years old), there is a greater chance of finding above-ground features and locating relevant historical documents. Therefore, architecture, gravestones, and other surviving material are important and integral artifacts in understanding the complexity of culture. In his broad definition of material culture, Deetz (1977) also includes music, dance, and even speech. Documents are a necessary and complementary component of historic cultures. Along with such records as deeds, court records, and wills, probate inventories serve as important documents for studying colonial material culture.

Deetz et al. (1987) examine changing functional use of space in the Plymouth colony. For instance, they note that display items were more often in halls than in parlors. By the late 17th century more standardized functional names and uses were employed. Other researchers have followed Deetz with a variety of analytical approaches to probate inventories. Using probate data, Brown (1973) tests Deetz's (1973, also see 1977) archaeologically based hypotheses of changing material culture in colonial Plymouth, Massachusetts. He documents the presence of specific ceramic categories and successfully compared them to Deetz's archaeological finds. Bowen (1978) uses probate inventories in conjunction with archaeologically recovered materials to study subsistence patterns and to

understand the total cultural complexity of a rural 18th-century farmstead, Mott Farm, in Portsmouth, Rhode Island. She successfully demonstrates the need of integrating historical and archaeological data. Beaudry's (1980, 1988) linguistic analysis of probate inventories retrieves folk taxonomies from 17th- and 18th-century Virginia. She quantifies and studies adjectives or modifiers that occur in inventory descriptions under the premise that changes in material classification will often indicate a dynamic cultural system. Yentsch (1980, 1988) uses probate inventory data in her ecological analysis of culture change in 18th-century Cape Cod communities. Her goal is to understand the complex relationships among culture, social action, and the environment by quantifying the presence of maritime-related items found in inventories. Bragdon (1988) studies acculturation by analyzing the probate inventories of Christian Indians in southern New England. These Indians used goods to maintain their distinctiveness as a subordinate group.

Probate inventories are instrumental in the Potomac Typological System for ceramic vessel identification (Beaudry et al. 1983). Realizing that most ceramic analyses in the Chesapeake ended at chronology, the authors create a typology system that uses a folk taxonomic system to achieve both a functional analysis and a basis of consistency for interassemblage analysis.

Other archaeologists use probate data to compliment archaeological data. In conjunction with archaeological data, Pendery (1987) uses probate data to examine the role of material goods in the changing social relations in 17th- and 18th-century Charlestown, Massachusetts. He demonstrates how consumer goods may have been strategically used to legitimize status. Little's (1987) goal is to study the effect of broad cultural changes on the craft of printing in the 18th century. While newspapers and excavated type indicate changes on a regional and international level, probate data helps to demonstrate these changes in the daily lives of the printer's family. Little (in press) also uses inventories to suggest gender-based differences in organizing household goods. I use probate inventory data in conjunction with etiquette books and archaeological data to analyze the changing attitudes towards dining and health- and hygiene-related behavior (Shackel 1987).

Research Goals for Understanding Meanings of Goods

There are a variety of ways to analyze probate data. Particularistic, functional, ecological, and linguistic analyses are all productive approaches to analyzing colonial material goods. Seldom have archaeologists, using archaeological or historical data, gone beyond these categories of analysis and attempted an ideological analysis of material goods.

Here I use both probate data and etiquette books to demonstrate how a socially dominant group manipulated material culture and a new personal discipline to exclude the encroaching lower wealth group and to create a culture in which modern inequalities are rooted. Even though this analysis focuses upon the unequal distribution of wealth, which intensified in the 18th century, its emphasis is the symbolic meanings of material culture and the use of those meanings in creating and reinforcing group boundaries and a disciplined behavior.

I use etiquette books found in Medieval and Renaissance western literature and probate inventory data from the city of Annapolis, Maryland from the late 17th century to the late 18th century to describe the development of a new discipline and an increasingly stratified society. I believe the changes seen are reactions to a series of social and economic adjustments including population increase, economic instability, inflation, and wealth consolidation. These socioeconomic instabilities produced an increasingly competitive society in which material goods took on specific uses and meanings, which helped to develop and reinforce a modern discipline and socially segmented society.

Material goods can be used to create and maintain social boundaries and legitimize the social order. Goods are not only an index of wealth, but also can be a medium that disguises social relations in the form of hegemony. They are visible displays of the established hierarchy of values (Douglas and Isherwood 1979:5). Material culture can communicate meaning and maintain intra- and intergroup social relationships through a nonverbal medium. Consumer goods create a system of meaning. However, if objects are taken out of context, that is, out of the intercourse of society in which they participate, they are meaningless. As early as the 18th century, Saint Simon remarked that what matters "...is not the thing itself but what it means in relations to certain people" (as quoted in Elias 1983:100). Whether and how goods are used or refused constitutes whether they maintain, create, or undermine social relations (Douglas and Isherwood 1979:72).

Goods communicate through a whole set of cues that elicit appropriate behaviors in specific situations and contexts, relaying the message of the behavior expected of people (Rapoport 1982:80). They create and maintain social boundaries that imply a commonality of understanding or common codes of communications within groups. It is through a social interactive process that their meaning is created (Rapoport 1982:15, 48, 59–60). Such interaction with goods indicates that symbolism is not a passive process but can be used to legitimize the social order, either explicitly or implicitly. "Communication and understanding of the world result

from the use of a common language — that is, a set of rules which identify both the way the symbols should be organised [sic] into sets, and the meaning of individual symbols in contrast to others" (Hodder 1982:7).

Douglas and Isherwood (1979:180) note that those within a group will synchronize their consumption activities with other group members who are being guided by similar circumstances (Douglas and Isherwood 1979:118). As information becomes "finely tuned" by members of a group, their behavior becomes standardized within that group (Douglas and Isherwood 1979:144; Douglas 1984:15). Whenever standardization in the form of precise rules and discipline is observed, one is probably near the center of a competitive system where deviation of even the smallest kind matters. Usually at high-ranking occasions behavior and goods are standardized, and if tampered with there is the danger of giving wrong signals (Douglas and Isherwood 1979:144–145; Rapoport 1982:183).

SOCIAL CONTEXT OF GOODS

One way of exploring increasing social competition in western society and the extent to which goods shaped and created social inequality is by examining the social context of the use of goods, that is, the accompanying codes or expected rules of behavior. From medieval times through the industrial revolution goods were used to help justify the social order, although the meanings of goods were radically different between these two eras. Behavioral guidebooks, commonly known as etiquette books, provide these rules of use for specific items.

Medieval customs for eating varied greatly from modern western civilization. Until the 16th century, a table setting usually consisted of knives, plates, and goblets. People usually helped themselves from a communal dish and solids were taken by the hand. Liquids were often drunk from ladles or spoons, and sometimes a communal glass was used. There were no special implements for different foods, rather the same knife or spoon was used for all foods at the meal. Soups and sauces were often drunk from plates and dishes lifted to the mouth. It was not uncommon to have two or more diners eating from the same plate or trencher (Elias 1978:67).

Goods also symbolized different meanings compared to our standards today. As objects became "minutely dented, chipped, oxidized, and worn away, they begin to take on 'patina'" (McCracken 1988:32). Patina authenticated status as it indicated a family's longevity of their position in society. Quality goods with patina demonstrated that the object was in the family for several generations and therefore the family could claim to be part of the established gentry, thus inflating their social standing. Lack of patina meant that the wealth was new and therefore the status was new (McCracken 1988:32).

In colonial Annapolis the adjective *old* is often seen

among the description of goods in the earliest inventories of the wealthy. Such designation may have implied a form of patina that legitimized the wealthy's position in society. Along with patina, the wealthy differentiated themselves from the poor by the quantities of goods they owned, rather than by types of goods.

After the War of the Roses in 16th-century England, membership of the old nobility dwindled and the new aristocracy grew in numbers and strength. Consumer goods played an increasing role in reinforcing new behaviors and creating and shaping social boundaries. Education was endorsed by Henry VIII and became acceptable among the aristocracy, thus creating a favorable environment for Renaissance ideas. With the development of this new socially competitive upper class, the questions of uniform material culture and good behavior became increasingly acute. Discipline began to create greater formality in eating. This new regimentation of all behavior, and specifically dining, was learned as though it were part of the laws of nature (Miller 1987).

During the reign of Louis XIV in the 17th century, France became the acknowledged leader of civility in western civilization. French authors added more complex and more disciplined rules than those set by their predecessors. Braudel (1979:203–209) explains that in 1654 Nicholas de Bonnefons described the new discipline and segmentation found among the upper classes with regard to etiquette. The meal became increasingly segmented, and the sharing of utensils was frowned upon. No longer was a person able to use a spoon to take food from the serving dish with their hands. De Courtin wrote a manners guide for use by a friend, and only other "well-bred people." He wrote for the court of Louis XIV and his writings were therefore popular among the elite (Elias 1978:100).

By the end of the first half of the 18th century profound alterations were made to the rules related to civility. They were changed beyond recognition of what they had been in the 17th century. Behavioral rules became more intricate and precise. This culture change penetrated wherever the Enlightenment was felt and became particularly prominent in England (Aresty 1970:129).

Aresty (1970:129) notes that the increasing preciseness in rules of behavior was an attempt by members of the upper class to prevent the upward mobility of the lower class. They therefore

...evolved a code of manners — regulations really — modeled on those that governed court life, but composed of numerous private ceremonies observed in certain cliques and sets. Each ceremonial was an invisible bar against intruders and by the end of the century these had been codified into rules of etiquette.

By the beginning of the second quarter of the 18th century in Annapolis, the meaning and context of goods changed. Elias (1983:68) notes that in 17th- and 18th-century Western Europe, particularly in France and England, competition for status and prestige led to an overt expression of behavior and material culture. Once a hierarchy was established, it was maintained by the competition of people within that group: "[E]ach being understandably anxious to preserve any privilege however trivial, and the power it conferred" (Elias 1983:85).

In 1729 La Salle (in Elias 1978) also prescribed the formation of an increasingly disciplined diner and segmented dinner. The use of three different utensils, a plate instead of a trencher, and a napkin were all prescribed for the table. The rules associated with each of the utensils — knife, fork, and spoon — were defined.

Rules associated with dining became increasingly more disciplined from the late Medieval times through the Renaissance. With this changing behavior came an increase in the forms of material culture, prescribed with a set of more complex rules to actively produce a disciplined and stratified society. These rules, which were accompanied by a new set of goods, were promoted as being embedded in nature and as being natural for the development of civility. An examination of material goods from probate inventories provides an indication of the transmission of this new behavior in the colonial Chesapeake.

Analysis of Probate Inventories From Annapolis, Maryland

The change from medieval to modern tradition occurred in Annapolis, not gradually, but rather suddenly in the 1720s, during times of social and economic tensions on the regional and local levels. For instance, during the second long period of growth of the tobacco industry, from 1715 to 1775, there was a tobacco depression (between 1722 and 1735) that is considered to have been the most persistent and most severe during colonial times (Hemphill 1985:54; Mccusker and Menard 1986; Kulikoff 1986). The tobacco depression and other factors may have combined to produce dramatically higher prices in the 1730s. Maryland currency also weakened during this era (Carr and Walsh 1977:12–14).

During the early 18th century Annapolis suffered the same tremendous economic fluctuations as the whole Chesapeake region. Wealth was dramatically consolidated in Annapolis from 1710 to 1732. The average wealth per estate among the poorest groups began to decrease dramatically, while the opposite is true for the wealthy (Russo 1983:3; Shackel 1987; Leone and Shackel 1987, 1990; Leone 1988) (Table 1). Four wealthy residents purchased and monopolized real estate, subjecting the poor and landless to a leasehold system (Baker 1986:5,9).

Table 1
PRESENCE OF FORMAL AND SEGMENTING DINING ITEMS (SALAD DISHES, TUREENS, DISH COVERS, FRUIT DISHES, CUSTARD CUPS, CASTORS, BUTTER BOAT, WINE GLASSES) IN ANNAPOLIS, MARYLAND

| Wealth in Pounds | Years | | | | | | | | | | | |
| | 1688–1709 | | | 1710–1732 | | | 1732–1754 | | | 1755–1777 | | |
	C	N	%	C	N	%	C	N	%	C	N	%
000–49	9	0	00	24	0	00	33	1	03	33	0	00
50–225	3	0	00	27	0	00	18	2	11	30	2	07
226–490	4	0	00	12	1	08	11	2	18	9	0	00
491+	1	0	00	9	3	33	15	1	07	17	7	41

C = Total number of cases.
N = Presence of item.
% = Percentage of cases.

Between 1720 and 1730, the city's population increased 65 to 70%, which is twice as fast as any other decade in the 18th century (Papenfuse 1975:14–15; Walsh 1983:6). During this era of social and economic tension, I would expect group behavior to standardize and power to consolidate. The wealthy should acquire a new behavior and goods to set themselves apart from an encroaching lower class. This new behavior would be dictated by the new discipline.

To test the idea I will use probate data and look for sets of forks and knives and particular formal dining items. I assume that *sets* imply a symmetry between individuals and dining equipment that implies segmenting and standardizing behavior around the table. Also, forks were introduced with the new etiquette. No longer did the hand make direct contact with the food; neither was the knife used to place food directly in the mouth. Rather this new specialized instrument was used. Sets of forks and knives imply that these objects were used by individual persons, and were not shared around the table, thus also segmenting the dinner and standardizing the behavior around the table. Formal and segmenting dining items (i.e., salad dishes, tureens, dish covers, fruit dishes, custard cups, castors, butter boats, and wine glasses) are also objects that help to create a more standardized and segmented dining process. No longer were communal dishes and bowls accepted as implements for dining, rather increasing amount of goods with specialized functions were introduced to increasingly define the different portions of the eating process. Separate vessels for salad, main course, dessert, and various liquids were now required.

To distinguish sets I used the criterion of six or more of one object (cf. Miller 1974:208). "Lots" and "parcels" of items were not counted as sets, because it was very unlikely that a true estimate of the quantities these terms represented could be determined. Therefore the item counts are a conservative measure of the new discipline.

A total of 255 Annapolis inventories were divided into four wealth groups. Wealth group I consists of the poorest of those inventoried. This includes all people with total estate values ranging between £0 and £49 at the time of death. Group II is composed of those with estate values ranging between £50 and £225; Group III consists of those with total estate values ranging between £225 and £490. The final category, Group IV, contains all estates valued equal to or greater than £491. These wealth divisions are the ones used by Chesapeake historians Carr and Walsh (1977, 1980, 1986). These categories were based on varying consumption patterns, which changed at specific points of wealth. To control for inflation in a diachronic comparison, I used a commodity price index illustrated by Carr and Walsh (1980:96). It demonstrates the proportional differences between prices of specific goods for different years. All values are adjusted to the value of money in 1700.

These data were examined to compare the rates of transmission of the new disciplining and segmenting behavior and possibly to determine if socioeconomic fluctuations correspond in shaping and creating this new order of behavior.

Formal and segmenting dining items were nonexistent in early Annapolis (Table 1). They first appeared in the 1710s and 1720s among the wealthiest groups. By the 1730s and 1740s the second and third wealth group had more of these items than the wealthiest group. Just prior to the American Revolution, the wealthy, once again, gained almost exclusive ownership of these goods.

None of the early Annapolitans owned sets of forks (Table 2). During the 1710s and 1720s estates from

Table 2
PRESENCE OF SETS OF FORKS IN ANNAPOLIS, MARYLAND

| Wealth in Pounds | Years | | | | | | | | | | | |
| | 1688–1709 | | | 1710–1732 | | | 1732–1754 | | | 1755–1777 | | |
	C	N	%	C	N	%	C	N	%	C	N	%
000–49	9	0	00	24	0	00	33	1	03	33	3	09
50–225	3	0	00	27	5	19	18	6	33	30	3	10
226–490	4	0	00	12	3	25	11	6	55	9	7	78
491+	1	0	00	9	4	44	15	2	13	17	12	71

C = Total number of cases.
N = Presence of item.
% = Percentage of cases.

Table 3
PRESENCE OF SETS OF KNIVES IN ANNAPOLIS, MARYLAND

| Wealth in Pounds | Years | | | | | | | | | | | |
| | 1688–1709 | | | 1710–1732 | | | 1732–1754 | | | 1755–1777 | | |
	C	N	%	C	N	%	C	N	%	C	N	%
000–49	9	0	00	24	0	00	33	0	00	33	3	11
50–225	3	1	33	27	5	19	18	5	28	30	4	30
226–490	4	0	00	12	3	25	11	6	55	9	7	78
491+	1	0	00	9	5	56	15	4	27	17	13	76

C = Total number of cases.
N = Presence of item.
% = Percentage of cases.

wealth groups II, III, and IV owned these items, although the wealthiest owned more. By the 1730s and 1740s all four wealth groups owned sets of forks, and the second and third groups owned more than the wealthy. By the eve of the American revolution the wealthy substantially increased their ownership of sets of forks, although the third wealth group owned slightly more.

Sets of knives were present in only one estate in early Annapolis (Table 3). By the 1710s and 1720s the three wealthiest groups owned sets of forks, and the wealthy owned the majority of these goods. By the 1730s and 1740s wealth group IV decreased its ownership of sets of knives, and the second and third wealth groups had proportionately more estates with these goods. From 1755 to 1777 the third and fourth wealth groups had substantially increased their proportional ownership of sets of knives, although wealth group III had slightly more.

According to the probate data collected, all coded items were found in Annapolitan society by 1710 to 1732 and were found in the greatest proportions among the wealthiest estates of the city. Consumer goods were accessible to New World markets prior to the 1710s, but it appears that during a time of many social and economic crises (i.e., tobacco depression, wealth restructuring, and increased population), the wealthiest consumed more of these disciplining and segmenting items, which facilitated the creation and reinforcement of a modern discipline. This new order of behavior distanced the upper wealth group from other groups, while the members were creating and consolidating their own identity. This modern discipline, especially in the form of complex manners, was foreign and to some extent nonexistent in Annapolis around 1700. But during times of socioeconomic fluctuations, the elite increasingly subscribed to a new behavior, which became both part of the natural order of the new distinct upper class and a social strategy of power and domination. An examination of probate data also indicates that etiquette books were found in only the libraries of the wealthiest Annapolitans (Inventories 4 1720, 12 1727, 84 1764). This indicates that the elite subscribed to some of the most recent rules of etiquette.

In most cases, there was a general leveling off or decrease in the ownership of these segmenting and disciplining items during the 1740s and 1750s. I have argued elsewhere (Little and Shackel 1989:499–501) that the elite used material culture, such as architecture and formal and segmenting dining items, during times in which the elite consolidated their social, economic, and political strength in the community. After this reaffirmation of the social order, there may have been little reason for using disciplining items to explicitly assert social differentiation. But in the decades just prior to, and during, the American Revolution, there was another sharp increase of the ownership of these disciplining dining items. The elite acquired this ostentation to create and maintain the hierarchy, and to distance themselves from the lower class. The elite created a bond with the lower classes and inspired the American Revolution. They convinced the rest of the population that they understood the natural order, and therefore had the natural right of power and domination. Manners also were believed to be natural and embedded in the laws of nature. The elite ostentatiously displayed their knowledge of the natural and material order and became the new ruling class in America (Isaac 1982; Leone 1984, 1987).

An analysis of probate data indicates that material culture is more than an index of wealth, but can also actively structure social relations. Goods and a new disciplined behavior were manipulated by a socially dominant group to create and maintain social inequalities. In Annapolis, Maryland the elite began to use formal dining items and a new exacting behavior during times of social and economic stress.

Toward an Archaeological Analysis of Context and Meaning

Probate data analysis provides a vehicle to measure the development of a new discipline by using goods that cannot be recovered archaeologically. An archaeological analysis may also reveal similar trends of developing social segmentation. In one sense the archaeological data are more limited, since dining items such as forks and knives are rarely found in the archaeological record. The archaeological database may be limited to ceramics and glass, since these are most commonly found in colonial and early American contexts. On the other hand, a vessel analysis based on archaeologically recovered materials may provide more detailed information than that provided in household inventories.

Therefore, a contextual approach, such as that used above for analyzing items listed in probate inventories,

has applicability to archaeological analyses only if archaeologists are willing to go beyond a functional analysis of artifacts and consider ideological uses. Changing archaeological patterns are important only if they are continually analyzed in the context of their use and meaning. Increasing or decreasing diversity of intra- and intersite assemblages is usually related to local or broad cultural contexts. To study tableware assemblages it is important to analyze ceramic type variation and to show the degree of segmentation present in the dining assemblage of a household. I initially developed a formula to give segmentation some measurable comparison for intra- and intersite assemblages (Shackel 1987). The formula

$$(\text{Type size/type})(\text{size}) = \text{index value}$$

is an indicator of the variability and changing segmentation of each ceramic assemblage. In this formula the value for "type" is the amount of standard ceramic wares present (i.e., creamware, shell edges, whiteware etc.). "Type size" is the total number of sizes present within the x-y coordinates of the table, and "sizes" are the number of different plate sizes present. A presence/absence table needs to be constructed. Indicating presence or absence is a valid way of representing tableware in the archaeological record. An assemblage with 15 tea cups and 4 dinner plates does not necessarily represent the true proportion of activities at the site, but may be a result of breakage and disposal. Therefore a presence/absence table does not create a false sense of precision by weighting different functional types. I expect values ranging from 1.0 and greater on an open-ended scale, with a value closer to 1.0 indicating low assemblage variability and greater values indicating increasing variation and segmentation. Therefore the following model indicates a low index value:

Plate Sizes

Type				
Creamware			x	Type = 4
Pearlware		x		Type size = 4
Whiteware		x		Size = 3
Ironstone	x			
Size (in.)	8	9	10	

Therefore, (4/4) (3) = 3.

An example of relatively higher variability would look like this:

Plate Sizes

Type					
Creamware	x	x	x	x	Type = 1
					Type size= 4
					Size = 4
Size (in.)	8	9	10	11	

Therefore, (4/1) (4) = 16.

In the case of Annapolis, Maryland, the degree of segmentation increased sharply at the beginning of the 19th century. (For more detail of this analysis, see Shackel 1987; Leone, Potter, and Shackel 1987; and Little and Shackel 1989.) This increasing segmentation is more than an indication of changing manufacturing techniques, but is also an indication of the development and acceptance of a new discipline that affected dining and served as a training ground for an increasingly segmented life.

To best use this formula, many sites should be analyzed for comparison. For a more complete analysis of the archaeological assemblage, other artifact categories also need to be considered.

The above formula, developed to measure variability among plate sizes, can be easily expanded to include different functional serving vessels. To expand the categories related to dining segmentation, a change to the formula is required and can be stated in the following formula:

$$(\text{Type function}/\text{type})(\text{function}) = \text{index value}$$

"Type" still represents the standard ceramic ware, and "type function" represents the various sizes and functions in the assemblage present within the x-y coordinates of the table. "Function" includes the various sized functional serving vessels and includes such items as 10-in. plates, 12-in. plates, tea cups, saucers, bowls, pitchers, soup plates, etc. The following is an example of the segmentation formula to measure variability in the entire ceramic assemblage:

Assemblage Variability

Type

Creamware, queensware	x	x	x					
Creamware, undecorated				x	x			
Pearlware, hand painted						x	x	
Pearlware, transfer print								x

| Functional categories: | 10-in. d, | 12-in. d, | 9-in. p, | 7-in. m, | 5-in. t, | 3-in. tc, | 5-in. s, | 7-in. pit |

Key: d = dish; p = plate; m = muffin; t = tureen; tc = tea cup; s = saucer; pit = pitcher.
Type size = 8; type = 4; function = 8.

The above formula can be easily applied to sites dating from the beginning of mass-produced ceramics, the mid-18th century, as long as there is an adequate sample size and recovery strategy. Due to new manufacturing techniques, glass was mass produced and mass consumed from the late 19th century. Therefore glass tableware assemblages may also be integrated into the analysis of increasing behavioral segmentation and personal discipline. As in the case of the ceramic analysis, it is also important to place the changing patterns of consumption of tableware in a historic and symbolic context.

Discussion

A consumer revolution in the Chesapeake in the 1710s to 1720s introduced a shift in consumption patterns among the wealthy and the poor. The advent of consumerism in the Chesapeake region can be partially explained by increased methods of transportation and better production methods, but the social context must also be set for the acceptance of cultural material and behavioral change. Generally in the Chesapeake, and more specifically in Annapolis, there were tremendous social and economic fluctuations during the 1710s and 1720s. During this era, a newly formed gentry who based their wealth on mercantile capitalism began to compete against the old guard. This unstable order was reordered by providing new meanings to new consumer goods. The concept of patina, which was once used to justify the hierarchy, was replaced by a new concept of consumerism. New and fashionable goods became the goal of consumption. Associated with these goods was a new behavior, which encouraged discipline, regimentation, and segmentation. Although members of lower wealth groups were able to acquire these goods, the wealthy created the rules for using these objects as an exclusionary tactic to identify outsiders and to prevent them from entering their social circles.

Although probate data serve contextual analysis, this approach also can be applied to archaeological contexts. Historical archaeologists should not confine themselves to solely functional analyses. When examining archaeological assemblages in historical and symbolic contexts, new questions may be asked of the data. Goods can be more than passive objects that reflect relative wealth. Objects also can be manipulated to negotiate contexts and their meanings. A vessel analysis may indicate more than the types of foods consumed, but may also be a reflection of how goods create and reinforce behaviors and establish social groups.

Scholars of material culture must pay attention to the significant interdependencies between culture and consumption. Consumer goods "express cultural categories and principles, cultural ideals, create and sustained lifestyles, construct notions of self, and create social change" (McCracken 1988:xi). In order to understand the patterns of consumption it is important to understand the social context in which goods are desired and used and eventually fall out of favor.

Acknowledgments

I am indebted to Barbara Little for comments and encouragement during all phases of writing this essay. Parker Potter and Barbara Little provided feedback during the development and experimentation of the ceramic formula. Barbara Little provided input and encouraged me to expand the latest version of the ceramic segmentation formula. Much of the probate data was collected while working for Archaeology in Annapolis, a cooperative project between the University of Maryland and the Historic Annapolis Foundation, and I owe Mark Leone a special thanks for his comments and criticisms during this data collection. Lois Carr also provided valuable guidance while I collected the inventory data. Although we disagree on interpretations, she always provided me with assistance to aide my understanding of the inventories.

References

Aresty, E. B. (1970) *The Best Behavior: The Course of Good Manners from Antiquity to the Present — As Seen through Courtesy and Etiquette Books.* Simon and Schuster, New York.

Baker, N. (1986) Annapolis, Maryland 1695–1730. *Maryland Historical Magazine* 81(3):191–209.

Baumgarten, L. (1975) The Textile Trade in Boston, 1650–1700. In *Arts of the Anglo-American Community in the Seventeenth Century,* I. Quimby, Ed. The University Press of Virginia, Charlottsville, pp. 219–273.

Beaudry, M. C. (1988) Words for Things: Linguistic Analysis of Probate Inventories. In *Documentary Archaeology in the New World,* M. Beaudry, Ed. Cambridge University Press, New York, pp. 43–50.

— (1980) *"Or What Else You Please to Call It" Folk Semantic Domains in Early Virginia Probate Inventories.* University Microfilms International, Ann Arbor, MI.

Beaudry, M. C., J. Long, H. Miller, F. Neiman, and G. W. Stone (1983) A Vessel Typology for Early Chesapeake Ceramics: The Potomac Typological System. *Historical Archaeology* 17(1):18–43.

Bowen, J. (1978) Probate Inventories: An Evaluation from the Perspective of Zooarchaeology and Agricultural History at Mott Farm. In *Historical Archaeology: A Guide to Substantive and Theoretical Contributions,* R. Schuyler, Ed. Baywood Publishing Company, Farmingdale, NY, pp. 149–159.

Bragdon, K. (1988) The Material Culture of the Christian Indians of New England, 1650–1775. In *Documentary Archaeology in the New World,* M. Beaudry, Ed. Cambridge University Press, New York, pp. 43–50.

Braudel, F. (1979) *Perspectives of the World: Civilization and Capitalism; 15th–18th Century.* Harper and Row, New York.

Brown, M. (1973) Ceramics from Plymouth, 1621–1800: The Documentary Record. In *Ceramics in America,* I. Quimby, Ed. The University Press of Virginia, Charlottsville, VA, pp. 41–74.

Candee, R. (1987) First-Period Domestic Architecture of Southern Maine and New Hampshire. Paper presented at the Dublin Seminar for New England Folklife, Early American Inventories, Boston, July 11–12.

Carr, L. (1983) Methodological Procedures for Inventory Analysis. In *Annapolis and Anne Arundel County, Maryland: A Study of Urban Development in a Tobacco Economy; 1649–1776.* L. Walsh, Ed. NEH Grant Number RS 20199-81-1955. On file at Maryland State Archives, Annapolis, MD.

Carr, L. and L. Walsh (1986) Lifestyles and Standards of Living in the British Colonial Chesapeake. Paper Presented at the International Economic History Association Meetings, Bern, Switzerland.

— (1980) Inventories and the Analysis of Wealth Consumption Patterns in St. Mary's County, Maryland, 1658–1777. *Historical Methods* 13(2):81–104.

— (1977) Inventories and the Analysis of Wealth and Consumption Patterns in St. Mary's County, Maryland, 1658–1777. The Newberry Papers in Family and Community History, paper 77–46. The Newberry Library.

— (n.d.) Changing Lifestyles and Consumer Behavior in the Colonial Chesapeake. Manuscript on file at the Maryland Hall of Records, St. Mary's City Commission, Annapolis, MD.

Cummings, A. L. (1986 [1964]) Inside the Massachusetts House. In *In Common Places: Readings in American Vernacular Architecture,* D. Upton and J. Vlatch, Eds. University of Georgia Press, Athens, GA, pp. 219–239.

Deetz, J. et al. (1987) Plymouth Colony Room-by-Room Inventories, 1633–1684. Paper presented at the Dublin Seminar for New England Folklife, Early American Inventories, Boston, July 11–12.

— (1977) *In Small Things Forgotten: The Archeology of Early American Life.* Doubleday, New York.

— (1973) Ceramics from Plymouth, 1635–1835: The Archaeological Evidence. In *Ceramics in America,* I. Quimby, Ed. University Press of Virginia, Charlottsville, VA, pp. 15–40.

— (1970) Archaeology as a Social Science. In *Contemporary Archaeology,* M. P. Leone, Ed. Southern Illinois University Press, Carbondale, IL, pp. 108–117.

Douglas, M. (1984) Standard Social Use of Food: Introduction. In *Food in the Social Order: Studies in Food and Festivities in Three American Communities.* Russell Sage Foundation, New York.

Douglas, M. and B. Isherwood (1979) *The World of Goods.* Basic Books, New York.

Elias, N. (1983) *The Court Society.* Random House, New York.

— (1978) *The History of Manners: The Civilizing Process, Volume I.* Translated by E. Jephcott, Pantheon Books, New York.

Hemphill, J. M. II (1985) *Virginia and the English Commercial System 1689–1733.* Garland Publishing.

Hodder, I. (1982) Theoretical Archaeology: A Reactionary View. In *Symbolic and Structural Archaeology,* I. Hodder, Ed. Cambridge University Press, Cambridge.

Inventories (1720) 4:197–207. Annapolis, Maryland. On file at the Maryland State Archives, Annapolis, MD.

Inventories (1727) 12:71–91. Annapolis, Maryland. On file at the Maryland State Archives, Annapolis, MD.

Inventories (1764) 84:53. Annapolis, Maryland. On file at the Maryland State Archives, Annapolis, MD.

Kulikoff, A. (1986) *Tobacco and Slaves: The Development of Southern Culture in the Chesapeake, 1680–1800.* The University of North Carolina Press, Chapel Hill, NC.

Leone, M. P. (1988) The Georgian Order as the Order of Merchant Capitalism in Annapolis, Maryland. In *The Recovery of Meaning: Historical Archaeology in the Eastern United States,* M. P. Leone and P. B. Potter, Eds. Smithsonian Institution Press, Washington, D.C., pp. 235–262.

— (1987) Rule by Ostentation: The Relationship between Space and Sight in Eighteenth-Century Landscape Architecture in the Chesapeake Region of Maryland. In *Method and Theory for Activity Area Research,* S. Kent, Ed. Columbia University Press, New York, pp. 604–633.

— (1984) Interpreting Ideology in Historical Archaeology: Using Rules of Perspective in the William Paca Garden in Annapolis, Maryland. In *Ideology, Power And Pehistory,* D. Miller and C. Tilley, Eds. Cambridge University Press, Cambridge, pp. 25–35.

Leone, M. P., P. B. Potter, and P. A. Shackel (1987) Toward a Critical Archaeology. *Current Anthropology* 28(3):283–302.

Leone, M. P. and P. A. Shackel (1987) Forks, Clocks and Power. In *Mirror and Metaphor: Material and Social Constructions of Reality,* D. Ingersoll and G. Bronitsky, Eds. University Press of America, Lathem, MA, pp. 45–62.

— (1990) The Georgian Order in Annapolis, Maryland. In *New Perspectives on Maryland Historical Archaeology,* R. J. Dent and B. J. Little, Eds. *Maryland Archaeology* 26:69–84.

Little, B. (1987) *Ideology and Media: Historical Archaeology of Printing in Eighteenth-Century Annapolis, Maryland.* University Microfilm International, Ann Arbor, MI.

— (in press) "She was...an example to her sex"; Possibilities for a Feminist Archaeology in the Historic Chesapeake. In *The Historic Chesapeake: Archaeological Contributions,* P. A. Shackel and B. J. Little, Ed. Smithsonian Institution Press, Washington, D.C.

Little, B. and P. Shackel (1989) Scales of Historical Anthropology: An Archaeology of Colonial Anglo-America. *Antiquity* 63(240):495–509.

Main, G. (1977) Inequality in Early America: Evidence from Probate Records of Massachusetts and Maryland. *Journal of Interdisciplinary History* 7(4):559–581.

— (1975) Probate Records as a Source for Early American History. *William and Mary Quarterly* 32:89–99.

McCracken, G. (1988) *Culture and Consumption: New Approaches to the Symbolic Character of Consumer Goods and Activities.* Indiana University Press, Bloomington.

McCusker, J. J. and R. R. Menard (1985) *The Economy of British America:1607–1789.* The University of North Carolina Press, Chapel Hill, NC.

Miller, G. (1974) A Tenant Farmer's Tableware: Nineteenth-Century Ceramics from Tabb's Purchase. *Maryland Historical Magazine* 69 (2):197–210.

Papenfuse, E. (1975) *In Pursuit of Profit: The Annapolis Merchant in the Era of the American Revolution, 1763–1805.* Johns Hopkins University Press, Baltimore.

Pendery, S. (1987) *Symbolism of Community: Status Differences and the Archaeological Record in Charlestown, Massachusetts, 1630–1760.* University Microfilm International, Ann Arbor, MI.

Rapoport, A. (1982) *The Meaning of the Built Environment: A Nonverbal Communication Approach.* Sage Publications, London.

Russo, J. (1983) Economy of Anne Arundel County. In *Annapolis and Anne Arundel County, Maryland: A Study of Urban Development in a Tobacco Economy; 1649–1776.* L. Walsh, Ed. NEH Grant Number RS 20199-81-1955. On file at Maryland State Archives, Annapolis, MA.

St. George, R. B. (1986) "Set Thine House in Order": The Domestication of the Yeoman in Seventeenth-Century New England. In *In Common Places: Readings in American Vernacular Architecture,* D. Upton and J. Vlatch, Eds. The University of Georgia Press, Athens, GA, pp. 336–364.

Shackel, P. (1987) *A Historical Archaeology of Personal Discipline.* University Microfilms International, Ann Arbor MI.

Shammas, C. (1980) The Domestic Environment in Early Modern England and America. *Journal of Social History* 14(1):1–24.

Smith, D. S. (1975) Underregistration and the Bias in Probate Records: An Analysis of Data from Eighteenth-Century Hingham, Massachusetts. *William and Mary Quarterly* 32:100–112.

Stone, G. W. (1970) Ceramics in Suffolk County, Massachusetts, inventories, 1680–1775, a preliminary study, with diverse comments Theron, and Sundry suggestions. *The Conference on Historic Site Archaeology Papers 1968* 3(2):73–90.

Sweeney, K. (1988) Furniture and the domestic environment in Wethesfield, Connecticut, 1639–1800. In *Material life in America, 1600–1860.* R. B. St. George, Ed. Northeastern University Press, Boston, pp. 261–290.

Teller, B. (1968) Ceramics in Providence, 1750–1900. *Antiques* 94(4):570–577.

Tratman, P. (1987) Dress in Seventeenth-Century Cambridge, Massachusetts. Paper presented at the Dublin Seminar for New England Folklife, Early American Inventories, Boston, July 11–12.

Vallette, E. (1774) *The Deputy Commissionary's Guide within the Province of Maryland.* Printed by Anne Catherine Green and Son, Annapolis, MA.

Walsh, L. S. (1983) Anne Arundel County Population. In *Annapolis and Anne Arundel County, Maryland, A Study of Urban Development in a Tobacco Economy, 1649–1776.* L. S. Walsh, Ed. NEH Grant Number RS 20199-81-1955. On file at the Maryland State Archive, Annapolis, MA.

Yentsch, A. E. (1988) Farming, Fishing, Whaling, Trading: Land and Sea as Resource on Eighteenth-Century Cape Cod. In *Documentary Archaeology in the New World,* M. Beaudry, Ed. Cambridge University Press, Cambridge, pp. 138–160.

— (1980) *Expressions of Cultural Diversity and Social Reality in Seventeenth-Century New England.* University Microfilm International, Ann Arbor, MI.

17: Texts, Images, Material Culture

Barbara J. Little
University of Maryland, College Park, Maryland

There has been, and continues to be, a great deal of discourse by anthropologists about discourse, text, signifiers and signified (e.g., Clifford and Marcus 1986; Keesing 1987; Marcus and Fischer 1986; O'Meara 1989; Sangren 1988; Sherzer 1987; Spencer 1989; as well as Geertz, e.g., 1973, 1983). Much that is provocative and productive is being written and said about both the ethnographic and the archaeological records and the ways they might be represented, interpreted, and perhaps even explained. The use of text as a metaphor for cultural institutions and behaviors may be useful in some of the ways analogy tends to be useful, not as an end in itself, but as a way to begin (O'Meara 1989; cf. Binford 1967).

In some sense we all talk about the archaeological record as something that can be "read," suggesting an analogy between material culture and text. Perhaps better would be an analogy between reading and interpretation. I want to be both cautionary and optimistic about the analogy between material culture and text: cautionary about taking it too seriously and optimistic for comprehending objects, including texts, as meaningful in their own terms. Although I am reacting to some of the ideas of post-structuralism and post-modernism that have come to archaeology through post-processualism, I do not intend to be understood as reactionary against this most recent epistemological debate in archaeology. Post-processualism, with its emphases on human action and on past and present social contexts, is a good thing for archaeology; its insights will allow us greater interpretive power for both texts and things.[1]

The post-structuralist idea that originally provoked me is that all things may be understood as text. This idea takes form in archaeological writing, both implicitly and explicitly (e.g., Hodder 1986, 1987a, 1987b; Tilley 1990). Writing that "Archaeologists produce texts. Archaeologists depend on texts," Michael Shanks and Christopher Tilley (1987:16) explore some of the implications of archaeological publication as a *translation* of material objects into written language. They write of "textual conversion": "Objects depend on being incorporated into texts; they are internally constituted by the changing script of social relations into which they fit" (1987:21). By assuming that social relations are necessarily text-like (or script-like) and by subsuming objects within texts, Shanks and Tilley reinforce the primacy of texts: the superiority of the translation (words) over the original source (objects).

I think I must agree with the essence of a recent article by Roger Keesing in which he writes, "A theory that takes social formations as cultural texts to be read leads, I think, to seductive but spurious, even absurd conclusions" (Keesing 1987:169). One source for this focus on texts is Jacques Derrida's "grammatology" (Derrida 1976; Mitchell 1986:29), which makes writing the basis for all language and all signs. Also, Michel Foucault's work can be interpreted as opening up the idea of text to encompass *as discourse* all forms of cultural institutions and behaviors (Foucault 1965, 1970, 1975, 1980; Wuthnow et al. 1984). There *is* valuable insight here. This analogical view of culture as discourse may help in some cases to interpret material culture in terms of written language, but we need to understand that Foucault's and Derrida's insights are only partial and may prevent us from understanding material culture in its own terms. Archaeologists need to think not only about interpreting material culture as text, but also about interpreting text and other discourse as material culture. We need a way to turn around the primacy of text and also to see material culture as a principal informant.

This observation is more than semantic fiddling; it brings to light an important conceptual and methodological problem that is rooted in presentism. It is easy to see text as a natural and obvious category with which to organize the world because we are literate. Our world is written and read. If all arenas of communication may be considered as text, then it is because we wish to make them so. Archaeologists organize questions, research, and discussions as text. We privilege text because that is the primary, explicit way in which we understand the world. Archaeology does indeed produce texts and its dependence on texts is clear (Shanks and Tilley 1987:17). However, as long as text constitutes the basis for our authority and the metaphor for our understanding, material culture, seen as much more ambiguous, will remain secondary, reflective, and supportive, rather than informative.

The recognized reliance on text leads to the cautionary note that analytic categories are not universal and must be transported to other times and places with the understanding that they are abstractions that may be misleading. This caution is familiar to archaeologists as well as ethnographers who have struggled with making sense of cross-cultural comparisons and generalizations. Descriptive and analytic categories, including deeply embedded ones such as gender (e.g., Moore 1989; Gibbs 1987), are transported from one culture to another at the risk of obscuring realities by forcing new data into old models. Because the post-processualist emphasis on specific historical contexts and their long-term development (e.g., Hodder 1987a, 1987b) is meant to help identify appropriate categories and descriptive contexts, it is somewhat ironic that text is adopted out of context.

In a view that uses text to model perceived reality, all human action follows the rules and the logic of writing. As archaeologists we are looking at the material remains of human behaviors as being made comprehensible through the application of textual analysis. What meaning does text have in interpreting the nontextual? What meaning could text have in a nonliterate society? Using text as a model to understand representations in a nonliterate society in the past is purely etic. Such analysis, even if it is purposefully and explicitly set in the present, may have much to contribute to epistemological and political discussions of contemporary social science, but it must be recognized as completely foreign to the society under study. In a partially literate society the analogy of text is partially useful but also potentially misleading. In a fully literate society the analogy must still be partial, since nontextual "discourse" is unlikely to be isomorphic with text, even if ways of thinking are predictably much affected by literacy.

To believe that textual analysis is not necessarily appropriate for most interpretations of nontext, one needs to be convinced of three things. The first is that the models we use affect what we "discover" from our data; the second is that we want to use flexible models that not only imply how other times and places are similar to our own, but also how they are different; the third, which I will discuss, is that our practice is recursive, or simply that literacy makes a difference.

Oral culture, scribal culture, and print culture are unequal. Oral culture is changed by the addition of writing. Scribal culture is changed by the addition of printing. Yet all three can coexist in modified forms (e.g., Goody 1986). Marshall McLuhan (e.g., 1962) wrestled with the problem of how media affect language, communication, and rationality. So did Plato. For McLuhan, the medium is the vital aspect of the message. For Plato, writing was a threat to memory and meditation and threatened the real purposes of thought.

Archaeologists and others can agree that literacy affects language and thought in important ways, but in spite of much intelligent work on the topic, find it difficult at best to isolate and specify those effects (e.g., Olson et al. 1985:3). The distinctions among oral, scribal, and print culture are not altogether clear, partly because such cultures have overlapped with every change in the technology of language. Transitions have been slow and uneven. On one level, literacy allows new organization for the economics of trade and business, for education, for religion, for law. On another level, literacy and the symbolism of letters changes perceptions and changes emphases on memory, inference, abstract thought, and classification. Ivan Illich and Barry Sanders note the affects of the alphabetization of the western mind. They write, "The self is as much an alphabetic construct as word and memory, thought and history, lie and narration" (1988:71). In other words, the creation of an alphabet and a writing system and their widespread familiarity created new categories, new priorities, and new perceptions. Just as writing affected perception, printing did also, but on a more widespread scale and with far-reaching consequences (see Eisenstein 1979, 1983 for a discussion of the influence of print culture). The material culture and technology of text created new contexts within which perceptions were created and actions carried out.

Although there have generally been low rates of literacy until 19th-century Western emphasis on universal literacy, literacy had widespread effects. Oral culture within a literate society could hardly be pristine. In his work on 18th-century Virginia, Rhys Isaac (1983) writes about the symbolic potency and authority of books in the life of a whole community, even where that community is largely illiterate. The great so-called speaking books — the Bible and the Law — are communicated through constant oral performance. The unlettered are unconcerned in an immediate way with exactly what is written, but ultimately respect learning and literacy because they form the basic authority of their world, both sacred and profane.

Material culture undoubtedly contains signs and symbols, not to mention variable messages, but it is structured differently than text. In nonliterate societies it is likely to be completely different, even if we insist on seeing it as text. In literate societies, where ways of thinking and categorizing are much affected by the attributes of writing and printing, then material culture communication may become more analogous to text, but it is not clear that it does so.

One way in which material culture probably *is* analogous to text is in the ambiguity of its meaning. Text is ambiguous. Its meanings are neither fixed nor universal. Interpretation relies on social context and situation, not only of the author, but also of the reader and listener (see, e.g., Eagleton 1983 for overview of contemporary literary theory). The post-modernist insight that text does not necessarily contain intentional, explicit information lends some optimism to an archaeologist's search to effectively use both material culture and textual evidence. Accepting such ambiguity and context-dependent, socially constituted meaning for text, which includes both historical documentation and archaeological interpretation, implies that archaeologists need not apologize for the ambiguous nature of our material culture data. Such acceptance allows an approach to both the documentary and archaeological records that assigns to neither clear authority and allows us to take advantage of different aspects of both textual and nontextual data.

Archaeologists need methodologies that will decrease dependence on the authority of text and increase possibilities for interpreting material culture more directly, placing the forms of our data on a more equal footing. The idea of "image" is useful for formulating a broad view that encompasses both text and material culture. Images may be verbal, mental, perceptual, optical, or graphic (Mitchell 1986:10). Written or printed representations of images are graphic and can be made verbal through speech or mental through reading. Images are also represented graphically through art and design projects, including the material culture of everyday life. Images in any form act in many ways and on many levels of meaning. They exist in the material world, fulfill some function or functions, react to what already exists, respond to other images, respond to real and perceived needs, and further create the material world, which forms the context for images, representations, things, and their interrelationships. Whether verbal, mental, perceptual, optical, or graphic, images affect.

The idea of image is useful for pulling together representations or reifications of the world. Mitchell writes of image that it is "not simply a particular kind of sign but a fundamental principle of what Michel Foucault would call 'the order of things.' The image is the general notion, ramified in various specific similitudes...that holds the world together with 'figures of knowledge'" (Mitchell 1986:11). Images embody a way of seeing that is affected by what is known or believed (Berger et al. 1972:7–11). That is, images are embedded in social and political contexts and, in turn, influence those contexts. John Berger's comment on the power of images is provocative, even though image is narrowly defined as two-dimensional art: "No other kind of relic or text from the past can offer such direct testimony about the world which sur-

rounded other people at other times. In this respect images are more precise and richer than literature" (Berger et al. 1972:10).[2] As an archaeologist, I would argue that 'relics' also offer rich testimony.

If we look at objects, including texts, as images, as representations of the world as it is or as it ought to be, as images of common cultural understanding, of common sense (however judged), we can see material culture and text as codependent. They may be both complementary and contradictory, but they are each an essential agent in teaching people how to structure their lives and thoughts. Things and text, as images and as representations, form the context for enculturation, which entails absorbing the normative rules of cultural common sense. Such enculturation does not form a rigid system. The rules of human behavior are not natural law and are therefore quite subject to individual or group strategies, carried out according to personal perceptions, perspectives, interests, and power. Images of all kinds form the basis for Bourdieu's *habitus* (1984, 1977) and Giddens' *structuration* (1979, 1981), each of which has been adopted to structure archaeological interpretation. Habitus is conditioned by the conditions of existence, that is, by social, political, and historical contexts, and contains both systems of practice and systems of judgment ("taste"). Bourdieu writes of these systems:

> [systematicity] is found in all the properties — and property — with which individuals and groups surround themselves, houses, furniture, paintings, books, cars, spirits, cigarettes, perfume, clothes, and in the practices in which they manifest their distinction, sports, games, entertainments, only because it is in the synthetic unity of the habitus, the unifying, generative principle of all practices (1984:173).

Much of the communication involved in material culture is about interpersonal relationships; relationships that are real, but not necessarily visual, can be represented, imagined, taught, and learned, through messages of the created environment.

Texts may give rise to various sorts of images, and they share with other sorts of material culture graphic representation. If we see material culture as text, or see a textual analogy as useful for interpretation, then we also have to acknowledge that text is very often material culture. In any literate society written language is necessarily concrete. It becomes an artifact with form and style. It is subject not only to the poetics of language, but also to the poetics of space, that is, to cultural ideals, dreams, and designs (cf. Bachelard 1964). The medium becomes message-laden (cf. McLuhan 1967).

The possibility exists for an archaeology of text in its material form, as well as an archaeology of text of the sort practiced by Foucault in *The Archaeology of Knowledge* (1972) and his other texts that use "archaeological" methods (1975, 1970). Acknowledging this material side of textual meaning may help emphasize the interpretive potential of material culture. Text can be interpreted as material culture, but its primary force comes from acting in its own terms, as text. Similarly, material culture may be interpreted as text, but its primary force is understood when it is interpreted in its own terms, not as text but as material culture.

The speaking books of the Bible and the Law provide a good example with which to conclude. In understanding Isaac's description of early 18th-century oral-print coexistence, it is important to realize that the symbolic potency of the book derives in some part from its place as a prop in the ritual reinforcement of hierarchy. Here we see these speaking books specifically as material culture, as is all recorded text. Clearly these texts are not influential merely by their presence, but have a great deal of meaning in the "information" they contain in their interpreted content. In both ways they are representations of the world. Both text and material culture can be interpreted as representational images that create the perceptual and material world. That world created by people contains everything from subsistence decisions to social relationships to religious judgements. Using the idea of images in this way requires thinking less about texts as having primary authority and more about the continual mediation of the world through all available media, including verbal, written, graphic, or material images.

I have reacted to the emergence of a new crosscultural, universalizing model in archaeology. "Reading" material culture implies a textual model for interpreting objects. Although archaeological discourse per se may require textual analysis, it does not follow that the material remains of human action require the same. The model of textual analysis, born in a climate of academic discourse and literacy that may have little relevance outside its own setting, may threaten to predetermine the structures that we see in the materials we study. Literacy has changed structures of thought; it is not a universal model. Attempting to apply textual models to nontext will not help access the meanings and insights that material culture holds. However, adopting the insight that text is ambiguous and subject to endless interpretation should allow archaeology to put its principal sources of data on a more equal footing. Using the idea of images helps to achieve this and avoids the necessity of dichotomizing text and nontext.

Notes

1   For some of the growing debate, see Hodder 1985, 1986; Shanks and Tilley 1987; Patterson 1990; Earle and Preucel 1987; Watson and Fotiadis 1990.

2   I must acknowledge that by promoting "image" as a useful metaphor for interpreting material culture, I am unavoidably guilty of presentism. There is no interpretation of the past that is not constrained by the present. Because the social context in which I write is one in which there is a seemingly endless reproduction of images, my understanding of images may be quite constrained and constraining, and my interpretation of any "image" cannot be identical with that of another age. Walter Benjamin's comment on art in the age of mechanical reproduction may be applicable to all sorts of images. He writes that mechanical reproduction releases art from its dependence on ritual, which requires a unique aura of authenticity. When authenticity is no longer applicable, as when reproduction destroys uniqueness and specific use-value, "the total function of art is reversed. Instead of being based on ritual, it begins to be based on another practice — politics" (Benjamin 1955:226). I offer the possibility that because archaeology already implicitly deals in such images, it is necessarily political. Shanks and Tilley write, "archaeology is rhetorical, historically situated, part of contemporary society and inherently political" (1987:66).

References

Bachelard, G. (1964) *The Poetics of Space*. Trans. by M. Jolas. Beacon Press, Boston.

Benjamin, W. (1955) The Work of Art in the Age of Mechanical Reproduction. In *Illuminations*. Trans. by H. Zohn (1968). Harcourt, Brace and World, New York.

Berger, J., S. Blumberg, C. Fox, M. Dibb, and R. Hollis (1972) *Ways of Seeing*. British Broadcasting Corporation and Penguin Books, London.

Binford, L. G. (1967) Smudge Pits and Hide Smoking: The Role of Analogy in Archaeological Reasoning. *American Antiquity* 32(1)1–12.

Bourdieu, P. (1984) *Distinction, a Social Critique of the Judgement of Taste*. Trans. by R. Nice. Harvard University Press, Cambridge, MA.

—(1977) *Outline of a Theory of Practice*. Cambridge University Press, Cambridge.

Clifford, J. and G. E. Marcus, Eds. (1986) *Writing Culture: The Poetics and the Politics of Ethnography*. University of California Press, Berkeley.

Derrida, J. (1976) *Of Grammatology*. Trans. by G. C. Spivak. Johns Hopkins Press, Baltimore.

Eagleton, T. (1983) *Literary Theory, an Introduction*. University of Minnesota Press, Minneapolis.

Earle, T. K. and R. W. Preucel (1987) Processual archaeology and the radical critique. *Current Anthropology* 28(4)501–538.

Eisenstein, E. (1983) *The Printing Revolution in Early Modern Europe*. Cambridge University Press, Cambridge.

— (1979) *The Printing Press as an Agent of Change: Communication and Cultural Transformations in Early Modern Europe.* Cambridge University Press, Cambridge.

Foucault, M. (1980) *Power/Knowledge.* Pantheon, New York.

— (1975) *The Birth of the Clinic: An Archaeology of Medical Knowledge.* Random House, New York.

— (1972) *The Archaeology of Knowledge.* Pantheon, New York.

— (1970) *The Order of Things: An Archaeology of the Human Sciences.* Random House, New York.

— (1965) *Madness and Civilization: A History of Insanity in the Age of Reason.* Random House, New York.

Geertz, C. (1983) *Local Knowledge: Further Essays in Interpretive Anthropology.* Basic Books, New York.

— (1973) *The Interpretation of Cultures.* Basic Books, New York.

Gibbs, L. (1987) Identifying Gender Representation in the Archaeological Record: A Contextual Study. In *The Archaeology of Contextual Meanings.* I. Hodder, Ed. Cambridge University Press, Cambridge, pp. 79–89.

Giddens, A. (1979) *Central Problems in Social Theory.* MacMillan, London.

— (1981) *A Contemporary Critique of Historical Materialism.* MacMillan, London.

Goody, J. (1986) *Logic of Writing and the Organization of Society.* Cambridge University Press, Cambridge.

Hodder, I. (1987a) The Contribution of the Long Term. In *Archaeology as Long-Term History*, I. Hodder, Ed. Cambridge University Press, Cambridge, pp. 1–8.

— (1987b) The Contextual Analysis of Symbolic Meanings. *The Archaeology of Contextual Meanings*, I. Hodder, Ed. Cambridge University Press, Cambridge, pp. 1–10.

— (1986) *Reading the Past.* Cambridge University Press, Cambridge.

— (1985) Postprocessual Archaeology. In *Advances in Archaeological Method and Theory.* M. B. Schiffer, Ed. Academic Press, New York.

Illich, I. and B. Sanders (1988) *The Alphabetization of the Popular Mind.* North Point Press, San Francisco.

Isaac, R. (1983) Books and the Social Authority of Learning: The Case of Mid-Eighteenth-Century Virginia. In *Printing and Society in Early America.* W. L. Joyce, D. D. Hall, R. D. Brown and J. B. Hench, Eds. American Antiquarian Society, Worcester, MA, pp. 228–249.

Keesing, R. M. (1987) Anthropology as Interpretive Quest. *Current Anthropology* 28(2)161–176.

McLuhan, M. (1967) *Medium is the Massage.* Random House, New York.

— (1962) *The Gutenberg Galaxy: The Making of Typographic Man.* The University of Toronto Press, Toronto.

Marcus, G. E. and M. M. J. Fischer (1986) *Anthropology as Cultural Critique, an Experimental Moment in the Human Sciences.* University of Chicago Press, Chicago.

Mitchell, W. J. T. (1986) *Iconology; Image, Text, Ideology.* University of Chicago Press, Chicago.

Moore, H. (1988) *Feminism and Anthropology.* University of Minnesota Press, Minneapolis.

Olson, D. R., N. Torrance and A. Hildyard, Eds. (1985) *Literacy, Language, and Learning; the Nature and Consequences of Reading and Writing.* Cambridge University Press, Cambridge.

O'Meara, J. T. (1989) Anthropology as an Empirical Science. *American Anthropologist* 91(2)354–369.

Patterson, T. (1990) History and the Post-Processual Archaeologies. *Man* 24:555–566.

Sangren, P. S. (1988) Rhetoric and the Authority of Ethnography: "Postmodernism" and the Social Reproduction of Texts. *Current Anthropology* 29(3)405–435.

Shanks, M. and C. Tilley (1987) *Re-constructing Archaeology.* Cambridge University Press, Cambridge.

Sherzer, J. (1987) A Discourse-Centered Approach to Language and Culture. *American Anthropologist* 89(2)295–309.

Spencer, J. (1989) Anthropology as a Kind of Writing. *Man* (N.S.) 24(1)145–164.

Tilley, C., Ed. (1990) *Reading Material Culture.* Basil Blackwell, Oxford.

Watson, P. J. and M. Fotiadis (1990) The Razor's Edge: Symbolic-Structuralist Archaeology and the Expansion of Archaeological Inference. *American Anthropologist* 92(3)613–629.

Wuthnow, R., J. D. Hunter, A. Bergesen, and E. Kurzweil, Eds. (1984) *Cultural Analysis.* Routledge & Kegan Paul, London.

Index

Index

Soconusco and, 85, 86
Ceramic scalings, creation of, for Rockbridge, 15–17
Change, boundaries of, defining, 179–192
Chapels, medieval, 142
Chesapeake, probate inventory studies in, 206, see also
　　　Probate inventories
Chiefdom, southeastern, 16th-century, 123–130
Christians, medieval history and, 136, 141–142
Church Order, Shakers, 196
Church sources, 3
Classical Greece, 149
Classical Rome, 149
Classics, 1
Climate
　　agriculture and, California missions and, 70
　　Sardinian, 153
Clothing
　　California missions and, 79
　　slave, 62
　　Soconusco and, 85, 90–91
Coevalness, 33
Cognitive patterns, oral history and, 33
Collaboration, oral history and, 28
Colonial Soconusco, New Spain, see Soconusco
Colonization, European, sites of, 26
Combined Caesarea Expeditions, 115
Community
　　alternative, 195, see also Shakers
　　material world and, 25
　　oral history and, 27, 28, see also Oral history
Company sources, 3
Concrete, Caesarea and, 103, 117
Connecticut, probate inventory studies in, 207
Consumer goods, see Goods
Contact period sites, 25
Contadini-guerrieri, Copper and Bronze Age, evidence for,
　　149–152
Context
　　archaeological analysis of, 212–213
　　social, of goods, 205, 208–209
　　text and, 5
Contradictory data, 3
Coosa chiefdom, 123
　　age-at-death distributions, 126, 127
　　age determination, 126
　　archaeological sample and, 125
　　burial phasing, 126
　　ethnohistoric and archaeological background of, 124–
　　　　125
　　health status in, 126
　　life tables, 126–127
　　methodology of study, 126–127
　　periosteal reactions in, 127–128
　　results of study, 127–128
　　sex determination, 126
Copper Age *contadini-guerrieri*, evidence for, 149–152
Critical theory, 26, 33
Crops, see Agriculture
Crusaders, Caesarea and, 103, 108, 110, 115–116
Cultivation, Sardinia and, 150, 151
Cultural critique, 33

Cultural relativity, 33
Cultural resource management, oral history and, 26, 27

Data
　　contradictory, 3
　　documents and, relationships between, 4
　　supplementary, 3
Daybooks, general store, 10, 11, 13–20
Decorative arts, probate inventory studies and, 206–207
Deetz, Jim, 175
de Luna, Tristan, 123
Demography
　　16th-century southeastern chiefdom, 123–130
　　slave, 59–60
de Soto, Hernando, 123
Diaries, 3
Diet, slave, 58, 61
Discourse, 217, 218
Disease, slave, health care and, 62–63
Documentary myths, 4
　　Sardinia and, 149, see also Sardinia
Documentary record
　　household differentiation and, in colonial Soconusco,
　　　　New Spain, 83
　　oral history and, 27
Documents
　　archaeological data and, relationships between, 4
　　historic, focused historic research and, 45–46
　　oral history and, 28
　　transient, 3
Drawings, Shaker, 198, 200, 201
Dressed burial element, 138

Ecology, California missions and, 77
Economic differentiation, household inventories and,
　　　　Soconusco, 84–92
Economy, California missions, 68–69
England, probate inventory studies in, 206–207
Environment, built, Shaker, 195–202, see also Shakers
Epigraphy, 1, 149
Epistemology, oral history and, 28
Ethical guidelines, oral history and, 27
Ethnicity
　　barbarian invasions and, 136–138
　　Butler Island Plantation, 58
Ethnoarchaeology, 25
Ethnographers, 26, 218
Ethnographic present, 33
Ethnography, 1, 2, 26, 28, 32–33
Ethnohistory, 25–26
　　California missions and, 78
　　Coosa chiefdom and, 124–125
　　Ottawa and Ojibwa and, 92–102
Etiquette books, meanings of goods and, 208
Etowah site, 123, see also Coosa chiefdom
European colonization, sites of, 26
Evaluation criteria, Oral History Association, 27
Exchange networks, craft, 181
Explorers, Spanish, 123
Exports, California missions and, 70
Ex-slave testimony, 55